T0213690

Lecture Notes in Computer Science 10216

Commenced Publication in 1973
Founding and Former Series Editors:
Gerhard Goos, Juris Hartmanis, and Jan van Leeuwen

More information about this series at http://www.springer.com/series/7407

Stephan Wong · Antonio Carlos Beck
Koen Bertels · Luigi Carro (Eds.)

Applied Reconfigurable Computing

13th International Symposium, ARC 2017
Delft, The Netherlands, April 3–7, 2017
Proceedings

 Springer

Editors
Stephan Wong
Delft University of Technology
Delft
The Netherlands

Koen Bertels
Delft University of Technology
Delft
The Netherlands

Antonio Carlos Beck
Federal University of Rio Grande do Sul
Porto Alegre
Brazil

Luigi Carro
Federal University of Rio Grande do Sul
Porto Alegre
Brazil

ISSN 0302-9743   ISSN 1611-3349 (electronic)
Lecture Notes in Computer Science
ISBN 978-3-319-56257-5   ISBN 978-3-319-56258-2   (eBook)
DOI 10.1007/978-3-319-56258-2

Library of Congress Control Number: 2017935847

LNCS Sublibrary: SL1 – Theoretical Computer Science and General Issues

Printed on acid-free paper

This Springer imprint is published by Springer Nature
The registered company is Springer International Publishing AG
The registered company address is: Gewerbestrasse 11, 6330 Cham, Switzerland

Preface

Reconfigurable computing technologies offer the promise of substantial performance gains over traditional architectures via customizing, even at runtime, the topology of the underlying architecture to match the specific needs of a given application. Contemporary adaptive systems allow for the definition of architectures with functional and storage units that match in function, bit-width, and control structures the specific needs of a given computation. They aim to exploit these novel and innovative resources to achieve the highest possible performance and energy efficiency.

Many are the challenges faced by reconfigurable computing in these days: design methods and tools, which include high-level languages and compilation, simulation and synthesis, estimation techniques, design space exploration, and run-time systems and virtualization; architectures, which may be self-adaptive and evolvable, heterogeneous, low-power, approximate, fine/coarse grained, embedded in an MPSOC and use an NOC, or even resilient and fault tolerant; applications that comprise security and cryptography, big data and HPC, embedded and DSP, robotics and automotive, mission critical, among many others; and trends in teaching, benchmarks, and other emerging technologies.

Over the past 12 years, the International Applied Reconfigurable Computing (ARC) Symposium series (www.arc-symposium.org) has provided a forum for dissemination and discussion of this transformative research area. The ARC symposium was first held in 2005 in Algarve, Portugal. The second edition took place in Delft, The Netherlands, in 2006, and was the first edition to have its proceedings published by Springer as a volume in its *Lecture Notes in Computer Science* series. Subsequent ARC yearly editions were held in Rio de Janeiro, Brazil (2007); London, UK (2008); Karlsruhe, Germany (2009); Bangkok, Thailand (2010); Belfast, UK (2011); Hong Kong, China (2012); Los Angeles, USA (2013); Algarve, Portugal (2014); Bochum, Germany (2015); Rio de Janeiro, Brazil (2016).

This LNCS volume includes the papers selected for the 13th edition of the symposium (ARC 2017), held in Delft, The Netherlands, during April 3–7, 2017. The symposium succeeded in attracting a significant number of high-quality contributions related to reconfigurable computing. A total of 49 papers were submitted to the symposium from 22 countries: Algeria (1), Brazil (5), Canada (1), China (9), Denmark (1), France (3), Germany (7), Greece (1), India (1), Iran(1), Italy(1), Japan (2), South Korea (1), Malaysia (1), The Netherlands (2), Pakistan (1), Poland (2), Singapore (2), Switzerland (1), Turkey (1), UK (4), and USA (1). All submissions were carefully evaluated by at least three members of the Program Committee. In all, 17 papers were accepted as full papers (acceptance rate of 34.7%) and 11 as short papers (global acceptance rate of 57.1%). The accepted papers composed a very interesting symposium program, which we consider to constitute a representative overview of ongoing research efforts in reconfigurable computing.

We would like to acknowledge the support of all the members of this year's Steering and Program Committees in reviewing papers, in helping with the paper selection, and in giving valuable suggestions. Special thanks also to the additional researchers who contributed to the reviewing process, to all the authors who submitted papers to the symposium, and to all the symposium attendees.

Last but not least, we are especially indebted to Juergen Becker from the University of Karlsruhe and to Alfred Hoffmann and Anna Kramer from Springer for their support and work in publishing this book as part of the LNCS series.

February 2017

Stephan Wong
Antonio Carlos Beck
Koen Bertels
Luigi Carro

Organization

General Chairs

Koen Bertels   Delft University of Technology, The Netherlands
Luigi Carro   Federal University of Rio Grande do Sul, Brazil

Program Chairs

Stephan Wong   Delft University of Technology, The Netherlands
Antonio Carlos Beck   Federal University of Rio Grande do Sul, Brazil

Finance Chair

Joost Hoozemans   Delft University of Technology, The Netherlands

Proceedings Chair

Hamid Mushtaq   Delft University of Technology, The Netherlands

Sponsorship Chair

Pedro Diniz   USC Information Sciences Institute, USA

Publicity Chairs

Sorin Cotofana   Delft University of Technology, The Netherlands
Pedro Diniz   USC Information Sciences Institute, USA
Chao Wang   University of Science and Technology of China, China

Web Chair

Johan Peltenburg   Delft University of Technology, The Netherlands

Steering Committee

Hideharu Amano   Keio University, Japan
Jürgen Becker   Universität Karlsruhe (TH), Germany
Mladen Berekovic   Braunschweig University of Technology, Germany
Koen Bertels   Delft University of Technology, The Netherlands
João M.P. Cardoso   University of Porto, Portugal
Katherine Morrow   University of Wisconsin-Madison, USA
George Constantinides   Imperial College London, UK

Pedro C. Diniz   USC Information Sciences Institute, USA
Philip H.W. Leong   University of Sydney, Australia
Walid Najjar   University of California Riverside, USA
Roger Woods   Queen's University Belfast, UK

Program Committee

Hideharu Amano   Keio University, Japan
Zachary Baker   Los Alamos National Laboratory, USA
Juergen Becker   Karlsruhe Institute of Technology, Germany
Mladen Berekovic   TU Braunschweig, Germany
Joao Bispo   Universidade Técnica de Lisboa, Portugal
Michaela Blott   Xilinx, Ireland
Vanderlei Bonato   University of Sao Paulo, Brazil
Christos Bouganis   Imperial College London, UK
João Canas Ferreira   University of Porto, Portugal
Cyrille Chavet   Université de Bretagne-Sud, France
Daniel Chillet   Université de Rennes, France
Rene Cumplido   Inst. Nacional de Astrofísica, Óptica y Electrónica, Mexico
Florent de Dinechin   Université de Lyon, France
Steven Derrien   Université de Rennes, France
Antonio Ferrari   Universidade de Aveiro, Portugal
Ricardo Ferreira   Universidade Federal de Vicosa, Brazil
Roberto Giorgi   University of Siena, Italy
Diana Goehringer   Ruhr University Bochum, Germany
Marek Gorgon   AGH University of Science and Technology, Poland
Frank Hannig   Friedrich Alexander University Erlangen-Nürnberg,
                          Germany
Jim Harkin   University of Ulster, UK
Dominic Hillenbrand   Karlsruhe Institute of Technology, Germany
Christian Hochberger   TU Darmstadt, Germany
Michael Huebner   Ruhr University Bochum, Germany
Waqar Hussain   Tampere University of Technology, Finland
Fernanda Kastensmidt   Federal University of Rio Grande do Sul, Brazil
Krzysztof Kepa   GE Global Research, USA
Georgios Keramidas   Technological Educational Institute of Western Greece,
                          Greece
Andreas Koch   TU Darmstadt, Germany
Dimitrios Kritharidis   Intracom Telecom, Greece
Tomasz Kryjak   AGH University of Science and Technology, Poland
Vianney Lapotre   Université de Bretagne-Sud, France
Philip Leong   The Chinese University of Hong Kong, SAR China
Eduardo Marques   University of Sao Paulo, Brazil
Konstantinos Masselos   University of the Peloponnese, Greece
Cathal McCabe   Xilinx, Ireland
Daniel Mesquita   Universidade Federal do Pampa, Brazil
Antonio Miele   Politecnico di Milano, Italy

Takefumi Miyoshi	e-trees.Japan, Inc., Japan
Razvan Nane	Delft University of Technology, The Netherlands
Horacio Neto	Technical University of Lisbon, Portugal
Smail Niar	University of Valenciennes, France
Seda Ogrenci-Memik	Northwestern University, USA
Kyprianos Papadimitriou	Technical University of Crete, Greece
Monica Pereira	Universidade Federal do Rio Grande do Norte, Brazil
Christian Pilato	Columbia University, USA
Thilo Pionteck	Otto-von-Guericke Universität Magdeburg, Germany
Kyle Rupnow	Advanced Digital Sciences Center, Singapore
Kentaro Sano	Tohoku University, Japan
Marco D. Santambrogio	Politecnico di Milano, Italy
Yuichiro Shibata	Nagasaki University, Japan
Cristina Silvano	Politecnico di Milano, Italy
Dimitrios Soudris	University of Patras, Greece
Dirk Stroobandt	Ghent University, Belgium
David Thomas	Imperial College London, UK
Tim Todman	Imperial College London, UK
Chao Wang	University of Science and Technology of China
Roger Woods	Queen's University Belfast, UK
Yoshiki Yamaguchi	University of Tsukuba, Japan

Additional Reviewers

Ahmed, Nauman
Allouani, Ihsen
Anantharajaiah, Nidhi
Baklouti, Mouna
Bapp, Falco
Barber, Paul
Bileki, Guilherme
Blochwitz, Christopher
Chaib Draa, Ismat Yahia
Del Sozzo, Emanuele
Di Tucci, Lorenzo
Durelli, Gianluca
Fraser, Nicholas
Gambardella, Giulio
Gottschling, Philip
Hernández-Munive, Roberto
Joseph, Moritz
Jung, Lukas
Kalb, Tobias
Kalms, Lester
Korinth, Jens

Martin, George
McCarroll, Niall
Melo Costa, Thadeu A.F.
Migliore, Vincent
Oliveira de Souza Junior, Carlos Alberto
Oliveira, Cristiano B. De
Perina, Andre B.
Procaccini, Marco
Reder, Simon
Rettkowski, Jens
Rohde, Johanna
Rosa, Leandro
Scolari, Alberto
Siddiqui, Fahad Manzoor
Stock, Florian
Wehner, Philipp
Wenzel, Jakob
Yu, Jintao
Zhang, Kaicheng
Özkan, M. Akif

Invited Talks

Rethinking Memory System Design (and the Computing Platforms We Design Around It)

Onur Mutlu

ETH Zurich, Zurich, Switzerland

Abstract. The memory system is a fundamental performance and energy bottleneck in almost all computing systems. Recent system design, application, and technology trends that require more capacity, bandwidth, efficiency, and predictability out of the memory system make it an even more important system bottleneck. At the same time, DRAM and flash technologies are experiencing difficult technology scaling challenges that make the maintenance and enhancement of their capacity, energy efficiency, and reliability significantly more costly with conventional techniques. In fact, recent reliability issues with DRAM, such as the RowHammer problem, are already threatening system security and predictability. In this talk, we first discuss major challenges facing modern memory systems in the presence of greatly increasing demand for data and its fast analysis. We then examine some promising research and design directions to overcome these challenges and thus enable scalable memory systems for the future. We discuss three key solution directions: (1) enabling new memory architectures, functions, interfaces, and better integration of memory and the rest of the system, (2) designing a memory system that intelligently employs emerging non-volatile memory (NVM) technologies and coordinates memory and storage management, (3) reducing memory interference and providing predictable performance to applications sharing the memory system. If time permits, we will also touch upon our ongoing related work in combating scaling challenges of NAND flash memory. An accompanying paper, slightly outdated (circa 2015), can be found at http://people.inf.ethz.ch/omutlu/pub/memory-systems-research_superfri14.pdf.

Acceleration Through Hardware Multithreading

Walid Najjar

Department of Computer Science and Engineering,
University of California Riverside, Riverside, USA

Abstract. Long memory latencies, as measured in CPU clock cycles, is probably the most daunting challenge to modern computer architecture. In multicore designs, the long memory latency is mitigated with the use of massive cache hierarchies. This solution pre-supposes some forms of temporal or spatial localities. Irregular applications, by their very nature, suffer from poor data locality that results in high cache miss rates and long off-chip memory latency. Latency masking multithreading, where threads relinquish control after issuing a memory request, has been demonstrated as an effective approach to achieving a higher throughput. Multithreaded CPUs are designed for a fixed maximum number of threads tailored for an average application. FPGAs, however, can be customized to specific applications. Their massive parallelism is well-known, and ideally suited to dynamically manage hundreds, or thousands, of threads. Multithreading, in essence, trades off memory bandwidth for latency. In this talk I describe how latency masking multithreaded execution on FPGAs can achieve a higher throughput than CPUs and/or GPUs on two sets of applications: sparse linear algebra and database operations.

Enabling Software Engineers to Program Heterogeneous, Reconfigurable SoCs

Patrick Lysaght

Xilinx Research Labs, San Jose, USA

Abstract. In this talk, modern software trends will be explored with a focus on how we can enable software developers to exploit the benefits of reconfigurable hardware. This talk introduces PYNQ, a new open-source framework for designing with Xilinx Zynq devices, a class of All Programmable Systems on Chip (APSoCs) which integrates multiple processors and Field Programmable Gate Arrays (FPGAs) into single integrated circuits. The main goal of the framework is to make it easier for designers of embedded systems to use APSoCs in their applications. The APSoC is programmed in Python and the code is developed and tested directly on the embedded system. The programmable logic circuits are imported as hardware libraries and programmed through their APIs, in essentially the same way that software libraries are imported and programmed. The framework combines three main elements:

- The use of a high-level productivity language, Python in this case
- Python-callable hardware libraries based on FPGA overlays
- A web-based architecture incorporating the open-source Jupyter Notebook infrastructure served from Zynq's embedded processors

The result is a programming environment that is web-centric so it can be accessed from any browser on any computing platform or operating system. It enables software programmers to work at higher levels of design abstraction and to re-use both software and hardware libraries for reconfigurable computing. The framework is inherently extensible and integrates coherently with hardware-dependent code written in C and C++. The talk concludes with an outline of areas for continued development, and a call for community participation.

Contents

Adaptive Architectures

Improving the Performance of Adaptive Cache in Reconfigurable
VLIW Processor 3
   Sensen Hu, Anthony Brandon, Qi Guo, and Yizhuo Wang

LP-P^{2}IP: A Low-Power Version of P^{2}IP Architecture
Using Partial Reconfiguration 16
   Álvaro Avelino, Valentin Obac, Naim Harb, Carlos Valderrama,
   Glauberto Albuquerque, and Paulo Possa

NIM: An HMC-Based Machine for Neuron Computation 28
   Geraldo F. Oliveira, Paulo C. Santos, Marco A.Z. Alves,
   and Luigi Carro

VLIW-Based FPGA Computation Fabric with Streaming Memory
Hierarchy for Medical Imaging Applications. 36
   Joost Hoozemans, Rolf Heij, Jeroen van Straten, and Zaid Al-Ars

Embedded Computing and Security

Hardware Sandboxing: A Novel Defense Paradigm Against Hardware
Trojans in Systems on Chip 47
   Christophe Bobda, Joshua Mead, Taylor J.L. Whitaker,
   Charles Kamhoua, and Kevin Kwiat

Rapid Development of Gzip with MaxJ 60
   Nils Voss, Tobias Becker, Oskar Mencer, and Georgi Gaydadjiev

On the Use of (Non-)Cryptographic Hashes on FPGAs 72
   Andreas Fiessler, Daniel Loebenberger, Sven Hager,
   and Björn Scheuermann

An FPGA-Based Implementation of a Pipelined FFT Processor
for High-Speed Signal Processing Applications. 81
   Ngoc-Hung Nguyen, Sheraz Ali Khan, Cheol-Hong Kim,
   and Jong-Myon Kim

Simulation and Synthesis

Soft Timing Closure for Soft Programmable Logic Cores:
The ARGen Approach   93
   Théotime Bollengier, Loïc Lagadec, Mohamad Najem,
   Jean-Christophe Le Lann, and Pierre Guilloux

FPGA Debugging with MATLAB Using a Rule-Based Inference System. . . .   106
   Habib Ul Hasan Khan and Diana Göhringer

Hardness Analysis and Instrumentation of Verilog Gate Level Code
for FPGA-based Designs   118
   Abdul Rafay Khatri, Ali Hayek, and Josef Börcsök

A Framework for High Level Simulation and Optimization
of Coarse-Grained Reconfigurable Architectures   129
   Muhammad Adeel Pasha, Umer Farooq, Muhammad Ali,
   and Bilal Siddiqui

Design Space Exploration

Parameter Sensitivity in Virtual FPGA Architectures   141
   Peter Figuli, Weiqiao Ding, Shalina Figuli, Kostas Siozios,
   Dimitrios Soudris, and Jürgen Becker

Custom Framework for Run-Time Trading Strategies   154
   Andreea-Ingrid Funie, Liucheng Guo, Xinyu Niu, Wayne Luk,
   and Mark Salmon

Exploring HLS Optimizations for Efficient Stereo Matching
Hardware Implementation   168
   Karim M.A. Ali, Rabie Ben Atitallah, Nizar Fakhfakh,
   and Jean-Luc Dekeyser

Architecture Reconfiguration as a Mechanism for Sustainable Performance
of Embedded Systems in case of Variations in Available Power   177
   Dimple Sharma, Victor Dumitriu, and Lev Kirischian

Fault Tolerance

Exploring Performance Overhead Versus Soft Error Detection in Lockstep
Dual-Core ARM Cortex-A9 Processor Embedded into Xilinx Zynq APSoC . . .   189
   Ádria Barros de Oliveira, Lucas Antunes Tambara,
   and Fernanda Lima Kastensmidt

Applying TMR in Hardware Accelerators Generated by High-Level
Synthesis Design Flow for Mitigating Multiple Bit Upsets
in SRAM-Based FPGAs   202
   André Flores dos Santos, Lucas Antunes Tambara, Fabio Benevenuti,
   Jorge Tonfat, and Fernanda Lima Kastensmidt

FPGA-Based Designs

FPGA Applications in Unmanned Aerial Vehicles - A Review   217
   Mustapha Bouhali, Farid Shamani, Zine Elabadine Dahmane,
   Abdelkader Belaidi, and Jari Nurmi

Genomic Data Clustering on FPGAs for Compression   229
   Enrico Petraglio, Rick Wertenbroek, Flavio Capitao, Nicolas Guex,
   Christian Iseli, and Yann Thoma

A Quantitative Analysis of the Memory Architecture of FPGA-SoCs.   241
   Matthias Göbel, Ahmed Elhossini, Chi Ching Chi,
   Mauricio Alvarez-Mesa, and Ben Juurlink

Neural Networks

Optimizing CNN-Based Object Detection Algorithms on Embedded
FPGA Platforms   255
   Ruizhe Zhao, Xinyu Niu, Yajie Wu, Wayne Luk, and Qiang Liu

An FPGA Realization of a Deep Convolutional Neural Network
Using a Threshold Neuron Pruning   268
   Tomoya Fujii, Simpei Sato, Hiroki Nakahara, and Masato Motomura

Accuracy Evaluation of Long Short Term Memory Network
Based Language Model with Fixed-Point Arithmetic   281
   Ruochun Jin, Jingfei Jiang, and Yong Dou

FPGA Implementation of a Short Read Mapping Accelerator   289
   Mostafa Morshedi and Hamid Noori

Languages and Estimation Techniques

dfesnippets: An Open-Source Library for Dataflow Acceleration on FPGAs . . .   299
   Paul Grigoras, Pavel Burovskiy, James Arram, Xinyu Niu, Kit Cheung,
   Junyi Xie, and Wayne Luk

A Machine Learning Methodology for Cache Recommendation   311
   Osvaldo Navarro, Jones Mori, Javier Hoffmann, Fabian Stuckmann,
   and Michael Hübner

ArPALib: A Big Number Arithmetic Library for Hardware and Software
Implementations. A Case Study for the Miller-Rabin Primality Test   323
   *Jan Macheta, Agnieszka Dąbrowska-Boruch, Paweł Russek,
   and Kazimierz Wiatr*

Author Index   331

Adaptive Architectures

Improving the Performance of Adaptive Cache in Reconfigurable VLIW Processor

Sensen Hu[1(✉)], Anthony Brandon[2], Qi Guo[3], and Yizhuo Wang[1]

[1] School of Computer Science and Technology, Beijing Institute of Technology,
Beijing, China
{foresthss,frankwyz}@bit.edu.cn
[2] EEMCS, Delft University of Technology, Delft, The Netherlands
A.A.C.Brandon@tudelft.nl
[3] University of Science and Technology of China, Heifei, China
guoqiustc@hotmail.com

Abstract. In this paper, we study the impact of cache reconfiguration on the cache misses when the issue-width of a VLIW processor is changed. We clearly note here that our investigation pertains the local temporal effects of the cache resizing and how we counteract the negative impact of cache misses in such resizing instances. We propose a novel reconfigurable d-cache framework that can dynamically adapt its least recently used (LRU) replacement policy without much hardware overhead. We demonstrate that using our adaptive d-cache, it ensures a smooth cache performance from one cache size to the other. This approach is orthogonal to future research in cache resizing for such architectures that take into account energy consumption and performance of the overall application.

Keywords: VLIW · Cache · Cache resizing · Downsizing · Reconfiguration · Issue-width · ρ-VEX

1 Introduction

ρ-VEX processor [1] is a reconfigurable and extensible softcore very long instruction word (VLIW) processor. It differs from traditional VLIW processors, in that the issue-width is parameterized from 2 to 4 to 8 - the core contains a maximum of 8 datapaths. A key motivation of the ρ-VEX processor design is to utilize only the necessary resources when needed. The dynamic nature of the ρ-VEX processor requires an adaptive cache organization that can combine several caches into a larger sized one, or separate a larger cache into smaller sized ones as depicted in Fig. 1—this is commonly referred to as cache resizing.

With these considerations, we investigated the effects of cache resizing triggered by the issue-width mode changes (caused by external factors) of the ρ-VEX

This work is supported in part by the National Natural Science Foundation of China under grant NSFC-61300011 and NSFC-61300010. The authors would like to thank the China Scholarship Council (CSC) for their financial support.

© Springer International Publishing AG 2017
S. Wong et al. (Eds.): ARC 2017, LNCS 10216, pp. 3–15, 2017.
DOI: 10.1007/978-3-319-56258-2_1

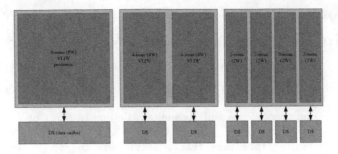

Fig. 1. The dynamic architecture of ρ-vex.

core in different scenarios. In the case of upsizing (combining multiple ways to form a larger cache), no detrimental effects are expected as no live data was removed and the additional cache resources will gradually decrease the cache miss rates. However, in the case of downsizing (disabling one or more ways), we observe immediately increases in the cache miss rates. The main reason for the increased miss rates is the elimination of live data when disabling certain ways in the downsizing process.

We reiterate here that the resizing decision is made by an external source, i.e., either by the processor or by the operating system. In both cases it is a fact that a transition time can be introduced between the decision for a (processor) mode change and the actual moment of change. Furthermore, we propose a mechanism to dynamically adapt the d-cache replacement policy to reduce the negative effects of downsizing in set-associative caches. We exploit this transition time to bolster the amount of live data in the (cache) ways that remain active by giving them a higher preference when loading new data (when a miss occurs) and by moving data to these ways from the to-be-disabled ways (when a hit occurs). To the best of our knowledge, this paper is the first to propose a dynamic adaptation of the cache replacement policy in relation to core reconfiguration. Moreover, we are not attempting to reduce the overall single application performance or energy consumption as other cache resizing approaches do. We are considering scenarios in which mode changes occur frequently (due to external factors) and attempt to limit the impact of these mode changes on the d-cache performance per occurrence. Consequently, our approach is orthogonal to other cache resizing approaches.

Our approach reduces the (sudden) increase in cache misses during a cache downsizing event in order to reduce (locally in time) the performance impact of such an event. The experimental results show that we can reduce the number of cache misses by between 10% and 63% compared to immediate cache downsizing without taking any measures. More specifically, the contributions of this paper are as follows:

- To the best of our knowledge, our proposal is the first to take the issue-width mode change of VLIW processor event as an external trigger to reconfigure the d-cache instead of monitoring the cache miss ratio, and resizes the d-cache to react to varying demand for cache size both within and across applications.

- We propose a transition period before the actual moment of resizing. This period of preparation before the actual cache resize ensures a smooth cache performance from one cache size to the other. In particular, we demonstrate that our main results can be achieved with a transition period of just 2000 clock cycles up to 4000 clock cycles.
- We implement a novel, simple, yet effective cache replacement policy, which migrates the accessed data to the enabled (active) cache ways after resizing, to reduce the transition cache misses in order to smoothen and thereby improve the performance (of the application) during the transition period and right after the downsizing event.
- Our approach allows for immediate cache downsizing without the need to maintain "live" portions of the cache after the downsizing event. In the ρ-VEX processor design philosophy, the "disabled" cache ways can be immediately used by other tasks as they are logically connected to other cores.

2 Related Work

Previous studies on the strategy of "when to resize" almost all relied on the miss ratio or profiling to determine the correct time to resize the cache. In [3,4], these methods made the decision solely based on monitoring cache miss rate, which are all miss-driven resizing approaches. [5] used dynamic profiling for predicting cache usage and energy efficiency of the application under multiple cache configurations. However, cache miss rate is not always a good performance indictor [3]. While many factors can affect the cache miss rate, even the minor changes in program behavior or available cache size probably causes large changes in miss rate [2,6]. Such miss-driven resizing approach probably thrashes the performance. The profiling approaches increase the overheads of hardware or software as well as miss-driven approaches. Unlike prior work, as far as we are aware, our work is the first to introduce two events as external trigger to dynamically reconfigure cache when the issue-width mode of VLIW processor changes. Meanwhile, our method considers reducing the miss rate while downsizing cache in order to decrease miss penalty and to smoothen the performance.

Finally, our work is implemented on the ρ-VEX VLIW processor [1,7], which is open-source and has a complete tool chain (compiler, simulator and assembler). The issue-width of ρ-VEX can be reconfigured dynamically to be 2-issue, 4-issue and 8-issue at run-time [8]. In [9], the authors implemented generic binaries, which can execute the same binary on different issue-width processors without much hardware modifications. This design allows for maintaining live data within existing cache blocks when the amount of computing resources in the core are changed. This by itself already results in an improvement of the execution times by on average 16% (with outliers of 0.7% and 42%) for the MiBench benchmark suite (also used in this paper) compared to a case in which each resizing event results in cold starts of the d-cache (and not taking into account i-cache misses).

3 General Approach

3.1 When to Resize

In some cases, more frequent reconfiguration may be desirable due to frequent context switches between applications or aggressive adaptive reconfiguration for the same application. As mentioned earlier, we assume that external factors (from the d-cache's point of view) determine whether the d-cache should be resized. At the same time, our approach relies on the possibility that there is enough time given to our approach to "prepare" the caches before the actual resizing action in order to minimize the negative effects.

First, an operating system (OS) can claim resources to execute kernel thread, but instead of completely switching out the context of the running program, it can temporarily reduce the resources for the running program. In this manner, the running program remains responsive. This simple fact must not be overlooked as it represents a key aspect of the ρ-VEX core design. Single core context switching always results in huge context switching overheads and the active application being swapped out, therefore, not responsive at all. Second, applications running on the ρ-VEX processor most likely will have different phases in which the ILP varies. Low ILP within the running application can lead the core to decide to reduce resource utilization in order to save core power. In both cases, the core resizing will lead to a corresponding cache resizing.

3.2 How to Resize

In the case of upsizing (combining multiple ways to form a larger cache), no detrimental effects are expected as no live data was removed and the additional cache resources will gradually decrease the cache miss rates. The key idea to reduce the cache misses after downsizing is to maintain as much as possible the live data within the downsized d-cache. In order to achieve this goal, we first have to find a way to identify the live data and subsequently decide how to treat the live data.

Before we discuss these two objectives we introduce the terminology used throughout this paper. For simplicity, we take a switching of mode from 8-issue to 4-issue to illustrate the transition mechanism in Fig. 2. There are two crucial instant times in the graph. One is $t_{decision}$, the other one is t_{switch}. $t_{decision}$ indicates the moment in time the decision is taken to perform the mode change of the core. t_{switch} indicates that the actual moment that the core switches its mode. The interval from $t_{decision}$ to t_{switch} is the transition period proposed in this paper. In Fig. 2, way0 and way1 will remain active after downsizing. Hence, the state of way0 and way1 during the transition period remains in the enabled state, while the state of way2 and way3 go to the transition state. Note that when $t_{decision}$ equals t_{switch}, our strategy equals the traditional strategy of cache resizing, i.e., immediate cache resizing.

In order to identify the live data, we can use active methods as outlined by [10] that require an additional address correlation table. This adds hardware

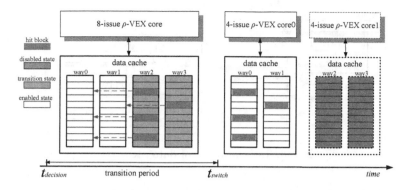

Fig. 2. Migration mechanism from 8 issue-width to 4 issue-width.

overhead and in turn increases power consumption. In our opinion, it is much easier to perform this identification by exploiting the temporal likelihood of re-accessing data—this information is already kept by the least recently used (LRU) replacement policy. We therefore correlate the most live data with the most recently used data.

4 Framework of Cache Resizing

4.1 Hardware Implementation

As depicted in Fig. 3, the way-selection logic (WSL) is in charge of carrying the active/inactive way-enable signal to each way. The way-mask register is provided to set which way is assigned to the corresponding core. It is a 4-bit vector that equals the associativity of cache. Each combination of bits in the way mask register is responsible for the corresponding cache ways. Given the core of 8 issue-widths, the value of way mask register is 1111, which denotes all of the ways are available. In such case, the d-cache acts as a four-way set-associative cache. If the issue-width of core is specified as 4, the available values of the way mask register are 1100 or 0011, which denotes the left ways or the right ways of the way-associative cache, respectively. In such case, the d-cache acts as a two-way set-associative cache. The core0 can hold the value 0011, while the core1 to take the value 1100. When the issue-width is specified as 2, there are four available values (0001, 0010, 0100, and 1000) since the four 2-issue cores can be run independently. The d-cache acts as a direct-mapped cache. Similarly, one core can hold one of 4 values while the rest of cores to hold the other values.

4.2 Resizing-LRU Replacement Algorithm

We have designed a novel replacement algorithm based on LRU and way-resizing, called resizing-LRU (R-LRU), which satisfies the cache downsizing requirement during the transition period. The key idea of this new policy is to migrate the

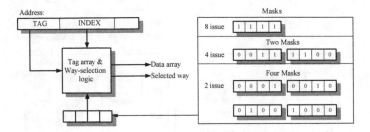

Fig. 3. Tag and index of data cache.

accessed block to the enabled part of cache during the transition period while consider the intrinsic temporal locality of the workloads. There are three cases in the R-LRU replacement algorithm, as Algorithm 1 shows:

- Case 1: hit in the disabled part.
- Case 2: hit in the enabled part.
- Case 3: miss in the whole d-cache.

R-LRU maintains a LRU list L. More precisely, a block in the head of L means it has been accessed recently while the one in the rear of L means it has the least access recently. Let *block* be the referenced cache block. We introduce three states: taking state enabled (E) to denote a cache way that one core can access, taking state disabled (D) to denote a cache way that one core can not access, and taking state transition (T) to denote a cache way that is in the transition period when downsizing the cache. Therefore, the transition state is a transient state to downsize the d-cache.

MRU	1	2	LRU	hit in enabled part	hit in disabled part	miss in whole cache
				–	evict LRU block	–
				–	evict LRU block	–
				–	evict block 2	evict block 2
				–	evict LRU block	–
				–	evict block 2	evict block 2
				–	evict block 1	evict block 1

| block in transition state | block in enabled block | performance maintain case | performance promoted case |

Fig. 4. Benefit from R-LRU algorithm.

To show the benefit of the R-LRU algorithm, we explain the advantages using LRU-based stack as depicted in Fig. 4. There are six different LRU stacks for R-LRU during the transition period. On the left of the graph, MRU position stands

---

Algorithm 1. Resizing-LRU Replacement Algorithm

Input: *block*: memory reference address. *L*: LRU list.
Output: *L*: LRU list.
// *LRU* The pointer to the LRU position
// *MRU* The pointer to the MRU position
$ptr = \text{FindBlock}(block, L)$;
if $(ptr! = NULL)$ **then**
    if $(ptr-> state == T)$ **then**   /* case1, hit in the disabled part of cache */
        $Block * tmp = LRU$;
        while $(tmp-> state! = E)$ **do**   /* find the last enabled block in L */
            $tmp = tmp-> prev$;
        end
        Evict(tmp);
        $ptr-> invalid = true$;
        $tmp = ptr$;
        $MRU = tmp$;
    else   /* case2, hit in the enabled part of cache */
        $MRU = ptr$;
    end
  else   /* case3, miss in the whole cache */
    $Block * tmp = LRU$;
    while $(tmp-> state! = E)$ **do**   /* find the last enabled block in L */
        $tmp = tmp-> prev$;
    end
    Evict(tmp);
    $tmp = ptr$;
    $MRU = tmp$;
end
Update(L);
return L;

---

for the most recently used block while LRU position stands for the least recently used block. The position next to MRU in the recency position is referred as position 1 and the next position as position 2. The shaded block is in transition state while switch to disabled state after the transition period. On the right of the graph, the 18 scenarios of cache accesses are listed. In the following, we will discuss the three cases individually:

Case 1 (hit in the disabled part). A hit in the disabled part is identical to a miss in the enabled part. The last enabled block of the LRU list is evicted and we replicate the hit data of to-be-disabled part to this position. Although the capacity of the hit set probably decreases, R-LRU only replicates the hit data rather than accessing the next level cache. Hence, the cost of this case is less than a real miss. Furthermore, there are three scenarios that evict the LRU block and only one scenario that evict block located the secondary of the LRU list, as shown in the second column of the table. An accessed block exhibits temporal locality if it is likely to be accessed again in the near future. In this way, R-LRU increases the amount of most recently used data in the enabled part, which suggests a benefit from R-LRU replacement algorithm.

Case 2 (hit in the enabled part). For a hit in this part, the R-LRU algorithm just need to update the LRU list, moving the hit blocks to the head of list. This is not different from traditional LRU replacement algorithms. The more hits in the enabled part, the better the locality is in this part. It is effortless to maintain the performance after downsizing. There is no extra overhead using R-LRU in this case. As a result, R-LRU maintains cache performance as shown in the first column of the table.

Case 3 (miss in the whole d-cache). While on a cache miss, the referenced block is only brought into the enabled part. R-LRU finds the last enabled block in the LRU list and evicts it. In this case, there are three scenarios that the evicted blocks occur in the LRU position, which are the same as the conventional LRU replacement policy. In the rest of three scenarios, there is one eviction occurring at Position1 and two evictions occurring at Position2. Considering the LRU block is evicted immediately, R-LRU slightly adjusts the sequence of the LRU list and brings the new block into the enabled way in advance. In this manner, we are able to benefit from the R-LRU replacement policy if the LRU block is no longer accessed before being evicted.

In our framework, the R-LRU policy allows in the transition period to transfer the accessed data from the to-be-disabled way of cache to the enabled way or boost the live-ness of the data in the enabled way. Ideally, all the enabled blocks will be included in the first N nodes of the LRU list after the transition period. In other words, the entire recently used nodes are located at the head of the LRU list. When the t_{switch} approaches, this optimization minimizes cache miss penalty introduced by downsizing.

5   Evaluation

5.1   Experimental Platform Setup

Our baseline of 8-issue core configuration is presented in Table 1. As explained above, the largest ρ-VEX core has a four-way set-associative d-cache in the 8-issue mode. While in the 4-issue mode, the cache is divided over the two cores and therefore also half cache size (32 Kbytes, 2-way) for each core. Similarly, in the 2-issue mode each core has a 16 Kbyte direct-mapped cache. We choose MiBench benchmark suite [11]. The benchmarks were compiled with the vex-3.43 compiler (Hewlett-Packard compiler) using -O3 optimization level and -fno-xnop -fexpand-div flags. Our experimental platform comprises the following elements:

– ρ-VEX prototype: We use an FPGA to prototype the ρ-VEX and run applications on actual hardware. The design runs on a Virtex 6 (ML605 development

Table 1. System configuration

Parameters	8-issue core
Processor frequency	37.5MHz
ALUs	8
MULs	4
Load/Store unit	1
Branch unit	1
L1 I-cache	32 Kbytes, 4-way, 32 bytes 1 cycle latency
L1 D-cache	64 Kbytes, 4-way, 32 bytes 1 cycle latency write-through
Memory access time	10 cycles

board) at 37.5 MHz. A hardware trace unit collects all the executed instructions for each benchmark on the FPGA prototype of ρ-VEX.

- Cache simulator: We extracted the memory read and write operations from this traces for use as input to the cache simulator. We extended the DineroIV [12] cache simulator, which is a sequential trace-driven cache simulator, to be able to simulate the reconfigurable cache as presented in Sect. 3.
- Core phase predictor [13]: We implemented a simple phase predictor to measure the ILP of the benchmark traces and predict/decide the most suitable mode for the ρ-VEX core to execute in. In addition, this predictor takes into account the trade-offs in terms of delay, energy consumption, and the energy delay product (EDP) to make the phase predictions.

5.2 Methodology

Our framework supports the dynamic reconfiguration of both cache downsizing and cache upsizing. When the cache upsizing occurs, which means the associativity is increased, tags and data arrays keep the data residing in it without degrading the performance. Henceforth, we only evaluate the scenario of d-cache downsizing. According to the trigger signal of the mode change, we perform the reconfiguration of d-cache downsizing in the framework proposed which combines the R-LRU replacement policy with varying transition periods. For the sake of fair comparisons, we also simulate the benchmark with the immediate d-cache upsizing/downsizing method at the same (time) points. Finally, we perform several different measurements after skipping the initialization part and warming up of the cache and the ρ-VEX processor is always initialized to the 8-issue mode.

6   Results

6.1   The Impact of the Interval of Transition

Figure 5 depicts how the interval of transition affects the performance, i.e., the cache downsizing occurs when the mode switched from 8-issue mode to 4-issue mode, from 8-issue mode to 2-issue mode and from 4-issue mode to 2-issue mode, respectively. The y-axis of three graphs represents the decreasing number of misses in 2000 cycles (bundles) after the actual downsizing compared to the immediate cache downsizing (normalized to immediate cache downsizing in the same execution point). We vary the interval of transition period ranging from 10 cycles to 10000 cycles (x-axis).

In the three scenarios of downsizing, our framework presents the same decreasing tendency of cache misses, which clearly demonstrates an advantage over the immediate cache downsizing approach. The longer the transition period is, the more the reduction in cache miss rate is. When the transition period is set to 2000 cycles, the majority of the benchmarks result in a near-optimal performance. More specifically, as shown in Fig. 5, our framework achieves a reduction

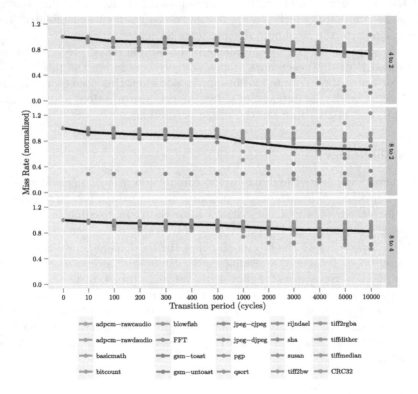

Fig. 5. The impact of the transition interval on cache misses with the mode change. The black lines indicate the average for all benchmarks.

in misses of on average 13% for 8-issue to 4-issue, 26% for 8-issue to 2-issue and 16% for 4-issue to 2-issue, respectively. The figure shows that for switches from 8-issue to 4-issue, for 16 benchmarks, the number of cache misses continuously decrease. It is also true for 11 benchmarks in when switching from 8-issue to 2-issue and for 12 benchmarks when switching from 4-issue to 2-issue.

6.2   About the Lasting Effect

Figure 6 depicts the MiBench benchmark's cumulative lasting effect for every mode change given the transition period is 2000 (bundle) cycles, from which we can observe that the cache misses curve of our approach (normalized to the cache miss rate due to immediate cache resizing without using our approach) gradually approaches $y = 1$ (the immediate resizing curve) rather than jumps to it directly. The area between every curve and $y = 1$ shows the advantages by using our framework.

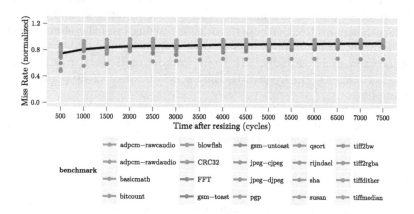

Fig. 6. The lasting effect with execution time. The black line indicates the average for all benchmarks.

For all the benchmarks, we can also achieve the decline of cache miss by about, on average, 16% (2000 cycles after resizing), 14% (4000 cycles) and 9% (7500 cycles after resizing). From our experiments, our framework can improve the performance of the cache more than 6000 (bundle) cycles after cache resizing given the transition interval is 2000 (bundle) cycles. Such framework could be particularly useful in the scenario from a four-way set-associative cache to a two-way set-associative cache.

Without the transition period provided by our framework, the downsizing moments will result in sharp jumps in cache misses ($y = 1$ in Fig. 6). The upsizing moments will not result in immediate recovery of the cache miss rates either as the newly added cache resources need to be populated again. Using our framework, we smooth the cache miss rate graph and when an upsizing event happens before the (lasting) effect of our approach subsided, the cache miss rate can improve again from a much lower point. For example, the recovery can start from any point on the cache miss curve. In this manner, our approach can greatly reduce the cache miss rates in a dynamic environment in which the cache must be resized very quickly. This point is further strengthened by our measured result that a transition period of about 1000–3000 cycles is adequate to reach the main results of our approach.

7   Conclusions

In this paper, we presented a novel reconfigurable d-cache framework combined with an adaptive R-LRU replacement policy without additional hardware overhead. We demonstrated that our framework has the capability to maintain a low miss rate with a transition period up to 6000 cycles while a period of 2000 cycles is enough to achieve good results. Moreover, our approach prevents the sharp miss rate increase as a result of the cache downsizing by on average between 10% to 63%. The short periods in which we achieved our results can lead to computing systems that more frequently perform core resizing (and therefore also cache resizing) in order to maintain a high level of responsiveness without sacrificing performance too much. Finally, when our framework is used in a scenario in which mode changes occur frequently, the improvement of cache performance is further amplified.

Acknowledgement. We would like to thank Prof. Wong for his valuable suggestions and kind help. We also thank TU Delft for their ρ-VEX platform.

References

1. Anjam, F., Wong, S., et al.: Simultaneous reconfiguration of issue-width and instruction cache for a VLIW processor. In: Embedded Computer Systems (SAMOS) (2012)
2. Zang, W., Gordon-Ross, A.: A survey on cache tuning from a power/energy perspective. ACM Comput. Surv. **45**(3), 32 (2013)
3. Keramidas, G., Datsios, C.: Revisiting cache resizing. Int. J. Parallel Program. **43**(1), 59–85 (2015)
4. Yang, S., Powell, M., et al.: Exploiting choice in resizable cache design to optimize deep-submicron processor energy-delay. In: High Performance Computer Architecture (2002)
5. Mittal, S., Zhang, Z.: EnCache: improving cache energy efficiency using a software-controlled profiling cache. IEEE EIT (2012)
6. Beckmann, N., Sanchez, D.: Talus: a simple way to remove cliffs in cache performance. In: High Performance, Computer Architecture (HPCA) (2015)
7. Wong, S., Van As, T., et al.: p-VEX: a reconfigurable and extensible softcore VLIW processor. In: FPT 2008 (2008)
8. Anjam, F., Nadeem, M., et al.: Targeting code diversity with run-time adjustable issue-slots in a chip multiprocessor. In: Design, Automation and Test in Europe Conference Exhibition (DATE) (2011)

9. Brandon, A., Wong, S.: Support for dynamic issue width in VLIW processors using generic binaries. In: Design, Automation Test in Europe Conference Exhibition (DATE) (2013)
10. Kharbutli, M., Sheikh, R.: LACS: a locality-aware cost-sensitive cache replacement algorithm. IEEE Trans. Comput. **63**, 1975–1987 (2014)
11. Guthaus, M., Ringenberg, J., et al.: MiBench: a free, commercially representative embedded benchmark suite. In: 2001 IEEE International Workshop on Workload Characterization, WWC-4, December 2001
12. Hill, M., Edler, J.: Dineroiv trace-driven uniprocessor cache simulator (2015)
13. Guo, Q., Sartor, A., et al.: Run-time phase prediction for a reconfigurable vliw processor. Design, Automation Test in Europe Conference Exhibition (DATE) (2016)

LP-P²IP: A Low-Power Version of P²IP Architecture Using Partial Reconfiguration

Álvaro Avelino[1(✉)], Valentin Obac[2], Naim Harb[3], Carlos Valderrama[3], Glauberto Albuquerque[3], and Paulo Possa[3]

[1] Technology and Science of Rio Grande do Norte,
Federal Institute of Education, Nova Cruz, RN, Brazil
alvaro.medeiros@ifrn.edu.br
[2] Electrical Engineering Department,
Federal University of Rio Grande do Norte, Natal, RN, Brazil
[3] Electronics and Microelectronics Department, Université de Mons, Mons, Belgium

Abstract. Power consumption reduction is crucial for portable equipments and for those in remote locations, whose battery replacement is impracticable. P²IP is an architecture targeting real-time embedded image and video processing, which combines runtime reconfigurable processing, low-latency and high performance. Being a configurable architecture allows the combination of powerful video processing operators (Processing Elements or PEs) to build the target application. However, many applications do not require all PEs available. Remaining idle, these PEs still represent a power consumption problem that Partial Reconfiguration can mitigate. To assess the impact on energy consumption, another P²IP implementation based on Partial Reconfiguration was developed and tested with three different image processing applications. Measurements have been made to analyze energy consumption when executing each of three applications. Results show that compared to the original implementation of the architecture use of Partial Reconfiguration leads to power savings of up to 45%.

Keywords: Energy efficiency · Low-power consumption · FPGA · Partial reconfiguration · Embedded real-time video processing system

1 Introduction

The Programmable Pipeline Image Processor (P²IP) is a systolic Coarse-Grained Reconfigurable Architecture (CG-RA) for real-time video processing embedded in FPGA. It features low-latency systolic array inherent structures, runtime reconfigurable data-path, high-performance CG operators and short compilation times of software applications. Its data path, operating at the pixel clock frequency, can deliver, after the initial latency of a 3-line pipeline, one processed pixel per clock cycle [2–4]. The architecture processing core consists of identical

© Springer International Publishing AG 2017
S. Wong et al. (Eds.): ARC 2017, LNCS 10216, pp. 16–27, 2017.
DOI: 10.1007/978-3-319-56258-2_2

Processing Elements (PEs). Each PE contains an optimized set of essential image processing operators (see Fig. 1) that can be parameterized in run time by software, using virtual reconfiguration. The number and content of PEs is defined before synthesis. Thus, although available and contributing to the overall power consumption, not all PEs are in use depending on the processing performed on the video stream.

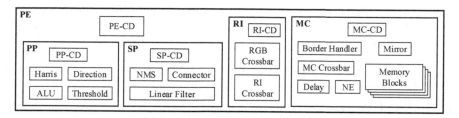

Fig. 1. Processing Element (PE) and its internal blocks. The main blocks are the Pixel Processor (PP), Memory Controller (MC), Spatial Processor (SP), Reconfigurable Interconnection (RI) and Configuration Decoder (PE-CD).

Applications for which there are power consumption restrictions, or where it is not possible to replace the battery that powers the circuit, such as a drone or a satellite, require circuit components with the highest energy-efficiency possible. Indeed, the use of smaller devices or a small number of enhanced devices reduces system cost and power consumption. On some modern FPGA devices, Partial Reconfiguration (PR) is a feature that allows changing the configuration of part of the device while the rest continues to operate. This feature can improve logic density by removing functions that do not operate simultaneously in the FPGA. In the context of P²IP, PR could lead to power savings by just replacing the content of an idle PE by a bypass using PR. This implies the use of a PE that implements no functionality other than a latched input driving its output. In a certain application, if there is one or more idle PEs, these can, using PR, assume the bypass configuration, reducing the overall power consumption.

We propose in this article a novel FPGA-based P²IP implementation using PR to reduce energy consumption. During configuration, the content of a PE can now be replaced by a bypass core, plus the possibility of assigning an optimized functionality. The latter represents a future enhancement as heterogeneous PEs can extend the architecture to support novel processing capabilities. To validate our proposal, we show comparative results concerning resources allocation, energy consumption and reconfiguration latency for three reference applications.

2 Energy Efficiency in FPGAs

Power consumption is a combination of static (which depends on the temperature T) and dynamic power, as stated by (1). The static power is caused by leakage currents inside transistors and the dynamic power is caused by the switching activity when charging and discharging the load capacitance C, as well as short-circuit currents when transistors commute.

$$P_{total} = P_{static}(T) + P_{dynamic}(f) \qquad (1)$$

Dynamic power, as stated in (2), has linear dependency on the clock frequency f and a quadratic dependency on the supply voltage V. In an FPGA, the load capacitance depends on the number of logic and routing elements used. The factor α is the activity or toggle rate of an element; it depends on the topology and its input stimuli.

$$P_{dynamic} = \alpha \times C \times V^2 \times f \qquad (2)$$

2.1 Related Works

The Partial Reconfiguration capability can be beneficial to P^{2}IP in two aspects, not only it can help to reduce power consumption but also extend its original functionality. Indeed, we report many related techniques that can be used in FPGAs to achieve more efficient power consumption while preserving functionality. However, while PR allows the reuse of the underlying logic, design granularity, reconfiguration support infrastructure and reconfiguration speed may be limiting factors.

One way to compensate the power consumption increase during PR is to maximize the partial bitstream transfer bandwidth from external memory to the PR interface [6]. In [5], the authors propose an intelligent Internal Configuration Access Port (ICAP) controller using DMA for a Virtex-4 board. This is a good solution for Virtex-4, which does not support DMA when copying partial bitstreams, but imposes additional logic to synthesize the modified ICAP interface. [18] describes an alternative way to load a partial bitstream in a Virtex-5 board. A customized PR controller is developed, which uses DMA to load the partial bitstream from external memory (DDR) to the ICAP interface, being more efficient than the traditional approach from Xilinx for the Virtex-5 family.

Concerning granularity and reconfiguration speed, in [7] it is proposed a 1-cycle reconfiguration scheme, although all reconfigurable elements are mapped into DSP48E1 cells. Thus, a fast reconfiguration can be carried out by updating the parameters of the DSP cells, but at the cost of high power consumption and high-end (and therefore costly) FPGA. Another approach, [1], proposes an alternative ICAP interface (called AC-ICAP) capable of applying PR to single LUTs without requiring pre-computed partial bitstreams. According to the authors, it imposes an acceleration of 380x with respect to the Xilinx ICAP controller. The disadvantage is that it consumes 5% additional cells on a Virtex-5 FPGA. With regard to structures using more complex PR components, the authors in [8] implement a FIR filter applied to Software-Defined Radio and conclude that using PR leads to a half of the original power consumption.

Compared to the works mentioned above P^{2}IP is already a software-configurable and customizable hardware architecture. This implies that it is already inherently scalable and flexible, so we assume a very small resources overhead by supporting PR. Due to requiring few or no additional controllers, when extended, its impact on energy consumption will be limited. As demonstrated by previous works, granularity has an impact on the size of partial bit-streams as well as on reconfiguration speed. The proposed architecture using regular components of intermediate granularity (greater than a DSP cell or a LUT) maintains PR time and partial bit-streams restricted. Moreover, the scalable aspect of the architecture makes it possible to combine various strategies to save static and dynamic power. However, this is a real-time configurable architecture, so, PR time can have an impact on the resulting image stream processing. Since the reconfiguration task is executed by the software side and several partial bitstream loading strategies are already available, the potential need to speed up the PR process is left out of the scope of this work.

3   Modifications on P^{2}IP

The original P^{2}IP architecture was enhanced to be used as AXI compliant IP for an FPGA implementation with extended configurable functionality including PR (for details about the original implementation refer to [4]).

3.1   Configuration Mechanism

The configuration mechanism allows to enable/disable operators as well as the input/outputs of a PE. It consists of a configuration tree composed by Configuration Decoders (CDs) organized hierarchically. In the original version it' communicates via an 8-bit serial interface [3]. The extended version provides an AXI4-Lite 32-bit interface clocked at 100 MHz and the configuration word carries two bytes of data (instead of one in the original implementation), as shown in Fig. 2.

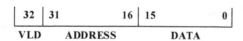

32	31	16	15	0
VLD	ADDRESS		DATA	

Fig. 2. Configuration word. The Configuration Block reads the word when the VLD bit is high. ADDRESS corresponds to the operator ID, and DATA is the configuration info.

On Fig. 1 it is possible to see the PE Configuration Decoder (PE-CD) and four (Module + Register) dedicated CDs (for the PP, RI, SP and the MC modules). Each CD can decode one (e.g. NE), two (e.g. ALU) or three words of data (e.g. Reconfigurable Interconnect crossbar), and this limit is defined during instantiation of the component.

3.2   PR Applied on P²IP

The runtime flexibility of P²IP requires that the number of PEs and the provided functionality be enough to withstand all possible stream operations. For that reason, the number of PEs is defined before synthesis. Although, depending on the video processing algorithm to be executed, PEs are not completely in use. Considering, for instance, basic algorithms such as Edge Sharpening (*Sharp*), Canny Edge Detection (*Edge*) or Harris Corner Detection (*Corner*), they just share some operations. *Sharp* uses just three PEs to data processing, while the others use five (*Edge*) and seven (*Corner*), respectively. In that context, unused PEs still contribute to both, dynamic and static power consumption. For details about mapping each application onto P²IP refer to [3].

To make possible the execution of the three aforementioned applications, seven PEs are defined. This number is chosen according to the *Corner* application, which, among the three, requires the greatest amount of PEs [3]. At runtime, the PEs or its content cannot simply be removed: it would interrupt the video stream continuity. Thus, in addition to the regular content of a PE core (all the blocks as shown in Fig. 1), a modified version (core+bypass) is proposed, in which the output buffers the input, to ensure a continuous video stream before removing the core. Indeed, the core of each PE is contained in a Reconfigurable Region (RR), as suggested in [4]. So, seven RRs are defined in the FPGA area. PEs are equal in size and content, hence, all RRs resource requirements are the same. However, resources allocated to each RR may vary, depending on where the RR is allocated in the FPGA area (and, consequently, the available resources in the referred area).

To achieve the three mentioned applications examples using PR, three configurations are defined:

- *Sharp*: RR1, RR2, RR3 in default configuration; RR4, RR5, RR6 and RR7 bypassed;
- *Edge*: RR1, ..., RR5 in default configuration; RR6 and RR7 bypassed;
- *Corner*: RR1, ..., RR7 in default configuration.

Figures 3, 4 and 5 show, respectively *Sharp*, *Canny* and *Corner* applications mapped onto P²IP using PR. The software-driven configuration mechanism is responsible for activating the inputs, outputs and internal blocks of each PE.

4   Methodology

The new architecture is able to allocate resources (PEs) to reconfigurable regions (RRs) defined in the FPGA area. Resources allocated to each RR can be of type bypass or original PE core.

Fourteen partial bitstreams (Default RR1..7 and Bypass RR1..7, in Fig. 6) are initially stored in an SD card. During boot, the ARM processor copies these partial bitstreams to the DDR memory.

After that, the ARM also loads a full bitstream (the initial configuration containing static and dynamic parts) before the FPGA starts running.

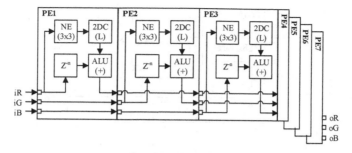

Fig. 3. *Sharp* application mapped onto P²IP: the first three PEs are in default configuration; the four last are configured as bypass.

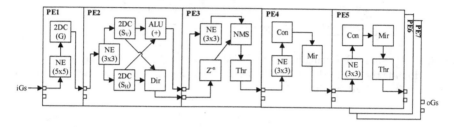

Fig. 4. *Canny* application mapped onto P²IP: the first five PEs are in default configuration; the two last are configured as bypass.

By default, the Xilinx Zynq platform offers two options to load a bitstream into the FPGA: the Internal Configuration Access Port (ICAP) or the Processor Configuration Access Port (PCAP). The first one is in use, for a long time, by the previous FPGA families [1,5,17,18]. It consists of an IP softcore and, consequently, spends some FPGA resources. The PCAP interface is native, does not consume any FPGA resources and uses a DMA engine [10]. This process is more efficient than the one adopted by the previous Xilinx FPGA families, since these generations did not use DMA natively, turning the partial bitstream transfer slower [9] while forcing the designer to consume more FPGA resources to allocate a custom DMA engine or the ICAP interface [17].

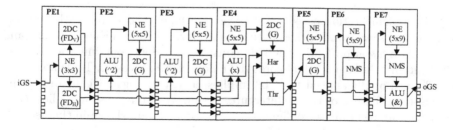

Fig. 5. *Corner* application: all PEs are in default configuration.

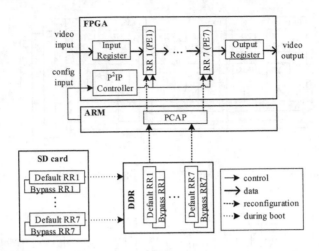

Fig. 6. P^2IP using PR: during boot, the ARM reads the partial bitstreams from the SD Card and loads them into the DDR. On demand, during runtime, the partial bitstreams are loaded from DDR into the RRs.

More details about the bitstream copy from the SD card to the DDR memory and from the DDR memory to the PCAP interface (valid for the Xilinx 7-series FPGAs) can be found on [19].

Since the purpose of this work is to reduce energy consumption, additional logic must be minimized, therefore the PCAP interface was chosen to transfer (static and partial) bitstreams from the memory to the FPGA, under the ARM supervision. The ARM is also used to activate the inputs/outputs, internal interconnections and blocks of each PE via an AXI4-Lite [14] interface.

For details about how the configuration mechanism works refer to [3]. Since all the video processing is done on the FPGA side, we have chosen to use a baremetal implementation on the ARM side, instead of using an Operating System. Figure 6 shows the block diagram of the architecture using PR, detailing how the ARM loads a partial bitstream into P^2IP.

5   Results

A P^2IP implementation based on PR was developed and tested with multiple configuration scenarios. Synthesis has been performed using Vivado 2015.2.1 and Zynq 7020 System on Chip (SoC). It consists of a SoC containing an Artix-7 FPGA, from Xilinx, and a dual-core ARM Cortex-A9 processor. To demonstrate that the use of PR applied to P^2IP implies energy savings without disrupting the real-time feature of the architecture, results regarding resource allocation, power measurement and reconfiguration time analysis are shown in this section.

5.1   Resource Analysis

Among the three applications, *Sharp* requires less resources, since four out of seven PEs are partially reconfigured as bypass. *Edge* still uses less logic resources than the static implementation, since the two last PEs are bypassed. *Corner* is more resource-consuming than the static implementation because all PEs are in the default configuration.

This application demands a higher number of resources than the original implementation, but in the worst case the resource increase is less than 5%, due to the extra logic added when using PR, and, in the best case, there is a resource utilization reduction of more than 50%.

The left side of Table 1 shows the resources utilized by each application compared to the static implementation. *Sharp* requires less than a half resources, when compared to the original implementation. *Edge* uses less than 80% of the resources required by the static implementation. *Corner* introduces almost 5% more FFs and 2% LUTs than the static implementation.

Table 1. Allocated resources, compared to the original implementation (left side) and measured power, in mW (right side).

	Allocated resources			Measured power, in mW		
	LUTs	FFs	RAMB18	Original	PR	Δ
Sharp	43.59%	48.31%	42.85%	371	204	−45.01%
Edge	70%	76.62%	71.42%		280	−24.52%
Corner	101.94%	104.73%	100%		373	+0.54%

5.2   Power Consumption Measurement

Previously, it has been shown that *Sharp* and *Edge* use less active resources than the static implementation. It leads to energy savings. To measure the energy consumption, we used the ZC702 board from Xilinx, which has current and voltage monitoring circuits [11]. One of these circuits is able to measure current and voltage applied to the FPGA core, as shown in Fig. 7. $VCCINT$ is a $1\,V$ voltage applied to the FPGA core. The voltage drop across a $5\,m\Omega$ is fed to an Instrumentation Amplifier (IA), whose gain is 23.7. The IA output serves as input to an I^{2}C DC/DC converter, which monitors $VCCINT$ and turns the analog voltage into digital data (I^{2}C). Since there are other I^{2}C components on the board, an 1-to-8 channel I^{2}C multiplexer is present.

Data can be accessed by the ARM [12], the FPGA or by means of a USB Interface Adapter, from Texas Instruments [13]. As stated before the monitored information is accessed through I^{2}C protocol. Getting data using the FPGA is not the most efficient solution, since it means adding logic resources to define in hardware I^{2}C communication interface and, consequently, it would contribute to power consumption increasing. Using the ARM is a good alternative if the USB Interface Adapter is not available.

In this work we have used the USB Interface Adapter. Fusion Power Digital Design software, from Texas Instruments, links to the USB Interface Adapter and gets voltage and current information, making possible to calculate the power consumption. It is possible to define measurement parameters and acquisition rate. Minimum acquisition rate is 10 ms, but it is important to highlight that the USB Interface Adapter is plugged to a computer running Microsoft Windows, which is not a Real Time Operating System (RTOS), and, thus, there is no guarantee that the acquisition rate will be respected. Due to this restriction during tests the minimum acquisition rate used was 100 ms. An advantage of this method compared to the ARM reading current and voltage is that the first does not interfere in the ARM power consumption [15].

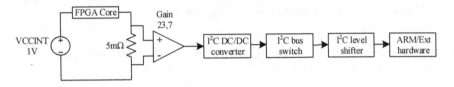

Fig. 7. FPGA core current measurement circuit on ZC702 board. Current can be read by the ARM processor or by an external hardware from Texas Instruments, both through the I²C bus.

The right side of Table 1 shows the measured power for the three configurations using PR (third column), compared to the original implementation (second column). The last column of the referred Table shows how much power savings it is possible to achieve using PR into P²IP. For each configuration 200 samples have been acquired using a sample rate of 100 ms, totalizing a 20 s acquisition (for each application). The values shown on Table 1 are the average of the 200 samples.

As can be seen in the previous Table, the power overhead for the *Corner* algorithm, due to the extra partial reconfiguration logic, is negligible.

5.3 Reconfiguration Latency

Another important point to be discussed is the amount of time necessary for changing configurations. Transitions require loading two partial bitstreams (such as from *Sharp* to *Edge*) or four partial bitstreams (such as from *Sharp* to *Corner*). According to Xilinx the bitstream transfer rate using PCAP interface in non-secure mode is 400 MB/s [16]. Partial bitstream size for RR1, RR2 and RR3 is 306 KB; for RR4, 309 KB; and, for RR5, RR6 and RR7, 409 KB. To measure the time necessary to load one partial bitstream a 64-bit general purpose ARM timer was used. Time to reconfigure each partial bitstream was measured and the average data rate is 128.51 MB/s.

Table 2 shows the time necessary to change configurations. To load one partial bitstream it is necessary: 2.381 ms, for RR1, RR2 or RR3; 2.404 ms, for RR4; and 3.175 ms for RR5, RR6 and RR7.

Table 2. Latency, when changing configurations, in ms.

	Sharp	Edge	Corner
Sharp	-	5.579	11.929
Edge	5.579	-	6.350
Corner	11.929	6.350	-

To assure that, using PR, the system remains a real time one, the following Equation is used:

$$t_{total} = t_{reconfig} + t_{config} \tag{3}$$

where t_{total} is the total reconfiguring latency, $t_{reconfig}$ is the time necessary to apply PR to the RRs and t_{config} is the time necessary to configuring internal PE blocks.

Time necessary to apply PR depends on how many RRs will be configured and is described in (4):

$$t_{reconfig} = \sum t_{RR_i} \tag{4}$$

where t_{RR_i} is the time necessary to apply PR to each RR.

Time necessary to apply PR to one RR depends on the external memory (which stores the partial bitstream) access and also on the time to load the partial bitstream on the respective RR and is shown in (5):

$$t_{RR_i} = t_{DDR} + t_{load_{PB}} \tag{5}$$

To maintain the real time feature of the system the following Equation must be respected:

$$t_{total} < t_{frame} \tag{6}$$

If (6) is respected then only one frame will be lost during reconfiguration, using PR or not. If the time overhead introduced by PR is less than the frame timing the extra time necessary to apply PR is admissible and does not imply in additional delay, that is, the system remains real time.

It is necessary $t_{config} = 0.27\,\mu s$ for each operator to be configured. In terms of latency the worst case is to change from *Sharp* to *Corner*, in which it is necessary to apply PR to four RRs and configure 21 operators (see Fig. 5). In this case $t_{total} = 11.935\,ms$. So, only one frame will be lost when applying PR. When changing the configuration (the number of active PEs or event an internal block) of the architecture (using PR or not) one frame will be lost. This work proves that it is possible to apply PR without losing additional frames.

6   Conclusions

In this article we have presented a low-power P^2IP architecture based on the use of the PR strategy. The original architecture was extended to support PR: processing elements were designated as PR components resulting on less than 5% resources overhead. To demonstrate the advantages of this novel architecture in terms of power consumption, three image processing algorithms were mapped and executed on both architectures. Power consumption comparison of original and PR implementations has been carried out and attested that PR implementation leads to power savings of up to 45%. The worst-case scenario, which takes into account the use of all available resources, implies an additional energy cost of less than 1%. Furthermore, PR latency does not affect the real-time feature of the system.

The PR strategy should not only be applied to lower the power consumption, it also serves to combine multiple alternative implementations of PEs that can be interchanged according to particular execution and quality requirements. Thus, future work should investigate the balance between power saving and required processing power.

Acknowledgments. The authors would like to thank the support from the Coordination of Superior Level Staff Improvement (CAPES), brazilian sponsoring agency, and also the Electronics and Microelectronics Department from the University of Mons, Belgium, for the support offered to the development of this work.

References

1. Cardona, L.A., Ferrer, C.: AC_ICAP: a flexible high speed ICAP controller. Int. J. Reconfigurable Comput. (2015). doi:10.1155/2015/314358
2. Possa, P.R., Mahmoudi, S.A., Harb, N., Valderrama, C., Manneback, P.: A multi-resolution FPGA-based architecture for real-time edge and corner detection. IEEE Trans. Comput. **63**, 2376–2388 (2014). doi:10.1109/TC.2013.130
3. Possa, P., Harb, N., Dokládalová, E., Valderrama, C.: P^2IP: a novel low-latency programmable pipeline image processor. Microprocess. Microsyst. **39**, 529–540 (2015). doi:10.1016/j.micpro.2015.06.010
4. da Cunha Possa, P.R.: Reconfigurable low-latency architecture for real-time image and video processing. UMONS (2013)
5. Liu, S., Pittman, R.N., Forin, A.: Minimizing partial reconfiguration overhead with fully streaming DMA engines and intelligent ICAP controller. In: Microsoft Research (2009)
6. Liu, S., Pittman, R.N., Forin, A.: Energy reduction with run-time partial reconfiguration. In: Microsoft Research (2009)
7. Ihsen, A.: Conception de Systèmes Embarqués Fiables et Auto-réglables. Universit de Valenciennes, Applications sur les Systèemes de Transport Ferroviaire (2016)
8. Becker, T., Luk, W., Cheung, P.Y.K.: Energy-aware optimization for run-time reconfiguration. In: 18th IEEE Annual International Symposium on Field-Programmable Custom Computing Machines (FCCM), pp. 55–62 (2010). doi:10.1109/FCCM.2010.17

9. Blodget, B., Bobda, C., Huebner, M., Niyonkuru, A.: Partial and dynamically reconfiguration of Xilinx Virtex-II FPGAs. In: Becker, J., Platzner, M., Vernalde, S. (eds.) FPL 2004. LNCS, vol. 3203, pp. 801–810. Springer, Heidelberg (2004). doi:10.1007/978-3-540-30117-2_81
10. Xilinx: Vivado Design Suite Tutorial - Partial Reconfiguration (2015)
11. Xilinx: ZC702 Evaluation Board for the Zynq-7000 XC7Z020 All Programmable SoC User Guide (2015)
12. Srikanth, E.: Zynq-7000 AP SoC Low Power Techniques part 3 - Measuring ZC702 Power with a Standalone Application Tech Tip (2014)
13. Texas Instruments: USB Interface Adapter Evaluation Module User's Guide (2006)
14. Xilinx: AXI4-Lite IPIF v3.0 (2016)
15. Nunez-Yanez, J.L., Hosseinabady, M., Beldachi, A.: Energy optimization in commercial FPGAs with voltage, frequency and logic scaling. IEEE Trans. Comput. **65**, 1484–1493 (2016). doi:10.1109/TC.2015.2435771
16. Xilinx: Partial Reconfiguration of a Hardware Accelerator on Zynq-7000 All Programmable SoC Devices (2013)
17. Silva, C.A.A., Neto, A.D.D., Oliveira, J.A.N., Melo, J.D., Barbalho, D.S., Avelino, A.M.: Definition of an architecture to configure artificial neural networks topologies using partial reconfiguration in FPGA. IEEE Latin Am. Trans. **15**, 2094–2100 (2015)
18. Dondo, J.D., Barba, J., Rincón, F., Moya, F., López, J.C.: Dynamic objects: supporting fast and easy run-time reconfiguration in FPGAs. J. Syst. Archit. **59**, 1–15 (2013). doi:10.1016/j.sysarc.2012.09.001
19. Muhammed, A.K., Rudolph, P., Gohringer, D., Hubner, M.: Dynamic and partial reconfiguration of Zynq 7000 under Linux. In: 2013 International Conference on Reconfigurable Computing and FPGAs, ReConFig 2013 (2013). doi: 10.1109/ReConFig.2013.6732279

NIM: An HMC-Based Machine
for Neuron Computation

Geraldo F. Oliveira[1(✉)], Paulo C. Santos[1], Marco A.Z. Alves[2],
and Luigi Carro[1]

[1] Informatics Institute, Federal University of Rio Grande do Sul,
Porto Alegre, Brazil
{gfojunior,pcssjunior,carro}@inf.ufrgs.br
[2] Department of Informatics, Federal University of Paraná,
Curitiba, Brazil
mazalves@inf.ufpr.br

Abstract. Neuron Network simulation has arrived as a methodology to help one solve computational problems by mirroring behavior. However, to achieve consistent simulation results, large sets of workloads need to be evaluated. In this work, we present a neural in-memory simulator capable of executing deep learning applications inside 3D-stacked memories. With the reduction of data movement and by including a simple accelerator layer near to memory, our system was able to overperform traditional multi-core devices, while reducing overall system energy consumption.

Keywords: Processing in memory · Near-data processing · Neuron simulator · Neural networks · Hybrid memory cube · Vector operations

1 Introduction

Neuron simulation has become a popular tool used to try to reproduce human brain's behavior, and a resource used to solve problems that require a learning capability from the system. For a given neuron in a Neural Network (NN), its Natural Time Step (NTS) defines the maximum time it has to read data from its neighbors, operate over input data, and output the resulted computation to subsequent neurons. Currently, the NTS for an Inferior-Olivary Nucleus (ION) neural arrangement is $50\,\mu s$ [1]. To keep up with system constraints, today neural simulators aim to explore available application parallelism by using HPC devices, usually composed of a mix of multi-core processors [2], GPU devices [3], and accelerator units based on FPGAs [4]. However, those setting are highly expensive and not energy efficient. A significant part of system energy consumption comes from data movement throughout the whole system [5]. For a neuron, data from its neighbors travel throughout the entire memory system until it gets to the computational target core. Therefore, a neuron simulation system presents a small rate of memory reuse, since only data from a single layer would

© Springer International Publishing AG 2017
S. Wong et al. (Eds.): ARC 2017, LNCS 10216, pp. 28–35, 2017.
DOI: 10.1007/978-3-319-56258-2_3

be useful for other neurons. This almost data-streaming behavior, intrinsic of neuron simulators, motives moving computational resources closer to the memory system.

Processing-in-Memory (PIM) aims to reduce system consumed energy and improve performance by including computational units inside or close to memory elements [6]. Several commercial 3D-stacked memories are available in the market nowadays, as Hybrid Memory Cube (HMC) [7], and High Bandwidth Memory (HBM) [8]. We have chosen to work with HMC memory because it has a concise public documentation, and also because it is technologically independent of any DRAM implementation. In the latest HMC specification [7], one device is composed of four high-speed serial links, a logic layer of 32 vault controllers, and four layers of DRAM memories connected via TSV through the vault controller. A single HMC device can provide a total bandwidth up to 320 GB/s.

In this work, we proposed a PIM reconfigurable accelerator implemented inside a HMC that can simulate biologically meaningful neural networks of considerable size. We highlight two distinct neuron's model, one proposed by Hodgkin-Huxley [9], and another by Izhikevich et al. [10], since both works present a complete and well accepted neural model, yet being different in structure and complexity. The Neuron In-Memory (NIM) mechanism presented is capable of simulating up to 12288 neurons inside the NTS of 50 μs.

2   NIM: A Neuron in Memory Approach

In a generic NN architecture, each network layer is composed of several neurons, which are connected throughout a fixed number of layers. In each layer, a given neuron receives data from previous layers, and potentially from the external world. This structure exposes both the available parallelism between neurons from a single layer, as also the computational demand required for simulating about the number of neurons per layer. One can notice that all neuron's input parameters can be arranged in a vector structure, positioning each neuron parameter in sequential order. This arrangement enables to execute vector operations over NN data. Also, the vector structure can be exploited directly by HMC devices, both by taking advantage of its internal parallelism, as also by implementing a PIM module, which can provide acceleration to NN applications.

Figure 1 shows in black boxes our mechanism distributed among HMC vaults. Our work is based on the device presented in [11], which implements an HMC accelerator capable of vector operations over up to 8KB chunks of data, and it can also be reconfigured to work with different ranges of data as the work proposed by [12]. However, due to the particularity of NNs applications, minor changes in the [11] mechanism were necessary to accomplish the proposed tasks.

2.1   Computation: Minor Changes

The work presented in [11] provides plain FUs capable of computing data directly from main memory. In our work, more complex FUs have been implemented

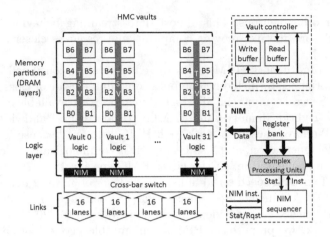

Fig. 1. NIM mechanism overview.

to execute NN task-intensive operations, such as exponentiation and division, which can be reconfigurable at runtime. Our mechanism operates at a frequency of 1 GHz. It is composed of 2,048 functional units (integer + floating-point), and a small register file with 8×16 registers of 32 bits each per vault. The integer FUs have a latency of 1 cycle for ALU, three cycles for multiplication, 20 cycles for the division, and ten cycles for exponentiation. For the floating-point FUs, the latencies are five cycles for ALU, five cycles for multiplication, 20 cycles for the division, and 18 cycles for exponentiation.

We also included support to perform fast vector elements operation. [11] counts with up to 64 FUs per HMC vault. Thus, all its FUs could be accessed in parallel to execute a single vector addition. Nevertheless, the original register file does not allow such operation, since each process occurs between different registers. To avoid a slow execution that would be constituted by a sequence of *SHIFT* and *ADD* commands, [11] data path was modified to execute intra-register operations, and a new *SUM* instruction was added to [11] ISA. One single vector operation unit can have different ranges of elements, from 64 B to 256 B.

Also, to schedule a given NN into our device, we simply travel through the neuron parameters' vector, placing each element evenly between memory banks, in an interleaving fashion.

3   Experimental Methodology and Evaluation of NIM

This section describes all performed experiments and its following results. To better understand all presented results, it is important to notice that the total number of neurons simulated in a NN is equivalent to the product of the number of neurons per layer N/L by the total number of layers L.

3.1   Methodology

To evaluate our work, we have made use of a cycle-accurate HMC simulator [13]. We aimed to simulate the maximum number of neurons while respecting the 50 µs NTS. Besides, we investigated how many neurons our device was able to simulate in a more relaxed time window of 1ms. At both sets of experiments, we considered as the best configuration result the total number of neurons that could fit its simulation time window, while taking into account a tolerance factor of 3% for 1ms experiments, and 1% for 50 µs.

The baseline considered was inspired by Intel SandyBridge processor microarchitecture. The SandyBridge is configured with up to 8 cores and AVX2 instruction set capabilities (512 bits of operands per core), and in all cases, the main memory used was a HMC device.

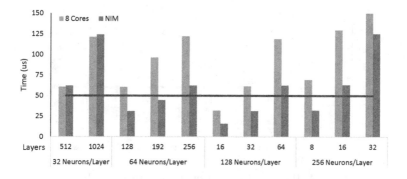

Fig. 2. Izhikevich Equations - 50 µs results

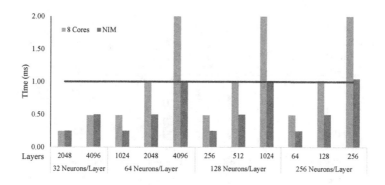

Fig. 3. Izhikevich Equations - 1 ms results

3.2   Performance Results

Izhikevich Application: Figure 2 depicts the results for NNs using Izhikevich equations. As the amount of N/L increases, the number of connections between neurons at different layers grows, therefore requiring more computational power from the system. During simulation, our NIM mechanism was able to simulate up to 12288 neurons within the $50\,\mu s$ NTS (64 N/L, 192 L). In contrast, for the same configuration, the baseline spent almost x2 more time than our NIM device. It is important to notice that for a small number of N/L, the baseline system performed better than our device. That happened because of two main factors. First, the baseline's CPU cores could execute instructions twice as fast as our NIM device. Second, and more important, the number of N/L is responsible for the amount of parallelism available. With more parallelism, a bigger array composed of neuron's input parameters can be sent to out device, thus providing data for more FUs to operate upon (an ideal array size would be of 8 KB, where all FUs would be operating).

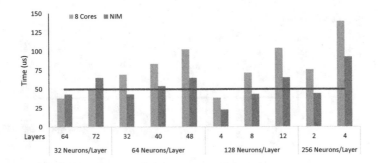

Fig. 4. Hodgkin-HuxkeyEquations - $50\,\mu s$ results

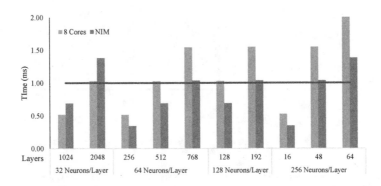

Fig. 5. Hodgkin-Huxkey 1 ms results.

Figure 3 shows the simulating results for the more relaxed scenario. When the time limit ranges to 1ms, the performance of the NIM mechanism showed the same behavior for N/L configured with up to 32 neurons. However, when the NN is configured with more than 64 N/L, the number of layers becomes less significant. The baseline can represent a maximum of 131072 neurons (64 N/L,

2048 *L*) while our NIM mechanism is capable of simulating the same amount of neurons at half the baseline time. For 1ms, the NIM simulated up to 262144 neurons in total (64 *N/L*, 4096 *L*).

Hodgkin-Huxkey (HH) Application: Figure 4 shows the results for the HH model with the time limit of 50 μs for both the baseline processor and for our mechanism. For a small number of *N/L*, the baseline showed a better performance than our device because of the little amount of parallelism available in the network. However, with more parallelism available, NIM achieves a better result. Within 50 μs NTS, the baseline can simulate up to 2304 neurons (32 *N/L*, 72 *L*). In contrast, within the same time, our device can simulate up to 2560 neurons (64 *N/L*, 40 *L*).

Figure 5 illustrates that the operational frequency of the baseline impacts the total number of neurons simulated. For the 1ms experiments, the baseline could simulate up to 65536 neurons (32 *N/L*, 2048 *L*), while at the best NIM configuration our device was able to simulate 49152 neurons (64 *N/L*, 768 *L*).

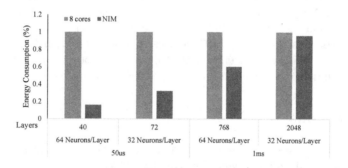

Fig. 6. Hodgkin-Huxkey energy results

3.3   Energy Consumption

To measure system energy consumption, we used the McPat [14] tool, configured to use 32 nm technology for both systems. We have chosen to estimate energy consumption for HH applications since their results showed a more heterogeneous scenario. We compared the baseline and NIM configurations that represented the maximum number of neurons simulated in each case.

Figure 6 depicts the percentage of energy consumed by our system when compared to the baseline. One can notice that the amount of *N/L* impacts the energy reduction our system can provide. For NNs with more *N/L*, our device mitigates unnecessary data movement from main memory to cache devices, since more *N/L* represent less data reuse. In contrast, increasing the number of layers reduces NIM impact over energy consumption, once that the number of hit access at cache memories will increase.

4   Related Work

In this section, we list several works that aim to simulate NNs. Each work targets distinct neuron models and networks topologies, making it not possible to compare the presented work directly with others. However, our evaluation metric (number of neurons in determined simulation time) can be used to approximate our gains over previous ones. We have classified the presented related works into four categories: GP-based, GPU-based, FPGA-based, and PIM-based.

In the first class, one could find works as [15] and [2]. Despite the large processing capability provided by these works, they both suffer from the same issue: neuron communication. In those cases, it is not possible to simulate NN within the natural time step.

[3] is an example of GPU-based neuron simulators. However, the timing constraint needed to represent biologically accurate NN on a large scale is a challenge for GPUs. Besides, GPUs are inefficient regarding energy and power.

In the third category, one could fit an extended number of works, as [4, 16], and [17]. Even though using dedicated hardware to simulate large NN is an effective approach, it is not as flexible as the other ones cited here.

Finally, similarly to our work, [18] aims to accelerate deep learning applications by exploiting PIM capabilities. In their work, the authors present an architecture composed of four HMC devices incremented with CPU and GPU modules at their logic layer. Even though [18] achieved good results, their module is computationally expensive, and it is not energy efficient as our device.

5   Conclusions

In this paper, we presented Neuron In-Memory (NIM), a computational mechanism able to simulate large Neural Networks (NNs). Our work is based on the vector processing capabilities extracted from NN applications that can be implemented directly in memory, taking advantages of the broad bandwidth available in modern 3D-stacked memory devices. To conclude, the presented NIM module is capable of simulating NN of significant sizes in an embedded environment. When compared with traditional multi-core environments, our mechanism provides system acceleration for large NN, while reducing overall energy consumption. In future works, we aim to extend our device to enable networks with layers of different sizes, thereby reducing data movement in small NN topologies.

References

1. De Gruijl, J.R., Bazzigaluppi, P., de Jeu, M.T., De Zeeuw, C.I.: Climbing fiber burst size and olivary sub-threshold oscillations in a network setting. PLoS Comput. Biol. **8**(12), e1002814 (2012)
2. Hines, M., Kumar, S., Schürmann, F.: Comparison of neuronal spike exchange methods on a Blue Gene/P supercomputer. Front. Comput. Neurosci. **5**, 49 (2011)

3. Wang, M., Yan, B., Hu, J., Li, P.: Simulation of large neuronal networks with biophysically accurate models on graphics processors. In: The 2011 International Joint Conference on Neural Networks (IJCNN), pp. 3184–3193, July 2011
4. Smaragdos, G., Isaza, S., van Eijk, M.F., Sourdis, I., Strydis, C.: FPGA-based biophysically-meaningful modeling of olivocerebellar neurons. In: Proceedings of the 2014 ACM/SIGDA International Symposium on Field-Programmable Gate Arrays, FPGA 2014, pp. 89–98. ACM, New York (2014)
5. Zenke, F., Gerstner, W.: Limits to high-speed simulations of spiking neural networks using general-purpose computers. Front. Neuroinform. **8**, 76 (2014). http://journal.frontiersin.org/article/10.3389/fninf.2014.00076
6. Balasubramonian, R., Chang, J., Manning, T., Moreno, J.H., Murphy, R., Nair, R., Swanson, S.: Near-data processing: insights from a MICRO-46 workshop. IEEE Micro **34**(4), 36–42 (2014)
7. Hybrid Memory Cube Consortium. Hybrid Memory Cube Specification Rev. 2.0 (2013). http://www.hybridmemorycube.org/
8. Lee, D.U., Hong, S., et al.: 25.2 a 1.2v 8GB 8-channel 128GB/s high-bandwidth memory (HBM) stacked DRAM with effective microbump I/O test methods using 29nm process and TSV. In: 2014 IEEE International Solid-State Circuits Conference Digest of Technical Papers (ISSCC), pp. 432–433, February 2014
9. Hodgkin, A.L., Huxley, A.F.: A quantitative description of membrane current and its application to conduction and excitation in nerve. Bull. Math. Biol. **52**(1), 25–71 (1990)
10. Izhikevich, E.M.: Simple model of spiking neurons. Trans. Neur. Netw. **14**(6), 1569–1572 (2003)
11. Alves, M.A.Z., Diener, M., Santos, P.C., Carro, L.: Large vector extensions inside the HMC. In: 2016 Design, Automation Test in Europe Conference Exhibition (DATE), pp. 1249–1254, March 2016
12. Santos, P.C., Oliveira, G.F., Tome, D.G., Alves, M.A.Z., Almeida, E.C., Carro, L.: Operand size reconfiguration for big data processing in memory. In: 2017 Design, Automation Test in Europe Conference Exhibition (DATE), March 2017
13. Alves, M.A.Z., Diener, M., Moreira, F.B., Villavieja, C., Navaux, P.O.A.: Sinuca: a validated micro-architecture simulator. In: High Performance Computation Conference (2015)
14. Li, S., Ahn, J.H., Strong, R.D., Brockman, J.B., Tullsen, D.M., Jouppi, N.P.: The McPAT framework for multicore and manycore architectures: simultaneously modeling power, area, and timing. ACM Trans. Archit. Code Optim. (TACO) **10**(1), 5 (2013)
15. Sakai, K., Sajda, P., Yen, S.-C., Finkel, L.H.: Coarse-grain parallel computing for very large scale neural simulations in the NEXUS simulation environment. Computers in Biology and Medicine, vol. **27**(4), 257–266 (1997)
16. Zhang, Y., Mcgeehan, J.P., Regan, E.M., Kelly, S., Nunez-Yanez, J.L.: Biophysically accurate foating point neuroprocessors for reconfigurable logic. IEEE Transact. Comput. **62**(3), 599–608 (2013)
17. Beuler, M., Tchaptchet, A., Bonath, W., Postnova, S., Braun, H.A.: Real-time simulations of synchronization in a conductance-based neuronal network with a digital FPGA hardware-core. In: Villa, A.E.P., Duch, W., Érdi, P., Masulli, F., Palm, G. (eds.) ICANN 2012. LNCS, vol. 7552, pp. 97–104. Springer, Heidelberg (2012). doi:10.1007/978-3-642-33269-2_13
18. Xu, L., Zhang, D.P., Jayasena, N.: Scaling deep learning on multiple in-memory processors. In: WoNDP: 3rd Workshop on Near-Data Processing (2015)

VLIW-Based FPGA Computation Fabric with Streaming Memory Hierarchy for Medical Imaging Applications

Joost Hoozemans[✉], Rolf Heij, Jeroen van Straten, and Zaid Al-Ars

Delft University of Technology, Delft, Netherlands
{j.j.hoozemans,j.van.straten-1,z.al-ars}@tudelft.nl,
r.w.heij@student.tudelft.nl

Abstract. In this paper, we present and evaluate an FPGA acceleration fabric that uses VLIW softcores as processing elements, combined with a memory hierarchy that is designed to stream data between intermediate stages of an image processing pipeline. These pipelines are commonplace in medical applications such as X-ray imagers. By using a streaming memory hierarchy, performance is increased by a factor that depends on the number of stages (7.5× when using 4 consecutive filters). Using a Xilinx VC707 board, we are able to place up to 75 cores. A platform of 64 cores can be routed at 193 MHz, achieving real-time performance, while keeping 20% resources available for off-board interfacing.

Our VHDL implementation and associated tools (compiler, simulator, etc.) are available for download for the academic community.

1 Introduction

In contemporary medical imaging platforms, complexity of image processing algorithms is steadily increasing (in order to improve the quality of the output while reducing the exposure of the patients to radiation). Manufacturers of medical imaging devices are starting to evaluate the possibility of using FPGA acceleration to provide the computational resources needed. FPGAs are known to be able to exploit the large amounts of parallelism that is available in image processing workloads. However, current workflows using High-Level Synthesis (HLS) are problematic for the medical application domain, as it impairs programmability (increasing time-to-market) and maintainability. Additionally, some of the image processing algorithms used are rather complex and can yield varying quality of results. Therefore, in this paper, we propose a computation fabric on the FPGA that is optimized for the application domain, in order to provide acceleration without sacrificing programmability. By analyzing the structure of the image processing workload type (essentially a pipeline consisting of multiple filters operating on the input in consecutive steps), we have selected a suitable processing element and designed a streaming memory structure between the processors.

The image processing workload targeted in this paper consists of a number of filters that are applied to the input data in sequence. Each filter is a stage

© Springer International Publishing AG 2017
S. Wong et al. (Eds.): ARC 2017, LNCS 10216, pp. 36–43, 2017.
DOI: 10.1007/978-3-319-56258-2_4

in the image processing pipeline. The input stage of a filter is the output of the previous stage - the stages *stream* data to each other. Making sure these transfers are performed as efficiently as possible is crucial to provide high throughput.

The processing element used in this work is based on a VLIW architecture. These type of processors are ubiquitous in areas such as image and signal processing. They are known for their ability to exploit Instruction-Level Parallelism (ILP) while reducing circuit complexity (and subsequently power consumption) compared to their superscalar counterparts. In the medical imaging domain, power consumption is not a main concern, but as image processing workloads can be divided into multiple threads easily, a reduction in area utilization will likely result in an increase in total throughput.

The remainder of this paper is structured as follows: Sect. 2 discusses related work, Sect. 3 discusses the implementation details, Sects. 4 and 5 present the evaluation and results, and Sect. 6 provides conclusions and future work.

2   Related Work

A prior study on using VLIW-based softcores for image processing applications is performed in [1], showing that a VLIW-based architecture has advantages over a scalar architecture such as the MicroBlaze in terms of performance versus resource utilization. In [2], an FPGA-based compute fabric is proposed using the LE-1 softcore (based on the same Instruction Set Architecture - VEX), targeting medical image processing applications. This work focuses solely on offering a highly multi-threaded platform without providing a memory hierarchy that can sustain the needed bandwidth through the pipeline. A related study on accelerating workloads without compromising programmability is [3], with one of the design points being a convolution engine as processing element. A well-known prior effort, and one of the inspirations of this work, uses softcores to provide adequate acceleration while staying targetable by a high level compiler is the Catapult project [4]. The target domain is ranking documents for the Bing search engine. A related effort that aims to accelerate Convolutional Neural Networks is [5]. However, this project did not aim to conserve programmability (only run-time reconfigurability), as the structure of this application does not change enough to require this. In the image processing application domain, [6] provides a comparison of convolution on GPU or FPGA using a Verilog accelerator, [7] and [8] present resource-efficient streaming processing elements, and [9] introduces a toolchain that targets customized softcores.

3   Implementation

The computation fabric developed in this work consists of two facets; the processing elements and the memory hierarchy, as shown in Fig. 1. The implementation of both will be discussed in this section. Then, the process of designing a full platform using these components is discussed.

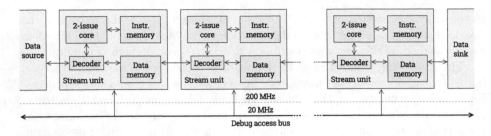

Fig. 1. Organization of a single stream of processing elements (Stream unit) and the streaming connections that link the data memories. Each processor can access the memory of its predecessor. Each processor's memories and control registers can be accessed via a bus that runs on a low clock frequency to prevent it from becoming a timing-critical net.

3.1 Processing Elements

This section describes the design and implementation of our fabric. The processor cores in the fabric are derived from the ρ-VEX processor [10]. The ρ-VEX processor is an VLIW processor based on the VEX ISA introduced by Fisher et al. [11]. The ρ-VEX processor has both run-time and design-time reconfigurable properties, giving it the flexibility to run a broad selection of applications in an efficient way.

Image processing tasks are highly parallelizable in multiple regards; (1) The code is usually computationally dense, resulting in high ILP, and (2) Every pixel can in theory be calculated individually and it is easy to assign pixels to threads (by dividing the image into blocks). In other words, there is an abundance of Thread-Level Parallelism (TLP). Exploiting TLP is usually more area efficient than exploiting ILP - increasing single-thread performance comes at a high price in power and area utilization and will quickly show diminishing returns. This is why GPUs exploit TLP as much as possible by using many small cores. Therefore, the processing elements of our fabric will use the same approach and we will use the smallest 2-issue VLIW configuration as a basis. This will still allow it to exploit ILP by virtue of having multiple issue slots and a pipelined datapath.

By placing multiple instances of our fabric on an FPGA, TLP can be exploited in two dimensions; by processing multiple blocks, lines or pixels (depending on the filter) concurrently, and by assigning each step in the image processing pipeline to a dedicated core (pipelining on a task level in contrast to the micro-architectural level).

To explore the design space of the processor's pipeline organization, we have measured code size and performance of a 3×3 convolution filter implemented in C. This convolution code forms a basis with which many operators can be applied to an image depending on the kernel that is used (blurring, edge detection, sharpening) so it is suitable to represent the application domain. The main loop can be unrolled by the compiler using pragmas. Figure 2 lists the performance using different levels of loop unrolling for different organizations of a 2-issue ρ-VEX pipeline; the default pipeline with 5 stages and forwarding, one with 2 additional pipeline stages to improve timing, and one using the longer pipeline and with Forwarding (FW) disabled to further improve timing and decrease FPGA resource utilization. Loop unrolling will allow the compiler to fill the pipeline latency with instructions from other iterations. The performance loss introduced is reduced from 25% to less than 2% when unrolling 8 times. Additionally, disabling forwarding reduces the resources utilization of a core allowing more instances to be placed on the FPGA (see Fig. 3).

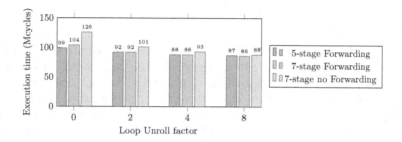

Fig. 2. Execution times of a 3×3 convolution filter on a single processor using different loop unrolling factors.

Pipeline organization		Cores	Resource utilization			Freq.
Forwarding	Stages		LUT	FF	BRAM	(MHz)
Enabled	7	64	99%	29%	81%	149
Enabled	5	64	93%	26%	81%	103
Disabled	7	75	96%	33%	95%	162
Disabled	5	75	98%	30%	95%	143
Disabled	7	4	5%	2%	5%	200
Disabled	7	64	82%	28%	81%	193

Fig. 3. Resource utilization and clock frequency of different platform configurations on the Xilinx VC707 FPGA board. The layout of the 64-core, 193 MHz platform on the FPGA is depicted on the right. Manually created placement constraints were used to group each stream together.

3.2 Memory Hierarchy

In our fabric, processing elements are instantiated in 'streams' of configurable length. This length should ideally be equal to the number of stages in the image processing pipeline. Each stage will be executed by a processor using the output of the previous processor. A connection is made between each pair of ρ-VEX processors in a stream, so that a core can read the output of the previous step (computed by the previous core in the stream) and write the output into its own data memory (making it available for reading by the next core in the stream). The memory blocks are implemented using dual-port RAM Blocks on the FPGA. Each port can sustain a bandwidth of one 32-bits word per cycle per port, so both processors connected to a block (current, next) can access a block without causing a stall. The blocks are connected to the processors by means of a simple address decoder between the memory unit and the data memories.

The first and last core should be connected to DMA (Direct Memory Access) units that move data to and from input and output frame buffers (eventually going off-board).

3.3   Platform

The VHDL code of the components is written in a very generic way and there are numerous parameters that can be chosen by the designer. First of all, the ρ-VEX processor can be configured in terms of issue width, pipeline configuration, forwarding, traps, trace unit, debug unit, performance counters, and caches. Secondly, there is an encompassing structure that instantiates processors in streams. The number of streams and length per stream are VHDL generics.

4   Experimental Setup

Since the target application of the designed system is related to medical image processing, an X-ray sample image is used as input for the evaluation. Typical medical imagers work with images that have a size of 1000 by 1000 pixels. The dimensions of our benchmark images are 2560 by 1920 pixels. The image is resized to other dimensions in order to determine the scalability of system performance. Each pixel is represented by a 32-bit value (RGBA). Using a technique described in the following section, the image may be scaled down to 1280 by 960 and 640 by 480 pixels.

A workload of algorithms based on a typical medical image processing pipeline is used. The first step in the image processing pipeline is an interpolation algorithm used to scale the size of the source image. The bi-linear and nearest neighbor interpolation algorithms both have the same computational complexity making them equally feasible. Because of its slightly higher flexibility, we select the bi-linear interpolation algorithm for the evaluation. Secondly, a gray scaling algorithm is applied. This algorithm is selected because it operates on single pixels in the input dataset. The third stage is a convolution filter that sharpens the image, followed by the final stage, an embossing convolution filter.

5   Evaluation Results

5.1   Resource Utilization

We have synthesized the platform using various configurations targeting the Xilinx VC707 evaluation board. As stated, the pipeline organization of the processing elements has influence on the resource utilization and timing. In

Figs. 3 and 4 options have been evaluated using the standard synthesis flow (unconstrained). With forwarding enabled, the platform completely fills the FPGA using 64 cores. When forwarding is disabled, this can be increased to 75.

Additionally, we have performed a number of runs where we created simple placement constraints that steered the tool towards clustering the cores per stream so that they are aligned on the FPGA in accordance with their streaming organization. A single stream consisting of 4 cores achieves an operating frequency of 200 MHz. Using 16 streams, timing becomes somewhat more difficult as the FPGA fabric is not homogeneous (some cores will need to traverse sections of the chip that are reserved for clocking, reconfiguration and I/O logic, and the distribution of RAM Blocks is not completely uniform). Still, this configuration achieves an operating frequency of 193 MHz at 80% LUT utilization, leaving room for interfacing with off-board electronics.

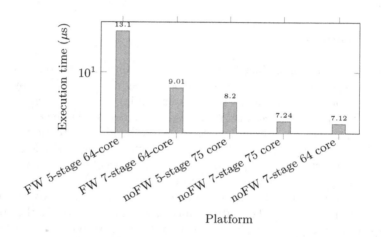

Fig. 4. Execution times of a convolution 3×3 filter for the platforms in the design-space exploration as listed in Fig. 3 using 8x loop unrolling (from Fig. 2).

5.2   Image Processing Performance

Figure 4 depicts the execution times of a 3×3 convolution filter on the various platforms, taking into account the number of cores, execution frequency, code performance on the pipeline organization (using 8x loop unrolling).

The results on using the streaming architecture for consecutive filters versus the same system with caches and a bus are depicted in Fig. 5. Enabling streaming of data results in speedup of 7.5 times. Processing an image sized 1280 by 960 requires 94.72 million clock cycles (see Fig. 5). Using 16 streams consisting of 4 cores (64 cores in total) at an operating frequency of 193 MHz, this would mean that our fabric can process approximately 34 frames per second.

Note that the difference will increase with the number of stages, so the fabric will perform better with increasingly complex image processing pipelines.

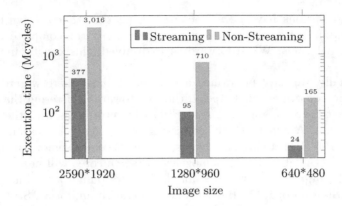

Fig. 5. Execution times of a 4-stage image processing pipeline on a streaming versus non-streaming platform using different image sizes

6   Conclusion

In this paper, we have introduced and evaluated an implementation of a FPGA-based computation fabric that targets medical imaging applications by providing an image processing pipeline-oriented streaming memory hierarchy combined with high-performance VLIW processing elements. We have shown that the streaming memory hierarchy is able to reduce bandwidth requirements and increase performance by a factor of 7.5 times when using a single stream of only 4 processing stages. The platform stays fully targetable by a C-compiler and each core can be instructed to perform an individual task. The platform is highly configurable and designers can modify the organization to best match their application structure. For future work, there is room for further design-space exploration of the processing elements in terms of resource utilization versus performance, introducing design-time configurable instruction sets, increasing the clock frequency, and other architectural optimizations. The platform, simulator and toolchain are available for academic use at http://www.rvex.ewi.tudelft.nl.

Acknowledgment. This research is supported by the ARTEMIS joint undertaking under grant agreement No. 621439 (ALMARVI).

References

1. Hoozemans, J., Wong, S., Al-Ars, Z.: Using VLIW softcore processors for image processing applications. In: 2015 International Conference on Embedded Computer Systems: Architectures, Modeling, and Simulation (SAMOS), pp. 315–318. IEEE (2015)
2. Stevens, D., Chouliaras, V., Azorin-Peris, V., Zheng, J., Echiadis, A., Hu, S.: BioThreads: a novel VLIW-based chip multiprocessor for accelerating biomedical

image processing applications. IEEE Trans. Biomed. Circuits Syst. **6**(3), 257–268 (2012)

3. Nowatzki, T., Gangadhan, V., Sankaralingam, K., Wright, G.: Pushing the limits of accelerator efficiency while retaining programmability. In: 2016 IEEE International Symposium on High Performance Computer Architecture (HPCA), pp. 27–39. IEEE (2016)

4. Putnam, A., Caulfield, A.M., Chung, E.S., Chiou, D., Constantinides, K., Demme, J., Esmaeilzadeh, H., Fowers, J., Gopal, G.P., Gray, J., et al.: A reconfigurable fabric for accelerating large-scale datacenter services. IEEE Micro **35**(3), 10–22 (2015)

5. Ovtcharov, K., Ruwase, O., Kim, J.-Y., Fowers, J., Strauss, K., Chung, E.S.: Accelerating deep convolutional neural networks using specialized hardware. Microsoft Research Whitepaper, vol. 2 (2015)

6. Russo, L.M., Pedrino, E.C., Kato, E., Roda, V.O.: Image convolution processing: a GPU versus FPGA comparison. In: 2012 VIII Southern Conference on Programmable Logic, pp. 1–6, March 2012

7. Wang, P., McAllister, J., Wu, Y.: Soft-core stream processing on FPGA: an FFT case study. In: 2013 IEEE International Conference on Acoustics, Speech and Signal Processing, pp. 2756–2760, May 2013

8. Wang, P., McAllister, J.: Streaming elements for FPGA signal and image processing accelerators. IEEE Trans. Very Large Scale Integr. (VLSI) Syst. **24**, 2262–2274 (2016)

9. Bardak, B., Siddiqui, F.M., Kelly, C., Woods, R.: Dataflow toolset for soft-core processors on FPGA for image processing applications. In: 2014 48th Asilomar Conference on Signals, Systems and Computers, pp. 1445–1449, November 2014

10. Wong, S., Anjam, F.: The Delft reconfigurable VLIW processor. In: Proceedings of 17th International Conference on Advanced Computing and Communications, (Bangalore, India), pp. 244–251, December 2009

11. Fisher, J.A., Faraboschi, P., Young, C.: Embedded Computing: A VLIW Approach to Architecture, Compilers, and Tools. Morgan Kaufmann Publishers, San Francisco (2005). 500 Sansome Street, Suite 400, 94111

Embedded Computing and Security

Hardware Sandboxing: A Novel Defense Paradigm Against Hardware Trojans in Systems on Chip

Christophe Bobda[1], Joshua Mead[1], Taylor J.L. Whitaker[1(✉)],
Charles Kamhoua[2], and Kevin Kwiat[2]

[1] University of Arkansas, JBHT Building, Fayetteville, AR 72701, USA
{cbobda,jpmead,txw043}@uark.edu
[2] Air Force Research Lab, Cyber Assurance Branch,
525 Brooks Road, Rome, NY 13441, USA
{charles.kamhoua.1,kevin.kwiat}@us.af.mil

Abstract. A novel approach for mitigation of hardware Trojan in Systems on Chip (SoC) is presented. With the assumption that Trojans can cause harm only when they are activated, the goal is to avoid cumbersome and sometimes destructive pre-fabrication and pre-deployment tests for Trojans in SoCs, by building systems capable of capturing Trojan activation or simply nullifying their effect at run-time to prevent damage to the system. To reach this goal, non-trusted third-party IPs and components off the shelf (COTS) are executed in sandboxes with checkers and virtual resources. While checkers are used to detect runtime activation of Trojans and mitigate potential damage to the system, virtual resources are provided to IPs in the sandbox, thus preventing direct access to physical resources. Our approach was validated with benchmarks from trust-hub.com, a synthetic system on FPGA scenario using the same benchmark. All our results showed a 100% Trojan detection and mitigation, with only a minimal increase in resource overhead and no performance decrease.

Keywords: Hardware sandbox · Hardware verification · Virtual resources · Hardware Trojan

1 Introduction

To tackle system complexity, and reduce costs and time-to-market system-on-chip (SoC) design, third-party Intellectual Property (IP) cores are used as integral parts of SoC design. Major parts of the IP design and IC production are outsourced to non-trusted facilities distributed across the globe, thus opening the door for Trojan insertion. Hardware Trojan insertion into an IC can occur at any stage of the IP integration process (3PIP) [5,16], including the specification, design, verification and manufacturing stages. Approaches to Trojan mitigation in SoCs have been so far statical using intense simulation, verification, and physical tests to detect the presence of malicious components before

© Springer International Publishing AG 2017
S. Wong et al. (Eds.): ARC 2017, LNCS 10216, pp. 47–59, 2017.
DOI: 10.1007/978-3-319-56258-2_5

system deployment. While statical methods take place at all levels of the integration process, post-fabrication testing based on side-channel observation have so far received more attention in the research community. The number of test patterns needed to activate with certainty potential hidden Trojans is very large for complex IPs and SoCs with dozens of inputs, outputs, states, and memory blocks, thus limiting the effectiveness of static testing methods. Run-time approaches such as [13] that have been proposed to monitor signal behavior and detect potential Trojan rely solely on using checkers and do not address generalization.

In this work, we propose a novel approach, the *Hardware Sandboxing* for Trojan mitigation in SoCs. Our approach is based on the well known concept of sandbox already in use in software, whose goal is to contain the execution and resources needed by components of non-trusted pieces of code in isolated environments, and deploying guards to prevent damaging actions to the rest of the system. Isolation of malicious IPs can increase system security while reducing fabrication costs, pre-deployment verification and testing efforts. Our concept will be enforced by dividing the system into a trusted area and a non-trusted area. Components in the trusted area are designed under strict control of the system integrator (e.g. the military) and trustworthy partners. These components are assumed to be safe and can access any system resource. Components in the non-trusted area are designed by non-trusted sources, and because they may contain hardware Trojans, they must be placed in a sandbox along with virtual resources they need. Trojans can be hidden in IPs and ICs, but as long as they do not manifest, the system can be considered secured. *The rationale of our work is therefore the same as fault-tolerant systems, namely to design and build systems along with dynamic methods that are capable of detecting manifestation of Trojans at run-time and prevent potential damage to the system.* To the best of our knowledge, this is the first work that addresses security in systems-on-chip through a containment of potential malicious components into sandboxes, which includes resources needed by the components in virtualized form, along with rule enforcement modules to detect malicious activities at run-time and prevent damage to the system.

The rest of the paper is organized as follows. Section 2 presents a short review of existing hardware Trojan mitigation methods. In Sect. 3, we present a general organization of SoC devices for a secured integration of non-trusted components. Using software as reference, sandboxing concepts and their feasibility in SoCs is investigated in Sect. 3.1. We then devise the structure of a Hardware Sandbox in Sect. 3.2, which leads to a design flow that starts with a systematic characterization of security properties and automatic generation of Hardware Sandboxes in Sect. 4. Our method is validated in Sect. 5 with examples from the trust-hub (www.trust-hub.com) benchmark leading to 100% protection of the system. Section 6 concludes the work and provides some indications of our future work.

2   Related Work

A comprehensive state of the art review of hardware Trojan mitigation approaches is provided in [5]. Thereafter protection and countermeasures can be done at three levels: at design time, at test time before deployment, and during system operation. Design time approaches mitigate Trojans either by hiding functional or structural properties of IPs to potential Trojan attackers through modification of IPs and ICs operation [7], thus making it difficult to insert Trojans in IPs, or by filling all non-used resources with non-functional components to prevent their use for Trojan insertion [19]. Side channel analysis has been widely investigated. It assumes that additional circuits needed for Trojan implementation and monitoring of activation conditions will have an observable impact on physical properties of the IC such as power behavior [18], area [3], temperature profile [8], path delays [12], or a combination of many physical parameters [6]. Deviation from behavior of a golden and Trojan free model is interpreted as a Trojan activity. Increasingly, verification approaches are being used to ensure correctness of some trust properties [15,20]. The idea is to characterize proper IP behavior and exercise functional verification with high coverage factor to catch deviations from normal IP behavior. One main problem with static approaches is the need for a golden model. Hardware Trojans are inserted most of the time because companies buy COTS and IPs that they cannot design in house, thus the non-existence of a golden model. Even in the presence of extensive tests and functional verification, activating test patterns may still not be exercised at testing time.

In this work, we are more interested in run-time approaches that can dynamically understand and assert IPs' properties to identify Trojans and prevent potential damage to critical systems. Online methods that rely on side channel analysis have the advantage of monitoring all devices' behavior at run-time and are therefore able to catch Trojans as they unfold. However, they still need a physical profile that only a golden model can provide. Security Monitoring has been discussed in [4] as a means to check signal behavior at run-time and identify deviation that might be attributed to malicious activities. The idea is to use assertions as a mean to describe signal behavior along with reconfiguration for reuse of area needed for the checker. Unfortunately, further details were not provided on conceptual and implementation realization of such strategy. A checker based on the use of parity information for online verification of potential security deviation has been presented in [13]. The checker is a classic parity checker, protected by a randomization procedure to prevent attacks from potential Trojans. Even though the authors achieved 99.98% success rate, no systematic approach has been provided for the design of generalized checkers. In [11] an isolation mechanism was presented with the goal to monitor and analyze traffic flow between an embedded device and the network for detection of potential DDoS activities. As in previous case, the approach does not involved virtual resource, which is a main component of hardware sandboxes considered here.

The approach proposed here is motivated by the observation that a better and cheaper IP protection can be achieved by focusing on a small set of security properties instead of the IP's internals. By focusing on components at their boundary and using checkers to track non-authorized behavior, a 100% protection of the rest of the system is possible. However, the use of checkers alone cannot be considered a sandbox. We therefore extend our protection strategy by providing isolated resources to non-trusted components. The combination of checkers and isolated virtual resources provided to non-trusted, third-party IPs is what makes our Hardware Sandbox. Our approach can be seen as the inverse of TrustZone [2] paradigm available in ARM processors. While ARM's Trust-Zone isolates sensitive parts of the system into a trusted zone and gives unlimited access to the rest of the system to non-trusted IPs, our approach does the inverse by giving unlimited access to all system resources to trusted components and encapsulates non-trusted components within Hardware Sandboxes.

3   Hardware Sandboxing Concepts in SoCs

As illustrated in Fig. 1 our proposed approach for designing secure SoCs partitions the chip in two zone types: a trusted region in which all components have direct access to system resources including communication components, peripherals and memory, and one or more non-trusted regions in which components execute in a sandbox. The trusted zone is tightly controlled by the system integrator and all resources are

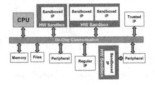

Fig. 1. Non-trusted IP integration in secured SoC using hardware sandboxing.

developed only by trusted contractors. Components Off The Shelf (COTS) and IPs designed by non-trusted contractors are only given indirect access to system resources over the sandbox. The proposed approach can be realized at all levels of the chip design cycle.

At system specification and register transfer level (RTL) implementation levels, the integrator will design the sandbox along with all resources under tight control and provide an interface to IP designers to integrate their IPs in the SoC. At the manufacturing level, split-manufacturing process [13] can then be used to manufacture the trusted areas and sandbox on one hand and the non-trusted parts separately in different facilities. The system-on-chip of Fig. 1 features a processor, memory, peripherals and two hardware accelerators in the trusted area. There are four non-trusted IPs encapsulated in three sandboxes with two IPs each using one sandbox exclusively and two IPs sharing a sandbox as a result of resource optimization.

Feasibility. The use of sandboxes between IPs and the rest of the system comes at the cost of *performance* and *resource overhead*. However, this is not an issue in today's SoCs as the evaluation in Sect. 5 will prove. Despite the high speed of hardware accelerators in SoCs, systems on chip always operate at the speed of the slowest peripheral. Consequently, buffers are always used between slower and faster modules to alleviate the effect of slower peripherals. For instance, many image capture and display modules operate only at a speed of 25 MHz but still work with hardware image compressors and renders that operate above 1GHz. The inclusion of buffers in sandbox can be used to alleviate potential slowdown by the intermediate sandbox components. Resource overhead is also not an issue in the area of transistor miniaturization and growing chip capacities.

3.1   Sandboxing Concepts in Software

Like many other technologies, such as network on chip, that originated from software before finding their way into hardware, we will first look into the details of sandboxing in software and devise a structure that fulfills hardware requirements. We rely on the taxonomy provided in [17], which places sandboxes in one of the following categories, depending on their operation mode.

Managed Code. Non-trusted applications are compiled into intermediate code (Java Bytecodes or Microsoft's Common Intermediate Language (CIL)), which is executed under the control of a virtual machine (VM) such as Java VM or Microsoft Common Language Runtime (CLR). This approach, while providing controlled access to system resources, cannot be applied to hardware IPs since hardware is not executed as a sequence of instructions that can be emulated by a virtual machine, but as a structure of interconnected blocks whose actions are visible only at their interface.

In-line Reference Monitor. This approach inserts resource access policies in the code of the non-trusted IP, which guarantees the enforcement of security policies even in case of bugs. Many verification tools allow for the insertion of assertions in IP specification for the purpose of verification only. While synthesizable assertion components are provided in libraries like OVL, they target a more coarse-grained integration at the interface of components. Extension of in-line reference monitor to the interface of IPs is more attractive for non-trusted IPs, many of which are COTS where the integrator has no access to the internals and therefore limits the interaction to the interface.

System Call Sandbox. Here, applications within the sandbox access system resources using system calls, which are caught and executed by the VM or the sandbox manager. This approach is similar to the previous in-line reference monitor, with the only difference being that the emulation takes place at the interface of the application and not within the code lines. This approach can be used to contain the execution of subsystems with processor and code used to access system resources.

Hardware Memory Isolation. The idea is to provide segments of isolated resources to non-trusted IPs within the sandbox, thus removing all memory access check mechanisms from the sandbox manager and only focusing on data transfer between memory segments in the sandbox and the rest of the system. We will make use of this approach, not only for memory, but for resource such as peripheral virtualization within the sandbox in general.

3.2   Structure of a Hardware Sandbox

With the previous discussion, we are now in position to devise the structure of our hardware sandbox (Fig. 2). The goal is to provide an environment with tools and capabilities for one or more non-trusted IPs to execute without jeopardizing secure parts of the system. We therefore propose the following components for a hardware sandbox.

Checkers. One or more checkers used for run-time enforcement of security rules defined by the system integrator at compile time. A checker is devised from the properties of an IP component in the sandbox and can be limited to only a subset of IP signals and properties for overhead reduction.

Virtual Resources. The concept of the sandbox requires that resources needed by IPs are provided in virtual form within the sandbox, where they can be used by an IP without damaging the rest of the system. In the sandbox of Fig. 2, the virtual UART (V-UART), virtual USB (V-USB), and virtual VGA (V-VGA) along with virtual memory V-MEM are provided to the IP in the sandbox. The main advantage here is that the interface between virtual resources within the sandbox and physical resources follows a secured protocol and can never cause a denial-of-service. Any attempt from a Trojan to alter a peripheral will be nullified by the virtual peripheral.

Sandbox Manager. The manager is in charge of data exchange between virtual resources and their physical counterparts, handling results from the checkers as well as configuration of the sandbox.

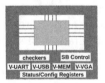

Status and Configuration Registers. A set of status and configuration registers will be used for the communication between sandbox manager and the rest of the system. Statistics on the behavior of IPs in the sandbox can be recorded for further analysis. IP that triggers a Trojan at run-time will cause a log on the processor side, which can then be used to exclude some vendors from the integrator's contractors' list.

Fig. 2. Structure of the hardware sandbox.

4   Design Flow

The structure of the hardware sandbox devised in
the previous section gives us a design flow consisting of (1) selecting the virtual resources to be used
along with their connection to IPs in the sandbox, (2)
generating checkers for IPs' signals and behavior to
observe and rules to enforce over time, and (3) designing the sandbox controller to map virtual resources
to physical ones and to control the flow of data to

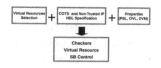

Fig. 3. Hardware sandbox
design flow.

and from the sandbox. While it is possible to perform all those tasks manually
on small examples, the complexity of today's designs requires tools that can
automatize the whole design process and produce efficient and secure systems.
The design flow we propose is illustrated in Fig. 3 and starts with the specification of IPs in the sandbox, the security properties and rules to be enforced at
run-time on selected signals, and the resources to be virtualized in the sandbox.
The flow produces the sandbox.

Virtual Resource Selection. Resources to be included in the sandbox can be
manually or automatically selected from a library of pre-implemented resources
according to the interfaces used by the IPs. For instance, if a non-trusted IP has
to be connected to a USB port on one side and to a UART port on the other side,
a virtual USB and a virtual UART can be automatically instantiated, configured
with the proper speed, clock, baud rate and placed into the sandbox. Building
a library of virtual resources to be included into a sandbox is not a challenging
task. Virtual resources have the same behavior as their physical counterparts,
thus the same specification used for the physical resource can be used with small
modifications. Since they act as intermediate between IPs in the sandbox and
the physical resource, they must offer the physical resource's interface to the IP
in the sandbox and the IP's interface to the virtual resource. Also a physical
resource controller must be used to manage the flow of data between interfaces.
In case a physical resource is used by many IPs in one sandbox, each IP will
be connected to its own virtual resource and data exchange between virtual and
physical resources will be coordinated by the physical resource controller in the
sandbox.

Checker Generation. The generation of run-time properties checkers and rule
enforcement components can be fully automatized, provided that we have a
means to capture desired and undesired behavior of IP components. Since we
are dealing with IP and COTS and have no details on their internal operation,
we only need to capture the desired properties of signals at their boundaries.
This raises the question of which language would be best appropriate for this
task. Fortunately, the verification community has been very active in this direction, designing languages and tools to capture properties of IPs at their interface,
mostly for verification purpose. We propose the use of the well established *properties specification language* (PSL) [1] as a starting point of our design flow
(Fig. 3).

Properties Specification. PSL is an Assertion Based Verification language that originated from the IBM Sugar language used for model checking, and evolved into an IEEE standard (1850–2005) [1]. PSL can be used to specify temporal properties of systems - i.e. properties that deal with the behavior of a system over time - through a combination of the temporal logic Linear Time Logic (LTL) [14] and regular expressions. PSL consists of 4 layers, the *Boolean layer*, the *temporal layer*, the *verification layer* and the *modeling layer*. Basic relationships among observable interface signals and state variables are defined at the Boolean layer. Expressions at this level are regular Boolean expression - either VHDL (*not* **reset** *and* **rd_en**) or Verilog flavor (**reset** && **rd_en**). The temporal layer is used to describe signals' behavior over finite or infinite sequence of states. A sequence is built from basic Boolean operators combined with sequence operators. PSL supports Sequential Extended Regular Expression (SERE) that allows for the evaluation of an expression across multiple clock cycles. Properties are then built on top of sequences and may contain Boolean expressions, and other sub-ordinate properties. Consider for instance a system with signals **req**, **ack**, **start**, **busy**, and **done**, each of which is true at a certain point in time [9]. The expression *always* **start** -> *next* **busy** states that whenever **start** is true at a time step, **busy** will be true at the next time step. Expression {[*]; **req**; **ack**} | => {**start**; **busy**[*]; **done**} states that for every occurrence of **req** that is immediately followed by **ack**, processing of the acknowledged request begins at the next time step after the **ack**. Expression **start**; **busy**[*]; **done**} is an example of sequential representation of event occurrences. It represents processing sequence that begins with **start**, which is followed by **busy** for some number of time points, and ends with **done**. PSL is primarily a verification language and the verification layer is where all directives are provided for a verification tool to check for the validity of a property. The *assert* directive for instance will instruct a verification tool to check that a certain property holds, and if not, a failure is reported. Using PSL or a subset of it to describe properties, we can now generate checker components automatically to guard security directives at run-time.

Even though our proposed design flow is based on PSL, our first experiments (Sect. 5) used Accelera's Open Verification Library (OVL) [10]. OVL is not a language, but a library of parameterizable assertion checkers, some of which can be synthesized directly into hardware. Instead of devising a global checker from properties specified in a language like PSL, the user must select signals that he wants to monitor and define an expression that can be evaluate in one or many steps.

Controller. The controller can be written by the user or generated from a behavioral description of the components in the sandbox. It must include actions to perform in case of security rule violation, reporting IP activities to the embedded processor and arbitrate data exchange between virtual resources and corresponding physical resources. The controller can vary from a simple finite state machine to a small processor that runs complex code in the sandbox.

5   Case Studies and Evaluation

The concepts previously discussed were tested with Trojan-free and Trojan-infected designs from the Trust-Hub (www.trust-hub.com) benchmark, which is now the reference in the hardware Trojan community. Besides simulation, we implemented various Trojan-free and Trojan-infected components from different classes (denial of service, functional change, information leakage) in FPGA for performance and overhead evaluation. We used the Digilent ZyBo (ZYnq BOard) FPGA board with the Zynq-7000 FPGA as processing engine. The dual core ARM Cortex-A9 processor along with Xilinx 7-series FPGA logic makes it an ideal platform to prototype systems-on-chip. The board also has a rich set of multimedia and connectivity peripherals (UART, USB, video and audio I/O, Ethernet, and SD), which makes it easier to exercise protection mechanisms for Trojans that access peripherals for denial-of-service or information leakage attacks.

Since Trojans from the Trust-Hub use the UART (RS232) for external connection, our tests were based on the RS232 interface. We were able to demonstrate that in 100% of cases our sandboxes were successful in containing and correctly identifying every RS232-based Trojan whose behavior deviated from the RS232 specification. The Trojan were from the classes denial of service, information leakage, and functionality change.

As shown in Tables 1 and 2, the resource overhead resulting from the addition of the sandbox resources is negligible (between 0.13% and 1.5%). This number is absolute and will not grow with the size of the circuit. The delay overhead is provided by the synthesis tool and shows negative values in the tables, which means that designs including sandboxes are not slower than the same designs without hardware sandboxes. The marginal improvement is due to the addition of registers in the sandbox, which breaks long combinational paths in the circuit into shorter paths, thus reducing delays and improving clock frequency.

The basis of our custom, run-time verification checkers consists of the Open Verification Library's (OVL) [10] synthesizable assertion checkers, specifically, the *Cycle Sequence component*. The heart of this component lies in a sequence signal as input with the signal, **fire**, as output. The Cycle Sequence accepts a signal of a sequence of bits, known as **test_expression**. Whenever the MSB of the sequence is evaluated to true, each subsequent bit in **test_expression** is checked on the next clock cycle edge to check for true evaluation. For the RS232-UART transmitter, this expression is derived from the following transmit signals: **xmit_data**, representing the data to be transmitted, **xmitH**, representing the signal to begin the transmission, **uart_xmit**, representing the serialized transmission line from the transmitter, and **uart_xmit_doneH**, representing the signal asserted when the transmission is complete. In total, we must check 177 bits across 177 clock cycles (CC) for the OVL Cycle Sequence to guarantee the UART transmission process is behaving expectantly. If even one of these bits is not high at the correct point of time in the full sequence, **fire** is asserted, indicating a problem exists; in our case, a hardware Trojan payload has been triggered. The following information gives the boolean expressions to create **test_expression** at each point in the sequence:

- $CC(0)$: **xmitH** == '1'
- $CC(1)$ to $CC(16)$: **uart_xmit_doneH** == '0' AND **uart_xmit** == '0'
- $CC(17+(16*i))$ to $CC(16+(16*(i+1)))$: **uart_xmit_doneH** == '0' AND **uart_xmit** == **xmit_data(i)**, where i is the index of **xmit_data**, range [0,7]
- $CC(145)$ to $CC(175)$: **uart_xmit_doneH** == '0' AND **uart_xmit** == '1'
- $CC(176)$: **uart_xmit_doneH** == '1'

This pattern follows the RS232 protocol used in the UART transmitter. Initially, **xmitH** is asserted to begin the transmission. For the next 16 clock cycles, **uart_tx** is always unasserted. Following that, the actual data is serialized and transmitted, starting from the LSB of **xmit_data**. Each of these bits being transmitted assumes 16 clock cycles. Once that is complete, the next 31 clock cycles of **uart_tx** are high followed by the **uart_xmit_doneH** signal being asserted to alert that the transmission process is complete. By checking if each of these signals is behaving as the protocol is given, we can build **test_expression** for the OVL Cycle Sequence. Additional checkers, such as one for the UART receiver, are created in the same manner.

Using the signal, **fire**, generated from the OVL component, we attach a series of memory-mapped, status and configuration registers to our sandbox to allow the processor the ability to read if a non-trusted IP is misbehaving, i.e. if our register reads 1 instead of 0. With this knowledge, appropriate action can thus be taken by the user.

Table 1. Evaluation of our hardware checkers with various RS232 designs from the Trust-Hub (www.trust-hub.com) benchmark.

Design	Trojan class	Checker type	Area overhead	Delay overhead
T-300	Info leak	Cycle sequence	243 LUT (1.38%)	−0.729 ns
T-400	Info leak	Cycle sequence	278 LUT (1.58%)	−0.046 ns
T-500	DoS	Cycle sequence	269 LUT (1.52%)	−0.174 ns
T-900	DoS	Cycle sequence	265 LUT (1.51%)	−0.149 ns

Another important feature of our sandbox is the virtualized resources. We build a case study in the FPGA as shown in Fig. 4 with one virtual VGA (V-VGA) and one virtual UART (V-UART), allowing our sandboxed IP the ability to see and use the corresponding transmitter and receiver without being directly connected to the physical UART device. Using the V-VGA is a simple process as it generates the correct vertical and horizontal sync signals based on the VGA protocol and return the pixel position on the

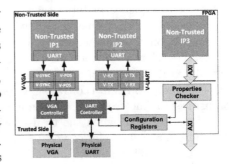

Fig. 4. Sandbox case study with two IPs and virtual UART.

screen to the sandboxed component. The V-UART is slightly more complex. However, mapping a non-trusted IP to the virtual UART to connect to the physical UART component is still a straightforward process.

Essentially, we invert the UART transmission and reception flow the non-trusted IP follows. The IP maps the potentially malicious transmission signals to the virtual UART receiver component, still on the non-trusted side. This receiver behaves exactly how the non-trusted IP allows and sees. The deserialized, received data, however, is passed to a virtual UART transmitter component on the trusted portion. Here, we check to make sure if the transmitted data should actually be sent via a simple finite state machine - i.e. if the non-trusted IP transmitting followed the correct procedure. If so, the data is transmitted to the physical UART component in the system. The reverse is true for mapping an IP receiver to allow communication with the physical receiver. Our implementation also allows for multiple IPs to exist in the same sandbox, mapping to their own virtual UARTs to a single physical UART through the use of an arbitration controller. In case of conflicts, the controller decides which component is allowed to use physical resource through priority, while the other IPs are forced to wait.

Table 2. Evaluation of our virtual resources.

Virtual resource	Area overhead	Delay overhead
VGA (V-VGA)	23 LUT (0.13%)	$-0.037\,$ns
RS232-UART (V-UART)	120 LUT (0.68%)	$-0.567\,$ns

After implementation, as shown in Tables 1 and 2, we found minimal overhead for both the RS232-UART checkers using the OVL Cycle Sequence and the virtual resources. Neither of these experienced any significant performance decrease either, proving our concept viable.

6   Conclusion

In this work we have demonstrated that the containment of non-trusted IPs using sandboxes with virtual resources and properties checkers can be efficient in fighting hardware Trojans in systems-on-chip, thus preventing high costs associated with pre-fabrication and pre-deployment tests. While our approach cannot detect information leakage though side-channel, we do not see this as a weakness. Because non-trusted IP are contained in the sandbox and therefore decoupled from the rest of the system, the possibility of stealing valuable information that they can leak through side channels is minimal to non-existent. Besides the design of a framework for automatic generation and optimization of hardware sandboxes, our future work will include the use of hardware sandboxes to provide more protection in multiprocessor systems-on-chip, where complete SoC subsystems, including a processor and other peripherals, may be isolated from secured parts using sandboxes.

Acknowledgment. This work was in part supported by the Air Force Summer Faculty Fellowship Program (SFFP 2015) at the Air Force Research Lab, Cyber Assurance Branch in Rome, NY. The authors would like to thank the Air Force and Information Institute for all the support they provided during the summer 2015.

References

1. IEEE standard for property specification language (PSL). IEEE Std 1850–2010 (Revision of IEEE Std 1850–2005) pp. 1–182, April 2010
2. ARM: Trustzone.   http://www.arm.com/products/processors/technologies/ trustzone/
3. Banga, M., Hsiao, M.: A region based approach for the identification of hardware Trojans. In: IEEE International Workshop on Hardware-Oriented Security and Trust, HOST 2008, pp. 40–47, June 2008
4. Bhunia, S., Abramovici, M., Agrawal, D., Bradley, P., Hsiao, M., Plusquellic, J., Tehranipoor, M.: Protection against hardware trojan attacks: towards a comprehensive solution. IEEE Des. Test **30**(3), 6–17 (2013)
5. Bhunia, S., Hsiao, M., Banga, M., Narasimhan, S.: Hardware trojan attacks: threat analysis and countermeasures. Proc. IEEE **102**(8), 1229–1247 (2014)
6. Çakir, B., Malik, S.: Hardware Trojan detection for gate-level ICS using signal correlation based clustering. In: Proceedings of the 2015 Design, Automation & Test in Europe Conference & Exhibition, DATE 2015, EDA Consortium, San Jose, CA, USA, pp. 471–476 (2015). http://dl.acm.org/citation.cfm?id=2755753.2755860
7. Chakraborty, R.S., Bhunia, S.: Security against hardware Trojan attacks using key-based design obfuscation. J. Electron. Test. **27**(6), 767–785 (2011). http://dx.doi.org/10.1007/s10836-011-5255-2
8. Forte, D., Bao, C., Srivastava, A.: Temperature tracking: an innovative run-time approach for hardware Trojan detection. In: 2013 IEEE/ACM International Conference on Computer-Aided Design (ICCAD), pp. 532–539, November 2013
9. Glazberg, Z., Moulin, M., Orni, A., Ruah, S., Zarpas, E.: PSL: beyond hardware verification. In: Ramesh, S., Sampath, P. (eds.) Next Generation Design and Verification Methodologies for Distributed Embedded Control Systems, pp. 245–260. Springer, Netherlands (2007). doi:10.1007/978-1-4020-6254-4_19
10. Group, O.W: Open verification library (OVL) working group.http://accellera.org/ activities/working-groups/ovl
11. Hategekimana, F., Tbatou, A., Bobda, C., Kamhoua, C.A., Kwiat, K.A.: Hardware isolation technique for IRC-based botnets detection. In: International Conference on ReConFigurable Computing and FPGAs, ReConFig 2015, Riviera Maya, Mexico, 7–9 December 2015, pp. 1–6 (2015). http://dx.doi.org/10.1109/ReConFig. 2015.7393319
12. Lamech, C., Rad, R., Tehranipoor, M., Plusquellic, J.: An experimental analysis of power and delay signal-to-noise requirements for detecting Trojans and methods for achieving the required detection sensitivities. IEEE Trans. Inf. Forensics Secur. **6**(3), 1170–1179 (2011)

13. Mitra, S., Wong, H.S.P., Wong, S.: Stopping hardware Trojans in their tracks. A few adjustments could protect chips against malicious circuitry. http://spectrum. ieee.org/semiconductors/design/stopping-hardware-trojans-in-their-tracks

14. Pnueli, A.: Special issue semantics of concurrent computation the temporal semantics of concurrent programs. Theoret. Comput. Sci. **13**(1), 45–60 (1981). http://www.sciencedirect.com/science/article/pii/0304397581901109

15. Sengupta, A., Bhadauria, S.: Untrusted third party digital IP cores: power-delay trade-off driven exploration of hardware Trojan secured datapath during high level synthesis. In: Proceedings of the 25th Edition on Great Lakes Symposium on VLSI, GLSVLSI 2015, NY, USA, pp. 167–172 (2015). http://doi.acm.org/10. 1145/2742060.2742061

16. Tehranipoor, M., Koushanfar, F.: A survey of hardware Trojan taxonomy and detection. IEEE Des. Test Comput. **27**(1), 10–25 (2010)

17. Venema, W.: Isolation mechanisms for commodity applications and platforms. Technical report RC24725 (W0901–048), IBM, January 2009

18. Wei, S., Potkonjak, M.: Scalable hardware Trojan diagnosis. IEEE Trans. Very Large Scale Integr. (VLSI) Syst. **20**(6), 1049–1057 (2012)

19. Xiao, K., Tehranipoor, M.: BISA: built-in self-authentication for preventing hardware trojan insertion. In: 2013 IEEE International Symposium on Hardware-Oriented Security and Trust (HOST), pp. 45–50, June 2013

20. Zhang, X., Tehranipoor, M.: Case study: detecting hardware Trojans in third-party digital IP cores. In: 2011 IEEE International Symposium on Hardware-Oriented Security and Trust (HOST), pp. 67–70, June 2011

Rapid Development of Gzip with MaxJ

Nils Voss[1,2(✉)], Tobias Becker[1], Oskar Mencer[1], and Georgi Gaydadjiev[1,2]

[1] Maxeler Technologies Ltd., London, UK
[2] Imperial College London, London, UK
n.voss16@imperial.ac.uk

Abstract. Design productivity is essential for high-performance application development involving accelerators. Low level hardware description languages such as Verilog and VHDL are widely used to design FPGA accelerators, however, they require significant expertise and considerable design efforts. Recent advances in high-level synthesis have brought forward tools that relieve the burden of FPGA application development but the achieved performance results can not approximate designs made using low-level languages. In this paper we compare different FPGA implementations of gzip. All of them implement the same system architecture using different languages. This allows us to compare Verilog, OpenCL and MaxJ design productivity. First, we illustrate several conceptional advantages of the MaxJ language and its platform over OpenCL. Next we show on the example of our gzip implementation how an engineer without previous MaxJ experience can quickly develop and optimize a real, complex application. The gzip design in MaxJ presented here took only one man-month to develop and achieved better performance than the related work created in Verilog and OpenCL.

1 Introduction

Gzip is a popular utility and widely used file format for lossless data compression. In this paper, we compare different implementations of the gzip compression on FPGAs using various languages. All implementations use very similar system architectures and are inspired by previous work by IBM [1].

This study provides an opportunity to show, how choices regarding the programming language offer distinct trade offs in productivity, performance and area utilization. This is of special interest, since FPGAs provide many possibilities to accelerate tasks while reducing energy consumption at the same time.

Designer productivity, and thereby development time, is a major cost factor in system design. While we acknowledge the challenges with accurately measuring productivity, especially in a comparable and quantified way, we still draw some claims on productivity advantages in the context of gzip development.

In recent years, different high-level synthesis tools emerged, in order to overcome the high complexity of hardware description languages such as VHDL and Verilog especially when targeting FPGAs. One of these tools provided by Altera is based on the OpenCL standard [2]. The programmer writes C-like code with additional OpenCL features to guide Altera's SDK in creating FPGA bitstreams.

© Springer International Publishing AG 2017
S. Wong et al. (Eds.): ARC 2017, LNCS 10216, pp. 60–71, 2017.
DOI: 10.1007/978-3-319-56258-2_6

A different approach are new languages for hardware description, which maintain the concepts known from high-level programming languages and thereby preserve their comfort while targeting hardware. One example is MaxJ by Maxeler and OpenSPL [3]. MaxJ is a Java based language with additional features and libraries to enable the rapid creation of FPGA designs.

To emphasize the OpenCL advantages Altera published the results of their gzip implementation [4] and compared them to results published by IBM. In this paper, an implementation of the same algorithm in MaxJ is presented and compared to related work in Verilog (IBM) and OpenCL (Altera).

The main contributions of this paper are:

- the analysis of various MaxJ advantages over OpenCL;
- a high-throughput gzip compression design;
- a productivity comparison of OpenCL, Verilog and MaxJ for gzip.

The paper is structured as follows. First in Sect. 2, we outline the background in high-level synthesis approaches, present MaxJ including its supporting ecosystem and give a short overview of OpenCL and Altera SDK. In Sect. 3 we briefly explain gzip, discuss existing gzip implementations and present the design considerations on implementing gzip on an FPGA. In Sect. 4 we study different implementation decisions and the differences between MaxJ and OpenCL. The performance of our design is compared against state-of-the-art implementations in Sect. 5. In Sect. 6 we examine the productivity advantages of the different languages and in Sect. 7 we draw our final conclusions.

2   Background - High-Level Design

FPGA designs are typically developed in low-level hardware description languages such as Verilog and VHDL. Designing in such languages can result in fast and efficient hardware implementations, but they require considerable skill and effort, which means that their productivity is low. There have been a wide range of approaches to raise the productivity of FPGA design. A typical approach to boost productivity is IP blocks reuse. Another possibility is to automatically generate FPGA designs from domain-specific tools such as Matlab Simulink or LabView but this is naturally limited to certain application types. It has also been proposed to increase productivity by using overlay architectures [5]. These provide a number of customisable templates that can be quickly used offering a compromise in efficiency, performance and development time.

Recently, various high-level synthesis tools have become available. These typically attempt to create FPGA designs from conventional programming languages, such as C, and often require some form of manual intervention in the transformation process.

Vivado HLS is a tool developed by Xilinx. It accepts C, C++ and System-C as inputs and supports arbitrary precision data types. Xilinx claims a 4× speed up in development time and a 0.7× to 1.2× improvement for the Quality of Result compared to traditional RTL design [6]. Vivado HLS is not a push-button C-to-FPGA synthesis tool and requires various manual transformations to customise the hardware architecture and achieve well performing designs.

Additionally Xilinx provides *SDAccel* which is a programming environment for OpenCL, C and C++. Additionally to the compiler, it also provides a simulator and profiling tools. Xilinx claims to achieve up to 20% better results than with hand-coded RTL designs and 3× better performance and resource efficiency compared to OpenCL solutions by competitors. SDAccel also supports partial runtime reconfiguration of FPGA regions without halting the remaining accelerators running on the chip [7].

IBM's *Liquid Metal* supports data flow and map-reduce. The *Lime* language is Java based and supports CPUs as well as FPGAs and GPUs. The hardware type is chosen at runtime based on available capacities in the datacenter [8].

Catapult C creates FPGA and ASIC designs from ANSI C++ and System-C descriptions [9]. Similar to other high-level synthesis tools, it requires the designer to perform iterations on the original C-code and manually tweak the hardware architecture in order to achieve a fast implementation.

Chisel is a Scala based hardware description language. Unlike other approaches focusing on synthesis from a C-like language, the concept behind Chisel is to add modern programming language features to a hardware description language. Design is still low level but the goal is to improve productivity by supporting high-level abstractions in the language [10].

The next section will explain the main advantages and differences of MaxJ.

2.1   MaxJ Development Ecosystem

MaxJ builds upon data-flow. A conventional processor reads and decodes instructions, loads the required data, performs operations on the data, and writes the result to a memory location. This iterative process requires complex control mechanisms that manage the basic operations of the processor.

In comparison, the data-flow execution model is greatly simplified. Data flows from memory into the chip where arithmetic units are organized in a graph structure reflecting the implemented algorithm.

In contrast to the majority of high-level synthesis tools, MaxJ is not generating hardware designs from control-flow oriented, and hence sequential, languages like C or C++. The programmer is expected to describe his/hers application as an inherently parallel data-flow graph structure in 2D space.

MaxJ is based on Java to benefit from its syntax while providing additional APIs for data-flow graph generation at scale. At build time the Java code creates the data-flow graph describing the hardware structure. This means that, for example, an *if-else* statement will be evaluated at build time to add either the nodes described in the *if* block or those in the *else* part to the data-flow graph and thereby to the hardware. This enables code fine tuning to different use cases and the creation of libraries covering many use-cases without overheads.

MaxCompiler translates MaxJ code into FPGA configurations. It also provides cycle accurate software simulation. In combination with

Maxeler's MaxelerOS and the SLiC library the simulation models or hardware configurations are tightly integrated into a CPU executable written in for example C, Fortran, Matlab or Python to allow rapid development of FPGA accelerated applications. The communication between FPGA and CPU is implemented using very high-level streaming primitives and there is no need for the user to worry about any of the low level details.

Maxeler's data-flow systems are built using its proprietary PCIe data-flow engines (DFEs). The MAX4 DFEs incorporate the largest Altera Stratix-V FPGAs as a reconfigurable computing substrate. This device is connected to a large capacity parallel DRAM (24-96 GB) to facilitate large in-memory datasets. Additionally DFEs for networking are available which offer additional connectivity via a maximum of three 40 GBits ports.

2.2   Altera OpenCL Compiler

OpenCL is a standard that aims at providing a single API to target different heterogenous computing platforms with a special focus on parallelization and allows a programmer to target different hardware platforms and instruction sets with the same code. While OpenCL does not guarantee optimal performance for the same code on all hardware platforms, it does guarantee correct functionality (if no vendor specific extensions are used) [11].

OpenCL uses a C-like syntax and provides many custom datatypes to enable easier access to SIMD instructions as well as additional syntax which takes the memory hierarchy used in modern hardware architectures into account. The workload can be distributed between multiple devices and is executed by processing elements on the available hardware. A scheduler distributes the computing tasks to the processing elements at runtime.

The first versions of OpenCL mainly targeted multicore CPUs, GPUs and DSPs but OpenCL can also be used for FPGA programming since Altera and Xilinx published their OpenCL SDKs for FPGAs [2,4,7].

The Altera OpenCL compiler supports the core OpenCL 1.0 features as well as extensions, which, for example, support streaming of data from an ethernet interface to a compute kernel. Altera OpenCL also provides an emulator for functional verification of the created designs in order to speed up the development time. In addition, a detailed optimization report and a profiler is provided to allow easier development of more efficient designs.

3   Gzip

Gzip is a utility [12] as well as a file format for lossless data compression [13]. For data compression DEFLATE [14] is used, which is a combination of Lempel-Ziv compression [15] and Huffman encoding [16].

The idea of the Lempel-Ziv compression algorithm is to replace multiple occurrences of equivalent byte sequences with a reference to the first sequence. This reference consists of a marker, showing that this data has to be interpreted as an index, a match length, indicating how many bytes are equal, and an offset, defining the distance to the first occurrence of the byte sequence.

Huffman coding replaces all data in a symbol stream with code words. It is an entropy encoder, which means that frequently used words will require less bits. A Huffman code is a prefix code which guarantees that no code word is a prefix of any other codeword and, as a result, unambiguous encoding.

The gzip standard knows two different forms of Huffman codes. The simpler one is the static Huffman code which is defined in the standard itself [14]. A different option is to create a customized Huffman code based on the actual input data. The Huffman code itself then needs to be encoded as well to enable the decompressor to correctly decode the data. Therefore the compressed Huffman code description is placed before the actual compressed data in the data-stream. While often providing better compression ratio this method is more complex to implement and leads to extra calculations at runtime.

Since gzip is so widely used, there are many different implementations of it. Intel published a high throughput CPU implementation achieving a throughput of $0.34\,\mathrm{GB/s}$ [17]. There are also many high-throughput FPGA implementations like the already mentioned implementations by Altera [4] and IBM [1] which achieve throughputs between 2.8 and $3\,\mathrm{GiB/s}$. A more recent FPGA based publication by Microsoft reports a throughput of $5.6\,\mathrm{GB/s}$ [18]. In addition, ASIC implementations of gzip exist with throughputs of up to $10\,\mathrm{GB/s}$ [19].

3.1 Gzip FPGA Implementation

The majority of gzip FPGA implementations struggle to process more than one byte per cycle, which severely limits throughput [20,21]. The problem is that the encoding of a symbol could also influence the encoding of the next one.

The approach used in this paper (the same as in [1,4]) enables processing of multiple byte per cycle using hash tables. In each cycle a fixed number of bytes is loaded and for each byte a hash key is computed. This hash key is usually based on the byte itself as well as a pre-defined number of following symbols.

These hash keys are used to address the hash tables. The hash tables store possible matches for a given hash value. There are as many hash tables as bytes read per cycle. So every computed hash key is used to update one of these tables. On the other side a parallel lookup is performed on all hash tables in order to find all possible matches. The whole process is depicted in Fig. 1.

The hash tables are also used to store the already seen data. If n bytes are read per cycle than n bytes have to be stored for each symbol in the hash table. These n bytes consist of the symbol itself followed by the next $n-1$ input bytes.

This avoids a large memory structure with many read ports holding all the previous data. Instead, only the data that can be referenced by the hash tables is stored. The disadvantage of this solution is that each symbol in the input window is stored n times. The hash table memory requires a wide word width and n read and one write ports, which strongly increases area usage.

In order to avoid the $O(n^2)$ memory usage complexity a different hash table architecture was proposed by Microsoft [18]. Instead of n hash tables with n read

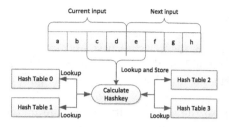

Fig. 1. Hash table implementation

ports they used a fixed number of hash tables with one read port each. The main idea is, that the possible hash keys are equally distributed onto different hash tables. Then if m hash tables are created, the least significant $log2(m)$ bits are used to determine which hash table is used for each hash value. In order to be able to save different data items for the same hash value, each hash table can be copied. So in order to avoid hash conflicts a different copy of the hash table can be used. The hash tables run at double frequency compared to the remaining design which effectively doubles the number of read and write ports.

The biggest problem with this implementation is that for a given set of least significant bits only two writes can be accomplished in one cycle. All other matches, which hash keys have the same least significant bits, have to be dropped slightly reducing the compression ratio. With this optimizations and a few other small changes Microsoft was able to increase the throughput significantly with limited impact on the compression ratio.

Since Microsoft did not report design time we can not directly compare against their design process and will focus on those used by Altera and IBM.

The hash table lookup provides n^2 possible matches, since we perform n lookups for each input byte. The first step is to perform the actual match search, which requires a comparison of the input data with the already processed data stored in the hash tables. The target is to find the longest match starting at each position in the input window, to allow encoding with as few bits as possible. In order to avoid complex inter-cycle dependencies the maximal match length is limited to the number of bytes read per cycle.

Since one byte may be covered by multiple matches, only a selection of all found matches has to be encoded. Decisions made here also impact the encoding in the next cycle, since a match might also cover symbols of the next input window. Since the design has to be fully pipelined, this inter cycle dependency has to be resolved within one cycle to prevent pipeline stalls.

If a match only covers a few symbols it might be cheaper to encode this as literals and not as a match. In this case the match will be ignored. A heuristic is applied on the remaining matches to resolve the inter-cycle dependencies.

This heuristics takes the match for the last symbol in the input window as the maximal match length into the input window of the next cycle. Since the maximal match length is n the last symbol is never covered by a match in a previous input window and thereby we do not have to consider any other inter cycle dependencies here. While this heuristic may decrease the compression ratio, it enables a fully pipelined design while limiting the design complexity.

In order to finally select the matches first all matches for symbols that were already covered by a match from the previous cycle are removed. Then the reach of each match is calculated, which is defined as the sum of the position of the current symbol and the match length. If two symbols have the same reach, they encode all symbols up to the same position and the match which covers more symbols in total is selected. In [4] a more detailed explanation is available.

At last, the data has to be encoded using Huffman coding. This can be done symbol-wise after the match selection. These code words then get combined using shifters and OR-gates to form the final output bitstream.

4   MaxJ Implementation Advantages

Our gzip implementation is similar to the implementation reported by Altera [4] to allow easier comparison between OpenCL and MaxJ implementations.

MaxJ custom datatypes offer a significant advantage. While C and OpenCL only support char (8 bit), short (16 bit), int (32 bit) and similar types, MaxJ allows programmers to define non-standard datatypes such as a 5 bit integer. Even for a byte-based algorithm like gzip many values do not need data types with power of 2 bit-widths. This applies for example for the Huffman code words, the match length, the match offset or the control signals.

The part of the architecture where the biggest number of similar modules exist is the match length calculation, since we have n^2 possible matches. The straight forward way of implementing this would be to byte-wise compare each byte of the input data with the data referenced by the lookup. As a result, if the bytes are equal and if all previous bytes were equal as well, the match length can be incremented as shown in Fig. 2. So if we process 16 Bytes per cycle we have to use 16 comparators, adders and MUXs per match and in total 4096 units of each element. Hence, the resource usage has a complexity of $O(n^3)$.

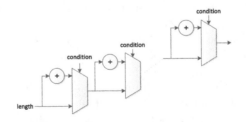

Fig. 2. Simple match length

Altera uses bit vectors instead so that for every similar byte a bit in the vector is set as shown in Listing 1.1 and Fig. 3. The advantage is that OR operations and shifters cost less than ADDs and MUXs. It also enables the scheduler to use less FIFOs to implement this part of the algorithm, since all OR operations can be scheduled in the same clock cycle and there is no dependency between the different iterations of the unrolled loop. As a result the OR operations can be scheduled in a tree like fashion which reduces the number of required FIFOs. By using this technique a 5% reduction of logic resources is claimed.

```
1  // compare current/comparison windows
2  #pragma unroll
3  for (char k = 0; k < LEN; k++)
4  {
5    if (curr_window[j + k] == comp_window[k][i][j])
6      length_bool[i][j] |= 1 << k;
7  }
```

Listing 1.1. OpenCL implementation of match length calculation

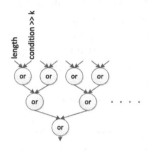

Fig. 3. Altera match length   **Fig. 4.** MaxJ match length

Writing the same code in MaxJ would already reduce resources, since the shifts are omitted in hardware as the result of these operations would be computed at build time instead. This, as stated in [4], is not done by the OpenCL SDK.

Listing 1.2 shows an equivalent MaxJ implementation with some additional improvements. The # operator is used to concatenate bits. So in this case we concatenate all results of the comparators bit-by-bit, which does not use any additional resources. Also we do not need any registers or FIFOs because the concatenation has no latency at all. The only costs come from the comparators. The result of that is also shown in Fig. 4.

```
1  // compare current/comparison windows
2  lengthBool[i][j] = currWindow[j] === compWindow[0][i][j];
3  for (int k = 1; k < LEN; k++) {
4    lengthBool[i][j] #= currWindow[j + k] === compWindow[k][i][j];
5  }
```

Listing 1.2. MaxJ implementation of match length calculation

Other MaxJ language features make it easier to meet timing. For example, the calculated hash keys are used at many different places and, as a result, have quite a large fanout. Since a huge chunk of the available memory resources on the FPGA are used for hash tables, the hash keys have to be routed to very distant locations of the chip. In order to compensate this and help meeting timing, an additional register was added after the hash key calculation as shown in Listing 1.3. The place and route tools can now duplicate this register, if needed, in order to distribute the signal to all hash tables, where it is used for addressing.

```
1 for (int i = 0; i < bytesPerCycle; i++) {
2    hashKey[i] = optimization.pipeline(calculateHashKey(currWindow, i));
3 }
```

Listing 1.3. Adding a Register to the hashKey signal, which is returned by the calculateHashKey() function. It is then passed into the optimization.pipeline() function to add the register.

On the FPGA platform used by Altera the input data gets transmitted over PCIe to DDR3 memory. The same principle applies to the encoded data which first is written into DDR3 memory before it is send back to the host via PCIe.

In the MaxJ design the data does not need to be buffered in external memory but can be send directly via PCIe to the FPGA where it is processed.

Since on-chip memory capacity is the limiting factor of the gzip design a different implementation of the Huffman encoding was used. Altera used a lookup table which can be changed by the CPU. In our design we calculate the Huffman code words on the fly and do not waste any on-chip memory.

This slightly limits the adaptability since only one fixed Huffman tree is available. This tree is optimized to all possible match lengths but could also be optimized for known payloads. While no big impact on compression ratio could be observed, this change is key in enabling our design to process 20 bytes per cycle. Both, IBM and Altera designs process only 16 Bytes per cycle.

5 Performance Evaluation

We now compare the performance and area utilization of the different designs. The area utilization is compared in Table 1. First, we are going to only compare the 16 byte per cycle MaxJ design with the designs implemented by IBM and Altera, since all these designs process the same number of bytes per cycle. The MaxJ design uses significantly less resources as the OpenCL design. The area utilization numbers for the IBM design shown here were estimated and reported by Altera based on a chip image [4]. So while we can only work with estimations, we can still assume that the logic utilization of the MaxJ design in comparison to the Verilog design is at least on par. Only the RAM utilization is higher which is probably caused by the scheduling overhead of 443 pipeline stages in contrast to the 17 stages of the Verilog design. Despite the fact that the OpenCL design uses only 87 pipeline stages the MaxJ design uses fewer memory resources.

Throughput and compression ratio differences are depicted in Table 2. The compression ratio for all designs was evaluated using the calgary corpus [22] and the geometric mean. While the compression ratio of the Intel, IBM and Altera designs are almost identical, the MaxJ design shows a slight improvement. The reason for this is probably a different hashing function (as described in [23]) which improves the compression ratio at the cost of additional logic resources.

Table 1. Area utilization of the gzip compression on Stratix V FPGA

	IBM (Verilog) [1]	Altera (OpenCL) [4]	MaxJ (16 Bytes)	MaxJ (20 Bytes)
Logic utilization	45%	47%	42.8%	51.1%
RAM	45%	70%	59.2%	88.6%

IBM implementation figures were estimated by Altera using a chip image [4]

Table 2. Compression ratio and throughput

	Intel (i5 650 CPU) [17]	IBM (Verilog) [1]	Altera (OpenCL) [4]	MaxJ (16 Byte)	MaxJ (20 Byte)
Compress. ratio	2.18	2.17	2.17	2.25	2.27
Throughput	0.338 GB/s	3.22 GB/s	3.05 GB/s	3.20 GB/s	5.00 GB/s
	0.315 GiB/s	3.00 GiB/s	2.84 GiB/s	2.98 GiB/s	4.66 GiB/s

While IBM reported a frequency of "just under 200 MHz" [1], Altera claims a frequency of 193 MHz. Our MaxJ design for 16 Bytes successfully runs at 200 MHz without any optimizations aimed to help meeting timing.

When we use the available space to process 20 bytes per cycle instead of 16 and additionally perform timing optimizations, our design achieved a throughput of 5 GB/s at 250 MHz. This makes our design nearly 15× faster than Intel's high throughput CPU implementation and nearly 1.8× faster than the OpenCL implementation by Altera [1, 4].

6   Productivity Discussion

In [4] Altera reported one month development time for their OpenCL gzip implementation. The MaxJ design presented here was performed by one intern student within a single month. The intern was novice to MaxJ and had only one week to work through the MaxJ tutorials. This clearly shows that learning MaxJ can be quick with a software development background in high-level languages.

An advantage of HLS in contrast to classical hardware description languages is, that the code is very readable and compact (the entire MaxJ gzip code is only 959 lines). This makes it easier to focus on optimizations and to make big changes in the architecture, since modern programming tools like unit tests can be used in combination with the simulator to quickly validate functionality. For example, the switch from the 16 byte per cycle design to 20 bytes was done by only changing a single constant in the code.

Because the MaxJ tools create deeply pipelined structures meeting timing is easier. While deep pipelining increases the overall memory usage it enables the designer to use more space of the chip productively.

As previously mentioned, Microsoft also reported an FPGA based gzip design using a slightly modified design architecture [18] achieving 5.6 GB/s on a Stratix

V FPGA. We were able to also create a design using their architecture and again achieve a higher throughput of 9.6 GB/s. Since we could reuse most of the already written MaxJ code, the actual implementation time went down to roughly one week. A few more weeks of not full-time effort were needed in order to fine-tune parameters like the used hash function and hash tables configuration as well as improve timing. It has to be noted that while meeting timing is time consuming it is not as costly as development time, since it mainly requires CPU time and not engineering effort.

When comparing to OpenCL, we can see that in a similar time far better results could be achieved with MaxJ. A reason for this is the more direct control over the hardware provided by MaxJ. This allows designers with good understanding of the underlying hardware to benefit from those additional improvements. For example, the option to directly insert registers in the design (as shown in Sect. 4) allows easier timing closure. Another good example is the direct impact that widths of the variables have on the hardware area utilization.

While it is possible to reuse existing OpenCL designs for CPUs and GPUs to target FPGAs it has to be noted, that the performance of the ported designs will be suboptimal in most cases. For example in [24] the same OpenCL code was executed on CPUs and FPGAs. The CPU versions all outperform the FPGA versions even though efficient hardware implementations for the tested algorithms exist. This shows that, similar to most other high-level synthesis frameworks (see Sect. 2), it is necessary to employ a series of code transformations in order to create efficient hardware designs. As a result a change of the programming language as well as the associated toolchain introduces only a limited overhead.

The above suggests that developing in MaxJ is significantly faster than in OpenCL since we had enough time to perform careful timing optimizations and compression ratio improvements. As a result this enabled us to deliver a significantly better bitstream in terms of throughput and compression ratio.

7   Conclusion

In this paper we presented a rapid FPGA implementation of gzip compression. We demonstrated that using MaxJ for high-level synthesis enabled us to achieve better results within the same amount of development time as compared to OpenCL. Furthermore, we showed that MaxJ and its development tools enable very competitive development times in comparison to classical hardware description approaches. Our design outperforms the OpenCL implementation by 1.8× in terms of throughput and delivers 5% better compression ratio by using only ~10% more resources. In addition, the presented design achieves a 1.7× higher throughput as compared to the Verilog implementation by IBM.

References

1. Martin, A., Jamsek, D., Agarwal, K.: FPGA-based application acceleration: case study with GZIP compression/decompression stream engine. In: International Conference on Computer-Aided Design (ICCAD), November 2013

2. Altera: OpenCL for Altera FPGAs: Accelerating Performance and Design Productivity (2012). http://www.altera.com/products/software/opencl/opencl-index.html
3. OpenSPL (2015). http://www.openspl.org
4. Abdelfattah, M.S., Hagiescu, A., Singh, D.: Gzip on a chip: high performance lossless data compression on FPGAs using OpenCL. In: International Workshop on OpenCL ACM, pp. 1–9 (2014)
5. Rashid, R., Steffan, J.G., Betz, V.: Comparing performance, productivity and scalability of the TILT overlay processor to OpenCL HLS. In: Field-Programmable Technology (FPT). IEEE, pp. 20–27 (2014)
6. Vivado HLS. http://www.xilinx.com/support/documentation/sw_manuals/ug1197-vivado-high-level-productivity.pdf. Accessed 18 Nov 2015
7. Xilinx: The Xilinx SDAccel Development Environment (2014). http://www.xilinx.com/publications/prod_mktg/sdx/sdaccel-backgrounder.pdf
8. Liquid Metal (2015). www.research.ibm.com/liquidmetal/
9. Catapult C (2015). http://calypto.com/en/products/catapult/overview/
10. Bachrach, J., et al.: Chisel: constructing hardware in a Scala embedded language. In: Design Automation Conference (DAC). ACM, pp. 1216–1225 (2012)
11. Stone, J.E., Gohara, D., Shi, G.: OpenCL: a parallel programming standard for heterogeneous computing systems. Comput. Sci. Eng. **12**(3), 66–73 (2010)
12. Gzip (2015). http://www.gzip.org
13. Deutsch, P.: Gzip file format specification version 4.3 (1996). http://tools.ietf.org/html/rfc1952
14. Deutsch, P.: RFC 1951 deflate compressed data format specification version 1.3 (1996). http://tools.ietf.org/html/rfc1951
15. Ziv, J., Lempel, A.: A universal algorithm for sequential data compression. IEEE Trans. Inf. Theory **23**(3), 337–343 (1977)
16. Huffman, D.A.: A method for the construction of minimum-redundancy codes. In: Proceedings of IRE, vol. 40, no. 9, pp. 1098–1101 (1952)
17. Gopal, V., Guilford, J., Feghali, W., Ozturk, E., Wolrich, G.: High Performance DEFLATE Compression on Intel Architecture Processors (2011). http://www.intel.com/content/dam/www/public/us/en/documents/white-papers/ia-deflate-compression-paper.pdf
18. Fowers, J., Kim, J.-Y., Burger, D., Hauck, S.: A scalable high-bandwidth architecture for lossless compression on FPGAs. In: 23rd IEEE International Symposium on Field-Programmable Custom Computing Machines, pp. 52–59 (2015)
19. AHA 378 (2015). http://www.aha.com/data-compression/
20. Huang, W.-J., Saxena, N., McCluskey, E.J.: A reliable LZ data compressor on reconfigurable coprocessors. In: Symposium on Field-Programmable Custom Computing Machines. IEEE, pp. 249–258 (2000)
21. Hwang, S.A., Wu, C.-W.: Unified VLSI systolic array design for LZ data compression. IEEE Trans. Very Large Scale Integr. (VLSI) Syst. **9**(4), 489–499 (2001)
22. Calgary Corpus (2015). http://corpus.canterbury.ac.nz/descriptions/#calgary
23. Sadakane, K., Imai, H.: Improving the speed of LZ77 compression by hashing and suffix sorting. IEICE Trans. Fundam. Electr. Commun. Comput. Sci. **E83–A**(12), 2689–2698 (2000)
24. Ndu, G., Navaridas, J., Lujan, M.: Towards a benchmark suite for OpenCL FPGA accelerators. In: Proceedings of 3rd International Workshop on OpenCL (IWOCL 2015), NY, USA, Article 10

On the Use of (Non-)Cryptographic Hashes on FPGAs

Andreas Fiessler[1]([✉]), Daniel Loebenberger[1], Sven Hager[2],
and Björn Scheuermann[2]

[1] Research and Project Development, genua GmbH, Munich, Germany
{andreas_fiessler,daniel_loebenberger}@genua.de
[2] Department of Computer Science, Humboldt University of Berlin, Berlin, Germany
{hagersve,scheuermann}@informatik.hu-berlin.de

Abstract. Hash functions are used for numerous applications in computer networking, both on classical CPU-based systems and on dedicated hardware like FPGAs. During system development, hardware implementations require particular attention to take full advantage of performance gains through parallelization when using hashes. For many use cases, such as hash tables or Bloom filters, several independent short hash values for the same input key are needed. Here we consider the question how to save resources by splitting one large hash value into multiple sub-hashes. We demonstrate that even small flaws in the avalanche effect of a hash function induce significant deviation from a uniform distribution in such sub-hashes, which allows potential denial-of-service attacks. We further consider the cryptographic hash SHA3 and other non-cryptographic hashes, which do not exhibit such weaknesses, in terms of resource usage and latency in an FPGA implementation. The results show that while SHA3 was intended for security applications, it also outperforms the non-cryptographic hashes for other use cases on FPGAs.

Keywords: FPGA · Packet processing · Hash table · Bloom filter · Hash function · Avalanche effect

1 Introduction

Hash functions are used to calculate a fixed-size hash value from a given input of arbitrary length. They have numerous applications, e.g., hash tables, integrity protection, Bloom filters, or authentication, making them a vital component in almost any computer system. These applications are built on top of standard CPU-based systems as well as dedicated hardware like FPGAs. Nevertheless, the requirements for a fast and efficient algorithm differ substantially between software for CPUs and hardware description for FPGAs. The advantage of a hardware implementation lies in the potential for massive parallelization at a comparatively low clock rate. In practice, many fast hash functions used for hash tables were designed originally for software and do not perform well when implemented in hardware [1].

© Springer International Publishing AG 2017
S. Wong et al. (Eds.): ARC 2017, LNCS 10216, pp. 72–80, 2017.
DOI: 10.1007/978-3-319-56258-2_7

This problem becomes even more relevant if the hash application requires multiple, independent hash values of the same key. Examples for these applications are hash tables with double hashing [2], cuckoo hashing [3], or Bloom filters [4]. The developer has to choose between re-using one hash module, which increases the latency for the calculation, or implementing multiple hash modules at the cost of higher resource usage. As both methods bear significant drawbacks, the question arises whether it is possible to exploit the fact that the required hash size is often significantly smaller than the actual size of the hash function's output. If there are no weaknesses in the output of a given hash function, the hash could be split into multiple sub-hashes. Although some authors argue that small flaws in the hash calculation are acceptable for hash tables when the full hash value is used [5], it is not clear if this is still the case when only parts of the hash are used.

Many non-cryptographic hash functions reveal issues when their *avalanche effect* is analyzed [6,7], in the sense that some input bits do not optimally propagate through the function. One of our goals is to determine the implications of those weaknesses with regard to our desired sub-hashes. It should be noted that a good avalanche effect of the function still does not necessarily imply there are no weaknesses in the hash, as can be seen for, e.g., the MurmurHash [8].

As previously mentioned, one must be aware that fast and efficient hash function designs for CPUs and hardware differ. Regarding the hardware implementation, the most important metrics of a hashing algorithm are resource utilization, latency l in clock cycles, and execution time as a result of the maximum possible clock rate. Typical hardware hash implementations are not fully pipelined, meaning they are blocked until one calculation finishes. A significant fraction of common hash functions suffer from large latencies when implemented in hardware [1], making them less suitable for, e.g., high-speed network applications. Furthermore, to gain full advantage of a highly parallelized processing pipeline, it is often necessary to process one key per clock cycle. In this case, the hash functions must be implemented l times in hardware in order to be used in a round-robin manner.

The growing importance of dedicated, feature-rich hardware components led to a shift in requirements when new standard algorithms are defined. For example, the winning candidate for the Secure Hash Algorithm 3 (SHA3) [9] was required to perform well in hardware. This opens the question whether such a hardware-optimized cryptographic hash function is more suitable than the non-cryptographic alternatives mentioned above.

The main contributions of this work are threefold: first, we show how statistical relevant weaknesses in the avalanche effect of a hash function can affect the uniformity of sub-hashes. Second, we examine the characteristics of several hash functions when implemented for a multi-hash FPGA use case. Third, based on these results, we demonstrate that SHA3 is currently a better choice for many FPGA use cases regarding these characteristics in comparison to non-cryptographic hashes.

2   Related Work

The key-value lookup accomplished by hash tables is important for a variety of networking tasks like stateful packet filtering, route lookup, or intrusion detection. Since dedicated hardware is increasingly used for these types of applications, hash table implementations for FPGAs have been widely discussed [5,10].

Bloom filters [4] can be a fast and efficient alternative when the only task is to query if a key is present in the filter. Since this is the case for many classification tasks in networking systems, Bloom filters experience wide application in this field [11]. Their feasibility on FPGAs has been shown in [10,12]. With memory lookups being the critical factor, Song et al. suggested using Bloom filters to reduce the amount of hash table operations by first probing a Bloom filter if the lookup is required in the first place [10]. If the query is negative, no expensive hash table lookup is necessary.

Good hash functions are also of major and ongoing interest [9]. Countless hash functions—cryptographically secure or not—have been introduced, quite a few of which have been shown to have significant flaws with regard to the expected qualities of a good hash function [8,13]. Hardware implementations of several hash functions were analysed in [1], with the result that most of them perform badly, causing a latency too high for network processing applications [10].

When hash functions are used for hash tables, the main issue derives from attackers being able to generate hash collisions with different keys. This can degrade the performance of hash tables and allow for denial-of-service (DoS) attacks [14]. Such flaws also led to security advisories, e.g., [8,15]. Bar-Yosef et al. were able to successfully attack the hash table in Linux' netfilter firewall [16], even though a randomization technique was implemented in place to protect against such attacks.

3   Use Cases and Attack Model

From the variety of applications for hash functions, we focus on FPGA use cases requiring multiple, independent hash values for, e.g., hash tables using *open addressing* by double hashing [2], cuckoo hashing [3], or Bloom filters [4].

There are different ways of generating such independent hash values out of the same key: (1) using different hashing algorithms, (2) using the method of double hashing, where two different hash functions are employed to compute the hashes, (3) mixing distinct seeds to the key *before* feeding it to the same hash function, and (4) splitting one hash value into non-overlapping sub-hashes.

The drawback of the first two options is that they either lead to higher resource usage or increased latency, due to the fact that multiple hash functions need to be computed. For the third option, it can be chosen whether to implement multiple hash modules at the cost of logic resources or re-use one implementation and thereby increasing the latency until all results are calculated. The last option is the only option that saves both space and latency, but requires a hash function of sufficient quality.

An attacker might try to generate *hash collisions* to degrade the performance for a DoS attack, since in case of collisions expensive computations must be performed [14]. If the hash function under consideration has statistical weaknesses in one of its sub-hashes, such collisions are more likely to occur than for a hash with uniformly distributed outputs.

If a Bloom filter is used to reduce the hash table workload as suggested in [10], an attacker would want to provoke false-positives by purposefully filling the filter with ones. In the worst case, each "real" query would then result in a false-positive, thereby enforcing an expensive hash table lookup. Also in this case, the likelihood and degree of the attacker's success strongly depends on the uniformity of the hash function's output. It is helpful for the attacker if he can make assumptions on how changes in the input data affect the output data other than a pseudorandom behavior, as it would be the case for a good hash function.

4   Hash Algorithms

Non-cryptographic hash-functions employed in practice are the Jenkins hash [17] as used in the Linux packet filter `netfilter` [18] or its successor SpookyHash [17]. Other examples include MurmurHash [8], CityHash [19], and SipHash [20]. The argument for using them are typically efficient implementations, and the mere requirement of uniform outputs. However, in applications like packet filters it is often not complicated to attack those kinds of functions if the attacker has control over their inputs [8]. In this work, we focus on a specific attack, where we exploit weaknesses in the so-called *avalanche effect* of the function [6] to actually generate hash values distributed in a non-uniform way, yielding a potential hash table DoS attack.

More formally, the avalanche probability for input bit i and output bit j of a hash function is the probability $p_{i,j}$ that output bit j changes when input bit i is flipped, i.e.,

$$p_{i,j} = \frac{1}{2^n} \cdot |\{x \in \{0,1\}^n \mid h(x)_j \neq h(x^{(i)})_j\}|,$$

where $x^{(i)}$ is x with bit i flipped and n is the (in our case always finite) input size for the hash function h. Ideally, this probability should be close to $1/2$ for all admissible choices of i and j. To measure the distance to this desired probability, we define the *bias* to be $|p_{i,j} - 1/2|$. Intuitively, when this bias is large, the avalanche effect for the function differs for input bit i and output bit j considerably from optimal.

A good hash function should not have statistical weaknesses in this regard. In fact, there are many hash functions available which do not suffer from this weakness, most prominently cryptographic hashes such as SHA3 [21]. These functions have the additional benefit that many other attacks (such as differential attacks) do not work either. A practical example of why even apparently small flaws can be problematic will be given in the next section.

5   Evaluation

We begin our evaluation with an analysis of an avalanche-weak hash function and show how the described method of splitting a hash value into sub-hashes is affected. Afterwards, different examples of hashing algorithms are implemented for an FPGA and the results are evaluated.

5.1   Impact of Weaknesses in the Avalanche Effect

We first demonstrate that small weaknesses in the avalanche probability of a hash function can be used to produce a non-uniform output distribution of the function, yielding potential hash DoS attacks. For illustration of the effect, we purposefully selected the avalanche-weak Jenkins hash function and split the 32 bit hash value in four one-byte chunks. The other considered non-cryptographic hash functions, i.e., SpookyHash and SipHash, do not have any known weakness in this regard. The Jenkins function family comprises of different algorithms. We considered the latest `lookup2` and `lookup3` in our analysis.

For our experiments, we selected in a first step for both routines an input/output bit pair with large bias for 34 byte inputs. To find such a pair, we empirically determined the bias for each input and each output bit by first selecting 10^5 random input values. We then successively flipped each input bit and counted the resulting flips over the 10^5 choices. We verified that this comparatively small number of samples is representative, since multiple runs of our experiments (with different random selections) gave comparable results. For further analysis, we selected a single input/output bit pair with bias larger than 0.025. Specifically, we considered for `lookup2` the pair $(i, j) = (248, 27)$ with bias 0.1685 and for `lookup3` the pair $(i, j) = (216, 25)$ with bias 0.03277. In a second step, now with the fixed input/output pair (i, j), we generated 10^5 random inputs to hash function, excluding those where the output bit j was 0. We then flipped the bit i of the input and computed the distribution of the last two bytes of the function. Note that one of them contains output bit j. The results are depicted in Fig. 1. Figures 1a and c show a clear non-uniform distribution of the byte containing the output bit j. For comparison, the byte not containing bit j is distributed close to the expected value $10^5/2^8 \approx 390$ for uniform distributions as can be seen in Fig. 1b and d. This shows that even the presence of a single input/output bit pair with large bias can be used to easily induce skewness in the output distribution of the resulting hash.

To counteract this attack, we argue that one should be careful with the selection of a hash function and that even small statistical weaknesses can be exploited in practice. Even though, we are aware that our experiments are rather a toy example than a fully-fledged attack on a concrete implementation.

5.2   FPGA Implementation Results

We selected four hash functions for implementation: (1) Jenkins (`lookup2`) [17], as it is used in Linux' netfilter firewall, (2) SpookyHash [17], the latest hash

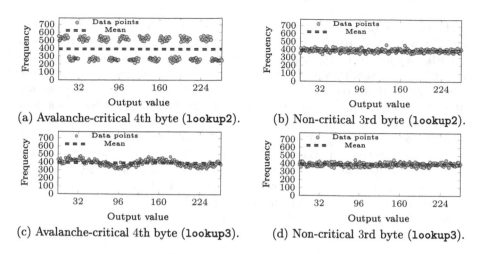

Fig. 1. Distributions of different Jenkins sub-hashes scaled by 10^5.

function of Bob Jenkins, (3) SipHash [20], the proposed alternative for hashes like MurmurHash and CityHash, and (4) SHA3 [21], as a current state-of-the-art cryptographic hash function. While the avalanche-weak Jenkins was included in our evaluation for reference, CityHash and MurmurHash were not further considered due to reported weaknesses [8,19].

All implementation results were determined for a fixed-size input key of 288 bit, correspondent to the quadruple of two IPv6-addresses and two port numbers. The targeted frequency for all implementations was 200 MHz. The results were determined using Xilinx Vivado 2014.4 with a Virtex 7 690t, speed grade −2 as the targeted FPGA. Both Jenkins and SpookyHash were implemented by ourselves natively based on the available source code [17]. For SipHash, we used the referenced Verilog implementation [22], for SHA3 a SHA3-512 core from [23]. The latency was identified by simulating the HDL implementation of each core.

Table 1. Virtex 7 690t FPGA resource utilization.

Hash	Size [bit]	LUTs	FFs	Lat. [CC/ns]	Use case LUTs	Use case FFs
Jenkins	64	2,874	3,419	76/380	436,848 (101.0%)	519,688 (56.0%)
SpookyHash	128	3,220	4,161	27/135	86,940 (20.1%)	112,347 (13.0%)
SipHash	32	944	789	52/260	196,352 (45.3%)	164,112 (19.0%)
SHA3-512	512	6,005	2,212	20/100	120,100 (27.7%)	44,240 (5.1%)

As can be seen in Table 1 for the evaluated hash functions and their hash value size, there are significant differences in terms of the usage of lookup tables (LUTs), flip-flops (FFs), and the inherent latency (CC, in clock cycles and ns at 200 MHz) for the calculation. To improve comparability, we included an example calculation for a use case requiring eight independent 16-bit hash values of the same key, with the capability of processing one key per clock cycle. This means the hash core has to be replicated $n = \lceil \frac{\text{desired hash size}}{\text{hash size}} \rceil \times$ latency times. Note that for SHA3, a smaller variant (e.g., SHA3-224) could be used since the hash size is larger that the required use case output size. Since this use case assumes that splitting the hash value bears no implications, the result for Jenkins is only given as a reference. The percentages illustrate clearly that a significant amount of the Virtex 7 FPGA resources are occupied for this use case. Moreover, a high latency alone can be a criterion for exclusion depending on the application. For comparison: in [10], the MD5 hash was deemed unsuitable for packet processing applications due to the latency of 64 clock cycles based on speed requirements present in the year 2005. Hence, from our evaluated candidates only SpookyHash and SHA3-512 can be considered suitable for high-speed FPGA applications.

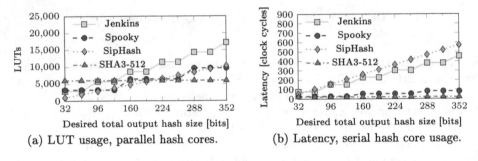

(a) LUT usage, parallel hash cores.   (b) Latency, serial hash core usage.

Fig. 2. FPGA utilization and latency for different hash value sizes.

As can be seen for the use case, the implementation results are dependent on the desired size and amount of independent hash values, as well as resource usage and latency of the hash functions. Two additional plots in Fig. 2 visualize this for different hash value sizes, provided that all can be split into independent sub-hashes of arbitrary size. Figure 2a assumes the total size is achieved by multiple, parallel hash modules. In contrast, Fig. 2b shows how the latency is affected if the necessary calculations are executed in series on one single hash module, thus maintaining almost constant resource usage. Combined with the demonstrated, possible implications of non-cryptographic hash functions, we argue that nowadays the cryptographic hash SHA3 should be the default choice for hardware implementations, also for non-cryptographic applications.

6   Conclusion

Good hash functions are essential for a variety of applications. Since the usage of FPGAs and dedicated hardware is increasing, the interest in fast hash-based data structures like hash tables and Bloom filters will likely continue to rise.

To make best use of limited hardware resources, it is advisable to find an efficient way to calculate the required hash values. In this paper, we described use cases where several independent hash values of the same key are commonly required. We demonstrated that the method of splitting one hash value into sub-hashes for multi-hash use cases can have non-optimal behavior if the used hash function suffers from non-optimal avalanche effect. Also, we analyzed the recent cryptographic hash SHA3 and compared it against common hash table hash functions as an alternative for hardware applications. Our results show that most hardware hash applications benefit from the use of SHA3 instead of non-cryptographic hashes optimized for CPU-based systems.

Acknowledgements. We would like to acknowledge the support of the German Federal Ministry for Economic Affairs and Energy.

References

1. Shi, Z., Ma, C., Cote, J., Wang, B.: Hardware implementation of hash functions. In: Tehranipoor, M., Wang, C. (eds.) Introduction to Hardware Security and Trust, pp. 27–50. Springer, Heidelberg (2012)
2. Bookstein, A.: Double hashing. J. Am. Soc. Inf. Sci. **23**(6), 402 (1972)
3. Pagh, R., Rodler, F.F.: Cuckoo hashing. In: Heide, F.M. (ed.) ESA 2001. LNCS, vol. 2161, pp. 121–133. Springer, Heidelberg (2001). doi:10.1007/3-540-44676-1_10
4. Bloom, B.H.: Space/time trade-offs in hash coding with allowable errors. Commun. ACM **13**(7), 422–426 (1970)
5. Broder, A., Mitzenmacher, M.: Using multiple hash functions to improve IP lookups. In: Proceedings of INFOCOM 2001, Twentieth Annual Joint Conference of the IEEE Computer and Communications Societies, vol. 3. IEEE (2001)
6. Feistel, H.: Cryptography and computer privacy. Sci. Am. **228**(5), 15–23 (1973)
7. Neustar Inc, "Choosing a Good Hash Function, Part 3," February 2012. https://research.neustar.biz/2012/02/02/choosing-a-good-hash-function-part-3/. Accessed 15 November 2016
8. oCERT.org, "#2012-001 multiple implementations denial-of-service via MurmurHash algorithm collision" (2012). http://www.ocert.org/advisories/ocert-2012-001.html. Accessed 14 November 2016
9. "Federal Register, vol. 72, no. 212". http://csrc.nist.gov/groups/ST/hash/documents/FR_Notice_Nov07.pdf. Accessed 14 November 2016
10. Song, H., Dharmapurikar, S., Turner, J., Lockwood, J.: Fast hash table lookup using extended bloom filter: an aid to network processing. ACM SIGCOMM Comput. Commun. Rev. **35**(4), 181–192 (2005)
11. Broder, A., Mitzenmacher, M.: Network applications of bloom filters: a survey. Internet Math. **1**(4), 485–509 (2004)
12. Attig, M., Dharmapurikar, S., Lockwood, J.: Implementation results of bloom filters for string matching. In: 12th Annual IEEE Symposium on Field-Programmable Custom Computing Machines, FCCM 2004, pp. 322–323. IEEE (2004)
13. Klima, V.: Tunnels in hash functions: MD5 collisions within a minute. IACR Cryptol. ePrint Arch. **2006**, 105 (2006)
14. Crosby, S., Wallach, D.: Denial of service via algorithmic complexity attacks. In: Usenix Security, vol. 2 (2003)

15. oCERT.org, "#2011-003 multiple implementations denial-of-service via hash algorithm collision" (2011). http://www.ocert.org/advisories/ocert-2011-003.html. Accessed 14 November 2016

16. Bar-Yosef, N., Wool, A.: Remote algorithmic complexity attacks against randomized hash tables. In: Filipe, J., Obaidat, M.S. (eds.) ICETE 2007. CCIS, vol. 23, pp. 162–174. Springer, Heidelberg (2008). doi:10.1007/978-3-540-88653-2_12

17. Jenkins, B.: Various publications on hash functions. http://www.burtleburtle.net/bob/hash/doobs.html, /hash/spooky.html, /c/lookup2.c, /c/lookup3.c. Accessed 15 November 2016

18. Das, A., Nguyen, D., Zambreno, J., Memik, G., Choudhary, A.: An FPGA-based network intrusion detection architecture. IEEE Trans. Inf. Forensics Secur. $3(1)$, 118–132 (2008)

19. Aumasson, J., Bernstein, D.: C++ program to find universal (key-independent) multicollisions for CityHash64. https://131002.net/siphash/citycollisions-20120730.tar.gz. Accessed 14 November 2016

20. Aumasson, J.-P., Bernstein, D.J.: SipHash: a fast short-input PRF. In: Galbraith, S., Nandi, M. (eds.) INDOCRYPT 2012. LNCS, vol. 7668, pp. 489–508. Springer, Heidelberg (2012). doi:10.1007/978-3-642-34931-7_28

21. Dworkin, M.: FIPS PUB 202. SHA-3 Standard: Permutation-Based Hash and Extendable-Output Functions, August 2015

22. Secworks Sweden AB, "Siphash verilog." https://github.com/secworks/siphash. Accessed 15 November 2016

23. Hsing, H.: http://opencores.org/project,sha3 (2012). Accessed 15 November 2016

An FPGA-Based Implementation of a Pipelined FFT Processor for High-Speed Signal Processing Applications

Ngoc-Hung Nguyen[1], Sheraz Ali Khan[1], Cheol-Hong Kim[2],
and Jong-Myon Kim[1(✉)]

[1] School of Electrical Engineering, University of Ulsan, Ulsan, South Korea
hungnguyenvldt@gmail.com, sherazalik@gmail.com,
jongmyon.kim@gmail.com
[2] School of Electronics and Computer Engineering,
Chonnam National University, Gwangju 61186, South Korea
cheolhong@gmail.com

Abstract. In this study, we propose an efficient, 1024 point, pipelined FFT processor based on the radix-2 decimation-in-frequency (R2DIF) algorithm using the single-path delay feedback (SDF) pipelined architecture. The proposed FFT processor is designed as an intellectual property (IP) logic core for easy integration into digital signal processing (DSP) systems. It employs the shift-add method to optimize the multiplication of twiddle factors instead of the dedicated, embedded functional blocks. The proposed design is implemented on a Xilinx Virtex-7 field programmable gate array (FPGA). The experimental results show that the proposed FFT design is more efficient in terms of speed, accuracy and resource utilization as compared to existing designs and hence more suitable for high-speed DSP applications.

Keywords: FFT · Radix-2 DIF · SDF architecture · Pipelined · FPGA · IP core

1 Introduction

The Fast Fourier Transform (FFT) is a widely used transform algorithm in signal processing applications, which is primarily a computational tool, used to efficiently calculate the Discrete Fourier transform (DFT) and its inverse using digital computers. Since its introduction by Cooley and Tukey [1], FFT has been the mainstay for spectral analysis of digital signals. Spectral analysis is extensively used in communication systems, signal processing, image processing, bio-robotics, intelligent maintenance and almost every branch of science and engineering [2–4], making FFT one of the most widely used algorithms on digital devices. With the advent of smart phones and hand held media and entertainment devices, the performance and cost of FFT processors has an ever greater significance. The computational speed, accuracy and chip area utilization of FFT has a direct bearing on the cost and performance of modern digital devices. Moreover, very high data rate applications such as real-time intelligent

© Springer International Publishing AG 2017
S. Wong et al. (Eds.): ARC 2017, LNCS 10216, pp. 81–89, 2017.
DOI: 10.1007/978-3-319-56258-2_8

maintenance require a high throughput FFT processor. Therefore, implementation of an accurate and efficient FFT processor is a great significant issue.

FFT algorithms are mostly implemented using technologies, such as Application Specific Integrated Circuit (ASIC) [5], Digital Signal Processors (DSP) [6] and Field Programmable Gate Arrays (FPGA) [2, 3] as they offer better performance in contrast to general purpose processors. FPGA being a programmable logic device offers more flexibility than an ASIC or a DSP; requires relatively less design time; has lower cost and therefore makes an excellent choice for implementing FFT processors [7, 8].

In this study, a high performance, pipelined FFT processor is implemented on an FPGA platform. The radix-2 decimation-in-frequency (R2DIF) algorithm is used to implement the FFT, which reduces the computational complexity of DFT. The proposed pipelined technique allows all stages of the architecture to execute concurrently thereby significantly increasing system performance [9, 10]. In this paper, the Single-path Delay Feedback (SDF) pipelined architecture is employed for hardware implementation of FFT as it requires less chip area and has a higher utilization rate and a rather simple control logic [11]. Common FFT implementations require a complex multiplier and an on-chip memory to store the twiddle factors; both of which consume large chip area thereby increasing the cost of these designs. The rising demand for larger-point FFT, which mandates a larger memory for storing the complex twiddle factors in multiplier based implementations, makes things worse as it increases their power consumption and degrades their performance because memory read operations are inherently slower [12, 13]. To address this issue, the proposed architecture exploits the symmetric property of twiddle factors to reduce the memory required for storing these complex factors, by half. It leads to substantial improvements in performance of design. In existing designs, complex twiddle factor multiplications are usually handled by embedded DSP blocks. These dedicated functional blocks occupy more area on FPGAs. In the proposed design, they are replaced with multipliers based on the shift-add method, which only use shifters and adders. This makes the proposed design more suitable for implementation as a dedicated ASIC. The proposed R2DIF, SDF-based pipelined FFT architecture (R2DIFSDF) is implemented on a Xilinx Virtex-7 FPGA using Verilog HDL.

The main contributions are exploiting the SDF-based pipelined technique for hardware implementation of Radix-2 DIF FFT, with improved resource utilization and computational speed. It uses the symmetric property of twiddle factors to reduce the memory required to store them by 50%, and uses the shift-add method for resource optimization of the twiddle factor multipliers, while getting rid of embedded DSP blocks.

The rest of paper is organized as follows. Section 2 gives an overview of FFT and the Radix-2 DIF algorithm. Section 3 discusses the hardware implementation of the proposed R2DIFSDF architecture and the optimization of complex twiddle factor multiplication. Section 4 shows the results of the proposed implementation and compares it with existing designs. Finally, Sect. 5 concludes this paper.

2 The Fast Fourier Transform and the Radix-2 DIF Algorithm

The FFT is an efficient algorithm for computing the DFT, which maps an input sequence $x(n)$ into its equivalent frequency domain representation $X(k)$. The N-point DFT of $x(n)$ is defined as follows:

$$X(k) = \sum_{n=0}^{N-1} x(n) W_N^{kn}; \qquad 0 \leq k \leq N-1 \tag{1}$$

where W_N^{kn} is often referred to as the twiddle factor, given by the relation in Eq. (2).

$$W_N^{kn} = e^{(-j2\pi kn/N)} = \cos\left(\frac{2\pi kn}{N}\right) - j\sin\left(\frac{2\pi kn}{N}\right) \tag{2}$$

The FFT effectively uses the symmetry and periodicity of the complex twiddle factors to compute the DFT. The Radix-2 DIF algorithm decomposes the N-point output $X(k)$ as given in Eq. (1) into even-numbered samples $X(2k)$, and odd-numbered samples $X(2k+1)$, as given in Eqs. (3) and (4) respectively.

$$X(2k) = \sum_{n=0}^{\frac{N}{2}-1} \left(x(n) + x\left(n + \frac{N}{2}\right) \right) W_{\frac{N}{2}}^{kn} \tag{3}$$

$$X(2k+1) = \sum_{n=0}^{\frac{N}{2}-1} \left(x(n) - x\left(n + \frac{N}{2}\right) \right) W_{\frac{N}{2}}^{kn} W_N^n \tag{4}$$

where $0 \leq k \leq N/2 - 1$. The FFT is calculated by replicating the Radix-2 butterfly operation, as shown in Fig. 1. The Radix-2 algorithm yields the smallest butterfly unit, which allows greater flexibility in the design space. The N-point FFT is computed in $\log_2 N$ stages, whereas each stage involves $N/2$ butterfly operations i.e. a total of $(N/2)\log_2 N$ butterfly units.

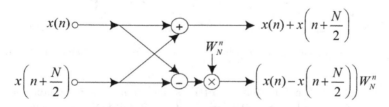

Fig. 1. The basic Radix-2 butterfly operation in DIF

3   Hardware Implementation of Radix-2 DIF FFT Algorithm

The FFT algorithms are often implemented using either memory based or pipelined architectures [14]. Memory-based FFT architectures consume fewer resources at the cost of lower speed, whereas, pipelined architectures achieve higher speed at the cost of more resources. In this study, the SDF-based pipelined architecture is chosen for hardware implementation on FPGA as it requires fewer hardwared resources, has a rather simple control logic and is adaptable to various FFT algorithms.

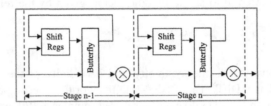

Fig. 2. Single-path delay feedback (SDF) architecture for Radix-2 DIF FFT

3.1   Implementation of Radix-2 SDF Pipelined FFT Architecture

The block diagram of a SDF-based pipelined architecture for R2DIF FFT algorithm is shown in Fig. 2. Each pipelined stage has a feedback data-path for write-back of immediate data into shift registers. The size of the next stage equals half of the previous stage and a complex multiplier is located on the data path between two stages.

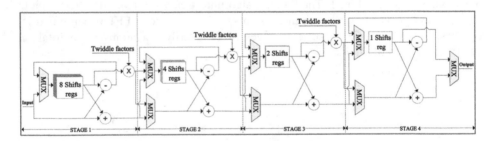

Fig. 3. The specified R2SDF pipelined architecture for 16-point FFT on harware

The pipelined design for 16-point FFT is shown in Fig. 3, whereas a R2DIF butterfly operation based on the SDF architecture (R2DIFSDF), is shown in Fig. 4, with a controller used to create the appropriate control signals for FFT computation. As shown in Fig. 3, the R2DIFSDF pipelined architecture has four stages and each stage includes two adders, a multiplier, shift registers for holding intermediate data and multiplexers to select data for the butterfly operation. The size of shift registers equals $N/2$ in the first stage and halves in the subsequent stages.

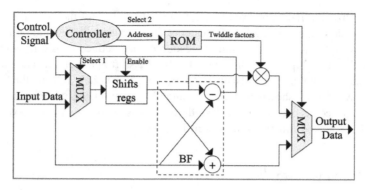

Fig. 4. The hardware architeture of a R2SDF pipelined stage or butterfly in FFT

The operation of the R2DIFSDF takes place in three phases. In the 1st phase, the multiplexer allows $N/2$ data points from the input to fill up the shift registers in $N/2$ clock cycles. During the 2nd phase, the butterfly computes FFT between the incoming $N/2$ data points and those already stored in the shift registers. The adder's output i.e. $x(n) + x(n+N/2)$ is directly forwarded to the next stage without any multiplication, whereas, the subtractor's output i.e. $x(n) - x(n+N/2)$, is fed back into the shift registers for temporary storage. This is done for all the data points, i.e. $0 \leq n \leq N/2$. In the 3rd phase, the buffered data is moved from the shift registers to the multiplier for complex twiddle factor multiplication and the product is directly forwarded to the next stage to complete the butterfly operation. The complex twiddle factors for FFT rotation are stored in a ROM. The N-point pipelined FFT architecture has the same SDF module repeated in its $\log_2 N$ stages. In general, a R2DIFSDF pipelined architecture for N-point FFT contains about $\log_2 N - 1$ multipliers, $2 \log_2 N$ adders and $N - 1$ shift registers.

3.2   Implementation of Twiddle Factor Multiplication in FFT

Optimal hardware implementation of twiddle factor multiplication requires careful consideration to minimize resource usage on FPGA and maximize the computation

$X \rightarrow$	*(8 bit)*					x_7	x_6	x_5	x_4	x_3	x_2	x_1	x_0
$55 \rightarrow$	*(6 bit)*							1	1	0	1	1	1
2^0 1						x_7	x_6	x_5	x_4	x_3	x_2	x_1	x_0
2^1 1					x_7	x_6	x_5	x_4	x_3	x_2	x_1	x_0	*1 bit*
2^2 1				x_7	x_6	x_5	x_4	x_3	x_2	x_1	x_0		*2 bits*
2^3 0			0	0	0	0	0	0	0	0			*3 bits*
2^4 1		x_7	x_6	x_5	x_4	x_3	x_2	x_1	x_0				*4 bits*
2^5 1	x_7	x_6	x_5	x_4	x_3	x_2	x_1	x_0					*5 bits*
$X*55 =$	$X \ll 5 + X \ll 4 + X \ll 2 + X \ll 1 + X$												

Fig. 5. Example of deployment for the constant multiplication based on the shift-add method

speed. If the size and radix are fixed for FFT, then the values of the twiddle factors are constants and determined using Eq. (2). Hence, the operation of FFT rotation is turned into constant multiplication. To optimize resources and reduce hardware complexity, the twiddle factor multipliers are implemented by the shift-add method. The number of shift and add operations depends on the number of non-zero bits in the constant; example of $X * 55$, as shown in Fig. 5. Using this method, only configurable logic blocks are required, as opposed to dedicated multipliers. This way, the proposed design saves 100% dedicated functional blocks in FPGAs.

4 Experimental Results

The proposed R2DIFSDF pipelined 1024-point FFT architecture, and the aforementioned architectures for comparison are implemented on a Xilinx Virtex 7 XC7VX485T FPGA using the Vivado Design Suite tool for functional and timing simulation and synthesis. A comparison of the two implementations for 1024-point FFT in terms of hardware complexity and performance is provided in Table 1.

Table 1. A comparison the achieved results on hardware based on two different designs

	(A)	(B)
# of Slices registers (CLB flip-flops)	2,046	1,591
# of Slices LUTs	3,159	16,275
# of IOBs	92	92
# of Block RAM/FIFO	4	0
# of Block DSPs	30	0
# of Clocking BUFGCTRLs	1	1
Total # of clock cycles for execution	2,066	2,058
Execution time (µS)	10.332	10.290

The best way to qualify a proposed design is to consider not only performance, but also area. It is necessary to have a clear measure for comparing area and performance of all designs. Hence, the area is measured in slices only, which is the main component in all FPGAs. In the Xilinx Virtex-7 FPGA family, each DSP block has a 25×18 multiplier and an accumulator, and it occupies around 500 slices. Whereas, the BRAM

Table 2. Results for 1024-point FFT with two different implementations

Designs	Resources							
	# of slices	DSP48		BRAM		Total # of slices	Frequency (MHz)	Execution time (µS)
		# of blocks	Equivalent slices	# of blocks	Equivalent slices			
(A)	5,205	30	15,000	4	6,800	21,800	200	10.332
(B)	17,866	0	0	0	0	17,866	200	10.290

block that is used for storing data, each has a capacity value that is equivalent to the area used by 1700 slices. Table 2 shows the experimental results for the two implementations of 1024-point FFT, and compares their efficiency in terms of area and execution time. The proposed design uses about 20% less slices and no dedicated functional blocks at all.

(A):   The traditional R2DIFSDF design based on memory using dedicated Xilinx logic core blocks (BRAMs, DSPs)

(B):   The proposed R2DIFSDF design with no dedicated functional blocks in the architecture

The precision of the proposed design is measured by calculating the average relative percentage error and comparing with baseline results obtained using Matlab. The results are presented in 16-bit fixed-point format with 10-bit precision, respectively. The average relative percentage error of the proposed architecture is very low, about 0.52%. The variation between results obtained using the proposed design and a 64-bit PC are not significant, especially in the face of gains made in hardware. The experimental results show the high precision of the proposed FFT implementation on FPGA hardware, which is better than Derafshi et al. [7] (1%) and Kumar et al. [15] (3.22%).

Table 3. Comparison the achieved results between the proposed design and the previous designs.

	Derafshi [7]	Harikrishna [3]	Xilinx [16]	Kumar [15]	The proposed design
# of points FFT	1,024	1,024	1,024	1,024	1,024
Operation clock frequency (MHz)	100	92.36	395	385	200
# of slices registers	2,472	3,155	2,264	2,633	1,591
# of slices LUTs	10,353	5,916	1,987	1,883	16,275
# of block RAM/FIFO	32	–	10	8	0
# of block DSPs	10	16	12	17	0
Total # of slices	43,225	22,617	27,251	26,616	17,866
Total # of clock cycles for execution	2,600	6,085	9,430	6,320	2,058
Execution time (µS)	26	65.89	23.87	16.376	10.290

A detailed comparison of the proposed design with others in terms of hardware complexity and performance is provided in Table 3. It is quite obvious that the proposed design takes the least amount of clock cycles and hence execution time, and requires fewer hardware resources to calculate 1024-point FFT. It operates 4.58× times faster than the FFT IP core by Xilinx, and totally removes embedded memory and DSP blocks in the architecture. It takes about 10.290 µs, at 200 MHz, to compute 1024-point FFT with better precision than existing designs.

5 Conclusion

In this paper, a high performance R2DIFSDF pipelined FFT processor designed as IP Logic-core for calculating 1024-point FFT is proposed and its implementation on a Xilinx Virtex-7 FPGA is discussed. The performance of the proposed architecture, in terms of speed, accuracy and hardware complexity, is compared with existing designs. The proposed design effectively exploits the R2DIF, SDF-based pipelined architecture and improves its performance and resource utilization by optimizing the complex twiddle factor multiplication using the shift-add operations. These improvements in the proposed architecture result in an FFT processor that is more accurate, faster, simpler, energy efficient and less costly. It delivers better performance and accuracy as compared to existing designs, using fewer resources and hence cost and power.

Acknowledgments. This work was supported by the Korea Institute of Energy Technology Evaluation and Planning(KETEP) and the Ministry of Trade, Industry & Energy (MOTIE) of the Republic of Korea (No. 20161120100350, No. 20162220100050), in part by The Leading Human Resource Training Program of Regional Neo industry through the National Research Foundation of Korea (NRF) funded by the Ministry of Science, ICT and future Planning (NRF-2016H1D5A1910564), in part by Business for Cooperative R&D between Industry, Academy, and Research Institute funded Korea Small and Medium Business Administration in 2016 (Grants No. C0395147, Grants S2381631), and in part by the development of a basic fusion technology in electric power industry (Ministry of Trade, Industry & Energy, 201301010170D).

References

1. Cooley, J.W., Tukey, J.W.: An algorithm for the machine calculation of complex Fourier series. Math. Comput. **19**, 297–301 (1965)
2. Sanchez, M.A., Garrido, M., Lopez-Vallejo, M., Grajal, J.: Implementing FFT-based digital channelized receivers on FPGA platforms. IEEE Trans. Aerosp. Electron. Syst. **44**, 1567–1585 (2008)
3. Harikrishna, K., Rao, T.R., Labay, V.A.: FPGA implementation of FFT algorithm for IEEE 802.16 e (mobile WiMAX). Int. J. Comput. Theory Eng. **3**, 197–203 (2011)
4. Chu, W., Champagne, B.: A noise-robust FFT-based auditory spectrum with application in audio classification. IEEE Tran. Audio Speech Lang. Process. **16**, 137–150 (2008)
5. Pitkänen, T.O., Takala, J.: Low-power application-specific processor for FFT computations. J. Sig. Process. Syst. **63**, 165–176 (2011)
6. Wang, Y., Tang, Y., Jiang, Y., Chung, J.-G., Song, S.-S., Lim, M.-S.: Novel memory reference reduction methods for FFT implementations on DSP processors. IEEE Trans. Sig. Process. **55**, 2338–2349 (2007)
7. Derafshi, Z.H., Frounchi, J., Taghipour, H.: A high speed FPGA implementation of a 1024-point complex FFT processor. In: 2010 Second International Conference on Computer and Network Technology (ICCNT), pp. 312–315. IEEE (2010)
8. Iglesias, V., Grajal, J., Sanchez, M.A., López-Vallejo, M.: Implementation of a real-time spectrum analyzer on FPGA platforms. IEEE Trans. Instrum. Meas. **64**, 338–355 (2015)
9. Zhou, B., Peng, Y., Hwang, D.: Pipeline FFT architectures optimized for FPGAs. Int. J. Reconfigurable Comput. **2009**, 1–9 (2009)

10. Garrido, M., Parhi, K.K., Grajal, J.: A pipelined FFT architecture for real-valued signals. IEEE Trans. Circ. Syst. I: Regul. Pap. **56**, 2634–2643 (2009)
11. Wang, Z., Liu, X., He, B., Yu, F.: A combined SDC-SDF architecture for normal I/O pipelined Radix-2 FFT. IEEE Trans. Very Large Scale Integr. (VLSI) Syst. **23**, 973–977 (2015)
12. Ma, Z.-G., Yin, X.-B., Yu, F.: A novel memory-based FFT architecture for real-valued signals based on a Radix-2 decimation-in-frequency algorithm. IEEE Trans. Circ. Syst. II: Exp. Briefs **62**, 876–880 (2015)
13. Luo, H.-F., Liu, Y.-J., Shieh, M.-D.: Efficient memory-addressing algorithms for FFT processor design. IEEE Trans. Very Large Scale Integr. (VLSI) Syst. **23**, 2162–2172 (2015)
14. Joshi, S.M.: FFT architectures: a review. Int. J. Comput. Appl. **116**, 1–5 (2015)
15. Kumar, M., Selvakumar, A., Sobha, P.: Area and frequency optimized 1024 point Radix-2 FFT processor on FPGA. In: 2015 International Conference on VLSI Systems, Architecture, Technology and Applications (VLSI-SATA), pp. 1–6. IEEE (2015)
16. Xilinx, Inc.: Logic core IP Fast Fourier Transform v8.0, Product specifications DS808 (2012)

Simulation and Synthesis

Soft Timing Closure for Soft Programmable Logic Cores: The ARGen Approach

Théotime Bollengier[1,2], Loïc Lagadec[2(✉)], Mohamad Najem[2],
Jean-Christophe Le Lann[2], and Pierre Guilloux[3]

[1] B-Com, Cesson-sévigné, France
[2] Lab-STICC UMR, 6285 Lorient, France
loic.lagadec@ensta-bretagne.fr
[3] IRISA UMR, 6074 Rennes, France

Abstract. Reconfigurable cores support post-release updates which shortens time-to-market while extending circuits' lifespan. Reconfigurable cores can be provided as hard cores (ASIC) or soft cores (RTL). Soft reconfigurable cores outperform hard reconfigurable cores by preserving the ASIC synthesis flow, at the cost of lowering scalability but also exacerbating timing closure issues. This article tackles these two issues and introduces the ARGen generator that produces scalable soft reconfigurable cores. The architectural template relies on injecting flip-flops into the interconnect, to favor easy and accurate timing estimation. The cores are compliant with the academic standard for place and route environment, making ARGen a one stop shopping point for whoever needs exploitable soft reconfigurable cores.

1 Introduction

As integrated circuits become increasingly complex and expensive to develop, the ability to apply post-fabrication changes appears all the more attractive. A direct gain lies in eliminating the cost and time associated with re-spinning silicon when fixing a bug or specializing the device to a specific application. Embedding reconfigurable logic in designs offers a solution to the semiconductor designers who need to update silicon post production.

In this context, several embedded FPGAs (eFPGA) have been developed as reported in [1–3]. EFPGAs are flexible logic fabrics, that, once programmed, implement digital circuits. But, unlike FPGAs, eFPGAs are intended to serve as pieces of a whole system-on-chip design. This approach allows:

- To support easy design specialization, while promoting reuse among several applications,
- To fix design issues that would have been belatedly detected (only after fabrication, if not post delivery),
- To add on-demand fleeting functionalities, such as assertion-based monitoring [4].

© Springer International Publishing AG 2017
S. Wong et al. (Eds.): ARC 2017, LNCS 10216, pp. 93–105, 2017.
DOI: 10.1007/978-3-319-56258-2_9

– To reflect changes in design specifications. This shortens time-to-market by allowing starting the design ahead of full specification availability (eg. to support changes in an evolving standard). The case of the H.264/AVC standard - that includes 22 revisions, corrigenda, and amendments spanning from May 2003 to February 2014 - helps assessing how serious this issue is.

This obviously comes at the cost of area and performance overheads, compared to a straight silicon implementation. However there are even more serious limitations [5].

First, every eFPGA embeds a fixed amount of reconfigurable resources. Any mismatch between theses resources and the applications needs (in terms of amount and nature of resources) is a serious issue. It may either prevent from using this support (if the application requirements exceed the eFPGA resources) or lead to a poor resources usage (internal fragmentation may nullify the advantage of using an optimized hard eFPGA core). Then, tailoring eFPGAs in order to set up a product line may seem attractive. Unfortunately, customizing eFPGA size and resources towards an application domain is likely to cause lengthy development cycles, as each new instance of hard eFPGA core must be silicon proven. However, Kuon et al. [6] demonstrated automation of circuit design, layout and verification, to cut off the required effort and time to design a new embedded hard FPGA core.

Second, eFPGAs are hard IP cores, which integration is complex and time consuming, and raises technology compliance issues, as all the cores must be provided with the same technology. As an example, the System-on-Chip of [7] was a scalable system infrastructure hosting heterogeneous reconfigurable accelerators, whose implementation required to migrate one of the accelerators to 90-nm, which resulted in a 6 months extra work.

This incites to move up a level of abstraction, based on soft macros that are process-independent. Some works have been reported in designing Soft Programmable Logic Cores (SPLCs) as summarized in Sect. 2. This paper complements these previous works by addressing some known issues in terms of scalability and timing closure.

The main contribution is ARGen, a generator of soft reconfigurable cores. ARGen supports core customization and trades a minor overhead against accurate timing closure. Also, SPLCs come along with their programming environment. As a result, the SPLCs' strengths (flexibility, just-fit dimensioning, performances predictability) outweigh disadvantages in term of performances.

The remainder of this paper is organized as follows: Sect. 2 summarizes related work on soft reconfigurable logic cores, Sect. 3 describes the structure of the proposed SPLC, aiming to simplify both SPLC synthesis and system integration, Sect. 4 presents the exploitation tool flow and circuit timing analysis, before Sect. 5.1 reports some results.

2   Background

Soft programmable logic cores (SPLC) have been introduced in [5,8] to empha-size flexibility and shorten development time, hence promote agility. Unlike hard core eFPGAs, synthesizable SPLCs are delivered as RTL descriptions, and syn-thesizing such cores is done using usual tools (standard ASIC or FPGA flows).

Integrating SPLCs in a design is easy: a flat synthesis of designs with one or many SPLCs requires no floorplanning.

Integrating SPLCs is safe: a whole design that contains SPLCs, can be ver-ified, simulated and emulated without additional complexity.

Integrating SPLCs is a just-fit process: SPLCs can be easily customized at the sole cost of updating the RTL description, with no need to silicon-proof each modified instance again, so that domain space exploration may be affordable.

Integrating SPLCs is reversible: the decision to use either a SPLC or fixed logic to implement any subpart of a design remains reversible until just before the chip goes to foundry. This decision stays on the designer who best knows which subsystem may/will need later modifications, and how much flexibility makes sense.

Integrating SPLCs supports optimization: authors in [9] demonstrated that soft core area overhead can be reduced by 58% and the delay overhead by 40% by creating custom standard cells (referred as *tactical cells*) that are more suitable for reconfigurable architecture implementations, and by using a tile-based approach to structure the layout of the hard macro.

As summarized above, SPLCs exhibit valuable features thanks to their RTL nature, nevertheless two difficulties emerge, that prevent from a wide broad adoption. First, the timing paths to explore are many. Second, the awareness of physical timings is poor.

Unlike regular designs, SPLCs present unusually large number of potential timing paths and combinatorial loops, due to their reconfigurable nature. This stresses the synthesis tool and may limit the size and nature of SPLCs [9]. To address this problem, authors in [5] propose to simplify the SPLC architecture by removing programmable flip-flops and by allowing the signal flow to go only in one direction, thus preventing combinatorial loops. As a consequence, the SPLCs exclusively target combinatorial applications; the proposed architecture is minimal which restricts the complexity and nature of applicative circuits to be implemented.

Moreover, performing timing analysis of a circuit mapped on a SPLC may be subject to a physical timing information miss. Exploiting the SPLCs goes through synthesizing applications on the reconfigurable cores. This relies on a synthesis tool -further referred as *virtual* synthesis tool- that is independent from the *physical* synthesis tool (the standard ASIC tool flow) used to implement the SPLC itself. As an example, in [5,8], the *virtual* synthesis tool is VPR [10]. The *virtual* synthesis tool executes timing-driven placement and routing, as well as timing analysis. These steps require the tool to be aware of every physical delay of SPLC resources. In [8], these physical delays are approximated using the conceptual representation of the SPLC. This results in an inaccurate circuit timing analysis, as adjacent resources in the conceptual SPLC representation may actually be positioned far apart in the silicon, thus tampering the delay estimation. In [5,9], timing exceptions are set to ignore the unused SPLC paths in the mapped circuit netlists when performing timing analysis according to the physical ASIC tools. This ensures the delay measures of the mapped circuits' critical paths are more reliable. However this comes at the cost of back and forth navigation between virtual and physical synthesis tools. Another option would be to extract an accurate information from the physical synthesis to feed the virtual tools. Yet, extracting this information means collecting the elementary delays of all arbitrary sub-segments of all combinatorial paths. This is of high complexity and must be processed for each new SPLC physical synthesis. Besides, this can only be considered a preliminary step, before the virtual synthesis tool actually exploits this information. As a consequence, even if back annotating the SPLC conceptual representation (used by the virtual tool flow) with actual physical delays is considered in [5,11], it has never been implemented in practice.

Our contribution goes one step beyond, and lifts these limitations. In this work, we propose a template for modifying SPLC architectures. This allows as easy SPLC integration as reported in [5] - but with no restriction on the SPLC architectures - while providing easy and accurate timing analysis of mapped circuits, solely using the virtual synthesis tool.

3   SPLC Design

Using an SPLC assumes three pre-requisite steps: generating the SPLC architecture, synthesizing this architecture to a physical target, and supporting system integration. Once generated, the SPLC module becomes a library element that can be instantiated within the application's RTL description, then the whole design is synthesized using an ASIC flow. The portable RTL description of the SPLC supports flat synthesis of the whole design without the need for specific steps such as floorplaning.

Then synthesizing and deploying applications onto the SPLC involve a dedicated software environment. This tool is independent from the physical technology, which in turn may require specific software development, as detailed in Sect. 4.

Figure 1 shows how these two flows, which together contribute to making SPLC a credible solution, relate and interact. The "ArGen" tool covers two aspects as detailled in the next section: architecture generation and bitstream production.

3.1   Overview of the SPLC Architecture

A SPLC architecture is composed of two layers:

- The *computation layer*, which is the set of reconfigurable elements that are available to applications, such as routing wires and function units.
- The *configuration layer*, which configures the computation layer.

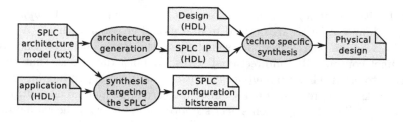

Fig. 1. Complete synthesis flow for using an SPLC.

The "ARGen" tool reads a specification of the computation layer, to automatically generate the SPLC's RTL description. This specification expresses the computation layer resources and their interconnections; the configuration layer is then automatically derived and eventually added to the model. Finally, a model transformation generates VHDL textual description of the architecture, allowing the SPLC module to be instantiated from a user design. The SPLC entity contains clock inputs, a vector of inputs and a vector of outputs, as well as a configuration interface. The generated RTL code is portable, simulation friendly, and synthesizable.

3.2 Detailed Computation Layer

The target SPLC computation layer that serves as a case study for this paper allows the synthesis of a large spectrum of applications. It is a fine-grained generic LUT-based architecture compatible with the standard architectures used in the academic Versatile Place and Route (VPR) tool [10]. This architecture is a simple *island-style* architecture as shown in Fig. 2, composed of Configurable Logic Blocks (CLBs) surrounded by routing channels.

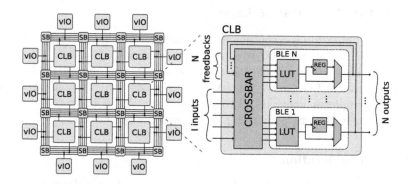

Fig. 2. An illustration of the proposed computation layer with 3×3 CLBs.

The SPLC has $Width \times Height$ CLBs, each of which has I inputs and N outputs. A CLB is composed of N BLEs (Basic Logic Element). A BLE has one LUT with K inputs and one register that can be bypassed (the *application register*). Inputs of BLEs are derived from a global crossbar with $I + N$ inputs (the I CLB inputs plus N feedback signals from the BLEs outputs). Each routing channel contains W unidirectional wires, in both directions, that can be connected to other wires from adjacent routing channels, depending on how the Switch Blocks (SB) are configured. Connections are implemented as multiplexers that are controlled through their *select signal(s)* coming from the configuration layer (as illustrated in Fig. 3).

The ARGen approach isolates the SPLC conceptual representation from its physical implementation on silicon. The proposed solution is to inject extra registers within the SPLC to latch the output of every configurable multiplexer that connects routing wire tracks. These registers are referred to as *Virtual Time Propagation Registers* (VTPRs). VTPRs break down physical logic chains into short segments, and prevent any combinatorial loop from appearing on the physical SPLC implementation, whichever its configuration. VTPRs are transparent for circuits mapped on the SPLC, and do not appear in the SPLC conceptual model.

VTPRs exhibit two decisive advantages. First, using VTPRs in a SPLC architecture alleviates the task of the physical synthesizer, as VTPRs reduce timing paths in the SPLC architecture and prevent combinatorial loops. This promotes architectures' scalability. There is no more need to limit size and complexity of synthesized architectures, nor to restrict the signal flow in one direction. This, however, rises the need for an extra and faster clock (Clk_{VTPR}), to allow signal propagation through VTPRs within one applicative clock cycle. Second, VTPRs favors timing closure, as reported in Sect. 4.2. VTPRs brings no improvement in term of performances of the synthesized SPLC. In that, VTPRs differ from C-slowing [12] which can be combined with retiming for sake of throughput increase.

3.3   Detailed Configuration Layer

The SPLC configuration is a contiguous sequence of bits that corresponds to the adequate configuration of SPLC resources (LUTs content, Crossbar, CLBs, and SBs) to implement a given application. The configuration layer is implemented as one or multiple shift registers. Once the transfer of the SPLC configuration to this register completes, every bit in the configuration layer is set to the desired value, resulting in the implementation of the synthesized circuit.

3.4   System Integration

When a design requires reconfigurability, the designer first isolates the part of the design which is subject to change apart from the static design, thus identifying the signals at the interface. The RTL of the static part instantiates the SPLC module, and connects the interface signals to the SPLC virtual inputs/outputs. A configuration controller drives the SPLC configuration interface, made of an

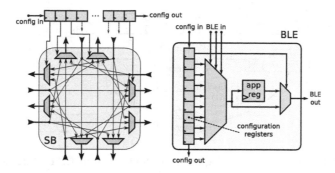

Fig. 3. Implementation of a Switch Box (left) and a BLE (right), whith their associated configuration registers from the configuration layer.

input `config_in` vector and an input `config_valid` bit. The number of configuration shift registers, forcing the size of the `config_in` vector, is determined to fit designer's needs (the wider the interface, the faster the configuration, the more area it consumes). The configuration controller can read the SPLC configuration bitstream from an internal memory, be mapped on a bus in case of a SoC, or even be accessible from outside the chip through the pinout.

4   SPLC Exploitation

When deploying applications onto SPLCs, no commercial tool fits the architecture, but some open-source academic works have been reported that offer a customizable solution for application synthesis. The ARGen approach relies on existing third parties tools, while offering a fast and accurate timing closure as a strong contribution. To this end, in addition to RTL code, the ARGen tool also generates VPR specific architecture description files. Additionally, ARGen generates bitstream and executes timing analysis.

4.1   Application Synthesis Targeting the SPLC Architecture

Hardware applications are designed as a RTL description within a Hardware Description Language (HDL). First, this description is used to produce a low-level netlist. Any tool can be supported as long as it outputs BLIF format [13] (e.g. the Odin II open-source CAD tool [14] that takes verilog as input). Then techno-mapping and optimizations take place. In this flow, ABC [15] is used to perform logic synthesis and optimizations, then map the netlist to the SPLC LUTs and produce a new netlist. Then, this netlist can be packed, placed and routed using VPR [10]. Finally, a timing report is generated along with the SPLC configuration bitstream by parsing VPR's outputs, and computing a portion of configuration per each SPLC resource. The synthesis flow of applications for the overlay is summarized in Fig. 4. This flow targets the SPLC architecture at various stages:

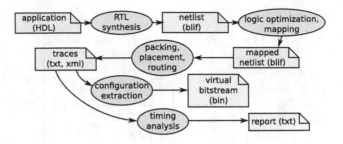

Fig. 4. Synthesis flow: from application RTL to an SPLC configuration

- LUT mapping respects the maximum number K of inputs per LUT;
- BLE packing into CLB respects N, the number of BLEs per CLB, as well as I, the number of inputs per CLB;
- Placement exploits the location of SPLC resources;
- Routing conforms to the SPLC routing graph;
- Configuration is compliant with the SPLC bitstream template;
- Timing analysis is specific to the SPLC architecture, as highlighted in the next section.

4.2   Timing Analysis

When synthesizing a SPLC, the timing reports indicate the F_{max} frequency at which the design may operate. F_{max} depends on the worst case propagation delay of SPLC atomic resources isolated between two VTPRs.

The virtual synthesis flow only relies on F_{max} to perform timing analysis. At the netlist level, assuming a net N_C connects two logic nodes L_A and L_B, the delay of the mapped net N_C can be computed as the number of VTPRs along the mapped path from L_A to L_B.

Adding VTPRs requires to operate two clocks: Clk_{VTPR}, the VTPRs clock, and Clk_{app}, clocking the application registers. To ensure that the mapped circuit properly runs on the SPLC, Clk_{VTPR} and Clk_{app} must abide by the relation:

$$F_{max} \geq F_{Clk_{VTPR}} \geq N_{VTPR} \times F_{Clk_{app}} \tag{1}$$

where

$$N_{VTPR} = \max_{\forall \ hypernet \ N_c} \left(\max_{N_c^i \in subnets(N_c)} (length(N_c^i)) \right) \tag{2}$$

In Eq. 2, the netlist is seen as a set of hypernets. These multi-terminal nets are spread as a collection of monoterminal nets, each of which goes from and reaches either an IO or a register.

This greatly simplifies and speeds up timing computation. Especially as the Manhattan distance is a smart approximation of *length*. Then Eq. 2 profitably replaces Elmore delay computation [16].

5   Experiments

The experiments rely on exploring the implementation cost of a parametric SPLC. Then, the use of this SPLC is demonstrated on a regular expression matching application.

5.1   SPLC Definition

The SPLC structure conforms to the previous specification, with dimensions ranging from $2*2$ to $14*14$ CLBs, with 4 BLEs per CLB (16 to 764 BLEs). The SPLC is synthesized using the J-2014-09-SP7 version of Synopys Design Compiler, on a ST 65 nm technology.

Figures 5, 6, and 7 illustrate some benefits of using VTPRs. Figures 5 and 6 illustrate the max frequency of the SPLC, regarding its dimensions, and the offered computing power respectively. What makes sense to be noticed here is first the top frequency (467 MHz) but also that the computing power ($\#BLE \times f_{max}$) exhibits scalability.

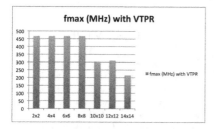

Fig. 5. VTPRs make timings predictable and lead to acceptable frequency

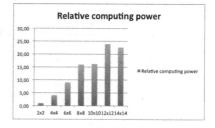

Fig. 6. Computing power exhibits scalability

The two following figures illustrate the feasibility of the approach.

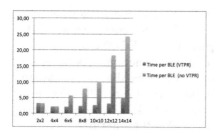

Fig. 7. VTPRs make the synthesis time affordable, hence promote scalability

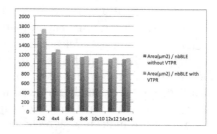

Fig. 8. VTPRs lead to a 3% average overhead in term of area

Figure 7 shows that the synthesis time ranges from 2.08 to 4.85 s per BLE, with 2.89 s/BLE in average when using VTPRs. Instead, this average rises up to 10.18 without VTPRs (ranging from 2.17 to 24.28). Besides, the standard deviation is reduced from 8.22 to 0.97 when introducing VTPRs. The lessons learned are two: first VTPRs save synthesis time, second VTPRs make synthesis time predictable. Figure 8 shows that VTPRs come almost for free in term of area (around 2% for bigger SPLCs). Also, as virtual prototyping usualy relies on FPGAs as an experimental platform, Table 1 reports results when implementing SPLCs -with and without VTPRs- on top of Xilinx FPGAs. Three stages are reported: XST (RTL synthesizer), MAP and PAR (logic synthesizer, placer and router), and TRCE (timing analyser).

VTPRs do not significantly impact synthesis time. On the opposite, MAP and PAR show unpredictable execution time unless VTPRs are used. This comes from the heuristics within these tools. In particular, the combinational loops within the SPLCs are broken down into smaller netlists undeterministicaly. TRCE seems to scale with regards to #*BLEs*. Again, the synthesis time is shorter and more predictable when using VTPRs, which preserves the FPGAs as a potential virtual prototyping platform when designing VTPR aware SPLCs.

Table 1. Synthesis time on Xilinx FPGA, with and without VTPR

Dimensions		XST time			MAP time			PAR time			TRCE time			Total synthesis time		
Size	BLEs	Raw	VTPRs	Ratio	Raw	VTPRs	Ratio	Raw	VTPRs	Ratio	Raw	VTPRs	Ratio	Raw	VTPRs	Ratio
2 × 2	16	32	32	1.00	133	120	1.11	103	66	1.56	35	33	1.06	303	251	1.21
4 × 4	64	68	61	1.11	228	238	0.96	344	138	2.49	71	39	1.82	711	476	1.49
6 × 6	144	159	146	1.09	530	298	1.78	60538	155	390.57	219	49	4.47	61446	648	94.82
8 × 8	256	328	354	0.93	909	524	1.73	3088	220	14.04	493	63	7.82	4818	1161	4.15
10 × 10	400	661	715	0.92	1842	763	2.41	4940	350	14.11	1208	84	14.38	8651	1912	4.52
12 × 12	576	1296	1371	0.94	4838	1179	4.10	39856	474	84.08	3289	105	31.32	49279	3129	15.75
14 × 14	784	2343	2487	0.94	4613	3904	1.18	18617	654	28.47	5007	154	32.51	30580	7199	4.24

5.2 Usage

Embedding a SPLC in a design adds some flexibility, which makes sense in various cases. First, this feature helps designers to fix bugs encountered in the design by offering post release Engineering Change Order (ECO) opportunities. Second, the SPLC can be used to implement transient functions. As an example, hardware probes and monitors may be useful when validating the design, although they are usually removed in a production phase. Last, SPLCs support incorporating new functions while updating some others. It is usually an iterative process to make a design change successfully, and SPLCs naturally support incremental compilation.

This paper focuses on the third item, and promotes the use of SPLC as a support for automata implementation. We consider a regex (regular expression) engine that generates logic to be implemented on a SPLC. The hardware template assumes an initial memory continuously streams data (one byte per cycle) to the generated design whose role is to detect a match with a reference pattern. The detection scheme relies on a non-deterministic finite automata (NFA) [17] to alleviate the need for backtracking (due to its multiple active states). Table 2 illustrates the implementation cost of representative expressions in terms of flip-flops and LUTs in the SPLC. The number of flip-flops only depends on the pattern size, while the number of LUTS does on the pattern complexity. The first five expressions score the cost of |, ?, + and ∗ constructs. The last two illustrate real cases. The *link* expression looks for hyperlinks with a known root. The full expression is: `/<a\s+href="/courses/[^ "]*"[^ >]*>/`. *ssh* is of higher complexity and corresponds to searching ssh traces in a log file. The full expression is: `/[^ ]+ +\d+ \d+:\d+:\d+ [^ ]+ sshd\[\d+\]:` `Accepted (password | publickey) for [^ ]+ from \d+\.\d+\.\d+\.\d+` `port \d + ssh/`.

Table 2. Synthesis results

Regex	SPLC FF	SPLC LUT	SPLC BLE	min N_{VTPR}	min size	W min
/abcdefgh/	8	12	12	10	2×2	4
/abcd|efgh/	8	15	15	12	2×2	4
/a(bcdefg)?h/	8	13	13	12	2×2	4
/a(bcdefg)+h/	8	14	14	10	2×2	8
/a(bcdefg)*h/	8	16	16	10	2×2	6
Link	23	44	44	14	4×4	12
ssh	76	99	100	18	6×6	12

The interesting point is that these expressions can be synthesized on modest SPLCs (6th column in Table 2), quickly enough (1 to 10 s, depending on the expression) to support design space exploration. Then, the circuit designer can dimension the SPLC in a just fit approach (last two columns) for a class of regex. The performances are only slightly impacted by the complexity of the expressions. N_{VTPR} denotes the factor by which the clock is divided due to the presence of VTPRs in the routing to generate the applicative clock Clk_{app}. The worst case still exhibits over 25 MHz $F_{Clk_{app}}$ applicative frequency.

6   Conclusion

The decision to include a reconfigurable IP in a design shortens time-to-market by allowing starting early development cycle before full availability of final applicative specifications. The design remains flexible, and the designers can partially update the circuit, even after silicon release. Integrating some Soft Programmable Logic Cores (SPLCs) is the easiest way to gain this flexibility, without affecting the ASIC design flow. However, timing analysis of circuits running on SPLCs usually comes to be inaccurate.

Our contribution tackles this issue by providing SPLCs decorated with VTPRs. VTPRs are extra registers, which break down loops in the interconnect in order to master the timings in the SPLC. This offers simplified timing closure (predictable and accurate timings). Besides, VTPRs ensure scalability when synthesizing the SPLC. Also, VTPRs make sense as an affordable feature, and come at the sole cost of 3% area overhead in average.

Finally, this approach has been demonstrated through implementing regex detection. This use case illustrates how SPLCs can support changing protocols. This work also closely relates to overlays, which are usualy virtual coarse-grain architectures, overlaying on top of fine-grained FPGA devices, for sake of improved productivity, portability, debugging capabilities, etc. ARGEN has demonstrated to suit designer's needs when adressing overlays. Future work will investigate how combining SPLC and overlays can drive new improvements.

Acknowledgement. This work has been supported by the French National Research Agency under the contracts ANR-11-INSE-015 (ARDyT) and ANR-A0-AIRT-07 (B-Com).

References

1. Menta - embedded Programmable Logic. http://www.menta-efpga.com
2. Nanoxplore. http://www.nanoxplore.com
3. ADICSYS - eFPGA (embedded FPGA) IP. http://www.adicsys.com
4. Abramovici, M., Bradley, P., Dwarakanath, K.N., Levin, P., Memmi, G., Miller, D.: In: Sentovich, E. (ed.) Proceedings of DAC 2006, pp. 7–12. ACM (2006)
5. Wilton, S.J., Kafafi, N., Wu, J.C., Bozman, K.A., Aken'Ova, V.O., Saleh, R.: Design considerations for soft embedded programmable logic cores. IEEE J. Solid-State Circ. **40**(2), 485–497 (2005)
6. Kuon, I., Egier, A., Rose, J.: Design, layout and verification of an FPGA using automated tools. In: Schmit, H., Wilton, S.J.E. (eds.) FPGA 2005, pp. 215–226. ACM (2005). http://doi.acm.org/10.1145/1046192.1046220
7. Voros, N., Rosti, A., Hübner, M. (eds.): Dynamic System Reconfiguration in Heterogeneous Platforms. LNEE, vol. 40. Springer, Heidelberg (2009)
8. Kafafi, N., Bozman, K., Wilton, S.J.: Architectures and algorithms for synthesizable embedded programmable logic cores. In: Proceedings of the 2003 ACM/SIGDA Eleventh International Symposium on Field Programmable Gate Arrays, pp. 3–11. ACM (2003)
9. Ova, V.A., Lemieux, G., Saleh, R.: An improved "soft" eFPGA design and implementation strategy. In: Proceedings of the IEEE 2005 Custom Integrated Circuits Conference, CICC 2005, pp. 179–182. IEEE (2005). http://dx.doi.org/10.1109/CICC.2005.1568636
10. Betz, V., Rose, J.: VPR: a new packing, placement and routing tool for FPGA research. In: Luk, W., Cheung, P.Y.K., Glesner, M. (eds.) FPL 1997. LNCS, vol. 1304, pp. 213–222. Springer, Heidelberg (1997). doi:10.1007/3-540-63465-7_226
11. Wiersema, T., Bockhorn, A., Platzner, M.: Embedding FPGA overlays into configurable systems-on-chip: ReconOS meets ZUMA. In: 2014 International Conference on ReConFigurable Computing and FPGAs (ReConFig), pp. 1–6, December 2014

12. Leiserson, C.E., Saxe, J.B.: Retiming synchronous circuitry. Algorithmica **6**, 5–35 (1991)
13. University of California Berkeley. (1992) Berkeley logic interchange format(blif). http://vlsi.colorado.edu/~vis/blif.ps
14. Jamieson, P., Kent, K.B., Gharibian, F., Shannon, L.: Odin 2 - an open-source verilog hdl synthesis tool for CAD research. In: FCCM 2010 (2010)
15. Brayton, R., Mishchenko, A.: ABC: an academic industrial-strength verification tool. In: Touili, T., Cook, B., Jackson, P. (eds.) CAV 2010. LNCS, vol. 6174, pp. 24–40. Springer, Heidelberg (2010). doi:10.1007/978-3-642-14295-6_5
16. Elmore, W.C.: The transient response of damped linear networks with particular regard to wideband amplifiers. J. Appl. Phys. **19**(1), 55–63 (1948)
17. Sidhu, R., Prasanna, V.K.: Fast regular expression matching using FPGAs. In: FCCM, ser. FCCM 2001, pp. 227–238. IEEE Computer Society (2001)

FPGA Debugging with MATLAB Using a Rule-Based Inference System

Habib Ul Hasan Khan$^{(\boxtimes)}$ and Diana Göhringer

Ruhr-University Bochum (RUB), Bochum, Germany
{habib.khan,diana.goehringer}@rub.de

Abstract. This paper presents an FPGA debugging methodology using a rule based inference system. Using this approach, the design stops a device under test (DUT), saves the data to external memory and then starts the DUT again. The saved data is used by MATLAB to debug the system by using a rule-based inference system. Normally, a debug system only displays the monitored data and then the decision making process is left to the user. But a rule-based inference system can be used to make the decision about the correct functionality of the system. The main benefits of this technique are no loss of debugging data due to an unlimited debug window, no use of HDL simulators for waveform viewing and shorter debugging time by using verification by a software technique.

Keywords: FPGA · Debugging · Simulation · Device start and stop · DSAS · Device under test · MATLAB · Rule-based inference system · DUT · Cross correlation

1 Introduction

The debugging process of current embedded systems is becoming tiresome because of the complexity of the design. Design complexity doubles every 18 months in comparison to the design productivity which doubles every 39 months [1]. This is because of the excessive efforts spent on verification of complex designs.

Normally, virtual prototyping is used for system verification but when the design is complex, virtual prototyping suffers due to speed issues. As stated in a report by IBM [2], the implementation of a design with a target frequency of 1.6 GHz faced a slow-down in the frequency when simulated on the HDL level. The report shows that only 10 Hz could be attained.

Due to such limitations of software-based verification methods, focus shifted to hardware simulation. But because of the hardware invisibility, only those signals can be monitored which are available at the pins of the FPGA. In order to resolve this issue, FPGA vendors introduced Integrated Logic Analyzer (ILA) [3] cores embedded in the design which can be set to trigger based on some preset conditions and offer limited debug window. But besides limited window, debugging is still difficult because user intervention is required to find out the problems. The difficulty of debugging therefore increases with the design complexity which increases the design cycle time. It is a practical necessity to test and debug any embedded design before physical deployment.

© Springer International Publishing AG 2017
S. Wong et al. (Eds.): ARC 2017, LNCS 10216, pp. 106–117, 2017.
DOI: 10.1007/978-3-319-56258-2_10

However, testing and debugging have associated time and cost implications. Furthermore, it is difficult to gather debugging data for complex designs when the amount of data is large and rapidly changing. However, if the simulation data can be linked to verification through a software environment, the testing and debugging process becomes much easier.

In this paper, a new methodology is introduced that addresses the visibility and limited window size issues. The paper presents a methodology to ease the debugging process with the help of a visual debugging tool implemented in MATLAB and hence using the power of MATLAB to debug a system. We have developed a new verification method based on hardware debugging using MATLAB as a tool and rule-based inference system as a verification method of the hardware design. We will be using a Gaussian filter based image processing system as a case study for illustrating the proposed verification method. In our verification system, a golden reference (GR) is utilized which can be defined using rule-based inference system or user defined. The goal is to find bugs without the need to run the system intermittently and debugging the complete window at one time utilizing the power of the MATLAB-based debugging system which will in turn reduce debugging time and hence the overall design cycle.

The rest of the paper is organized as follows. Section 2 presents related work and provides background information. Section 3 discusses the debugging by DSAS approach with Matlab using rule based inference system. In Sect. 4 the results are discussed. The paper is concluded in Sect. 5.

2 Related Work

Currently the main approaches for FPGA debugging are as follows.

2.1 Debugging Using Logic Analyzers and HDL Simulators

The internal logic analyzer is an additional logic added to the design which allows certain aspects of the running system to be measured, recorded or verified for possible error conditions. But active involvement of the designer is required for debugging of the design. Examples are SignalTap [4] from Altera and ChipScope [5] from Xilinx. These solutions offer selection of signals of interest and are based on triggering and sampling logic. The methodology is based upon trace buffers which use block memories to gather data by utilizing FPGA resources [6]. Data is saved to the BRAMs and extracted afterwards to use for debugging purposes. This debugging methodology is shown in Fig. 1. While this takes extra logic, this also requires trigger to monitor the verification data and still requires human intervention for debugging. One drawback in the commercially available tools is that the signal set for the trace buffer block has to be identified during design time. Therefore, any changes require re-synthesis of the design. This approach results in an increased design time for the system before the design can be debugged. ILA cores offered by the FPGA manufacturers also use trigger signals due to the limited debug window because the data utilizes scarce FPGA resources [7]. In other words, the trigger signal remains a major bottleneck since the data can be

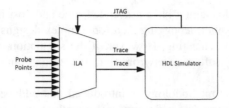

Fig. 1. HDL simulation design methodology

monitored only after the core has been triggered and even after the trigger, a limited debug window is available. Debugging with a small amount of sample data becomes cumbersome. Furthermore, debugging is done by HDL simulators which require cost and human intervention for debugging. Sometimes external logic analyzers can also be used along with the ILA cores for enhancing the debugging capabilities but the solution does not remain cost effective in such cases [8].

2.2   Debugging Using Emulation Systems

Emulation systems can also be used for debugging. Exostiv has offered an FPGA debugging solution [9] based upon a data collection and saving block technique. This solution requires a connection to the PC through its high speed port and then the data can be viewed on the PC. However, this system requires Exostiv hardware for debugging. Furthermore, HDL simulators (in case Xilinx Vivado simulator) are also required to carry out debugging.

2.3   Debugging Through Software

Verification by simulation is the main technique for functional verification of the design. MATLAB/Octave [10] functions can be used to build a debugging and testing environment. This method is flexible and sometimes only one RS-232 serial cable may be required [11].

Limited programming is used in this case. High level programming languages can automate the verification process and hence reduce the amount of user intervention required to verify and debug complex designs. Sometimes the manual work needed for analyzing the test results can constitute a bottleneck in the verification process. However, using high level programming software, debugging and verification of complex designs can be accelerated [12]. The main advantage of using MATLAB as verification software is that the complex programming tasks can be written, often, in few MATLAB commands [13] (Fig. 2).

Although this debugging method is simple, it suffers from the delay-time limitation. The main reason is the A/D conversion (or vice versa depending upon the design) and the transmission time between the DUT and the processing system. The delay may be less for Ethernet than for serial communication. However, this software debugging solution may not be appropriate for FPGA based designs which operate at very high frequencies.

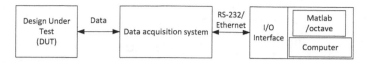

Fig. 2. Debugging through software

2.4 Hardware Co-simulation Based Debugging

A hardware co-simulation model is discussed in [14, 15]. In each of these papers, first the algorithm is proposed in MATLAB, system architecture based upon the algorithm is finalized and then the modules are built and verified in MATLAB/Simulink. After verification GR is obtained. Then the GR is used for RTL coding. Hardware co-simulation can then be carried out as shown in Fig. 3.

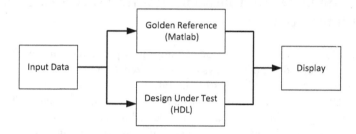

Fig. 3. Hardware co-simulation based debugging

But as obvious from Fig. 3, the design process has to start from MATLAB. However, if the algorithm is difficult or entirely impossible to implement in MATLAB, the process of hardware generation cannot start.

2.5 Knowledge Based Automated Debugging System

An expert system incorporates a knowledge base containing accumulated experience and an inference engine which applies the knowledge base to each particular situation described to the program based upon certain rules [16]. The system's capabilities can be enhanced by additions to the knowledge base or to the set of rules. Current systems may include machine learning capabilities that allow them to improve their performance based on experience, just as humans do.

Using a knowledge base for debugging a system is not new. An expert system was discussed in [17, 18] which could debug Pascal programs. This expert system was helpful in locating and correcting errors in Pascal programs. Furthermore, a knowledge based automated debugging system was discussed in [19]. The system was meant as an aid for more efficient debugging of Pascal based programs by determining possible causes for compiler, runtime, and logic errors (Fig. 4).

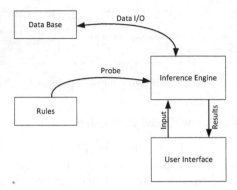

Fig. 4. Expert system [16]

3 Debugging by DSAS Approach with MATLAB Using Rule Based Inference System

In this section, a new methodology for debugging is presented. In the scope of this work, a processor-based debugging system is utilized (ARM in case of Xilinx Zynq device or Microblaze for rest of Xilinx FPGA families) to collect the data from onboard trace buffers (DSAS approach) [20]. Once the trace buffers are full, the DUT is stopped by the clock manager and then the data is transferred to the terminal through Ethernet. The saved data is used by MATLAB-based software debugging system utilizing a rule-based inference system approach. A block diagram of the hardware-software co-debugging methodology is shown in Fig. 5.

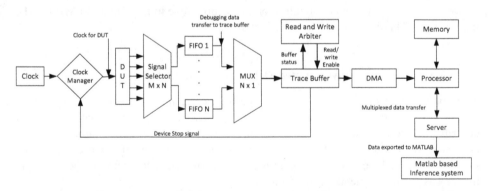

Fig. 5. Debugging by rule based inference system

Normally, a debug system can only show the monitored data (limited to the window size) and then the decision making process is left to the user. But if the debugging system has an unlimited window as promised by DSAS, monitoring millions of samples by the user may be tiresome. This necessitates the use of verification software for debugging. However, the main bottleneck for FPGA-based designs in using verification by software methods is the data transfer rate limitation. This is because the designs operate at very high frequencies and the data transfer between the FPGA and verification software cannot be as fast as the FPGA operating frequency. Adopting DSAS approach resolves the issue because the DUT is stopped during the data transfer from the FPGA to the terminal. Hence, rule-based inference system utilizing the power of MATLAB can be used very efficiently along with DSAS approach which cannot only monitor the output but also make the decision about the qualification of system as well.

The main benefits of this technique are no loss of debugging data due to an unlimited debug window, no use of HDL simulators for waveform viewing and shorter debugging time by using verification by a software technique.

3.1 Device Under Test (DUT)

The methodology has been validated by using two different DUTs.

3.1.1 The first DUT is a Gaussian filter [21] based image processing system. The filter has an adaptable window generator for which the image width, height and size of input pixel data can be specified. For the current research work, an input image of 1000×1700 pixels with 8 bits per pixel is used. The second stage of the Gaussian filter is a 7×7 kernel which is also adaptable. Output of the Gaussian kernel is a 16 bits image pixel. VHDL has been used for the design of both modules. After verification and qualification, the design is used as DUT for the debugging system (Fig. 6).

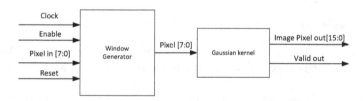

Fig. 6. Gaussian filter

3.1.2 The second DUT is a CORDIC core [22] used with a Microblaze soft processor. Microblaze reads data from a file and then sends the data to the CORDIC core. Different mathematical operations were performed by the CORDIC core before the data is sent back to the Microblaze (Fig. 7).

3.2 Interfacing

The debugging system hardware is connected to the terminal through Ethernet using UDP protocol [23]. Once the debugging data is received on the terminal platform, it is used by MATLAB for debugging. In order to control the whole process of debugging and streamlining the process, a graphical user interface has been developed using MATLAB GUIDE [24]. The GUI front panel is shown in Fig. 8.

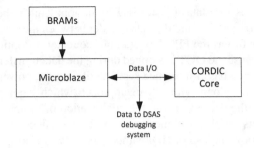

Fig. 7. Microblaze-based CORDIC design

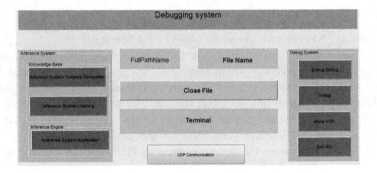

Fig. 8. Graphical user interface (GUI)

3.3   Rule-Based Inference System

Rule-based inference system is the core of the proposed debugging methodology. As shown in Fig. 9, it has three main parts namely Inference Engine, Knowledge base and Rules set.

The knowledge base can have one of the following three types of data. The first priority lies with the user defined data set. Since the user generally knows which type of

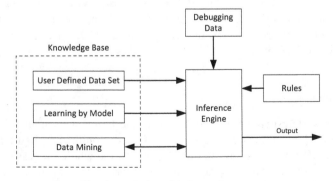

Fig. 9. Rule-based inference system

output is expected, it is most appropriate for the user to provide the data set for pattern matching. Based upon the rules set, the inference engine calculates the similarity between the debugging data and the dataset from the knowledge base. Depending upon the DUT type, regression (multiple linear regression), correlation (linear or rank correlation) or cross correlation can also be selected as a rule. For the current research work the inference engine calculates the cross correlation (rule) between the debugging data and user defined dataset and displays the result. A cross correlation of 1.0 depicts a match. In cases where the user does not know the output, it is also possible to make the debugging system learn from any available identical system. If either of the two data options are not available, the debugging system can mine for one in the database (if a similar system was debugged in the past and data saved to the knowledge base). If relevant dataset is not found then debugging data will be displayed without any overlay or rule application. In such cases the debugging data is saved in the data base for future reference if the debugging data has unique nomenclature.

Once the relevant data has been loaded to the inference engine, the engine calculates cross correlation between the debugging data and database. The result of cross correlation function is an array of values showing the similarity between debugging data and the database. The maximum cross correlation value is achieved when the two datasets match perfectly. Using the MATLAB functions, lag between the two datasets can also be found. A correlation of 0.0 depicts no match. A cross correlation of 1.0 depicts a perfect match that means one dataset can be derived from the other either directly or using a positive scale factor. A correlation of -1.0 depicts max negative correlation (that means one dataset can be derived from the other using a negative scale factor). Values between 0 and 1 show a partial match. A correlation value (>0.90) may indicate very good similarity between the two dataset [25] (depends upon the use case) but for debugging purposes a perfect match is required. The inference engine can also indicate the best match instance which can be used as a starting point for debugging. Hence by using rule-based expert system, debugging becomes easier and saves a lot of time.

The main advantage of this debugging methodology is that unlike limited window based debugging systems; the DSAS approach can have extremely large data set. It can monitor 16 signals (for the current research work but not limited to 16) simultaneously with each signal having millions of points; comparing such large number of transitions manually may become cumbersome because each transition needs to be checked with the corresponding clock cycle (sample number in this case). But adopting the rule-based inference system methodology, debugging becomes easy once the knowledge base has been populated with appropriate data; because the system carries out the cross correlation (or any appropriate rule) and displays the results. Furthermore, the debugging system plots the debugging data with relevant data overlay for easing the debugging process.

4 Results

The proposed debugging approach has been tested with 2 different designs: An image processing application and a Microblaze-based CORDIC application. MATLAB plot of the image processing design without inference system application is shown in

Fig. 10. The design was operated at 100 MHz. Hence each sample corresponds to a clock cycle of 10 ns. Input (*pixel in*) is shown in first subplot. After processing the input data, corresponding *Img out* is shown in the second subplot. In third subplot, the *Valid out* remains zero initially because the window generator needs to be filled before valid data can be acquired at the output. As can be seen in the third subplot, Valid data turns to 1 after (6w + 6) i.e. 6006 samples (where w is the image width) indicating that the filter has a valid output. The data remains valid for (w − 6) i.e. 994 samples and then again becomes invalid for 6 samples (kernel size −1). This pattern continues for the whole length of the image. If the design is required to be reset, the *reset* needs to be transitioned to 1. In order to keep the design enabled during debugging, the *enable* should be 1. It can be noticed that more than 135,000 samples of each signal has been acquired. (5 signals are shown in the figure however 16 signals were monitored for the current research work).

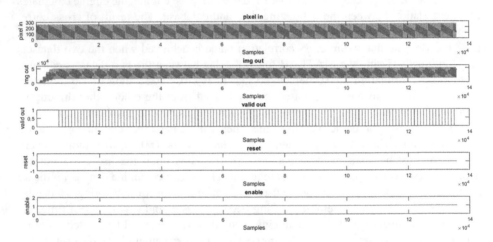

Fig. 10. MATLAB plots

In Fig. 11, debugging data has been plotted besides the dataset from knowledge base. MATLAB facilitates mathematical modelling of any system greatly. However, in case a mathematical model is not available or modelling is time consuming, data from any similar design can suffice for knowledge base generation. For the current research work, the knowledge base has been populated from the data acquired by learning from a similar system. However, if a similar system is not present, user can input his own template for populating the knowledge base because expected output is generally known.

Furthermore, if the knowledge base is devoid of any template, still the option for manual debugging is available in contrast to other verification by software debugging methodologies where debugging is not possible in absence of the GR model. When the user is satisfied with the output, the data base can be populated for future use.

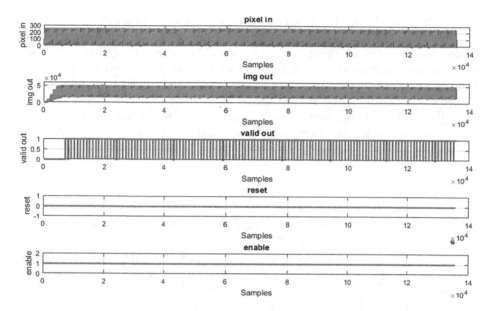

Fig. 11. MATLAB plots after expert system application

Once the knowledge base has been populated with corresponding dataset, inference engine calculates cross correlation between debugging data and the knowledge base dataset and displays the results. A plot of the output of rule-based inference system is shown in Fig. 12.

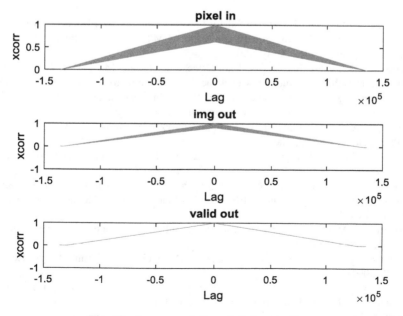

Fig. 12. Cross correlation plotted against lag

As can be seen in Fig. 12, the maximum cross correlation between the two datasets is 1.0 for the plotted data and the lag between the two datasets is zero, hence a perfect match exists between the debugging data and the knowledge base. However, if the maximum cross correlation is less than 1.0 which indicates some disparity between the debugging data and the knowledge base dataset, analyzing the data becomes important. In such cases, the lag against the maximum value can be used as a starting point for debugging. Manual comparison of such large datasets would have been time consuming. But rule-based inference system has made the debugging process fast and efficient.

5 Conclusions

The response of an FPGA-based embedded design needs to be verified. If a suitable debugging system is used, a lot of effort and time can be saved. Furthermore, besides the hardware debugging system, if a hardware-software debugging approach is used, debugging can become easier. In order to carry out the task, a hardware-software solution is introduced in this paper. When a problem on the hardware is encountered and debugging is required, DSAS approach along with a rule-based inference engine can be used. It will provide an un-limited debug window as promised by DSAS and MATLAB-based software solution to speed up the debugging process by allowing minimal human interaction.

References

1. Hung, E., Wilton, S.J.: Towards simulator-like observability for FPGAs: a virtual overlay network for trace-buffers. In: Proceedings of the ACM/SIGDA International Symposium on Field Programmable Gate Arrays (2013)
2. Asaad, S., Bellofatto, R., Brezzo, B., Haymes, C., Kapur, M., Parker, B., Roewer, T., Saha, P., Takken, T., Tierno, J.: A cycle-accurate, cycle-reproducible multi-FPGA system for accelerating multi-core processor simulation. In: Proceedings of the ACM/SIGDA International Symposium on Field Programmable Gate Arrays (2012)
3. Herrmann, A., Nugent, G.P.: Embedded logic analyzer for a programmable logic device. U. S. Patent No. 6,389,558, May 2002
4. Altera Inc.: On-chip design verification with Xilinx FPGAs, Agilent Application Note 1456, April 2003
5. Arshak, K., Jafer, E., Ibala, C.: Testing FPGA based digital system using XILINX ChipScope logic analyzer. In: IEEE 29th International Spring Seminar on Electronics Technology (2006)
6. Kuijsten, H.: Method and apparatus for a trace buffer in an emulation system. U.S. Patent No. 5,680,583, 21 October 1997
7. Woodward, J.: In-circuit debug of FPGAs. CMP Media LLC N. Y. Embed. Syst. Eur. **7**(49), 16–17 (2003)
8. Agilent Technologies Inc.: Deep storage with Xilinx ChipScope Pro and Agilent Technologies FPGA Trace Port Analyzer. Agilent Product Overview 5988-7352EN, February 2003

9. Exostive Inc.: FPGA debug reloaded. http://www.exostivlabs.com
10. Eaton, J.W., Bateman, D., Hauberg, S.: GNU Octave. Network Theory, London (1997)
11. Goris, M.J.: Using Matlab to debug software written for a digital signal processor. In: Proceedings of Benelux Matlab User Conference (1997)
12. Wang, Z.: Real-time debugging and testing a control system using Matlab. Open J. Appl. Sci. **3**(02), 61 (2013)
13. Hatnik, U., Altmann, S.: Using ModelSim, Matlab/Simulink and NS for simulation of distributed systems. In: Parallel Computing in Electrical Engineering, pp. 114–119 (2004)
14. Liang, G., He, D., Portilla, J., Riesgo, T.: A hardware in the loop design methodology for FPGA system and its application to complex functions. In: International Symposium on VLSI Design, Automation, and Test (VLSI-DAT), pp. 1–4 (2012)
15. Hai, J.C.T., Pun, O.C., Haw, T.W.: Accelerating video and image processing design for FPGA using HDL coder and simulink. In: IEEE Conference on Sustainable Utilization and Development in Engineering and Technology (CSUDET), pp. 1–5 (2015)
16. Waterman, D.: A Guide to Expert Systems. Addison-Wesley, Boston (1986)
17. Geis, D., Morscher, R., Kiper, J.: An expert system for debugging novice programmers' Pascal programs. In: Proceedings of the 17th Conference on ACM Annual Computer Science Conference (1989)
18. Looi, C.K.: Analysing novices programs in a prolog intelligent teaching system. In: European Conference on Artificial Intelligence (ECAI), pp. 314–319 (1988)
19. Zin, A.M., Aljunid, S.A., Shukur, Z., Nordin, M.J.: A knowledge-based automated debugger in learning system (2001). arXiv preprint: arXiv:cs/0101008
20. Khan, H.H., Göhringer, D.: FPGA debugging by a device start and stop approach. In: Proceedings of the International Conference on Reconfigurable Computing and FPGAs (Re-Config) (2016)
21. Muralikrishnan, B., Raja, J.: Gaussian filter. In: Muralikrishnan, B., Raja, J. (eds.) Computational Surface and Roundness Metrology, pp. 33–38. Springer, London (2009)
22. Xilinx Inc.: Cordic v6.0 IP core. http://www.xilinx.com
23. Postel, J.: User datagram protocol. No. RFC 768 (1980)
24. Qiu, J.H., Wang, Y.H., Li, Z.Q.: A new way to develop interface based on Matlab/GUI. Hebei J. Ind. Sci. Technol. **4**, 012 (2008)
25. Taylor, R.: Interpretation of the correlation coefficient: a basic review. J. Diagn. Med. Sonogr. **6**(1), 35–39 (1990)

Hardness Analysis and Instrumentation of Verilog Gate Level Code for FPGA-based Designs

Abdul Rafay Khatri$^{(\boxtimes)}$, Ali Hayek, and Josef Börcsök

Department of Computer Architecture and System Programming,
University of Kassel, Kassel, Germany
arkhatri@student.uni-kassel.de

Abstract. Dependability analysis and test approaches are key steps in order to test and verify system robustness and fault-tolerance capabilities. Owing to the shrinking size of components, it is very difficult to guarantee an acceptable degree of reliability. With the growing computational power of FPGAs and other diverse advantages, they have become indispensable solutions for embedded applications. However, these systems are also prone to faults and errors. Therefore, the testability and the dependability analysis are necessary. Both methods require the deliberate introduction of faults in the SUT. In this paper, a fault injection algorithm is proposed for Verilog gate level code, which injects faults in the design. Also, the method is proposed for finding sensitive locations of SUT. These methods are developed under a fault injection tool, with a GUI, for the ease of use, and it is named *RASP-FIT* tool. Benchmark circuits from ISCAS'85 and ISCAS'89 are considered to validate the both proposed methods.

Keywords: Dependability analysis · Instrumentation · Fault injection · FPGA · Verilog HDL · Fault tolerance

1   Introduction

Nowadays, Field Programmable Gate Array (FPGA) is a widely used technology in the field of embedded system designs. Owing to its remarkable features such as parallelism, reconfiguration, separation of functions, self-healing capabilities and increased overall availability [3], the FPGA has become the nucleus of many embedded applications over the last few decades. The major applications include aerospace, biomedical instrumentation, safety critical systems and spacecraft, to name a few [9].

However, FPGA-based devices are sensitive to Single Event Upsets (SEUs), which can be caused by various sources, such as α-particles, cosmic rays, atmospheric neutrons and heavy-ion radiations etc. Furthermore, since the capacity of FPGA technology is increasing, the size of components on a chip is

© Springer International Publishing AG 2017
S. Wong et al. (Eds.): ARC 2017, LNCS 10216, pp. 118–128, 2017.
DOI: 10.1007/978-3-319-56258-2_11

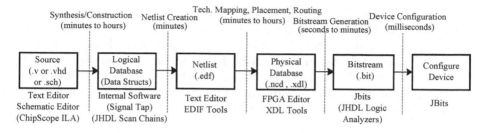

Fig. 1. Points of modification in the FPGA development flow [6] (Color figure online)

reduced as well. This makes the device more prone to soft errors [4]. For FPGA-based systems, simulation and emulation based methods are usually applied for testing, verification and validation of designs. Therefore, testing and the dependability analysis of such systems are crucial. These procedures require deliberate introduction of faults in target systems. The fault injection technique plays an important role in the dependability evaluation and is a widely accepted solution to perform SEU sensitivity analysis [2,5]. In the FPGA-based fault injection process, there are different points in the design process, where faults can be injected as shown by blue dashed lines in Fig. 1. Various tools have been devised in the past several years, to inject faults in FPGA-based designs at various locations for evaluating design characteristics. FPGA-based fault injection tools have advantages of both physical and simulation-based technique, such as speed and flexibility. There are two main groups of techniques, reconfiguration-based and instrumentation-based [9]. The fault injection tools that work on the net-list developed after the synthesis process are introduced in [10–12], and those based on the reconfiguration technique are presented in [1,5,10,15]. Additionally, there are some tools based on the instrumentation technique [13,17], and hybrid techniques (simulation/emulation) [7,14,16].

In this work, the instrumentation-based fault injection methodology is developed in Matlab, and an experimental approach is also proposed, which identifies the most sensitive part of the design for different fault models (e.g. bit-flip and stuck-at 1/0).

Contributions

The major contributions of this work can be summarized as:

- Injecting faults in designs at the coding phase
- Dealing with bit-flip and stuck-at 1/0 fault models individually
- Being capable of injecting faults at all possible locations along with the fault controlling unit (FISA)
- Generating any number of copies with evenly distributed faults
- Finding sensitive locations in the overall design of System Under Test (SUT) for fault models
- Developing an easy to use and portable GUI wizard.

The organization of this paper is as follows: Sect. 2 describes the in-depth technicalities of the proposed fault injection algorithm for the modification of Verilog gate level code. Section 3 presents the proposed methodology of finding sensitive locations of the design. Section 4 briefly describes the working flowchart of the proposed *RASP-FIT* tool. Section 5 shows the results and provides some discussion on the performed experiments. Finally, Sect. 6 concludes the paper and presents some further steps of our future work.

2   Fault Injection Methodology: How It Injects

The automatic fault injection algorithm is designed and developed in Matlab, which can be used for any combinational and sequential designs, written in Verilog HDL. There are many levels of abstraction in which designs are defined in Verilog, namely, behavioral or algorithmic, data flow level, gate level and switch level. Currently, we have considered the designs at the gate level for the fault injection methodology, whereas, the work at the behavioral and data flow levels (a.k.a RTL) will be implemented in the next phase of this research.

In this algorithm, the Verilog code of SUT is divided into two partitions: one consists of the declaration part where no faults are injected, and is defined by the library *ListNoFault* e.g. {'module', 'input', 'output', 'wire', 'endmodule', 'reg'}, whereas in the other partition, we have the list of some special or user defined instances, where the injection of faults are described by some predefined positions in the instance, and is defined by the library *ListSpecial* as shown in Fig. 2. For the second partition, a variable *ListInsert* defines the position in the instance, e.g. flipflop or multiplexer. These two lists are used, when the user does not wish to insert the fault in the whole design. For that case, the user puts an instance name in the first library and so on. This tool also has the flexibility to generate and evenly distribute faults in all different copies of the target system. In order to obtain different number of faulty copies *nSec*, the user must input this value during fault injection process. The controlling of faults in the copy of SUT, de-multiplexer based Fault Injection Selection and Activation (FISA) unit is generated and added [8]. Note that, these operators ($\hat{} $ = bit-flip, | = stuck-at 1, & = stuck-at 0) are specified as fault models in the Verilog code. More detail can be found in [9]. Furthermore, Fault Select (FS) signal is added to the faulty copy of SUT as a *select* input and its value is calculated by Eq. 1 as shown in Fig. 3, along with golden model of SUT, FISA unit and way of fault injection in instances.

$$FS = \lceil \log_2(N_{copy}) \rceil \qquad (1)$$

where N_{copy} denotes the number of faults injected per copy of the SUT.

All the generated files have different naming conventions for the uniqueness and understanding purposes by adding *SourceFileName_faultycopy(nSec).v* to the name of original source file name (e.g. *c17_faultycopy1.v*). Output ports naming conventions are also changed for the purpose of further comparison of responses in the fault injection experiment, the fault detection and the test analysis, also shown in Fig. 3.

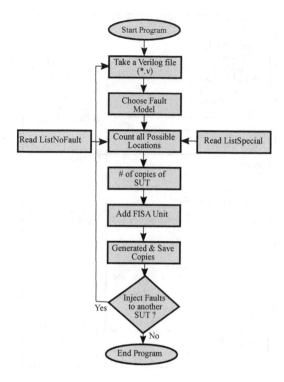

Fig. 2. Flow chart of fault injection methodology

Table 1. Instrumentation using fault injection methodology for different SUT

SUT	Type of SUT	# of faults injected (bf,sa1,sa0)	# of FISA inputs
c17	Combinational	12	4
c432	=	336	9
c499	=	408	9
c880	=	729	10
c1355	=	1064	11
c1908	=	1498	11
c2670	=	2076	11
c5315	=	4385	13
s27	Sequential	21	5
s344	=	284	9
s400	=	342	9
s510	=	430	9
s820	=	762	10
s1196	=	1027	11
s15850	=	14178	14

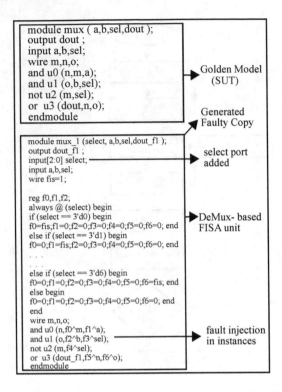

Fig. 3. Original and instrumented Verilog gate level code

3   Finding Fault Sensitive Locations: An Experimental Approach

The sensitive location is the location in a SUT, where occurrence of any type of fault results in a failure. The sensitive locations of the SUT are obtained using the following proposed experimental approach. According to this approach, these locations are more or less equally sensitive to bit-flip and stuck-at (1/0) faults. Some definitions must be considered in order to understand the proposed approach.

Definition 1. *A fault-experiment is a setup in which an input pattern is applied, all N faults are injected and activated one by one, and responses are gathered for each of the respective fault. The Total Output Responses (TOR) are calculated using Eq. 2,*

$$TOR = P \times N \tag{2}$$

where P is the number of qualified patterns applied in the whole experiment and N is the total number of faults in a target circuit.

Definition 2. *Fault-hardness 'H' defines the characteristics of hard to detect faults or faults which can be detected very rarely.*

$$H = \left(1 - \frac{\#\,of\,Fault\,Detections}{Total\,Patterns\,Applied}\right) \times 100\% \tag{3}$$

Definition 3. *A sensitive-threshold level is defined as a level that serves to illustrate whether the fault-hardness of a particular fault of all fault models is below that sensitive-threshold.*

In the proposed approach, the fault-hardness of individual faults is calculated, and subsequently divided into (1) hard to detect and (2) frequently detected faults, for all three fault models. We have used previously developed test method for the combinational digital system presented in [8] as an experimental setup. The *SetPoint* value is considered in the range of 20% to 50% of total faults N in a fault-experiment. When a fault-experiment is performed, the detections of faults are counted and compared to the *SetPoint* value. If the number of detections exceeds the *SetPoint* value, the input pattern is considered as the qualified pattern for the Fault Matrix. Fault Matrix is an arrangement of qualified input patterns and the detection of faults for the input pattern given in Eq. 4.

$$\text{Fault Matrix} = \begin{bmatrix} P_1 & F_{1,1} & F_{2,1} & \cdots & F_{N,1} \\ P_2 & F_{1,2} & F_{2,2} & \cdots & F_{N,2} \\ \vdots & \vdots & \vdots & \vdots & \vdots \\ P_i & F_{1,i} & F_{2,i} & \cdots & F_{N,i} \end{bmatrix} \tag{4}$$

Where P_1 to P_i are qualified input patterns obtained during fault-experiment, and the array of detected faults for a particular pattern are placed in a row of the matrix. When the specific fault is detected, it gets value '1', otherwise gets value '0'. In this approach, only 100 qualified input pattern are obtained, the value of i will reach a maximum of 100 and the value of total faults N depends on the faults injected by the fault injection algorithm described in Sect. 2 as given in Table 1. However, the random input patterns are generated using Linear Feedback Shift Register (LFSR). This method is a simple, computationally fast and memory efficient.

According to this methodology, the detection of each fault is summed up individually (column sum) for each fault model. In the next step, hardness of each fault is calculated by Eq. 3, and placed in a matrix, named *Hardness Matrix* as given in Eq. 5. All columns are compared with the different threshold values for a particular system or application in order to find the number of sensitive locations. Threshold values are used to obtain the number of the most sensitive locations to less sensitive locations. Results are illustrated tabularly and graphically in Sect. 5.

$$\text{Hardness Matrix} = \begin{bmatrix} H_{f_1,bf} & H_{f_2,bf} & \cdots & H_{f_N,bf} \\ H_{f_1,sa0} & H_{f_2,sa0} & \cdots & H_{f_N,sa0} \\ H_{f_1,sa1} & H_{f_2,sa1} & \cdots & H_{f_N,sa1} \end{bmatrix} \tag{5}$$

4   RASP-FIT Tool

RASP-FIT tool is designed in order to the test, the fault detection and the dependability analysis of FPGA-based systems. It stands for "RechnerArchitektur und SystemProgrammierung-Fault Injection Tool". It is developed in Matlab using its GUI environment. In general, the fault injection method should be highly effective for validating and demonstrating the design characteristics and robustness in the presence of faults [18]. In order to ease of use, a standalone Matlab GUI is developed for the proposed tool using *deploytool* command. The complete flow chart of the proposed tool is shown in Fig. 4.

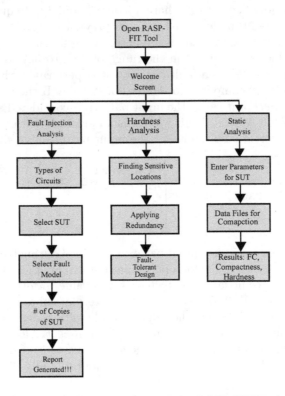

Fig. 4. Working flow chart of the *RASP-FIT* tool

5   Methodology and Discussion

The *RASP-FIT* tool accepts Verilog *.v file and injects bit-flip and stuck-at 1/0 faults in all possible locations in the SUT. These files contain the code for the original and faulty copies separately. Table 1 describes the results of the fault injection algorithm applied on various SUTs from ISCAS'85 and ISCAS'89 circuits for bit-flip and stuck-at 1/0 fault models. These benchmark circuits are widely used for different purposes e.g. testing and fault injection analysis.

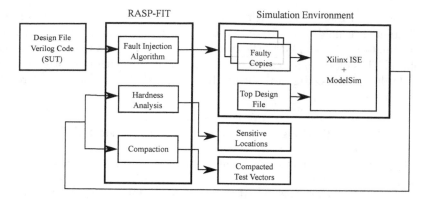

Fig. 5. Block diagram of the proposed experimental approach

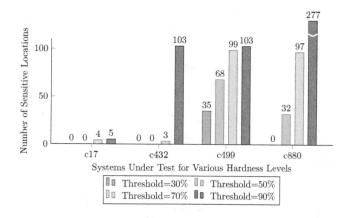

Fig. 6. Sensitive locations for different threshold values

The number of select pins required for *select* inputs is also shown in the table. In the previously proposed ATPG test method, faults were injected using this tool, and it was presented in our work [8].

RASP-FIT tool is developed in Matlab, while simulation environment is created using Xilinx ISE and ModelSim softwares as shown in Fig. 5. Combinational digital systems are considered for hardness analysis in this paper. If the hardness of a fault results in 100%, it means the fault is not detectable for any input; hence, it is called an untestable or undetectable fault. On the other side, a hardness of 0% shows the detection of fault for all test vectors, which means that the portion of the circuit where the fault has occurred is very sensitive to fault attacks.

We consider four threshold levels and find out the sensitive locations for each. Using these threshold values, we can obtain the most sensitive locations. Table 2 shows various threshold levels and their respective numbers of sensitive locations. These locations are obtained from the hardness matrix by comparing its value for each fault model with a particular threshold value. We have used four different threshold values to obtain different numbers of sensitive locations. This information will be used in the development of redundant technique in the next phase. These locations are obtained in a row vector with the corresponding specific fault numbers. Figure 6 shows the graphical illustration of the results provided in Table 2.

Table 2. Hardness analysis for different combinational SUTs

SUT	Type of SUT	# of sensitive LoCs threshold 30%	# of sensitive LoCs threshold 50%	# of sensitive LoCs threshold 70%	# of sensitive LoCs threshold 90%
c17	Combinational	0	0	4	5
c432	=	0	0	3	20
c499	=	35	68	99	103
c880	=	0	13	55	277
c1355	=	1	32	97	642
c1908	=	1	28	208	700
c2670	=	0	33	111	634

6   Conclusion

In this paper, some methodologies used in the development of the *RASP-FIT* tool have been presented, which includes fault injection algorithm, and the method for finding sensitive locations for FPGA-based designs. In this work, the proposed fault injection algorithm has been validated on the Verilog gate level designs for combinational ISCAS'85 and ISCAS'89 circuits. Also, the hardness analysis method has been presented for combinational ISCAS'85 benchmark circuits.

In the future, the fault injection algorithm will be developed for other abstraction levels and SoCs. Also, the hardness analysis method will be applied to the sequential and microprocessor designs. Currently, the validation of this proposed method and the redundant approach are in progress for these sensitive locations, making the design more robust and fault-tolerant, without major area overhead and power consumption.

References

1. Alderighi, M., Casini, F., D'Angelo, S., Mancini, M., Codinachs, D.M., Pastore, S., Poivey, C., Sechi, G.R., Weigand, G.S.R.: Experimental validation of fault injection analyses by the FLIPPER tool. In: 2009 European Conference on Radiation and Its Effects on Components and Systems (RADECS), Burges, Belgium, pp. 544–548, September 2009

2. Alexandrescu, D., Sterpone, L., López-Ongil, C.: Fault injection and fault tolerance methodologies for assessing device robustness and mitigating against ionizing radiation. In: 2014 19th IEEE European Test Symposium (ETS), Paderborn, Germany, pp. 1–6, May 2014

3. Corradi, G., Girardey, R., Becker, J.: Xilinx tools facilitate development of FPGA applications for IEC61508. In: 2012 NASA/ESA Conference on Adaptive Hardware and Systems (AHS), Erlangen, Germany, pp. 54–61, June 2012

4. Desogus, M., Sterpone, L., Codinachs, D.M.: Validation of a tool for estimating the effects of soft-errors on modern SRAM-based FPGAs. In: 2014 IEEE 20th International On-Line Testing Symposium (IOLTS), Platja d'Aro, Girona, Spain, pp. 111–115, July 2014

5. Gosheblagh, R.O., Mohammadi, K.: Dynamic partial based single event upset (SEU) injection platform on FPGA. Int. J. Comput. Appl. (0975–8887) **76**(3), 19–24 (2013)

6. Graham, P., Nelson, B., Hutchings, B.: Instrumenting bitstreams for debugging FPGA circuits. In: The 9th Annual IEEE Symposium on Field-Programmable Custom Computing Machines, FCCM 2001, Rohnert Park, CA, USA, pp. 41–50, March 2001

7. Jeitler, M., Delvai, M., Reichor, S.: FuSE - a hardware accelerated HDL fault injection tool. In: 5th Southern Conference on Programmable Logic, SPL, Sao Carlos, Brazil, pp. 89–94, April 2009

8. Khatri, A.R., Hayek, A., Börcsök, J.: ATPG method with a hybrid compaction technique for combinational digital systems. In: 2016 SAI Computing Conference (SAI), London, UK, pp. 924–930, July 2016

9. Khatri, A.R., Milde, M., Hayek, A., Börcsök, J.: Instrumentation technique for FPGA based fault injection tool. In: 5th International Conference on Design and Product Development (ICDPD 2014), Istanbul, Turkey, pp. 68–74, December 2014

10. Mansour, W., Aguirre, M.A., Guzmán-Miranda, H., Barrientos, J., Velazco, R.: Two complementary approaches for studying the effects of SEUs on HDL-based designs. In: 2014 IEEE 20th International On-Line Testing Symposium (IOLTS), Platja d'Aro, Catalunya, Spain, pp. 220–221, July 2014

11. Mansour, W., Velazco, R.: An automated SEU fault-injection method and tool for HDL-based designs. IEEE Trans. Nuclear Sci. **60**(4), 2728–2733 (2013)

12. Mansour, W., Velazco, R., Ayoubi, R., Ziade, H., Falou, W.E.: A method and an automated tool to perform SET fault-injection on HDL-based designs. In: 2013 25th International Conference on Microelectronics (ICM), Beirut, Lebanon, pp. 1–4, December 2013

13. Mansour, W., Velazco, R.: SEU fault-injection in VHDL-based processors: a case study. J. Electron. Test. **29**(1), 87–94 (2013)

14. Mohammadi, A., Ebrahimi, M., Ejlali, A., Miremadi, S.G.: SCFIT: a FPGA-based fault injection technique for SEU fault model. In: 2012 Design, Automation Test in Europe Conference Exhibition (DATE), Dresden, Germany, pp. 586–589, March 2012

15. Nápoles, J., Mogollón, J.M., Barrientos, J., Sanz, L., Aguirre, M.A.: FT-UNSHADES2: a platform for early evaluation of ASIC and FPGA dependability using partial reconfiguration. In: La Sociedad de Arquitectura y Tecnologa de Computadores, pp. 1–5 (2012)

16. Rahbaran, B., Steininger, A., Handl, T.: Built-in fault injection in hardware - the FIDYCO example. In: Second IEEE International Workshop on Proceedings of Electronic Design, Test and Applications, DELTA 2004, Perth, WA, Australia, pp. 327–332, January 2004

17. Shokrolah-Shirazi, M., Miremadi, S.G.: FPGA-based fault injection into synthesiz-
    able Verilog HDL models. In: Second International Conference on Secure System
    Integration and Reliability Improvement, SSIRI 2008, Yokohama, Japan, pp. 143–
    149, July 2008
18. Wulf, N., Cieslewski, G., Gordon-Ross, A., George, A.D.: SCIPS: an emulation
    methodology for fault injection in processor caches. In: 2011 IEEE on Aerospace
    Conference, Big Sky, MT, USA, pp. 1–9, March 2011

A Framework for High Level Simulation and Optimization of Coarse-Grained Reconfigurable Architectures

Muhammad Adeel Pasha[1]($\boxtimes$), Umer Farooq[2], Muhammad Ali[1],
and Bilal Siddiqui[3]

[1] Department of Electrical Engineering, SBASSE, LUMS, Lahore, Pakistan
adeel.pasha@lums.edu.pk
[2] LiP6, Sorbonne Universités, Paris, France
umer.farooq@lip6.fr
[3] Department of Electrical and Computer Engineering,
Purdue University, West Lafayette, IN, USA
siddiqu8@purdue.edu

Abstract. High-level simulation tools are used for optimization and design space exploration of digital circuits for a target Field Programmable Gate Array (FPGA) or Application Specific Integrated Circuit (ASIC) implementation. Compared to ASICs, FPGAs are slower and less power-efficient, but they are programmable, flexible and offer faster prototyping. One reason for the slow performance in FPGA is their finer granularity as they operate at bit-level. The possible solution is Coarse Grained Reconfigurable Architectures (CGRAs) that work at word-level. There already exists a myriad of CGRAs based on their architectural parameters. However, the CGRA research lacks in design automation since high-level simulation and optimization tools targeted at CGRAs are nearly non-existent. In this paper, we propose a high-level simulation and optimization framework for mesh-based homogeneous CGRAs. As expected, the results show that auto-generated homogeneous CGRAs consume 54% more resources when compared with academic FPGAs while providing around 63.3% faster mapping time.

1 Introduction

Reconfigurable architectures have evolved greatly in recent years. Some approaches use the standard fine-grained reconfigurable architectures like commercial FPGAs, while others contain hardcore processors coupled with softcore reconfigurable coprocessors (e.g., GARP [1]). Similarly, coarse-grained reconfigurable architectures (CGRAs) have attracted a lot of attention from the research community as well and there has been extensive work in the domain application to CGRA mapping (e.g. [2,3], etc.). CGRAs comprise of predefined hardcore Processing Elements (PEs) to provide computational power. Because the PEs are capable of doing byte or word-level computations, CGRAs can provide higher performance (in terms of latency) for data intensive applications,

S. Wong et al. (Eds.): ARC 2017, LNCS 10216, pp. 129–137, 2017.
DOI: 10.1007/978-3-319-56258-2_12

such as image, video and digital signal processing (DSP) when compared with fine-grained architectures like FPGAs. Moreover, being coarse grained in nature, CGRAs also incur smaller reconfiguration overheads.

However, there has been a parallel development in design automation of fine-grained architectures such as academic FPGAs. Manual design and optimization of reconfigurable architectures remains a daunting task and there is a need for automated design-flows that take a set of target applications at higher level (e.g. C or C++) and generate hardware descriptions of possible target reconfigurable platforms that can then be synthesized by any standard synthesis tool to get the final hardware.

On the other hand, if we look at design automation tools for CGRAs, extensive work has been done in the area of architecture optimization where people proposed various architectural templates suited for a set of target applications [4,5]. The other major research direction is application to architecture mapping where researchers have tried to optimize different design constraints like mapping time or resource optimization of a selected CGRA template [2,3]. To the best of our knowledge, there exists no high-level simulation and optimization design-flow targeted at CGRAs that start from C and ends at hardware description for a custom CGRA. In this work, we address this aspect through our proposed framework.

If we look at the architectural aspects of CGRAs, based on organization of PEs, the CGRAs can be classified into two types (i) linear array architecture and (ii) 2-D mesh-based architecture. In linear array architecture, PEs are organized in one or several linear arrays while in mesh-based architecture, the PEs are arranged in a two-dimensional space much like any standard FPGA. PipeRench [5] is an example from former class while PACT-XPP [4] represents one example from latter category.

In this paper, we propose a generalized framework that can be used for high-level simulation, optimization and resource (power & area) estimation of homogeneous mesh-based CGRAs. We used several codes from data/compute-intensive application benchmark suite MiBench [6] and generated custom homogeneous mesh-based CGRAs for target applications.

The rest of the paper is organized as follows: we start by presenting the related work in Sect. 2 and describe the details of proposed approach in Sect. 3. Section 4 details the implementation and simulation results for sample benchmark applications. We, then, conclude and draw future research directions in Sect. 5.

2   Related Work

Our focus, in the proposed framework, is on homogeneous mesh-based CGRAs since they provide more efficiency than linear arrays for DSP and multimedia applications. As far as the frameworks for mesh-based CGRAs mapping are concerned, Lee et al. [2] proposed an application mapping framework for 2-D mesh-based CGRAs supporting both integer and floating point arithmetic. They presented both optimal formulation using integer linear programming (ILP) as well as a fast heuristic mapping algorithm. Their experiments on randomly generated examples generate optimal mapping results using heuristic algorithm for 97% of the examples within a few seconds. They then extended the results for practical examples from multimedia and 3-D graphics benchmarks and got similar success with their proposed heuristic algorithm. Similarly, Peyret et al. [3] proposed automated design-flow to map C-code applications on CGRAs and they claim to have faster mapping than the state-of-the-art.

It is, however, interesting to note that all of these frameworks provide solutions for application to CGRA mapping and none of them provide a high-level simulation and optimization solution that can generate custom CGRAs suitable for a set of input applications/kernels. In our proposed framework, we extend the state-of-the-art in this direction and propose a basic framework that takes in a set of Data Flow Graphs (DFGs) and provide simulation and resource estimation results of the custom CGRA implementation.

3   Proposed Approach

3.1   Basic CGRA Template

Like the renowned homogeneous mesh-based CGRA, PACT-XPP [4], the basic Processing Element (PE) of our target CGRA architecture is an "arithmetic logic unit" (ALU) as shown in Fig. 1(a). This 8-bit ALU is capable of performing eight (8) distinct logic and arithmetic operations. These ALUs are surrounded by horizontal and vertical routing channels forming a generic routing fabric where the communication between PEs is ensured through programmable routing resources and connection with I/Os and memory is maintained through programmable I/O blocks. Figure 1(b) shows an abstract level view of an overall homogeneous CGRA fabric.

3.2   The Proposed Framework

The proposed framework takes ANSI-C applications as inputs and automatically generates the VHDL description of a custom 2-D mesh-based homogeneous CGRA. The complete design flow is shown in Fig. 2 and we discuss its detailed working in following sections.

C to Net-List Transformation. Our proposed framework leverages from GeCoS [7], an open source retargetable compiler framework for initial compilation of the input C applications. To be precise, we used GeCoS front-end to generate intermediate representations (IRs) that are in the form of CDFGs (Control and Data Flow Graphs). We then used the GeCoS DAG building facilities to convert the basic blocks of our application codes into DAGs. We then developed a parser that converts these DAG descriptions into CGRA-specific net-lists. Each operator node in the DAG is converted into a virtual ALU node that is going to perform a particular arithmetic or logic operation.

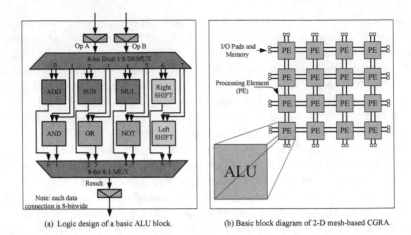

(a) Logic design of a basic ALU block.   (b) Basic block diagram of 2-D mesh-based CGRA.

Fig. 1. Block diagram of mesh-based CGRA and logic design of an ALU block.

Table 1. Placement and routing time comparison between CGRA and FPGA

Benchmark name	P and R time comparison		
	CGRA	FPGA	Gain
	(Sec)		(%)
BitCount	568	568	0
DC-Filter	528	756	30
FIR	280	868	68
IDCT	3786	11896	68

Net-List to CGRA Mapping. The CGRA-specific net-lists are placed onto a generic CGRA fabric (shown in Fig. 1(b)) using simulated annealing algorithm. The algorithm tries to minimize the bounding box cost of the architecture. Similarly, for routing purposes pathfinder routing algorithm is used which is a negotiation based congestion driven algorithm.

Once placement and routing phases are complete, area of the architecture is calculated using a generic area model where the total area of resultant CGRA is the sum of logic and routing areas of underlying architecture. Logic area of underlying architecture is calculated by combining the area of all the PEs in the architecture whereas routing area is calculated by combining area of all routing resources in the architecture.

4   Experimental Results

This section presents the experimental results of generating both custom CGRAs and FPGAs for different input applications. For CGRAs, we used our proposed design-flow while for academic FPGAs, an open-source tool targeted at FPGA

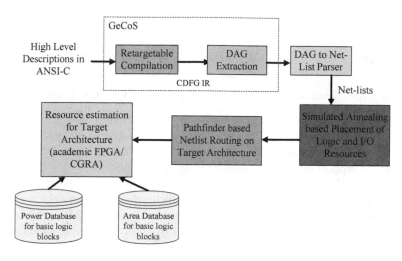

Fig. 2. Proposed design-flow for the generation of custom CGRAs.

generation [8] is used. In this work, we have considered homogeneous architectures due to fine-grained nature of available benchmarks. We also present the area and dynamic power consumption results of the two design-flows. The applications are taken from the famous Mibench [6] and other CGRA benchmarks available in the literature.

For experimental purposes, a spice-level device modeling was performed for resource profiling. Basic operators of the ALU were simulated in LTspice at functional level. Furthermore, capacitance of individual operators was measured using Hspice. Individual component capacitances were then used to calculate the total load capacitance of the complete architecture and total load capacitance was used to calculate the dynamic power consumption of target architecture using Eq. 1. The estimations were performed using the open-source 65 nm processing technology [9].

$$P = \alpha C V^2 f \qquad (1)$$

where V is the supply voltage, f the operating frequency, C the load capacitance and α the switching activity of the circuit. For power estimation, switching activity (α), frequency and voltage were assumed to be 0.5, 25 MHz and 1.2 V respectively. However, these values are arbitrary and can be changed that will lead to a scaling of the resultant power consumption through Eq. 1.

4.1 Computation Time Comparison for CGRA Vs. FPGA Implementations

In this work, we have used four benchmarks for our experimentation (as shown in Table 1). For CGRA mapping, the flow described in Sect. 3 is used whereas for FPGA mapping flow discussed in [8] is used. It can be seen that our proposed framework gives either equal or better mapping time results. Finally, if we consider average time taken for both architectures, CGRA framework takes 1290 s for four benchmarks while FPGA framework takes 3522 s. This gives an average mapping time gain of 63.3% for CGRAs over FPGAs.

4.2   Area and Power Results for CGRA vs. FPGA Implementations

For the sake of completeness, we also present the area and power consumption results of CGRAs and FPGAs. These results are obtained using respective flows of CGRAs and FPGAs, and they are summarized in Tables 2 and 3 for common benchmarks mapped on CGRAs and FPGAs respectively.

Table 2 shows that for each benchmark under consideration, individual CGRA architecture was created. Results of individual benchmarks are shown in lines 1 to 4 of the table. For each benchmark, first a CGRA architecture is defined that best suits the logic requirements of the benchmark. Benchmark is then placed and routed on the defined CGRA architecture using our proposed flow. The flow used in this work optimizes the resources of the architecture and culminates with the area and power estimations of the architecture. Area of a CGRA architecture in this work is mainly divided into two parts: logic area and routing area. Logic area of CGRA is calculated as the sum of logic area of all the ALUs present in the architecture. Routing area of CGRA is calculated as the sum of area of all the routing components in the CGRA architecture. When the design-flow of CGRA is terminated after optimization, number of routing components and their areas are combined together to give the overall routing area of the architecture (ref columns 2–4, and 6 of Table 2). Logic area and routing area values are finally combined to give total area of architecture (ref column 7 of Table 2). Dynamic power consumption values are given in column 8 of Table 2. Results shown in lines 1–4 of the table are individual benchmark results that give an idea about the area and power requirements of each benchmark separately. However, a combined CGRA architecture was also defined that satisfies the requirements of all the applications under consideration. The combined CGRA results are shown in line 5 of Table 2. It can be seen from this table that "IDCT" has the largest logic & routing resource requirements and a CGRA architecture satisfying the needs of this application can satisfy the needs of all the netlists of the set under consideration.

Area and dynamic power results of the common benchmarks for FPGAs are shown in Table 3. To have a fair comparison, we generated the results for both individual as well as combined FPGA architectures. It can be seen from Tables 2 and 3 that for combined architecture CGRAs consume 63% less SRAMs. This is because of the fact that due to bus-based routing structure of CGRAs, they have shared configuration memory cells for their routing switches which eventually leads to smaller number of SRAMs required for routing architecture.

However, due to this very nature of routing structure of CGRAs, channel width is significantly increased that results in much larger requirement of multiplexers. For combined architecture, CGRAs require 70% more multiplexers than FPGAs. Although smaller number of SRAMs are required for combined CGRA, but the area of individual SRAM is much smaller as compared to area of a

2×1 MUX; hence the area gain of SRAMs is far outweighed by additional area caused by large multiplexer requirement. These effects, combined together with buffer area, result in 63% smaller routing area for combined FPGA compared to combined CGRA implementation. As far as logic area is concerned, due to coarser granularity of CGRAs, number of ALUs required are much lesser than the number of CLBs required for FPGA-based implementations. Hence despite the fact that the area of individual ALU is larger than the area of a single CLB, we eventually get a 27.5% reduction in logic area for CGRAs when compared to FPGAs. However, it is important to mention, here, that routing area of CGRAs comprises of 90% of total area. Hence, smaller logic area of CGRA is overshadowed by larger routing area and finally gives 53.5% smaller FPGA architecture while consuming 54.8% less dynamic power when compared to CGRAs.

Table 2. Area and power results for CGRAs

Benchmark name	No. of MUXes	No. of SRAMs	Buffer area	Logic area	Routing area	Total area	Dynamic power consumption (mW)
			x10³ (μm^2)				
BitCount	19392	1470	0.195	0.663	4.8	5.46	0.7
DC-Filter	25280	1800	0.26	0.49	6.25	6.74	0.9
FIR	14312	990	0.14	0.34	3.53	3.87	0.45
IDCT	84840	5694	0.83	2.29	20.9	23.19	3.12
CGRA combined	84840	5694	0.83	2.29	20.9	23.19	3.12

Table 3. Area and power results for CGRAs

Benchmark name	No. of MUXes	No. of SRAMs	Buffer area	Logic area	Routing area	Total area	Dynamic power consumption (mW)
			x10³ (μm^2)				
BitCount	2332	1432	0.025	0.44	0.69	1.13	0.15
DC-Filter	1848	1144	0.02	0.35	0.55	0.9	0.12
FIR	2872	1752	0.03	0.55	0.85	1.4	0.19
IDCT	25668	15588	0.26	3.16	7.61	10.77	1.41
FPGA Combined	25668	15588	0.26	3.16	7.61	10.77	1.41

Results presented in this section suggest that CGRAs are, on average, 63.3% more efficient than FPGAs in terms of required placement and routing time. This is because of the less complex nature of CGRA fabric. However, contrary to [10], interconnect overhead of our proposed CGRA is relatively high. This is because of the fact that our proposed framework is based on a generic environment that uses architecture independent placement and routing algorithms. These algorithms can be used for exploration of logic and routing resources of CGRA architectures. Due to flexible nature of underlying algorithms, CGRAs in our work, are based on general purpose programmable interconnects when compared with fixed interconnects presented in the literature [10].

5   Conclusion

Compared to ASICs, FPGAs are slower and less power-efficient, but their edge over ASIC is their programmability and flexibility. One reason for their slow performance is their finer granularity. The potential solution is CGRAs who operate at word-level. However, high-level simulation tools targeted at CGRAs are nearly non-existent. This paper presents a complete high-level framework for simulation, optimization and resource estimation of mesh-based CGRAs. As a case study, we used embedded DSP and CGRA application benchmarks. The results show that auto-generated homogeneous mesh-based CGRAs consume 54% more area when compared with auto-generated academic FPGAs while providing around 63.3% faster mapping.

References

1. Hauser, J.R., Wawrzynek, J.: Garp: a MIPS processor with a reconfigurable coprocessor. In: Proceedings the 5th Annual IEEE Symposium on Field-Programmable Custom Computing Machines, pp. 12–21, April 1997
2. Lee, G., Choi, K., Dutt, N.D.: Mapping multi-domain applications onto coarse-grained reconfigurable architectures. IEEE Trans. Comput. Aided Des. Integr. Circ. Syst. **30**(5), 637–650 (2011)
3. Peyret, T., Corre, G., Thevenin, M., Martin, K., Coussy, P.: An automated design approach to map applications on CGRAs. In: Proceedings of the 24th Edition of the Great Lakes Symposium on VLSI, ser. GLSVLSI 2014, pp. 229–230. ACM, New York (2014)
4. Baumgarte, V., Ehlers, G., May, F., Nückel, A., Vorbach, M., Weinhardt, M.: PACT XPP - a self-reconfigurable data processing architecture. J. Supercomput. **26**(2), 167–184 (2003)
5. Goldstein, S.C., Schmit, H., Moe, M., Budiu, M., Cadambi, S., Taylor, R.R., Laufer, R.: PipeRench: a coprocessor for streaming multimedia acceleration. In: Proceedings of the 26th IEEE ISCA, pp. 28–39 (1999)
6. Guthaus, M.R., Ringenberg, J.S., Ernst, D., Austin, T.M., Mudge, T., Brown, R.B.: MiBench: a free, commercially representative embedded benchmark suite. In: IEEE International Workshop on Workload Characterization (WWC-4), pp. 3–14, December 2001
7. L'Hours, L.: Generating efficient custom FPGA soft-cores for control-dominated applications. In: Proceedings of the 16th IEEE ASAP, pp. 127–133 (2005)

8. Pasha, M.A., Farooq, U., Siddiqui, M.B.: A design-flow for high-level synthesis and resource estimation of reconfigurable architectures. In: 10th International Conference on Design & Technology of Integrated Systems in Nanoscale Era (DTIS), Naples, Italy, pp. 1–6. IEEE (2015)
9. Zhao, Y.C.W.: New generation of predictive technology model for sub-45nm early design exploration. IEEE Trans. Electron Devices **53**(11), 2816–2823 (2006)
10. Zhang, C., Lenart, T., Svensson, H., Öwall, V.: Design of coarse-grained dynamically reconfigurable architecture for DSP applications. In: International Conference on Reconfigurable Computing and FPGAs, pp. 338–343 (2009)

Design Space Exploration

Parameter Sensitivity in Virtual FPGA Architectures

Peter Figuli[1]([✉]), Weiqiao Ding[1], Shalina Figuli[1], Kostas Siozios[2],
Dimitrios Soudris[3], and Jürgen Becker[1]

[1] Institute for Information Processing Technology, Karlsruhe Institute of Technology,
Karlsruhe, Germany
{peter.figuli,shalina.ford,becker}@kit.edu, weiqiao.ding@student.kit.edu
[2] Department of Physics, Aristotle University of Thessaloniki, Thessaloniki, Greece
ksiop@auth.gr
[3] School of Electrical and Computer Engineering,
National Technical University of Athens, Athens, Greece
dsoudris@microlab.ntua.gr

Abstract. Virtual FPGAs add the benefits of increased flexibility and
application portability on bitstream level across any underlying commercial off-the-shelf FPGAs at the expense of additional area and delay
overhead. Hence it becomes a priority to tune the architecture parameters of the virtual layer. Thereby, the adoption of parameter recommendations intended for physical FPGAs can be misleading, as they are
based on transistor level models. This paper presents an extensive study
of architectural parameters and their effects on area and performance
by introducing an extended parameterizable virtual FPGA architecture
and deriving suitable area and delay models. Furthermore, a design space
exploration methodology based on these models is carried out. An analysis of over 1400 benchmark-runs with various combinations of cluster and
LUT size reveals high parameter sensitivity with variances up to ±95.9%
in area and ±78.1% in performance and a discrepancy to the studies on
physical FPGAs.

Keywords: FPGA · Virtualization · Cluster size · LUT size · Efficiency

1 Introduction

During the last three decades, Field Programmable Gate Arrays (FPGAs) have
evolved from less competitive and prototyping devices with as little as 64 logic
cells towards complex System on Chip (SoC) and massive parallel digital signal processing architectures. The functional density alone, however, is not the
unique selling point and there is still a considerable gap to ASICs in this regard.
Moreover, it is the flexibility and the comparably short design times along with
low NRE costs and low risks that make FPGAs so attractive. Currently, we are
witnessing a new movement towards general purpose computing. The signs are
conspicious considering the facts that (1) there is a trend towards heterogeneous

© Springer International Publishing AG 2017
S. Wong et al. (Eds.): ARC 2017, LNCS 10216, pp. 141–153, 2017.
DOI: 10.1007/978-3-319-56258-2_13

reconfigurable SoCs, (2) recently Intel as a major General-Purpose Processor (GPP) company acquired Altera and (3) there are serious efforts to employ FPGAs in data centers and cloud services, e.g. Intel Xeon+FPGA Integrated Platform [8] or the Microsoft Catapult project [13]. At this rate, FPGAs will become mainstream in the future and indispensable in our day-to-day systems and applications such as entertainment, communication, assistance, automation, cyber-physical systems, cloud services, monitoring, controlling, and many more. There will be the situation that FPGA based devices and applications change more often than how it is today, thereby making it necessary to loosen the bond between application and the execution platform.

Virtualization can be a key for instant **portability and migration** of applications even on bitstream level without redesigning or recompiling. Thereby, an optimized reconfigurable architecture as a virtual layer can be mapped onto an existing Commercial Off-The-Shelf (COTS) FPGA, while the application itself will be executed on the virtual layer, thus being independent of the underlying physical platform. We call this technique *virtual FPGA*. The eminent advantage is that the specification of the virtual architecture can persist, while the hosting physical platform can be exchanged by another one. Furthermore, virtual FPGAs can be utilized to (1) enable independent reconfiguration mechanisms, (2) prototype novel FPGA architectures without physical implementation and (3) emulate custom reconfigurable architectures. Despite a few related works [5,6,9,10,12], the field of virtual FPGAs is still considered unexplored. The design space gets extended by a new dimension as the virtual FPGA has the added flexibility to alter not only the application circuit but also the executing architecture. In this regard, the mapping efficiency of applications which is highly related to architectural parameters, is getting very important, especially as the additional layer adds a considerable overhead to the underlying platform. The practice of adopting parameter recommendations intended for physical FPGAs to the virtual domain is questionable as explained in this paper. Yet, due to lack of separate and detailed studies, they have been predominantly followed more or less blindly, accepting that it might not be the optimum solution.

The scope of this paper is to close these gaps and to examine the impact of main architectural parameters of virtual FPGAs on area and performance. Therefore, we propose a suitable design space exploration methodology with area and delay models representing the virtual layer and its realization, which can differ from platform to platform. The contributions of this paper are:

- introduction of an extended highly parameterizable version of *V-FPGA*
- analytical area and delay models for virtual FPGA architectures
- parametric design space exploration
- analysis of parameter tuning and resulting area and performance variance

The rest of the paper is organized as follows: Sect. 2 summarizes the related works. In Sect. 3 we introduce the extended *V-FPGA* architecture. Section 4 derives the area and delay models while the methodology for parametric design space exploration is presented in Sect. 5. Experimental results are presented in Sect. 6 and the conclusions are summarized in Sect. 7.

2   Related Works

2.1   Virtual FPGA Architectures

In [10] Lagadec et al. present a toolset for generic implementation of virtual architectures. The main focus of their work lies on the generic tool flow for architectural representation and place & route of application netlists onto various abstract virtual architectures. The virtualization aspects from hardware perspective, the mapping onto the underlying platform, the programming mechanisms and configuration management remain predominantly unaddressed.

Lysecky et al. introduced in [12] a simple fine grain virtual FPGA that is specifically designed for fast place and route. The architecture has a mesh structure with fixed-size Configurable Logic Blocks (CLBs) being connected to Switch Matrixes (SMs) as opposed to architectures where logic blocks are connected directly to the routing channels. The *V-FPGA* architecture used in this paper has a similar granularity and architecture class as the work of Lysecky et al. but is generic and highly flexibile, thus it can take over different shapes and be tailored towards the application needs.

In [6,9] we introduced a scalable island style virtual FPGA architecture with the primary focus on adding new features to an underlying FPGA, that are not supported natively. More specifically, we achieved to enable partial and dynamic reconfiguration on a flash based Actel ProASIC3 device. The *V-FPGA* architecture presented in this paper builds upon this preliminary work, yet offering a higher flexibility with a rich parameter set.

The ZUMA architecture by Brant and Lemieux [5] is a clustered LUT based FPGA with island style topology and targets to reduce the area overhead of the virtualization layer by utilizing LUTRAMs of the underlying platform. *V-FPGA* follows a different ideology as it concentrates on portability and easy mapping even onto ASIC processes, thus renouncing platform exclusive element usage of ZUMA approach.

The major drawbacks of all virtual FPGA architectures, including the one used in this paper, are higher chip area and larger path delays compared to physical FPGAs. This is due to the fact that each virtual logic cell is realized by a multitude of programmable logic cells of the underlying physical platform. The area overhead of virtual FPGA mainly depends on the granularity of the underlying platform as well as how well the virtual resources can be matched by the physical resources. Thus, the same Virtual FPGA has a different area efficiency on one underlying platform than on another and a change in its design parameters can turn the game.

2.2   Effects of Architectural Parameters on Area and Performance

With respect to architectural parameter choice in physical FPGAs, [3,14] indicate that a LUT size K between 3 and 4 provides the best area efficiency, while $K = 6$ gives the best performance. [7] shows similar results through a theoretical model, while [15] indicates that $K = 6$ is the best choice for area, delay and area-delay product in nanometer technology. However, those results are an average and in virtual architectures the area efficiency and performance depend also on how efficient a K-input LUT can be realized by the underlying platform, thereby making their recommendations not highly applicable.

Betz and Rose studied in [4] the relationship between cluster size and required number of inputs per CLB and also the optimal cluster size for 4-input LUTs. Later, Ahmed and Rose extended this study in [3] by varying both LUT size K and cluster size N in the range of $K = 2..7$ and $N = 1..10$ and concluded that $K = 4..6$ and $N = 3..10$ provide the best trade-off between area and delay. The findings in [3] have become a widely accepted reference and guideline in parameter choice for many academic FPGA architectures. While the experiments mentioned above rely on area and delay models on transistor-level, and thus scale smoothly, virtual FPGAs are mostly platform independent and the base units are multiplexers and flip-flops realized by underlying logic blocks. Consequently, these differences can lead to unmatched proportions in logic area, local routing area and global routing area as well as in path delays.

3   The Generic *V-FPGA* Architecture

The V-FPGA is a generic LUT-based FPGA architecture that can be mapped onto existing commercial off-the-shelf (COTS) FPGAs, such as Xilinx, Altera, Microsemi, etc. This extensively scalable and parameterizable architecture is implemented in a fully synthesizeable HDL code, utilizing hierarchy, modularity and generics. As illustrated in Fig. 1, the applications will be mapped and executed on the virtual layer rather than on the logic layer of the underlying COTS FPGA. The merit of this approach is that the specification of the virtual FPGA stays unchanged independent to the underlying hardware and adds new features such as dynamic reconfigurability which is for example not available with all COTS FPGAs. It also entitles the re-use of hardware blocks on other physical FPGA devices and enables portability of unaltered bitstreams among different FPGA manufacturers and device families, e.g. in order to overcome the problem of device discontinuation. In the following subsections the structure of the architecture and its tuneable parameters are presented.

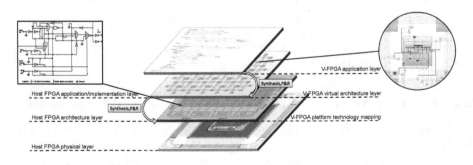

Fig. 1. Layer model of the *V-FPGA* approach

3.1   General Topology

The *V-FPGA* follows an island-style topology as depicted in Fig. 2(a), where CLBs are surrounded by routing channels that can be accessed through connection boxes. Programmable Switch Matrices (PSMs) at the intersections of routing channels control the global routing. I/O Blocks (IOBs) on the perimeter of the logic array enable interfacing with other (sub-)systems.

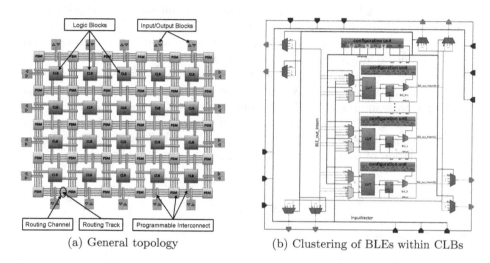

(a) General topology   (b) Clustering of BLEs within CLBs

Fig. 2. Structure of the *V-FPGA*

3.2   Clustered Logic Cells

The generic clustering architecture of *V-FPGA* is parameterizable with cluster size N and LUT size K as shown in Fig. 2 (b). The union of a K-input LUT, a flip-flop and a bypass MUX forms a Basic Logic Element (BLE). A CLB contains N BLEs. Each BLE also holds a configuration unit that sets the bits of the LUT and controls the bypass MUX. As proposed in [3], a CLB with N BLEs of K-input LUTs contains $I = K/2 \cdot (N + 1)$ inputs and $O = N$ outputs. The location pattern of in- and outputs of a CLB aims an equal distribution to improve routability. Input multiplexers for each BLE input can select signals either by using fully-connected multiplexers (all CLB inputs and all BLE outputs are selectable) or partially-connected multiplexers (only a fraction of 1/K CLB inputs and all BLE outputs are selectable). The latter version is more area efficient but is also dependant on outer routing. The multiplexers at the outputs of a CLB are optional as they can slightly ease the outer routing but cost additional area. It is recommended to use direct wiring of BLE outputs to CLB outputs, whereby the outer routing can be facilitated by reordering of BLEs.

3.3 Routing Infrastructure

Connection boxes around the CLBs consist mainly of multiplexers and their select signals are controlled by configuration registers. At the same time only one routing track can be connected to the input through CBr, whereas several tracks can be connected to the same output through CBw. PSMs realize the global routing of the signal paths by connecting tracks from different channels at the intersections. Therefore a 4:1 MUX is located at each output of a PSM as shown in Fig. 3(a). A PSM has on each side W in- and outputs, whereby W is the channel width. On the left and bottom sides, the first position of the MUX is the logic level '1', which is the defined idle value of the routing infrastructure, i.e. if there is no routing intended in this direction. The three remaining positions are each associated with an input from one of the three adjacent sides. The two select lines of the MUX are controlled by configuration registers set by the configuration unit during programming. On the top and right sides of the PSM, the inputs can be fed back to the outputs of the same sides by selecting the first position of the respective multiplexers. This technique, which we call *loopback propagation* enables emulation of bi-directional tracks using uni-directional tracks.

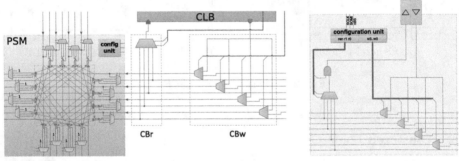

(a) Routing infrastructure with PSMs, CBr and CBw   (b) Schematic of I/O block

Fig. 3. Interconnects in *V-FPGA*

3.4 I/O Blocks

IOBs on the perimeter of the array have exactly one in- and one output and work in a similar way like the connection boxes of the CLBs. As shown in Fig. 3 (b), a MUX connects one of the tracks from the routing channel to the output pad. When an output is not assigned, logic '0' is issued by an AND gate connected between the MUX and the configuration register bit *ren*. In favour of higher routability, the input pad can be connected to several tracks in parallel through respective 2:1 MUXs. All the MUXs are controlled by configuration registers.

4   Area and Delay Models

Typically, the overall area requirement and performance of an application mapped onto a virtual FPGA is revealed after the synthesis, place and route (P&R) steps of both, the application and the virtual FPGA. Since the P&R steps are area and timing driven, area and delay models are required in order to find an optimized solution. For instance, our initial *V-FPGA* [9] used the physical parameters of the architecture file templates contained in MEANDER toolflow [1], which are based on 180 nm technology. Similarly, the technology parameters of ZUMA architecture in [2] are almost the same as that of the ones used in the 90 nm architecture templates of the VTR toolflow package [11]. While the application mapping will be still valid and the circuits operable, this practice might be deceitful for the purpose of design space exploration and optimization as the ratios of e.g. logic area to routing area or local routing to global routing will suffer accuracy. This might lead to non-optimal parameter choices and reduced mapping efficiency. To overcome this situation, area and delay models for the *V-FPGA* are derived based on the utilized resource types of the underlying platform. The idea is to decompose the *V-FPGA* into basic elements of minimum size, characterize these elements and in a bottom up approach derive area and delay models that are dependent on the parameters K, N, W, I, and O described in Sect. 3. The programmable units of *V-FPGA* are BLEs, CLBs (including connection boxes), PSMs and IOBs. A BLE is composed of 2^K:1 MUX (for the LUT), 2:1 MUX (for the bypass) and flip-flops (2^K for the configuration unit and one for bypass at the LUT output). The remaining CLB circuitry requires $(N + \lceil I/K \rceil)$:1 MUXs for BLE inputs, optionally N:1 MUXs at the outputs and D-FFs for the configuration unit. Additionally, the connection boxes require 2:1 MUXs for *CBw* and W:1 MUXs for *CBr*. Each PSM is composed of 4:1 MUXs for routing and D-FFs for configuration. An IOB needs a W:1 MUX and an AND gate for the output, 2:1 MUXs for the input and D-FFs for the configuration unit. Hence the Minimum Size Basic Elements (MSBEs) are 2:1 MUX, 2-input AND gate and D-FF with their corresponding areas and delays as A_{MUX2}, A_{AND2}, A_{FF} T_{MUX2}, T_{AND2}, T_{FF_setup}, $T_{FF\_clock\_to\_Q}$ and T_{net} respectively. All the other elements are composed of these MSBEs and are derived as follows:

$$A_{BLE} = \left(2^K + 1\right) \cdot A_{FF} + \left(\left(2^K - 1\right) + 1\right) \cdot A_{MUX2} \quad (1)$$

$$A_{BLE\_inMUX} = \left(N + \left\lceil \frac{I}{K} \right\rceil - 1\right) \cdot A_{MUX2} + \left\lceil log_2 \left(N + \left\lceil \frac{I}{K} \right\rceil\right)\right\rceil \cdot A_{FF} \quad (2)$$

$$A_{BLE\_outMUX} = (N - 1) \cdot A_{MUX2} + \lceil log_2 (N) \rceil \cdot A_{FF} \quad (3)$$

$$A_{CLB} = N \cdot K \cdot A_{BLE\_inMux} + N \cdot A_{BLE} + O \cdot A_{BLE\_outMUX} \quad (4)$$

$$A_{CBr} = (W - 1) \cdot A_{MUX2} + \lceil log_2(W) \rceil \cdot A_{FF} \quad (5)$$

$$A_{CBw} = W \cdot (A_{MUX2} + A_{FF}) \quad (6)$$

$$A_{PSM} = 4 \cdot W \cdot (3 \cdot A_{MUX2} + 2 \cdot A_{FF}) \quad (7)$$

$$A_{IOB} = (2W - 1) \cdot A_{MUX2} + A_{AND2} + (W + \lceil log_2(W) \rceil + 1) \cdot A_{FF} \quad (8)$$

The delays are obtained through characterizations of the MSBEs in a placed and routed design with the help of the timing analyzing tool. In addition to the MSBEs, the average delay of the short nets is also needed. The relevant delays of the other elements are estimated as follows:

$$T_{MUX4} = 2 \cdot T_{MUX2} + T_{net} \tag{9}$$

$$T_{LUT} = T_{net} + K \cdot (T_{MUX2} + T_{net}) \tag{10}$$

$$T_{BLE\_outMUX} = \lceil log_2(O) \rceil \cdot (T_{MUX2} + T_{net}) \tag{11}$$

$$T_{BLE\_inMUX} = \left\lceil log_2 \left(N + \left\lceil \frac{I}{K} \right\rceil \right) \right\rceil \cdot (T_{MUX2} + T_{net}) \tag{12}$$

$$T_{IOB\_in} = T_{MUX2} + T_{net} \tag{13}$$

$$T_{IOB\_out} = (\lceil log_2(W) \rceil - 1) \cdot (T_{MUX2} + T_{net}) + T_{AND2} + T_{net} \tag{14}$$

These models target a fine grained underlying platform (e.g. the 3-input Versa-Tiles in Actel ProASIC3) and need to be slightly modified when the underlying platform changes. For instance, for an underlying platform with 6-input LUTs, a 4:1 MUX becomes an MSBE as it will have the same area and timing as a 2:1 MUX (both can be realized by 1 LUT). Note that the additive MSBE based models are pessimistic as they don't reflect possible LUT sharing techniques.

5   Methodology of Parametric Design Space Exploration

The architecture level design space exploration is performed with combinations of varying cluster size N and LUT size K. Parts of the VTR toolset [11] are used for this purpose and are complemented by our custom scripts and architecture file generators. However Fig. 4 illustrates a more general view of the CAD flow independent from the actual tools. Starting with the smallest $K = 2$, technology independent netlists of presynthesized benchmark circuits are translated into netlists of K-input LUTs. Proceeding this is the packing process, where N LUTs are clustered into one CLB with an initial value of $N = 1$. The hypergraph nodes of the resulting netlist are placed onto an array of CLBs, whose size is not known at the beginning. One of the optimization goals of this placing step is to determine the required number of CLB columns and rows with minimum area consumption. The placed nodes are then swapped to achieve timing driven optimizations, aiming for minimum distance between connected nodes. The next step is to route the signal paths between the placed nodes by considering the routing capabilities of the architecture (PSMs, connection boxes, in- and output multiplexers). The channel width W is estimated beforehand based on the parameters K and N. This is not an accurate estimation since the minimum W depends also on the application. However, this is good enough to start an initial routing attempt, followed by iterative bisection of the estimated W to converge towards the minimum channel width with a reduced number of routing attempts. Once the minimum channel width is found, the usual timing driven optimizations follow. The steps of packing, placement and routing require information about the target virtual FPGA architecture and the parameters and constants related to area and delay models, which are provided through architecture files. Some of the area and delay model equations in Sect. 4 are dependent on W, which is known only after the routing process. Thus initially the estimated W is used. For an improved accuracy, a feedback is needed to update the architecture file with the actual channel width W and to re-run the area- and/or timing-driven P&R processes. The results in terms of array size, channel width, area, critical path delay are stored in a data base for assessing the figure of merit (FOM). Then the process is repeated with other combinations of N and K in a nested loop to span the design space of interest.

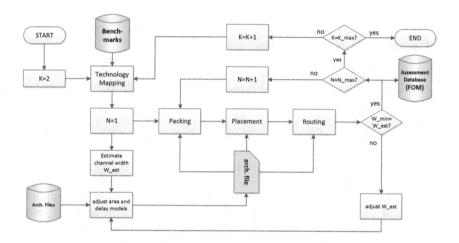

Fig. 4. Concept of parametric DSE Flow.

6   Experimental Results and Analysis

Design space explorations with the 20 largest MCNC benchmarks were performed to observe the parameter sensitivity. The effects of LUT size variation alone were examined in an unclustered architecture, followed by experiments with combinations of LUT size and cluster size. The analysis required 1400 benchmark-runs with the steps *logic optimization, LUT mapping, packing, placing* and *routing*. The first two steps were eased by reusing the pre-mapped versions of the MCNC benchmarks within the VTR package [11] and the latter steps were done with VPR (part of VTR) and with architecture files, that reflect the *V-FPGA* hosted by an Actel ProASIC3 device, including area and delay models from Sect. 4. The result graphs (Figs. 5, 6 and 7) are drawn according to the following scheme: For each benchmark, the variance is displayed with relative distances from the median centred between its best and worst result. This allows to compare the parameter sensitivity among all benchmarks, irrespective of their sizes and scales. The dotted curve represents the average over all benchmarks.

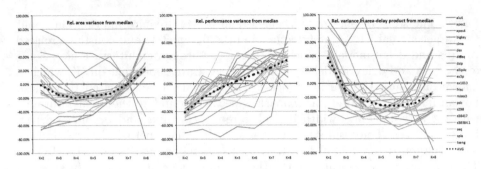

Fig. 5. Effects of LUT size K on (a) area (b) performance (c) area-delay product.

6.1   The Effects of LUT Size Tuning on Area and Performance in Unclustered Architectures

Figure 5 shows the variance of area, performance and area-delay product with different LUT sizes in the range of $K = 2..8$. The average curve (dotted line) of area variance has a smooth bathtub characteristic with a wide optimum for $K = 3..6$ and a degradation in area efficiency outside this range. Hence a LUT size of $K = 3..6$ will yield in average the best area efficiency for general purpose cases. However, the different benchmarks differ greatly in area variance over LUT size K and parameter sensitivity. This manifests not only by the variance range and the steepness but also by the smoothness of the curves. Some of the benchmarks are trending a higher area efficiency with rising K, while some show the opposite trend and others follow a bathtub characteristic. This shows that there is plenty of room for optimization through application specific customization and parameter tuning. Regarding performance variation, all benchmarks show an ascending performance trendline for increasing K with the average curve being almost linear from $K = 2$ to $K = 8$. Some of the benchmarks show relatively smooth curves that are oriented around the average curve, while others show a disturbed and inconsistent curve with alternating change of trend and few show a nearly exponential shape. Around 5% of the benchmarks have a performance maximum at $K = 5$, 10% at $K = 6$, 40% at $K = 7$ and 45% at $K = 8$, which indicates that $K = 7..8$ are in average the recommended choices for performance optimization in general purpose cases. LUT sizes between 5 and 7 show the best trade-off between area and performance with regard to area-delay product. These results differ from [3,7,14,15] and show that their findings based on transistor-level modelling are not certainly transferable to virtual architectures.

6.2   The Effects of Combined Cluster Size N and LUT Size K Tuning on Area and Performance

Clustering can have a significant effect on area and performance depending on how well it is tuned in conjunction with the LUT size. For adequate parameter tuning, the 20 largest MCNC benchmarks are re-evaluated for all combinations of cluster sizes with $N = 1..10$ and LUT inputs with $K = 2..8$. Figures 6, 7 present the resulting variances in area and performance. Interestingly, quite a few area curves have a sawtooth characteristic with minima at $N = 1$ for all K indicating that clustering is harmful for the respective benchmarks if area efficiency is the objective. For the average case starting with $N = 4$ and $K = 2$, N should decrease with increasing K for better area efficiency. On the whole, the performance increases with rising K and N. The evaluation also shows a strong parameter sensitivity with variances up to $\pm95.9\%$ in area and $\pm78.1\%$ in performance. Furthermore, the fluctuating benchmark curves confirm that application specific customization can yield high optimizations, rather than relying on average values for parameterization of the architecture.

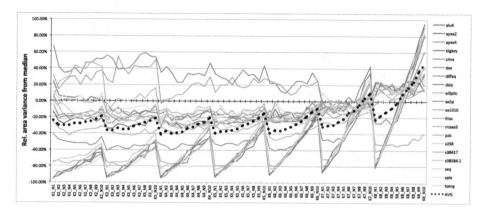

Fig. 6. Effects of LUT size K and cluster size N on area variance.

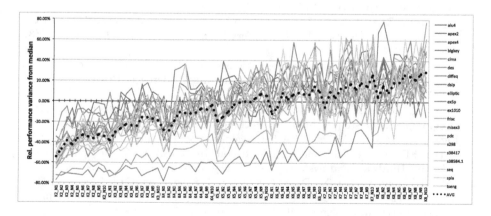

Fig. 7. Effects of LUT size K and cluster size N on performance variance.

7   Conclusions

In this paper an extended version of the *V-FPGA* has been introduced and the area and delay models suitable for vitualization have been derived by decomposing the architecture into MSBEs. In contrast to the existing models which are based on transistor-level, the new models adopt the characterization of MSBEs that are mapped onto the desired underlying COTS FPGA. Thus they represent a more realistic view to the new design space exploration methodology and also to the CAD tools for application mapping. The analysis of over 1400 benchmark-runs with various combinations of LUT size and cluster size reveals a high parameter sensitivity with individual variances up to $\pm95.9\,\%$ in area and $\pm78.1\,\%$ in performance. This proves a remarkable potential for application specific optimizations through parameter tuning. For general purpose cases, an averaging of area-delay products over the examined benchmarks leads to recommendations of $K = 5..7$ for unclustered logic CLBs and combinations of $K = 4..7$ with $N = 2..5$ for clustered CLBs. However if the target application field is narrow, it is not recommended to rely on averaging as the individual benchmarks differ tremendously from the average values. Furthermore, our results show some discrepancy in the parameter recommendations of physical FPGAs and discourage a 1:1 adoption to virtual FPGAs.

Acknowledgments. This work was partially supported by the German Academic Exchange Service (DAAD).

References

1. MEANDER Design Framework (2016). http://proteas.microlab.ntua.gr/meander/download/index.htm. Accessed 25 Nov 2016
2. ZUMA Repository 2016. https://github.com/adbrant/zuma-fpga/tree/master/source/templates. Accessed 25 Nov 2016
3. Ahmed, E., Rose, J.: The effect of LUT and cluster size on deep-submicron FPGA performance and density. IEEE Trans. Very Large Scale Integr. (VLSI) Syst. **12**(3), 288–298 (2004)
4. Betz, V., Rose, J.: Cluster-based logic blocks for FPGAs: area-efficiency vs. input sharing and size. In: Custom Integrated Circuits Conference, Proceedings of the IEEE 1997, pp. 551–554 (1997)
5. Brant, A., Lemieux, G.G.F.: ZUMA: an open FPGA overlay architecture. In: Field-Programmable Custom Computing Machines (FCCM), April 2012
6. Figuli, P., Huebner, M., et al.: A heterogeneous SoC architecture with embedded virtual FPGA cores and runtime core fusion. In: NASA/ESA 6th Conference on Adaptive Hardware and Systems (AHS 2011), June 2011
7. Gao, H., Yang, Y., Ma, X., Dong, G.: Analysis of the effect of LUT size on FPGA area and delay using theoretical derivations. In: Sixth International Symposium on Quality Electronic Design (ISQED 2005), pp. 370–374, March 2005
8. Gupta, P.K.: Accelerating datacenter workloads. In: 26th International Conference on Field Programmable Logic and Applications (FPL), August 2016

9. Huebner, M., Figuli, P., Girardey, R., Soudris, D., Siozos, K., Becker, J.: A heterogeneous multicore system on chip with run-time reconfigurable virtual FPGA architecture. In: 18th Reconfigurable Architectures Workshop, May 2011
10. Lagadec, L., Lavenier, D., Fabiani, E., Pottier, B.: Placing, routing, and editing virtual FPGAs. In: Brebner, G., Woods, R. (eds.) FPL 2001. LNCS, vol. 2147, pp. 357–366. Springer, Heidelberg (2001). doi:10.1007/3-540-44687-7_37
11. Luu, J., Goeders, J., et al.: VTR 7.0: next generation architecture and CAD system for FPGAs. ACM Trans. Reconfigurable Technol. Syst. **7**(2), 6:1–6:30 (2014)
12. Lysecky, R., Miller, K., Vahid, F., Vissers, K.: Firm-core virtual FPGA for just-in-time FPGA compilation. In: Proceedings of the 2005 ACM/SIGDA 13th International Symposium on Field-programmable Gate Arrays, p. 271 (2005)
13. Putnam, A.: Large-scale reconfigurable computing in a Microsoft datacenter. In: Proceedings of the 26th IEEE Symposium on High-Performance Chips (2014)
14. Rose, J., Francis, R.J., Lewis, D., Chow, P.: Architecture of field-programmable gate arrays: the effect of logic block functionality on area efficiency. IEEE J. Solid-State Circ. **25**(5), 1217–1225 (1990)
15. Tang, X., Wang, L.: The effect of LUT size on nanometer FPGA architecture. In: 2012 IEEE 11th International Conference on Solid-State and Integrated Circuit Technology (ICSICT), pp. 1–4, October 2012

Custom Framework for Run-Time Trading Strategies

Andreea-Ingrid Funie[✉], Liucheng Guo, Xinyu Niu, Wayne Luk,
and Mark Salmon

Imperial College London, London, UK
aif109@ic.ac.uk

Abstract. A trading strategy is generally optimised for a given market regime. If it takes too long to switch from one trading strategy to another, then a sub-optimal trading strategy may be adopted. This paper proposes the first FPGA-based framework which supports multiple trend-following trading strategies to obtain accurate market characterisation for various financial market regimes. The framework contains a trading strategy kernel library covering a number of well-known trend-following strategies, such as "triple moving average". Three types of design are targeted: a static reconfiguration trading strategy (SRTS), a full reconfiguration trading strategy (FRTS), and a partial reconfiguration trading strategy (PRTS). Our approach is evaluated using both synthetic and historical market data. Compared to a fully optimised CPU implementation, the SRTS design achieves 11 times speedup, the FRTS design achieves 2 times speedup, while the PRTS design achieves 7 times speedup. The FRTS and PRTS designs also reduce the amount of resources used on chip by 29% and 15% respectively, when compared to the SRTS design.

1 Introduction

In finance, a *trading strategy* is a fixed plan that is designed to achieve a profitable return by buying or selling stock on certain markets. Numerous trading strategies are employed in financial markets with many outcomes in mind - the most common being the identification of market trends. Understanding the different market characteristics is a first step towards being able to identify and measure them. This, in turn should link trend-following performance to the state of these market characteristics. Finally, this might be a step towards devising a way for a trend-following strategy to adapt to these changing market regimes.

Nowadays, with the advance of hardware acceleration devices such as field programmable gate arrays (FPGAs), it is possible to attain high component density and low power consumption, while achieving minimal latency [1]. Most of the existing solutions allow reconfiguration between different computations, but do not take advantage of their Partial Reconfigurability (PR): the possibility to reconfigure the device during the same computation. When using PR the application is represented as a sequence of operations that do not need to (or cannot)

© Springer International Publishing AG 2017
S. Wong et al. (Eds.): ARC 2017, LNCS 10216, pp. 154–167, 2017.
DOI: 10.1007/978-3-319-56258-2_14

overlap their execution: each operation corresponds to a distinct configuration that can be loaded into the FPGA at run-time. Many of the hardware acceleration solutions use full-reconfiguration (FR) to switch at run-time between multiple FPGA designs. Full-reconfiguration based implementations have a small advantage when the data to be processed needs the FPGA on-board memory, as after each reconfiguration the data must to be sent again to the FPGA, resulting in increased reconfiguration overhead time [2]. FR is however simpler since the complete chip is reconfigured, while it can be tedious to implement PR since much low-level detail is involved. Finally, it is also possible to use one or more multiplexers to switch between different circuits at run time; we call this Static Reconfiguration (SR). Clearly SR designs require the largest area but the least reconfiguration time compared to PR and FR designs.

Our study aims to provide the first generic framework for run-time customisation of trading strategies, with the following *contributions*:

1. Novel designs involving static reconfiguration, partial reconfiguration and full reconfiguration for multiple trading strategies.
2. Library of optimised trend-following trading strategies including fully-pipelined designs for Double Moving Average Crossover (TS1), Triple Moving Average Crossover (TS2), Price Rate of Change (TS3), and Bollinger Bands (TS4).
3. Demonstration of the proposed framework on both synthetic and historical market data points, showing a speedup of up to 11 times, 7 times and 2 times respectively for the SR, PR and FR designs when compared to an optimised multi-core CPU implementation.

2   Background and Related Work

The Foreign Exchange Market (FX) is tradable 24 h/day excluding weekends, which makes it the largest asset class in the world suitable for high-frequency trading (HFT). FX market's dynamics make it change in regimes that move fast or slow, thus requiring the trading strategy to adapt to reflect the regime. HFT involves complex tools and algorithms to move in and out of certain positions in seconds or even milliseconds [3]. The following presents three well-known trend-following strategies which are included in our trading strategy kernel library.

(1) *Exponential Moving Average (EMA)*: A *moving average* (MA) is a sequence of arithmetic means taken over a fixed interval which is then moved along consecutive data points. The regular time scale we are using could be interpreted either as fixed units of clock time units or fixed units of market time defined in some way for the strategy. An exponential moving average (EMA) is similar to a simple moving average, except that more weight is given to the latest data, using the following formula:

$$EMA_x = (\alpha * s_x) + (1 - \alpha) * EMA_{x-1} \tag{1}$$

where EMA_x is taken for each value $(x+n) < i < (x+k-n)$, s is the data set and α stands for the weight $\alpha = \frac{2}{movingAverageLength+1}$. In finance, it is often used to detect trends in price, in particular by comparing two simple moving averages: one over a long window and one over a short window [4]. Previous work has shown how to create a fully-pipelined simple 3-point moving average kernel [5]. However, this method has not been evaluated with market data [6] and it only provides small window moving averages, compared to what real-world applications need (e.g. 200-point moving average to predict financial trends [4]).

(2) *Price Rate of Change*: The price rate of change (PROC) is a trading strategy that measures the percentage change between the most recent price and the price "n" periods in the past, using the following formula:

$$\frac{p_{now} - p_n}{p_{today-n}} * 100 \tag{2}$$

where p_{now} stands for the value of the closing price now and p_n represents the closing price value "n" periods ago. It is used by traders to confirm price movements, detect divergences, and determine potential over-bought/oversold areas.

(3) *Bollinger Bands*: A Bollinger Band (BB) is a band plotted two standard deviations away from a simple moving average. Because standard deviation is a measure of volatility, BBs adjust themselves to the market conditions, as follows:

$$SMA_X \pm (STD_X * 2) \tag{3}$$

where SMA_X stands for simple moving average for the past X closing prices (we use EMA instead of SMA), and STD_X represents the standard deviation of the past X closing prices. The closer the prices move to the upper band, the more overbought the market, and the reverse is true for oversold market identification.

In our study, we employ a *BUY* trading strategy. Taking the example of a GBP/USD FX trading market, whenever we choose to BUY 50 units of GBP, we will take the reverse position [3]. We compute our *returns* (which represent the profit in \$M) on the CPU, after the FPGA provides the final trading position decision, using the following formula:

$$R_c = (-d_t * p_t^A + d_t * p_t^B) - tc_t \tag{4}$$

where d_t takes the value 50 in our case. p_t^A and p_t^B represent our two currency prices, GBP and USD at time t, while tc_t stands for transaction costs. Transactions costs are neglected for our simulated synthetic market data, however they are included within our historical tick data.

3   Framework for Reconfigurable Trading Strategies

We develop a framework to support different combinations of trading strategy kernels. Our framework includes: (1) a static architecture which makes use of multiplexers to switch strategy kernels. (2) a full-reconfiguration architecture which changes the entire FPGA configuration and DRAM data. (3) a partial-reconfiguration architecture which only changes some parts of the FPGA configuration, while the remaining parts stay the same.

One challenge due to run-time full-reconfiguration (RTR) architectures comes from the overhead related to DRAM transfer. Because many commercial platforms use a soft memory controller on the FPGA fabric, reconfiguring the FPGA fabric results in the loss of DRAM contents, since the DRAM controller is no longer available to refresh DRAM. Thus before reconfiguration any intermediary data must be saved, and after reconfiguration any problem data must be loaded on-chip. Depending on the problem size, this may become a bottleneck. Depending on the total run time, the impact of RTR may be significant and one common way to address this is by increasing problem sizes (i.e. processing large amounts of data in our case) so the reconfiguration overhead becomes negligible compared to the savings in execution time. We choose to offer PR as an option as it removes the need to reload DRAM and even though it is harder to implement and uses more resources than FR because of the reconfiguration module, it offers a good trade-off between resource usage and performance.

Our framework can be configured as one of the three architectures whose design will be described throughout this section. It also provides a *trading strategy (TS) library* which includes, at the time of writing, some of the most well-known trading strategies (whose parameters can be changed by the user) which adopt a trend-following approach. Their respective performance will be analysed in Sect. 6. *Our framework is configured generically, such that any user can add a new trading strategy kernel to the library and use it freely*. We can also configure the area where a trading strategy will be placed on-chip as well as customise the way we choose to place the trading strategies on the FPGA: for example, we can choose to run all strategies in parallel so we get multiple feedback, or run just a number of them in parallel and switch between some others (according to a switch condition set by the user). The number of trading strategies is not fixed, it varies with the chosen architecture, how we choose to use it and how complex each of the strategies' design is, all being highly dependent on resource usage.

Static Reconfiguration (SR) Architecture. It contains all the strategy kernels and places them on the FPGA. The SRTS design can choose a group of the strategy kernels to run: for example in Fig. 1, first the framework chooses TS_{x+1} to TS_n to run, and then it switches and chooses the group $TS_1 \ldots TS_x, TS_{m+1} \ldots TS_n$ to run. SRTS can run all the kernels at the same time, or use multiplexers to select some of the kernels. As it puts all the kernels on the FPGA, thus taking the most resources compared with other architectures. This architecture is the fastest because it uses multiplexers to do the switching within one cycle, although for more complex designs a pipelined multiplexer network can be used to reduce cycle time, at the expense of taking multiple cycles.

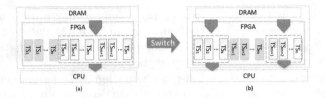

Fig. 1. SRTS: (a) choose TS group A to run. (b) choose TS group B to run

Full Reconfiguration (FR) Architecture. Figure 2 shows the overall FR architecture, which works as follows. (1) The data are collected on the CPU and are then transferred to the accelerator DRAM. (2) On each market data tick, the outcome of the evaluation (Buy, Switch or No Position to be taken) indicates what trading position the algorithm should take. (3) Every X number of cycles we check if the condition set by the user is met (i.e. in our case, the conditions stated in Sect. 5) and if it is a switch is performed (X corresponds to the market entry points from a particular trading window: e.g. 30-s trading window with a frequency of 1000 ticks per second and an FPGA clock rate of one tick/clock cycle, X = 30000). (4) Reload the market data onto accelerator DRAM. (5) Repeats steps (2) to (4) until there are no more data to evaluate. On the FPGA we used, we have to transfer the data to DRAM each time we switch between two FPGA designs. This is due to the limitations of the DRAM controller IP available for our device. If the controller had a user interface to issue commands for self refresh mode on DRAM, this data reloading would not be necessary. Each of the reconfigurable blocks from our architecture can contain multiple trading strategies. The transferring operation, the unload and the load operations of the FPGA designs add further overload to our solution, increasing the switch time and thus making it less feasible from a time constraint point of view to switch between strategies as often as possible. On CPU we check all outputs from each FR module and compute the returns according to Formula 4.

The total *reconfiguration overhead* time for our FR design is:

$$O_f = r_t + d_t \qquad (5)$$

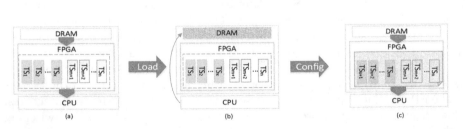

Fig. 2. FRTS: (a) kernel running, (b) data reload, (c) kernels reload

where O_f is the reconfiguration overhead, r_t stands for reconfiguration time and d_t is the data transfer time. The total *data transfer* time is computed as follows:

$$d_t = data_{size} * (n_{bytes})/bandwidth \tag{6}$$

Partial Reconfiguration (PR) Architecture. We employ partial reconfiguration tools [7] to develop our PRTS, which can switch between the multiple trading strategies at run-time. Our PR architecture links a reconfigurable block (which can contain many trading strategies) to multiple static ones (that can be used as trend-following momentum filters or just as different trading strategies). Figure 3(i) shows the overall PR architecture, which works as follows: (1) The market data are simulated on the CPU and are then transferred to the accelerator DRAM. (2) TS_i kernel reads data from DRAM. (3) If the switch condition is met, then every X number of cycles we perform the switch to TS_{i+1} kernel (respectively TS_i kernel if previous state was TS_{i+1} kernel). (4) Repeats steps (2), (3) until there are no more data to evaluate.

The *PR configuration region* used for our design and implementation is ((0, 0), (1, 2)) and corresponds to the area split shown in Fig. 3(ii). We choose this because we need to save area for data stored in DRAM - however the PR configuration area in our framework can be fully-customised by the user to accommodate its needs. The *common parts* of our design are the manager, the memory controller, the PCIe communication module and any other static kernel (e.g. TS3, TS4 in our case) that might be chosen to run in parallel with the partial-reconfiguration module. These static kernels stay fixed, and only the $TS_{n-1}..TS_n$ kernels switch at run-time (e.g. in our case TS1, TS2).

The total *reconfiguration overhead* time for our PR solution is given by:

$$O_p = r_t + t_e \tag{7}$$

where r_t stands for reconfiguration time and t_e stands for increased execution time due to reduced clock frequency. In our case, when we take the trading decision and perform the returns using Formula 4 on CPU, we take into consideration our two different filters as follows: if one of our main trading strategies (i.e. TS1 - TMAC) suggests a BUY position should be taken - we check if one

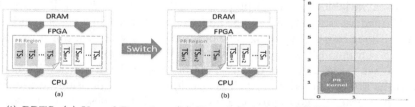

(i) PRTS: (a) Kernel Running, (b) Kernel Switch   (ii) PR Config. Region

Fig. 3. PR architecture and configuration region

of our filters (i.e. TS3 - PROC) suggests the same - if not, we decide not to pursue with the position. It is important to note that this is just one particular approach in which this framework could be used.

4   Implementation Details

The implementation of the proposed designs depends heavily on the properties of the target system. The accelerator system we use is a Maxeler MPCX node. If we were to use a different architecture than the one based on Maxeler's infrastructure, then the implementation and its respective performance would change according to the new accelerator's specifications: e.g. the reconfiguration time could change using a different reconfiguration methodology on different boards, or the communication channel may change among different architectures. The system properties are summarised in Table 1 and it consists of a CPU node in 32 nm transistor technology, and a DFE node with the FPGA in 40 nm transistor technology. The two are connected via Infiniband through a Mellanox FDR Infiniband switch. The implementation of the architectures follows thoroughly their design as presented in Figs. 1, 2 and 3.

Table 1. System properties

CPU/CPU DRAM	Intel Xeon CPU X5650@2.67GHz/48 GB
FPGA/FPGA DRAM	Virtex6 SXT475/24 GB
CPU to FPGA BANDWIDTH	2 GB/s

The Virtex-6 SX475T FPGA used in this work has 16 clock regions: *we do not place PR regions in the central clock regions of the chip as this could reduce the impact on the routing process for memory controllers.*

Input/Output/Operation. The data-flow engine (DFE) is optimised for relatively large transfer bursts from on-board DRAM and maximum DRAM transfer efficiency is achieved when more bursts are read in a linear access pattern: both our designs enable this, as all market data are read from DRAM in a sequential fashion. We can read up to 1536 bits per clock cycle from DRAM. Since our market data variables are single precision floating point values (32 bits wide), we could read up to $1536/32 = 48$ different market variables from on-board DRAM without causing the designs to become memory bound. Since we try to simulate a continuously streaming environment, we use only one market variable per clock cycle, thus the default memory controller frequency is enough. The returns are computed on the CPU considering every decision output from the FPGA. Because a good proportion of the market values will be reused for each trading strategy evaluated on every new market point entry, these will be stored in DRAM and only incur the transfer penalty over the slow interconnect between the CPU and FPGA once for both SRTS and PRTS. For FRTS we will however have to re-transfer the data every time we perform a switch.

CPU Implementation. This is built using C++11 and parallelised using OpenMP. We compile the CPU implementation using Intel c++ with flags `-O3 -march=native -fopenmp` to enable general performance optimisations, architectural optimisations for the Intel XEON and the use of multithreading.

FPGA Implementation. While both our run-time reconfiguration versions PRTS and FRTS are applicable to any number and combination of trading strategies, for the purpose of this paper we limit the trading strategies to the ones implemented in the provided library (see Sect. 5). The SRTS approach can contain as many trading strategies as we can fit on the available FPGA, thus being highly dependent on resource usage. We aim to set the basis of a generic framework which could include many more trading strategies in a lot of different combinations, depending on the user's trading interest, thus focusing on optimising the potential switch between trading strategies under different market conditions. Our proposed framework includes three different solutions: a PR, a FR approach as well as a SR one. The library designs included in our framework have fully-customisable parameters (e.g. different moving average lengths), thus allowing the potential users to be able to exploit the best financial returns.

5   Library of Trading Strategies

We propose to exploit the SR, PR and FR capability of FPGA technology by creating customisable designs which achieve the throughput rate of one data point per clock cycle. We implement the following trend-following strategies as an initial library for our framework:

(1) *Exponential Moving Averages on FPGA.* The FPGA design of our EMA consists of a series of statements defining input and output streams and computations on streams, as follows: As we store all data elements in memory, we have a register which stores the sum and at each tick it shifts in new data and multiplies it to the present sum following Formula (1). We use the exponential moving average in the following two strategies [4]:

   (a) *Double Moving Averages Crossover Trading Strategy (DMAC).* It involves two MAs: one short and one long. We pick the most encountered case in practice for short-term market fluctuations, thus having the short and long MAs computed over a 25-point respectively 200-point trading window of closing prices. The strategy trades when the short MA crosses the long MA from above and below. In our system, DMAC will exit and switch to the triple moving average crossover trading strategy when the moving averages cross.

   (b) *Triple Moving Averages Crossover Trading Strategy (TMAC).* It uses three MAs: one short, one medium, and one long. The most common MA lengths proven to give good results in practice are: 25-point trading window for the short MA, 100-point for the medium MA and 200-point for the long MA. The strategy takes a buy decision if: (i) Short MA is above the medium MA; (ii) Medium MA is above the long MA where the short MA is already over the medium MA.

(2) *Price Rate of Change Trading Strategy (PROC).* The most common period for PROC is 12-periods for short-term signals. We decide to use this value for testing, as it is aligned with our high-frequency trading strategy trend-following approach. Generally, a negative PROC value shows that the market is being oversold, while a positive PROC value observes the market as being overbought. In our case, when the PROC value $\leq -30\%$ we decide to take a Buy position [4].

(3) *Bollinger Bands Trading Strategy (BB).* We use a 20 period EMA as the "middle band" (one of the mostly used values for short-term trend identification in the financial markets), thus our "lower band" and "upper band" BB values being based on a 20 period prices standard deviation as well. This trading strategy acts as a filter on top of the other trading strategies, alongside the PROC trend-following strategy, for further trend direction strength optimisation [4].

6   Evaluation

Our PRTS implementation runs at a clock frequency of $150\,Mhz$, while our FRTS and SRTS implementation run at a clock frequency of $175\,Mhz$. For the PRTS approach an increase in clock frequency from $150\,Mhz$ to $175\,Mhz$ is difficult to obtain as it was hard to meet timing requirements. All the run times are measured by using the `chrono::high_resolution_clock` which is part of the C++11 standard library. Both CPU and FPGA times measured include the time to process the total market ticks (respectively the total market ticks between switches). We perform different experiments on both synthetically generated FX GBP/USD market data at different trading frequencies, as well as historical data: First, we analyse the speedup and returns for SRTS, PRTS and FRTS designs in an offline environment. Then, we identify the best trading opportunity when checking the obtained performance for multiple data set dimensions, and different trading-window switch frequencies. Last, we simulate a real-time trading environment, thus accounting for the data loss encountered during different trading-window switch durations when using FRTS and PRTS.

Resource Usage Results. We analyse what each of our framework configurations (SRTS, PRTS, FRTS) properties are, when using the trading strategies implemented. Table 2 presents the FPGA total resource usage expressed as a percentage of the total available resource on the chip for the single precision floating point implementation of all individual static trading strategies kernels. It also shows the FPGA total resource usage for the SRTS solution which implements all the presented trading strategies (TMAC, DMAC, PROC and BB) and runs them all in parallel. Our framework gives the users the flexibility for both SR and PR to pick if they want to run all strategies in the same time, or if they want to switch between a few of them and/or run others in the same time as well (possibly with different parameters - in practice, traders choose to run the same trading strategy with different parameters in parallel, so that they can identify its optimum coefficients at any point in time). Table 3 shows the resource usage for the generalised framework version as described previously.

Table 2. FPGA total resource usage for static kernels. Measurements are provided for 864M data points and 175 Mhz clock frequency

# Kernel	LUTs	FFs	BRAMs	DSPs	Total logic
TMAC	11.02%	14.02%	9.92%	1.19%	17.75%%
DMAC	10.65%	14.17%	9.92%	0.79%	17.79%
PROC	10.88%	14.13%	9.92%	0.20%	18.19%
BB	11.15%	14.48%	10.06%	0.74%	18.33%
All static	14.12%	17.27%	14.94%	2.98%	22.22%

Table 3. Resource usage for PRTS and FRTS provided for 864M data points

Property	PRTS	FRTS	Static
Compute clock frequency (MHz)	150	175	175
Memory clock frequency (MHz)	400	400	400
Total logic (4 trading strategies)	18%	15%	23%
Total logic (8 trading strategies)	32%	27%	38%

This framework can be used to provide guidance on which trading strategy performs best under different market regimes, but for this to be optimal many trading strategies would need to be implemented on-chip. Having just a static kernel solution would work as long as we have enough resources. However, adding new trading strategies kernels will quickly scale the total resource usage on-chip until it becomes completely unusable. Increasing the resources will further reduce the clock frequency thus making the FPGA approach slower as well. We can then use the FRTS approach to try and save area on-chip or we could use the PRTS solution to use many trading strategies to switch from, while still being able to run potentially a few more in parallel, as shown in Fig. 3(i).

Offline - Static Reconfiguration Trading Strategies on FPGA. We run all trading strategies in parallel, with the parameters presented in Sect. 5, and we employ a majority rule trading strategy - if the majority of the trading strategies tell us to BUY then we BUY. Table 4 shows that our SRTS approach obtains up to 11 times speedup when compared to its fully optimised CPU C++ software version. Also, the speedup increases with the number of market data points evaluated, thus confirming the FPGA choice for this compute-bound problem.

Table 4. All static - FPGA performance results

# Market ticks	1.152M	28.8M	86.4M	432M	604.8M	864M
CPU time (s)	0.05	1.38	4.15	24.51	32.97	54.23
FPGA time (s)	0.03	0.14	0.44	2.45	3.45	4.91
FPGA speedup	**1.67**	**9.85**	**9.43**	**10.00**	**9.55**	**11.04**
Returns (M)	**1.679**	**2.805**	**4.831**	**6.204**	**8.205**	**10.178**

Offline - Partial Reconfiguration Trading Strategy on FPGA. We evaluate our solution using TS1 (TMAC) and TS2 (DMAC) as part of the PR region and TS3 (PROC) and TS4 (BB) as the static kernels acting as momentum filters running in parallel with the partial reconfiguration module. Table 5 presents the DMAC and TMAC evaluation results using the partial reconfiguration solution on FPGA. Every X number of cycles (X corresponding to the market entry points from a particular trading window e.g. 5 min trading window) we have *the option to perform a switch*, which in our case it happens if the market conditions explained in Sect. 5 are met. As expected, Table 5 identifies that more frequent switches decrease our system's speedup, because for every switch to be performed during the run-time reconfiguration, we lose $70\,ms$ (see formula (7)).

Table 5. PRTS - FPGA performance results for 864M market data entries

Switch frequency (min)	0.5	1	5	15	30
# of switches	374	192	58	24	10
CPU time (s)	48.12	45.76	42.88	41.01	40.88
FPGA time (s)	31.90	19.15	9.81	7.43	6.42
PRTS speedup	**1.51**	**2.39**	**4.37**	**5.52**	**6.36**
PRTS returns (M)	**1.428**	**2.903**	**5.890**	**7.965**	**12.361**

Offline - Full Reconfiguration Trading Strategies on FPGA. Table 6 draws the same conclusion as the PRTS one, that more frequent switches decrease our system's speedup. This method shows a noticeable decrease in the speedup due to the fact that each time we perform a switch we need to unload the old FPGA design and reload a new one. All our designs depend on the use of DRAM: in the FRTS case we notice an additional DRAM average load time of 1.61 s (see Formula (6)), for the 864M data entries we need to transfer each time. After ignoring the communication latency over PCIe/Infiniband which is of the order of milliseconds, we obtain an average total transfer + load time of 1.66 s.

PRTS vs FRTS in a Trading Simulated Environment. Table 7 shows returns for both PR and FR approches when trying to simulate a continuously

Table 6. FRTS - FPGA performance results for 864M market data entries

Switch frequency (min)	0.5	1	5	15	30
# of switches	374	192	58	24	10
CPU time (s)	55.34	49.12	46.02	45.38	42.29
FPGA time (s)	607.02	314.03	98.28	44.62	21.18
FRTS speedup	**0.09**	**0.16**	**0.47**	**1.02**	**2.00**
FRTS returns (M)	**0.781**	**1.290**	**4.203**	**6.992**	**8.834**

streaming algorithm. We notice that when we lose access to the data corresponding to the switch time period, we seem to be decreasing our overall returns, as
well as encounter losses at times. However, the PRTS returns are higher than the
FRTS ones which shows that simply switching between trading strategies at different times is not good enough, but by introducing momentum filters (as in the
PRTS approach) we better account for the financial markets condition changes
and avoid under-performance of one particular selected trading strategy.

Table 7. PRTS vs FRTS return results for 864M market data entries

Switch frequency (min)	0.5	1	5	15	30
PRTS # of switches	302	240	78	44	25
PRTS returns (M)	**0.712**	**2.108**	**5.264**	**7.112**	**10.780**
FRTS # of switches	402	287	101	53	17
FRTS returns (M)	**−5.611**	**−2.889**	**1.017**	**3.859**	**7.513**

Figure 4(i) shows the different returns for both PRTS and FRTS solutions,
when we account for the data loss that would appear during the switch time.
This graph presents a 30 min trading strategied switch frequency over different
market data entries (i.e.: 28.8M). The "real-time" simulation of our trading
strategy shows that when losing access to the data corresponding to the switch
time period, returns decrease as data become less reliable and more volatile.

Figure 4(ii) shows the different switch times corresponding to each of the
respective number of market entries, when running both PRTS as well as FRTS,
using all the implemented trading strategies from the strategy kernel library. We
notice PR solution regardless the number of market entries, while it increases
with the increase of the market data points in the case of the FR implementation.

SRTS vs PRTS vs FRTS Returns for Historical FX Market Data.
We verify the applicability of our proposed approach by evaluating Historical GBP/USD tick-data from the Foreign Exchange Market which corresponds
to time-periods from 2003/2004. Our historical tick data include transaction

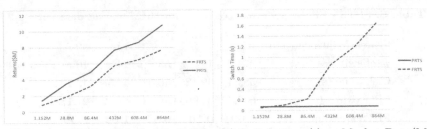

(i) Returns(M) vs Market Data(M)   (ii) Switch Time(s) vs Market Data(M)

Fig. 4. Returns and switch frequency for FRTS and PRTS

costs. Table 8 shows returns for all static, partial-reconfiguration as well as full-reconfiguration approach when trying to simulate a continuously streaming algorithm using historical market data. We can notice a slight decrease in the return levels from 2003 and 2004, being very much in accordance with the greater FX market efficiency in 2004 compared to 2003 (i.e. a growth in electronic high-frequency trading occurred during the 2003–2008 period).

Table 8. SRTS vs PRTS vs FRTS - March (10–14) 2003, 2004

Switch frequency (min)	0.5	1	5	15	30
2003					
SRTS returns (M)	0.412	0.402	0.899	0.594	0.656
PRTS returns (M)	0.335	0.484	0.805	0.661	0.579
FRTS returns (M)	0.147	0.388	0.689	0.570	0.601
2004					
SRTS returns (M)	0.360	0.321	0.680	0.694	0.557
PRTS returns (M)	0.272	0.301	0.760	0.612	0.514
FRTS returns (M)	0.082	0.258	0.516	0.432	0.491

7   Conclusion and Future Work

Our study aims to provide the first framework for developing and comparing multiple trading strategies for FPGA designs. Our tool offers the user multiple solutions for running their trading strategies. Three architecture types are supported: static, partial-reconfiguration and full-reconfiguration. Our approach offers alternative solutions when a static design becomes too large because of too many different trading strategies or the trading strategies themselves are very complex and occupy a significant amount of resources [8]. If the resources of a given device run out, a larger FPGA would be needed, but if not available, our framework offers the user a low-cost, resource and performance efficient solution.

We show that FPGAs can effectively accelerate a system based on multiple trend-following trading strategies which come as an initial library for our framework. Our SRTS design achieves 11 times speedup, the PRTS design achieves 7 times speedup, while the FRTS design achieves up to 2 times speedup, when compared to the corresponding multi-threaded C++11 implementation running on a six-core Intel Xeon CPU X5650 processor. After testing our tool on historical FX data, we show that trading strategies supported by the proposed design are reliable and, if further exploited, can increase profitability from high frequency FX markets trading. Thus, applying different trading strategies based on different market regimes would help the modeling process better reflect the reality.

Opportunities for further work include adding support for varying data representation and evaluating speedup/returns improvements on more recent financial market data. We could include multiple copies of trading strategies on-chip so that one could start processing without waiting for a previous computation to finish. We also aim to enhance the trading strategies kernel library, implementing additional effective strategies on the FPGA, as well as developing macroeconomic and news factors for stock and fixed income trading. We further plan to include designs to optimally detect regime change, such as those based on permutation entropy [9]. In the future, we will also make our framework available as open source, to allow developers to add their custom strategies to the library.

Acknowledgments. The support of UK EPSRC (EP/I012036/1, EP/L00058X/1, EP/L016796/1 and EP/N031768/1), the European Union Horizon 2020 Research and Innovation Programme under grant agreement number 671653, the China Scholarship Council, the Maxeler University Programme, Altera, Intel and Xilinx is gratefully acknowledged.

References

1. Wray, S., et al.: Exploring algorithmic trading in reconfigurable hardware. In: ASAP (2010)
2. Altera. FPGA Run-Time Reconfiguration: Two Approaches - White Paper. ftp://ftp.bittware.com/documents/fpga-run-time-reconfiguration.pdf
3. Driver, M.: Foreign Exchange: A Practical Guide to the FX Markets. CreateSpace, North Charleston (2012)
4. Aldridge, I.: High-Frequency Trading: A Practical Guide to Algorithmic Strategies and Trading Systems (Wiley Trading), 2nd edn. Wiley, Hoboken (2013)
5. Maxeler Technologies, MaxCompiler-WhitePaper (2001). https://www.maxeler.com/media/documents/MaxelerWhitePaperMaxCompiler.pdf
6. Leber, C., et al.: High frequency trading acceleration using FPGAs. In: FPL (2011)
7. Mastinu, M.: Design flow to support dynamic partial reconfiguration on Maxeler architectures. Politecnico di Milano (2012)
8. Funie, A.I., et al.: Reconfigurable acceleration of fitness evaluation in trading strategies. In: ASAP (2015)
9. Guo, C., et al.: Pipelined reconfigurable accelerator for ordinal pattern encoding. In: ASAP (2014)

Exploring HLS Optimizations for Efficient Stereo Matching Hardware Implementation

Karim M.A. Ali[1(✉)], Rabie Ben Atitallah[1], Nizar Fakhfakh[2], and Jean-Luc Dekeyser[3]

[1] LAMIH, University of Valenciennes, Valenciennes, France
{karim.ali,rabie.benatitallah}@univ-valenciennes.fr
[2] NAVYA Company, Paris, France
nizar.fakhfakh@navya-technology.com
[3] CRIStAL, University of Lille1, Lille, France
jean-luc.dekeyser@univ-lille1.fr

Abstract. Nowadays, FPGA technology offers a tremendous number of logic cells on a single chip. Digital design for such huge hardware resources under time-to-market constraint urged the evolution of High Level Synthesis (HLS) tools. In this work, we will explore several HLS optimization steps in order to improve the system performance. Different design choices are obtained from our exploration such that an efficient implementation is selected based on given system constraints (resource utilization, power consumption, execution time, ...). Our exploration methodology is illustrated through a case study considering a Multi-Window Sum of Absolute Difference stereo matching algorithm. We implemented our design using Xilinx Zynq ZC706 FPGA evaluation board for gray images of size 640 × 480.

Keywords: FPGA · High level synthesis · Stereo matching algorithms

1 Introduction

FPGA circuits have emerged as a privileged target platforms to implement intensive signal processing applications [3]. For this reason several academic and industrial efforts have been devoted in order to increase the productivity of FPGA-based designs by means of using High Level Synthesis (HLS) tools. HLS approach in Electronic Design Automation (EDA) is a step in the design flow aiming at moving the design effort to higher abstraction levels [6]. This evolution towards HLS-based methodologies can be easily traced along the history of hardware system design [2]. Although the first generations of HLS tools failed to produce efficient hardware designs, different reasons have motivated researchers to continue improving these tools. We can mention among these reasons: the huge growth in the silicon capacity, the emergence of IP-based design approaches, trends towards using hardware accelerators on heterogeneous SoCs, the time-to-market constraint which usually presses to reduce the design time,

© Springer International Publishing AG 2017
S. Wong et al. (Eds.): ARC 2017, LNCS 10216, pp. 168–176, 2017.
DOI: 10.1007/978-3-319-56258-2_15

etc [1]. Today several existing HLS tools have shown their efficiency for producing acceptable design performances and shortening time-to-market [6,8].

For a given design, defining the priority of constraints could vary from one application to another. For example, power consumption is a key factor for battery-based systems while hardware resources matter if several functionalities would be embedded on the same chip. In some other cases, timing is crucial for safety critical applications while Quality-of-Service is important for interactive or multimedia applications. During the design phase, it is the role of the designer to define the priorities of system constraints then to explore the design space for the implementation that could efficiently satisfy them. In this research work, the design space was built by applying a set of high level synthesis optimization steps. The obtained designs have different trade-offs in terms of hardware resources (FF, LUT or BRAM), power consumption, timing and operating frequency. Our objective is to explore the possible hardware designs then choose the one that most fit with our requirements. As a case study, we focus on the development of an FPGA-based system dedicated to streaming stereo matching applications. Our application considers Multi-Window Sum of Absolute Difference (Multi-Window SAD) algorithm [4] performed on input gray images of size 640×480 with maximum disparity $= 64$.

As a similar work targeting stereo matching domain, authors in [9] examined five stereo matching algorithms for their HLS implementation. Five optimization steps were applied to the SW code: baseline implementation, code restructuring, bit-width reduction, pipelining and parallelization via resource duplication. Our work differs from that presented in [9] as follows: (i) Baseline implementation is considered as step zero in our work because our input code is HLS-friendly. (ii) Dividing an image into strips can be achieved in three different ways with vast difference in terms of execution time and resource utilization (Optimization #1). (iii) Parallelism was exploited in both work at different levels. In our work, data-independent loops are executed in parallel by duplicating the input data stream (Optimization #3). We also increased the number of processed disparity lines at the same time either by enlarging the size of strip (Optimization #7) or by duplicating the top-level function (Optimization #8). While authors in [9] applied parallelism only by duplicating the disparity computation pipeline. Authors in [7] purposed an optimized C-code for Sobel filter in three steps. Although the design run on Zynq platform; no details were mentioned on how the HLS-based Sobel filter was interfaced and connected to the system. In this work, we will detail this point in Sect. 4. In addition to that two more optimization steps related to Zynq platforms are presented in Sect. 3 (Optimization #5 and #6).

The rest of this paper is organized as follows: Sect. 2 describes our case study related to Multi-Window SAD stereo matching algorithm. Section 3 represents our main contribution that explores high level optimization steps for an efficient implementation for our case study. System architecture and experimental results are presented in Sect. 4.

2   Multi-window SAD Matching Algorithm

Stereo matching is a correspondence problem where for every pixel X_R in the right image, we try to find its best matching pixel X_L in the left image at the same scanline. Figure 1a shows how the depth of objects is calculated in stereo matching problem. Assuming two cameras of focal length (f) at the same horizontal level, separated from each other by a distance *baseline* (b). Pixel (P) in the space will be located at point (X_R) and point (X_L) in the right and left image respectively. The difference between the two points on the image plane is defined as *disparity* (d). Therefore; the depth of pixel (P) from the two camera can be calculated from the following equation:

$$\text{depth} = \frac{baseline * focal\, length}{disparity} = \frac{b * f}{(X_R - X_L)} \tag{1}$$

Several methods in the literature were proposed to find the best matching [10]. In Multi-Window SAD [4], the absolute difference between pixels from the right and left images are aggregated within a window. The window of minimum aggregation is considered as the best matching among its candidates. In order to overcome the error that appears at the regions of depth discontinuity, the correlation window can be divided into smaller windows and only non-errored parts are considered in calculations. Figure 1b shows 5-window SAD configuration: pixel (P) lies in the middle of window (E) while it is surrounded by another four windows named (A, B, C and D). The four windows are partially overlapped at the border pixel (P). The score of any window is equal to the aggregation of its pixels. In 5-window SAD, the correlation score at pixel (P) is equal to the score value of window (E) in addition to the best minimum two score values of the other four windows (A, B, C and D). The minimum score among the candidates is considered as the best matching. Occluded objects are common to happen in stereo matching problem where sometimes the objects are only captured by

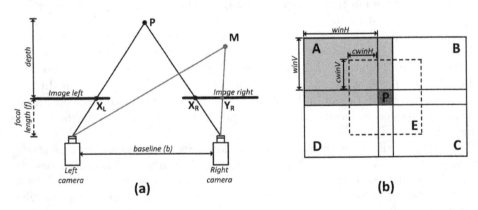

Fig. 1. (a) Calculating the depth of an object in stereo matching problem (b) 5-window SAD configuration

one camera. For example, pixel (M) in Fig. 1a was only captured by the right camera. Therefore, Left/Right consistency check is done in order to get rid of occluded objects from the final disparity image.

3 High-level Synthesis Optimizations

In this section, we are going to explore the possible optimization steps that could be done in order to achieve an efficient hardware implementation. The C code was written in HLS-friendly syntax with neither file read/write, nor dynamic memory allocation nor system calls. The optimization steps are incrementally applied to the design as listed in Table 1. From our point of view, a fair comparison between designs is valid only for adjacent rows in order to observe the impact of adding this optimization to the overall design performance. The SW code was synthesized by Vivado HLS to obtain the first synthesizable design (Design #1). Table 1 shows that Design #1 had an overuse for BRAM (BRAM_18K=7392) while using Xilinx Zynq ZC706 platform of maximum BRAM_18K=1090. This will lead to the first optimization step which is dividing an image into strips during processing in order to reduce the required memory usage.

Optimization #1: Dividing an image into strips. In strip processing, the code will be repetitively executed until one frame is completely processed. The pixels can be summed in three different ways: (i) Design #2 aggregates the pixels in the horizontal direction along the scanline then in the vertical one. (ii) While aggregation is done vertically along the column length then horizontally along the scanline for Design #3. (iii) However in Design #4, the pixels are aggregated within one window then box-filtering technique [5] is applied to get the summation of other windows along the horizontal direction. Table 1 reports the estimated hardware utilization for the three designs. By comparing, we can observe that Design #4 is more efficient in terms of BRAM usage as well as execution time (it was improved by 73% of that reported for Design #2). Therefore; we will consider Design #4 as a base for the next optimization steps.

Optimization #2: Using arbitrary precision data types. Vivado HLS supports arbitrary precision data types to define variables with smaller bit width. Using this optimization will produce systems of the same accuracy but with less area utilization. A complete analysis was done to know exactly the required number of bits for each variable. In Table 1, Design #5 showed around 31% reduction for LUT and 40% reduction for FF after applying optimization #2.

Optimization #3: Executing data-independent loops in parallel. Along the same scanline, the score for window (B) is used after ($winH+1$) pixel shift as a score for a new window (A). It is also the same case for windows (C) and (D). Therefore, only three score calculation loops are needed for windows (A/B, C/D and E). By duplicating the input data stream, the three loops can run in parallel. In Table 1, Design #6 reported the effect of optimization #3.

Optimization #4: Using HLS optimization directives. Using HLS optimization directives to tune the design performance is one of the fundamental

Table 1. Synthesis results reported by Vivado HLS for each optimization step

Design	Slice	FF	LUT	BRAM 18K	SRL	Freq. (MHz)	Exec. time (ms)	% change in Perf.
SW version	380 ms on core i7@ 2.7 GHz and 16 GB of RAM							
#1	X	2637	5918	7392	0	100	X	X
#2	898	1743	2735	155	0	100	30080	0
#3	859	1758	2659	113	0	100	22410	25.4
#4	1400	2552	3738	75	0	100	8163	72.8
#5	983	1525	2567	47	0	100	5786	29.1
#6	985	1713	2768	65	0	100	2679	53.7
#7	2695	6088	7611	57	0	100	328	87.7
#8	2688	6134	7661	59	0	100	331	−9.1
#9	2822	6365	8116	59	0	100	307	7.2
#10	7989	20256	24433	112	0	100	76	75.2
#11	7995	18765	24945	112	39	150	51	32.8
#12	8038	21250	26483	112	121	200	38	25.5

optimization steps. We examined three types of directives that gave a crucial improvement in performance: (i) Arrays were partitioned either into smaller arrays (partial) or as individual registers (complete) in order to boost the system throughput by increasing the number of available read/write ports. (ii) Loops were unrolled by factor = 2 to make profit from the existed physical dual-port for arrays implemented as BRAMs. (iii) Loops were pipelined with Initiation Interval (II) = 1 to enhance the system performance. In Table 1, Design #7 listed the estimated hardware resources and execution time after using optimization #4.

Optimization #5: Choosing I/O interface protocol for the top-level function. *HLS_SAD* core is synthesized for Zynq platform where pixels flow through DMA-based connections as shown in Fig. 2. We chose AXI-Stream for I/O ports while AXI-Lite was chosen for controlling the hardware core. AXI-Stream defined by Vivado HLS comes only with the fundamental signals (*TDATA*, *TREADY*, *TVALID*) but for DMA communications, *TLAST* signal is also needed. Therefore, Design #8 was modified such that the output port also includes a *TLAST* signal with 9% decrease in performance as listed in Table 1.

Optimization #6: Grouping pixels at I/O ports for DMA-based communication. Zynq platform has four High Performance bus (HP bus) between Processing System (PS) and Programmable Logic (PL) of 64-bit data width. The designer can benefit from this data width by merging pixels at I/O ports. In our design, the input pixel is 32-bit width while the output disparity pixel is only 8-bit. Thus we can merge up to 2 pixels at the input port and up to 8 pixels at the output port. This data merging requires an additional attention from the designer while separating the pixels at the input or merging them at the output. Design #9 showed 7% improvement in the execution time.

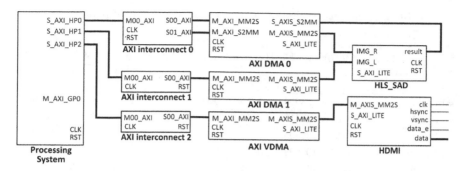

Fig. 2. System architecture block diagram

Optimization #7: Enlarging the size of strip. During strip processing, there is only one scanline difference between two strips when processing two adjacent disparity lines. From Fig. 1b, one disparity line needs a strip of size $= 2 * win\_V + 1$ while four adjacent disparity lines need a strip of size $= 2 * win\_V + 4$. In Design #10, four disparity lines are calculated using the same pipeline such that the execution time is reduced to the quarter (Table 1).

Optimization #8: Duplicating the top-level function. In this optimization step, we run multiple instances of Design #10 in parallel. Simply, we defined a new top-level function that contains multiple instances of the function defined in Design #10. In the experimental results, we will explore designs of 5, 6, 7 or 8 instances running in parallel at frequencies of 100, 150 or 200 MHz.

4   Experimental Results

The generated *HLS_SAD* IP was tested experimentally to validate both its proper functioning and the estimated results. During our experiments, we used Vivado 2015.2 design suite to implement our system over Zynq ZC706 FPGA evaluation board (XC7Z045-FFG900) with input grey images of size 640×480. The system was configured for 5-window SAD with the following parameters: $winH = 23$, $winV = 7$, $cwinH = 7$, $cwinV = 3$ and maximum disparity $= 64$.

Figure 2 illustrates the connection of *HLS_SAD* core to the other cores in the system. Pixels were transferred between the processing system (*PS*) and *HLS_SAD* block through two *AXI DMA* cores. *AXI VDMA* and *HDMI* cores were used to display the obtained disparity image on the output screen.

We obtained different design choices by exploring the effect of optimization #8 at different operating frequencies of 100, 150 or 200 MHz as listed in Table 2. During the experiments, we increased the level of parallelism up to 8 instances operating at the same time. We stopped at that level due to the limited LUT resources (design #23 consumed 95.37% of LUT). Default synthesis and implementation strategies were used by default for all designs. For design #18, *Flow_Perf_Optimized_High* and *Performance_Explore* were used as synthesis and

Table 2. Synthesis results for designs at different levels of parallelism

Design	Level of paral- lelism	Slice (54650)	FF (437200)	LUT (218600)	BRAM 18K (1090)	Freq. (MHz)	Frame exec. time (ms)	Power (W)	Energy (mJ)
#10	1	10534	28903	31163	131	100	83.91	0.852	71.49
#11	1	10111	27410	31140	131	150	57.74	0.949	54.80
#12	1	9642	29895	31184	131	200	45.02	1.043	46.96
#13	5	40326	109624	130262	579	100	20.56	1.512	31.09
#14	5	41208	102174	130571	579	150	14.37	1.795	25.79
#15	5	38980	114617	130917	579	200	11.44	2.109	24.13
#16	6	46337	129822	155728	691	100	17.83	1.612	28.74
#17	6	48752	120873	155822	691	150	12.5	1.943	24.29
#18	6	52670	141335	195408	691	200	9.98	2.519	25.14
#19	7	51022	150015	182108	803	100	15.75	1.667	26.26
#20	7	50592	139557	184409	803	150	11.08	2.047	22.68
#21	7	Timing constraints are not met @ 200 MHz							
#22	8	54470	170195	206273	915	100	14.42	1.794	25.87
#23	8	54636	158259	208993	915	150	10.17	2.115	21.51
#24	8	Timing constraints are not met @ 200 MHz							

implementation strategies respectively to meet the time constraints. For designs #21 and #24, although we tried several strategies, the tool failed to meet the time constraints for an operating frequency of 200 MHz.

The frame execution time was firstly estimated by Vivado HLS as shown in Table 1 then it was measured experimentally as listed in Table 2. For all designs, we could notice that Vivado HLS underestimated the frame execution time with an error range between 10–30%. The reason for this underestimation is that Vivado HLS did not consider the time spent for DMA communication while pixels are transferred from/to *HLS_SAD* core. Table 2 lists the required hardware resources to realize the system architecture depicted in Fig. 2. We could notice that at the same level of parallelism, changing the operating frequency led to different numbers for FF and LUT in order to satisfy the timing constraints. For example, in comparison with design #16, FF decreased by 6.9% and increased by 8.9% for designs #17 and #18 respectively while LUT was almost unchanged in design #17 and increased by 25% for design #18.

The power consumption was measured experimentally through UCD90120A power controller mounted on Zynq ZC706 FPGA board. Two factors mainly contribute to the power consumption: the used hardware resources and the operating frequency. Design #18 showed the maximum power consumption of 2.52 W at 200 MHz. Although design #23 utilized more hardware resources, it showed 16% less in power consumption (2.12 W) since it operates at 150 MHz. Calculating energy consumption showed that some design points were more energy efficient

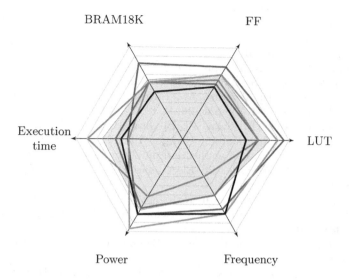

Fig. 3. Radar chart for designs #15 ▬, #16 ▬, #17 ▬, #18 ▬, #23 ▬ and system constraints ▬. (Color figure online)

than others even if they consumed more power. For example, design #23 had the lowest energy consumption of 21.51 mJ although it recorded one of the highest power consumption (2.12 W).

All design variations listed in Table 2 could be accepted as a solution but the applied system constraints will direct our final decision to choose one design among the others. Figure 3 depicts some of the candidate designs (#15, #16, #17, #18 and #23) along with the system constraints to guide the designer towards the efficient solution. The orange shaded area represents the system constraints defined by the designer which are: power consumption ≤ 2 W, execution time ≤ 15 ms, LUT ≤ 180000, FF ≤ 140000, BRAM ≤ 700 and frequency ≤ 150 MHz. From Fig. 3, we could deduce that design #17 succeeded to satisfy all the system constraints. Design #15 had relatively less hardware utilization and acceptable execution time in compare with design #17; however, it failed to meet two design constraints (power consumption and frequency).

5   Conclusion

Using HLS tools for complex system design becomes mandatory to increase the design productivity and to shorten the time-to-market. As a future work, we will automatically explore designs at higher level of parallelism. In addition to that we will build a model to predict if that design is feasible or not for a given set of system constraints.

References

1. Cong, J., Liu, B., Neuendorffer, S., Noguera, J., Vissers, K., Zhang, Z.: High-level synthesis for FPGAs: from prototyping to deployment. IEEE Trans. Comput. Aided Des. Integr. Circ. Syst. **30**(4), 473–491 (2011)
2. Coussy, P., Gajski, D.D., Meredith, M., Takach, A.: An introduction to high-level synthesis. IEEE Des. Test Comput. **26**(4), 8–17 (2009)
3. Gonzalez, I., El-Araby, E., Saha, P., El-Ghazawi, T., Simmler, H., Merchant, S.G., Holland, B.M., Reardon, C., George, A.D., Lam, H., Stitt, G., Alam, N., Smith, M.C.: Classification of application development for FPGA-based systems. In: IEEE National Aerospace and Electronics Conference, NAECON 2008, pp. 203–208, July 2008
4. Hirschmuller, H.: Improvements in real-time correlation-based stereo vision. In: IEEE Workshop on Stereo and Multi-Baseline Vision, (SMBV 2001), Proceedings, pp. 141–148 (2001)
5. McDonnell, M.: Box-filtering techniques. Comput. Graph. Image Process. **17**(1), 65–70 (1981)
6. Meeus, W., Van Beeck, K., Goedemé, T., Meel, J., Stroobandt, D.: An overview of today's high-level synthesis tools. Des. Autom. Embed. Syst. **16**(3), 31–51 (2012)
7. Monson, J., Wirthlin, M., Hutchings, B.L.: Optimization techniques for a high level synthesis implementation of the Sobel filter. In: 2013 International Conference on Reconfigurable Computing and FPGAs (ReConFig), pp. 1–6, December 2013
8. Nane, R., Sima, V.M., Pilato, C., Choi, J., Fort, B., Canis, A., Chen, Y.T., Hsiao, H., Brown, H., Ferrandi, F., Anderson, J., Bertels, K.: A survey and evaluation of FPGA high-level synthesis tools. IEEE Trans. Comput.-Aided Des. Integr. Circ. Syst. **35**(99), 1 (2016)
9. Rupnow, K., Liang, Y., Li, Y., Min, D., Do, M., Chen, D.: High level synthesis of stereo matching: productivity, performance, and software constraints. In: 2011 International Conference on Field-Programmable Technology (FPT), pp. 1–8, December 2011
10. Scharstein, D., Szeliski, R.: A taxonomy and evaluation of dense two-frame stereo correspondence algorithms. Int. J. Comput. Vis. **47**(1–3), 7–42 (2002)

Architecture Reconfiguration as a Mechanism for Sustainable Performance of Embedded Systems in case of Variations in Available Power

Dimple Sharma$^{(\boxtimes)}$, Victor Dumitriu, and Lev Kirischian

Ryerson University, Toronto, Ontario, Canada
{dsharma,vdumitri,LKIRISCH}@ee.ryerson.ca

Abstract. The paper presents a method for deriving high-level power consumption estimation (PCE) model for FPGAs with tile based architecture. This model can be used by systems having multi-task workloads to support run-time architecture-to-workload adaptation in order to sustain the performance of critical tasks in case of depleting power. The approach is based on reconfiguring implementation variants of tasks by estimating their power consumption at run-time using the derived model. This allows reduction of system power consumption by reducing performance of non critical tasks while maintaining critical task performance at required level. In turn, it allows prolongation of system activity for the required period. The paper demonstrates derivation of PCE model for the System on Programmable Chip (SoPC) deployed on Xilinx Zynq XC7Z020 FPGA and how this SoPC adapts to depleting power, sustaining the performance of its critical task for an additional hour.

Keywords: Architecture reconfiguration · Power consumption estimation model · Multi-task · Embedded systems · FPGA

1 Introduction

The main objective of the presented research has been to find an effective mechanism for autonomous embedded computing systems like systems deployed on satellites, robotic systems, stand-alone terrestrial and marine monitoring systems etc., to be able to sustain performance of their multi-task workloads in presence of significant variations in available power. The concept of the proposed approach is to adapt to a reduced energy budget by using architecture reconfiguration to appropriately reduce system power consumption. In [1], it was shown that, for a given task algorithm, a number of architecture variants can be obtained, which exhibit different performance, operating frequency, resource usage and power consumption. These architecture variants can be referred to as Application Specific Processing circuits (ASP circuits). Dynamically reconfiguring a suitable ASP circuit for each active task can provide the system with much greater control over its power consumption. Required performance of high priority tasks can be sustained by reconfiguring an ASP circuit which utilizes

© Springer International Publishing AG 2017
S. Wong et al. (Eds.): ARC 2017, LNCS 10216, pp. 177–186, 2017.
DOI: 10.1007/978-3-319-56258-2_16

more hardware resources at a reduced operating frequency. For tasks with lower priority, variants which use fewer resources can be reconfigured so that they can still continue their functionality at a reduced performance (e.g. lower video resolution or communication bandwidth). As a result, current power constraints are satisfied while maintaining the required performance for most important tasks.

Thus, when there is a change in the power budget, the system selects a suitable combination of ASP circuit variants for its active tasks such that the total power consumption is reduced. In order to do so, the system must be able to estimate at run-time, power consumption of the combination of ASP circuit variants under consideration. For a large system with say, 10 active tasks and 10 ASP circuit variants per task, the possible number of combinations of ASP circuits that can be deployed on the FPGA is 10^{10}! Measuring FPGA power consumption or estimating it using vendor tools for such a large number of combinations and maintaining a look up table for the purpose of adaptation is practically not feasible. Hence, a run-time PCE model which is general enough to estimate power consumption of the FPGA for any combination of ASP circuits, while maintaining a certain degree of accuracy needs to be developed.

Additionally, the proposed approach also requires the development of a special on-chip infrastructure to be deployed in partially reconfigurable FPGA devices, which provides flexible reconfiguration and re-location of ASP circuits. Multi-mode Adaptive Collaborative Reconfigurable self-Organized System, i.e. MACROS framework has been developed for this purpose. The framework is briefly described in this paper and is detailed in [2,3].

This paper has the following contributions: (a) It presents a generic procedure to derive a PCE model for any FPGA; (b) It discusses the mechanism of architecture reconfiguration of a suitable ASP circuit variant for each system task, based on system power consumption estimated by the model at run-time. This enables the system to adapt to varying power constraints at run-time.

Section 2 of the paper analyzes existing works in the field of controlling and modeling power consumption for FPGA-based systems. Section 3 discusses in brief, the MACROS framework introduced above. Section 4 presents in detail the method to derive PCE model for an FPGA using the example of Xilinx Zynq XC7Z020 device. Section 5 uses the extracted model to demonstrate how a system sustains its critical task's performance for a longer time in case of depleting power. Section 6 concludes the paper and discusses future work.

2   Related Works

Commonly adopted methods for reduction and control of power consumption in embedded systems are power gating [4,5] and Dynamic Voltage and Frequency Scaling (DVFS) [6,7]. Both the methods do not allow architecture variability and hence cannot take advantage of the potential trade-offs between parallelism and operating frequency. Use of Dynamic Partial Reconfiguration (DPR) coupled with frequency control can offer more power consumption flexibility.

DPR is used in [8] to control the number and type of computing circuits present in a power-aware system for efficient dynamic resource management.

However, here too, since tasks architectures are fixed, the system can only manage scheduling and allocation of the computing circuits to control power consumption. The authors of [9] use the concept of design variants which have different resource utilization and operating frequency. Although they analyze power consumption with respect to parallelism and frequency scaling, a fixed choice of an optimum variant is made by the designer at design time. Our approach on the contrary uses the concept of task architecture variants from [1] to adapt to dynamically changing power conditions at run-time.

A system using our proposed approach requires a model, which can estimate system power consumption for any combination of task variants at run-time. Most of the high level modeling methods are aimed towards specific entities like IP Cores [10] or arithmetic operators [11] or soft processors [12] etc. and are not generic for the FPGA as a whole. The run-time model presented in [8] is also based on intimate knowledge of the task architecture, and cannot be easily expanded to large numbers of architectures. Development of a high-level, simple and accurate model for the FPGA thus becomes inevitable.

3   MACROS Framework

To support run-time architecture adaptation, an embedded system requires a specialized framework which permits run-time deployment of tasks into a programmable fabric. To address this need, MACROS framework has been developed [2,3]. The general architecture of MACROS framework based system is shown in Fig. 1. It primarily consists of three elements: (I) a number of reserved partially reconfigurable regions (PRRs) in the FPGA device, referred to as slots, some connected to I/O blocks; (II) a distributed communication infrastructure, which incorporates a cross-switch matrix able to interconnect each slot with any other slot, and a control bus, which transfers control and synchronization information between slots; (III) a bit-stream and configuration management system.

An ASP circuit variant for each active system task is configured in the slots as shown in the three examples in Fig. 1. Each ASP circuit can be housed in one or multiple slots. Integration of an ASP circuit deployed in few slots is done automatically by self-integration procedures using control infrastructure described in [2,3]. Thus, a system only needs to select the appropriate ASP circuit for each task and the rest is taken care of by MACROS framework.

4   Derivation of Power Consumption Estimation Model

A system capable of run-time adaptation to changing power budget must incorporate an estimation model which predicts power consumption of any combination of ASP circuit variants under consideration. This section discusses a generic procedure to derive the model for any FPGA. Xilinx Zynq XC7Z020 [13] housed in the Zedboard [14] is used as an example to describe the process.

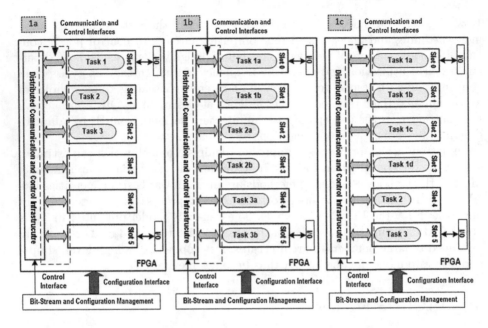

Fig. 1. Examples of ASP circuit configuration in MACROS framework

In case of any FPGA, reconfigurable resources can be broadly categorized into Logic Slices, Random Access Memory Blocks (BRAMs), Digital Signal Processing (DSP) slices and Input/Output Blocks (IOBs) [13]. For a combination of ASP circuit variants running on an FPGA, the total resource utilization in terms of these reconfigurable resources and the operating frequency can easily be made available for the system at run-time. We must therefore develop a model which is based on frequency and parameters of Logic, BRAMs, DSP slices and IOBs depending on which of these are used in ASP circuits of system tasks. To do so, power consumption behavior of each reconfigurable resource must be isolated. As the procedure is generic for each reconfigurable resource, it is discussed using only logic and BRAM slices for ease of explanation.

Step 1 - Identify General Equation for PCE Model: A test design is developed such that multiple test cases can be generated from it by varying logic utilization and/or memory. In the experiments conducted for the Zynq XC7Z020 device (further referred as Zynq), the test design is an integration of video stream processing IP cores for a 720p video frame standard. The design makes use of only logic and memory. It is well suited to permit variations up to 13300 logic slices and 140 BRAM slices available in the Zynq device [13]. For this step, 5 test designs are generated by varying only logic utilization from 3900 slices to 13100 slices in 5 steps. 10 BRAMs are used in the design, which remain constant throughout the test cases. Also for each of the 5 test designs, based on the 720p video standard, the operating frequency is varied in multiples of 37.125 MHz up to 185.625 MHz. Thus the 5 frequencies used are 37.125, 74.25,

111.375, 148.5 and 185.625 MHz. A maximum frequency of 185.625 MHz is used, as beyond this multiple, the timing requirements of the design start to fail for some test cases. Thus, a total of 25 test cases are generated for this step.

Dynamic power consumption (DPC) of Zynq is now measured for each test design. ZedBoard has an on-board current sense resister of 10 mΩ in series with its 12 V power supply [14]. Voltage across this resistor is measured using Agilent Technologies Digital Multimeter, U3401A. Current consumed by the board and its total power consumption is calculated from this voltage. Subtracting the static power of the board from the total power measured for a test case provides the DPC of Zynq for that case. Since the test design uses only FPGA resources, the calculated DPC corresponds to power consumed by Zynq alone.

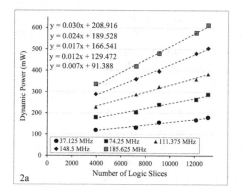 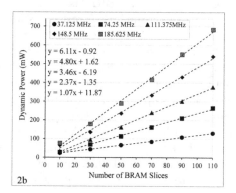

Fig. 2. Dynamic power consumption vs. logic slices and BRAMs

Although the obtained DPC is due to both, logic slices and BRAMs, variation in DPC is due to changes in number of logic slices. Hence, the obtained results are plotted with respect to logic slices at every frequency, as shown in Fig. 2a. From these plots, the linear equations representing the relation between power consumption and number of logic slices are obtained at every frequency, and are also shown in Fig. 2a. It can be observed that the linear coefficients are dependent on frequency. To add to that, the constant term in the equations is also seen increasing with frequency. This can further be split into a fixed constant and a frequency dependent offset, a portion of which is due to the 10 BRAMs in the design. Thus, the set of equations in Fig. 2a, can be summarized into one equation involving all parameters, namely, frequency, logic slices and BRAMs. This following general equation represents the model for DPC of any FPGA.

$$DPC_{(FPGA)}(mW) = \frac{F_{cc}}{F_{min}} \times \{C_{LS} \times N_{LS} + C_B \times N_B + C_F\} + B \qquad (1)$$

In (1), F_{cc} is current operating clock frequency and F_{min} is minimum operating frequency for the applications. C_{LS}, C_B and C_F are coefficients representing the individual effects of slices, BRAMs and frequency respectively. N_{LS} and N_B is the number of logic slices and BRAMs respectively. B is a constant offset.

In case of our experiments, F_{min} = 37.125 MHz. From Fig. 2a and (1), the model for DPC of Zynq XC7Z020 is obtained as:

$$DPC_{(FPGA)}(mW) = \frac{F_{cc}(MHz)}{37.125} \times \{0.006 \times N_{LS} + 30\} + 60 \qquad (2)$$

In (2), C_{LS} = 0.006, B = 60, N_B = 10 and 10 x C_B + C_F = 30. The individual values of C_B and C_F will be figured from the next step.

Step 2 - Isolate Behavior of BRAM Slices: In this step, both, BRAM and logic slices are increased simultaneously as opposed to increasing BRAM slices alone, as increasing BRAMs in the design will increase logic slices as well. For our set of experiments, 5 test cases are generated by varying logic and BRAM utilization on Zynq from 2900 slices and 20 BRAMs to 13100 slices and 120 BRAMs in 5 steps. Frequency is again varied in multiples of 37.125 MHz up to 185.625 MHz, thus generating a total of 25 test cases. DPC of Zynq is again obtained for each test case. Substituting the number of slices used in every test case in this step, in (2), and subtracting the calculated DPC values from the DPC values measured in this step, we get DPC of BRAMs alone. These values are plotted with respect to BRAM slices at different frequencies, as shown in Fig. 2b. From the set of equations in Fig. 2b, it is observed that the linear coefficients in this case too depend on frequency. Thus, the set of equations in Fig. 2b can be summarized into the following general equation which represents BRAM DPC.

$$DPC_{(BRAM)}(mW) = \frac{F_{cc}}{F_{min}} \times \{C_B \times N_B\} \qquad (3)$$

From Fig. 2b, in case of Zynq, dynamic power consumption of BRAMs is:

$$DPC_{(BRAM)}(mW) = \frac{F_{cc}(MHz)}{37.125} \times \{1.2 \times N_B\} \qquad (4)$$

Step 3 - Complete the Model Equation: From (4), C_B = 1.2. Substituting C_B in 10 x C_B + C_F = 30, obtained from (2), we get CF = 18. Thus, the combined model for power consumption due to logic slices, BRAM slices and frequency can be summarized for Zynq XC7Z020 as:

$$DPC_{(FPGA)}(mW) = \frac{F_{cc}(MHz)}{37.125} \times \{0.006 \times N_{LS} + 1.2 \times N_B + 18\} + 60 \qquad (5)$$

The first and second terms in (5) represent the individual effect of slices and BRAMs on power consumption. The third term is a frequency dependent constant and the last term is a constant offset. Using (5) and comparing the estimated results with the measured results, the maximum difference between the two is 30 mW. Thus, the model accurately represents the true DPC of Zynq XC7Z020. The same procedure can be followed to incorporate IOBs and DSP slices and also to derive a model for any FPGA.

From the derived PCE model, the following can be analyzed: Since the coefficient for logic slices is very small, the power consumed by the slices can be considered as a negligible constant, especially at low frequencies, for further simplification of the model. The BRAMs on the other hand have 200 times $(1.2/0.006 = 200)$ the impact of logic slices, which is a significant contribution to dynamic power. To add to that, power reduction due to reduction in frequency by a certain factor is more than due to reduction in resource utilization by the same factor. This means that if resource utilization is doubled and the frequency is halved, the power consumption reduces instead of staying the same.

The process from measurements for all test cases up to model derivation took around 8 h. Use of predictions from Xilinx Power Analyser (XPA) instead of measurements was also attempted. Default switching activity values resulted in a slope for increase in power due to increase in frequency, which was 60% higher than that from measurements. Generating SAIF file for an accurate activity factor took around 1 day for simulation per test case and hence was avoided. Using trial and error, when close to accurate activity factors were fed into XPA, the predicted slope for increase in power due to increase in frequency was equal to that from measurements. It can be concluded that XPA can be used if accurate activity factors are available, otherwise actual measurements is the most accurate and fastest method to obtain FPGA power consumption.

5   PCE Model Application Analysis

An application of the derived PCE model has been analyzed on the Zynq XC7Z020 device. The MACROS framework is deployed on the FPGA dividing it into 6 slots. The power source is a rechargeable battery with power budget of 2 A-h at 12 VDC. The workload comprises of three tasks: T1: Control and navigation task associated with GPS information processing at 400 MBps; T2: Video acquisition and processing video frames according to 720p standard at 120 frames per second (fps). This task can also be processed in 60 fps and 30 fps modes. T3: Communication and video-transmission task with maximum, intermediate and minimum bandwidth of 16 Mbps, 8 Mbps and 4 Mbps respectively. Among these, T1 is a critical task and needs to be active throughout the system life time providing un-compromised performance.

The system stores ASP circuit variants for each task. Each variant corresponds to a different set of performance, resource utilization, and operating frequency. At each performance specification, there can be multiple variants which have a different combination of resource utilization and operating frequency. A theoretical example of variants for the three tasks is presented in Table 1. The system estimates power consumption of each ASP circuit variant and its total consumption using the derived model. The system also needs spare slots to maintain a task's performance when frequency is reduced. So, in case of maximum available power, it chooses task variants at highest frequency and maximum performance to keep as many slots in reserve as possible. Decreasing task performance is considered only when system life time needs to be extended due to anticipated delay in battery recharge.

Table 1. ASP circuit variants for tasks T1, T2 and T3

Variant no.	No. of slots	F_{cc} (MHz)	Performance	No. of slices	No. of BRAMs	Power (mW)
T1 - 1	4	37.125	400 MBps	8591	80	226
T1 - 2	2	74.25	400 MBps	4312	40	244
T1 - 3	1	148.5	400 MBps	2200	20	281
T2 - 1	1	37.125	30 fps	1504	15	105
T2 - 2	2	37.125	60 fps	2950	30	132
T2 - 3	1	74.25	60 fps	1504	15	150
T2 - 4	4	37.125	120 fps	5853	60	185
T2 - 5	2	74.25	120 fps	2950	30	203
T2 - 6	1	148.5	120 fps	1504	15	240
T3 - 1	1	37.125	4 Mbps	2028	33	130
T3 - 2	2	37.125	8 Mbps	3960	66	181
T3 - 3	1	74.25	8 Mbps	2028	33	200
T3 - 4	4	37.125	16 Mbps	8046	132	285
T3 - 5	2	74.25	16 Mbps	3960	66	302
T3 - 6	1	148.5	16 Mbps	2028	33	339

Case 1: When the battery is fully charged at 100% capacity, variants TI-3, T2-6 and T3-6 are configured. They occupy one slot each and run at F_{cc} = 148.5 MHz at their maximum performance of 400 Mbps, 120 fps and 16 Mbps respectively. Thus, as seen in Fig. 1a, three slots can be used as spare resources for adaptation. From Table 1, DPC of the FPGA due to the three active tasks is equal to 860 mW. Adding the static power of 2200 mW, the total system power consumption is 3060 mW. Current consumption is therefore 255 mA, making the system sustainable up to 7.8 h.

Case 2: At the end of one hour, battery capacity reduces by 255 mA-h to around 87% of its capacity, as shown in Fig. 3b. System power budget shows that it can live for 6.8 h. If battery is recharged later than this period of time, the system can shut down. Suppose that the predicted time for battery recharge is 7 h. To adapt to the situation, the system, as shown in Fig. 1b, dynamically reconfigures variants T1-2, T2-5 and T3-5, all of which occupy two slots and operate at 74.25 MHz, maintaining their maximum performance. This adaptation of the SoPC architecture allows extension of active time without performance degradation. A calculation as above gives the current consumption as 245 75 mA. The system can now work for 7 h and 6 min and thus prevent its shut down before the battery can begin re-charging.

Case 3: After another hour, battery capacity is depleted to around 75% of its capacity, as shown in Fig. 3b. Based on system power budget, it can function up to 6.1 h. However, due to external conditions, the battery charge can

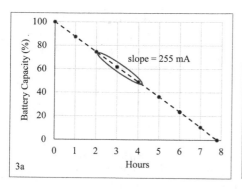
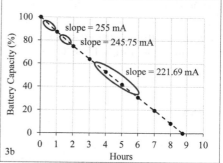

Fig. 3. System battery discharge without and with adaptation

now begin recharging only after 6.7 h: 42 min later than expected 6 h. The system should now dynamically reconfigure variants T1-1, T2-1 and T3-1 as shown in Fig. 1c, where $F_{cc} = 37.125$ MHz. ASP T1-1 occupies 4 slots to maintain its required performance. ASPs T2-1 and T3-1 occupy one slot each to provide a reduced performance of 30 fps and 4 Mbps respectively. The system now consumes a current of 221.69 mA to increase its active time by 40 min, again preventing shut down before the battery can begin re-charging.

If the system had continued at the initial 255 mA, it would function up to 7.8 h as shown in Fig. 3a. However, due to adaptation, the system sustains itself at the desired performance of T1 for around one hour more, as seen in Fig. 3b, while simultaneously preventing system shut down. This example thus demonstrates the system's ability to adapt to reduced power budget without performance degradation when reserved resources can compensate for lack of power. Also, when all resources are used, further reduction of the power budget can be compensated by reducing performance of non-critical tasks.

Configuring Zynq with a full bit-stream using JTAG consumes only 100 µW-h of energy. A dynamic reconfiguration cycle using partial bit-streams over the PCAP/ICAP port would consume much lesser energy and hence can be neglected compared to energy consumed by ASP circuits for their execution time.

6 Conclusion

A PCE model based architecture reconfiguration approach is presented for FPGA-centric systems such that they can adapt to changing power budget and continue execution of their critical tasks at required performance for extended time. The method for deriving the PCE model is presented using Xilinx Zynq XC7Z020 FPGA as an experimental platform but can be applied to any FPGA. An example of a FPGA-centric system was analyzed in light of sustaining its critical task performance with or without performance degradation of non-critical tasks according to available power. It was shown that the proposed approach also prevents system shut down before battery re-charge. The benefits of the presented adaptation mechanism can be better observed in case of a large system with more number of tasks and their implementation variants. However, this will require a special decision making mechanism, which selects ASP circuit variant for optimal SoPC implementation. This aspect is the next research objective.

References

1. Dumitriu, V., Kirischian, L., Kirischian, V.: Mitigation of variations in environmental conditions by sopc architecture adaptation. In: 2015 NASA/ESA Conference on Adaptive Hardware and Systems (AHS), pp. 1–8, June 2015
2. Dumitriu, V., Kirischian, L.: Sopc self-integration mechanism for seamless architecture adaptation to stream workload variations. IEEE Trans. Very Large Scale Integr. (VLSI) Syst. **24**(2), 799–802 (2016)
3. Dumitriu, V., Kirischian, L., Kirischian, V.: Run-time recovery mechanism for transient and permanent hardware faults based on distributed, self-organized dynamic partially reconfigurable systems. IEEE Trans. Comput. **65**(9), 2835–2847 (2016)
4. Tabkhi, H., Schirner, G.: Application-guided power gating reducing register file static power. IEEE Trans. Very Large Scale Integr. (VLSI) Syst. **22**(12), 2513–2526 (2014)
5. Hosseinabady, M., Nunez-Yanez, J.L.: Run-time power gating in hybrid arm-fpga devices. In: 2014 24th International Conference on Field Programmable Logic and Applications (FPL), pp. 1–6, September 2014
6. You, D., Chung, K.S.: Quality of service-aware dynamic voltage and frequency scaling for embedded GPUS. IEEE Comput. Archit. Lett. **14**(1), 66–69 (2015)
7. Khan, M.U.K., Shafique, M., Henkel, J.: Power-efficient workload balancing for video applications. IEEE Trans. Very Large Scale Integr. (VLSI) Syst. **24**(6), 2089–2102 (2016)
8. Rodríguez, A., Valverde, J., Castañares, C., Portilla, J., de la Torre, E., Riesgo, T.: Execution modeling in self-aware FPGA-based architectures for efficient resource management. In: 10th International Symposium on Reconfigurable Communication-centric Systems-on-Chip (ReCoSoC), pp. 1–8, June 2015
9. Ali, K.M.A., Atitallah, R.B., Fakhfakh, N., Dekeyser, J.L.: Using hardware parallelism for reducing power consumption in video streaming applications. In: 10th International Symposium on Reconfigurable Communication-centric Systems-on-Chip (ReCoSoC), pp. 1–7, June 2015
10. Jovanovic, B., Jevtic, R., Carreras, C.: Binary division power models for high-level power estimation of FPGA-based DSP circuits. IEEE Trans. Industr. Inf. **10**(1), 393–398 (2014)
11. Jovanovic, B., Jevtic, R., Carreras, C.: Triple-bit method for power estimation of nonlinear digital circuits in FPGAS. Electron. Lett. **46**(13), 903–905 (2010)
12. Senn, L., Senn, E., Samoyeau, C.: Modelling the power and energy consumption of NIOS II softcores on FPGA. In: 2012 IEEE International Conference on Cluster Computing Workshops, pp. 179–183, September 2012
13. Xilinx: Zynq-7000 All Programmable SoC Overview v1.10, September 2016
14. Xilinx: ZedBoard Hardware User's Guide v2.2 January 2014

Fault Tolerance

Exploring Performance Overhead Versus Soft Error Detection in Lockstep Dual-Core ARM Cortex-A9 Processor Embedded into Xilinx Zynq APSoC

Ádria Barros de Oliveira[✉], Lucas Antunes Tambara,
and Fernanda Lima Kastensmidt

Instituto de Informática - PGMICRO,
Universidade Federal Do Rio Grande Do Sul (UFRGS), Porto Alegre, Brazil
{adria.oliveira,latambara,fglima}@inf.ufrgs.br

Abstract. This paper explores the use of dual-core lockstep as a fault-tolerance solution to increase the dependability in hard-core processors embedded in APSoCs. As a case study, we designed and implemented an approach based on lockstep to protect a dual-core ARM Cortex-A9 processor embedded into Zynq-7000 APSoC. Experimental results show the effectiveness of the proposed approach in mitigate around 91% of bit flips injected in the ARM registers. Also, it is observed that performance overhead depends on the application size, the number of checkpoints performed, and the checkpoint and rollback routines.

Keywords: Fault tolerance · Embedded processors reliability · Lockstep · Soft error · Fault injection

1 Introduction

Heterogeneous computing architectures, which combine embedded processors and Field Programmable Gate Arrays (FPGAs), are increasingly being used for implementing mission-critical and reliable systems. In various fields of application, such as High Performance Computing (HPC) servers, non tripulated vehicles, and avionics systems, SRAM-based FPGA solutions are frequently used due the high reconfiguration flexibility, competitiveness costs, and capability of integrate complex systems on the same component. Embedded processors used in such systems can be based on soft- or hard-cores, in which the former are implemented in the logic elements of the FPGA and the latter are designed in dedicated silicon. FPGAs devices divided in Processing System (PS), which contain dedicated embedded processor in silicon, and the Programmable Logic (PL), the customizable logic, are called All Programmable System-on-Chip (APSoC).

Although modern commercial FPGAs offer a plethora of advantages, the ones that use SRAM-based technologies are very susceptible to soft errors caused by

© Springer International Publishing AG 2017
S. Wong et al. (Eds.): ARC 2017, LNCS 10216, pp. 189–201, 2017.
DOI: 10.1007/978-3-319-56258-2_17

radiation effects, as they are composed of millions of SRAM cells used to configure all the synthesized logic, the embedded processors, DSPs, and memories [1].
Embedded systems operating in aerospace applications are especially susceptible to radiation effects caused by ionized particles. Systems in avionics and at
ground level can also be affected by radiation-induced soft errors due to interaction with neutron particles present in the atmosphere [2]. These particles can
interact with silicon, provoking transient pulses in some susceptible areas. Such
episodes might lead to Single Event Upset (SEU) – or bit flips – in the sequential logic that could induce errors, generating Silent Data Corruption (SDC) and
other failures in the system, like hangs and crashes [3].

In this work, we developed an approach based on dual-core lockstep (DCLS)
technique to improve the dependability in the embedded dual-core ARM Cortex-
A9 processor of the Xilinx Zynq-7000 APSoC, and analyzed different setups in
terms of performance, execution time overhead, and soft error recovery. The
proposed DCLS architecture relies on two ARM cores running with independent
embedded BRAM memories to duplicate the application execution, and a checker
module to validate the processors' output and, in case of failure, rollback the
application. The novelty lies in to apply the DCLS to a hard-core ARM Cortex-
A9 in which, for the best of our knowledge, we have not seen a work that focus on
this processor. Besides, the use of an exclusive BRAM memory to each processor,
in order to avoid a single point of failure on the data memory increasing the
reliability. Results show that the overhead in the execution time strongly depends
on the number of checkpoints with the relation between the application size
and the size of checkpoint and rollback routines. A fault injection method was
developed to emulate soft errors in the dual-core processor to validate the DCLS
approach. Experiments indicate that the proposed DCLS approach for the dual-
core ARM-A9 is able to mitigate around 91% of the bit flips injected in the ARM
register file. Nevertheless, the proposed DCLS approach can be extendable to
other APSoC devices, such as Xilinx Zynq-7000 UltraScale and Intel Cyclone V.

2   Related Works

There are many fault-tolerance techniques to improve the dependability of
processors. They can be classified as hardware-based, software-based and hybrid
techniques [3]. DCLS is a hybrid fault-tolerance technique based on hardware
and software redundancy for error detection and correction. It uses the concepts
of checkpoint combined with rollback mechanism at software level, and processor
duplication and checker circuits at hardware level. The DCLS works by executing
the same application simultaneously and symmetrically in two identical processors, which are initialized to the same state with identical inputs (code, bus
operations and asynchronous events) during system start-up. So, during normal
operation the state of the two processors is identical from clock to clock. The
DCLS technique assumes that an error in either processor will cause a difference
between the states, which will eventually be manifested as a difference in the
outputs. Thus, the DCLS system monitors the outputs of both processors and

flags an error in the case of a discrepancy. Therefore, in an error-free execution, they are expected to perform the same operations allowing the monitoring of the processors' data, addressing, and controlling buses [4]. There is a checker module that monitors the processors and periodically compares the outputs to check for inconsistencies. Points of verification must be inserted in the program to indicate for the checker module when to stop execution and compare the outputs.

Several approaches of lockstep have been proposed over the years to improve the dependability of the systems in applications that require high reliability. The authors in [5,6] proposed a lockstep approach to protect the soft-core processor Leon2 programmed into a Xilinx Virtex device and concluded that the technique could detect and correct 99% of soft errors injected in the processor's registers. The authors focus on attacking the pipeline registers during fault injection, which originates a deterministic behavior with predictable results, thus the checker implementation can be adjusted to specific cases. The execution time overhead reported ranges from 17% to 54% depending on the amount of data. The authors irradiated the system for 24 h and observed 254 SEUs that resulted in rollback recovery and 13 SEUs resulted in device reconfiguration. In [7], the authors implemented a lockstep using an adapted 8-bit soft-core processor based on the PIC16 architecture and showed that the technique presented an area overhead of 300% and a high fault recovery rate. In [8], authors proposed an enhanced lockstep scheme using two soft-core MicroBlaze processors, which identifies the faulty core in case of an error. And then through a Configuration Engine, which is built using PicoBlaze cores, it is possible to recover from an upset by the combination of partial reconfiguration with roll-forward recovery technique. The lockstep scheme area overhead is around 297% against 384% using the TMR approach. A fault injection in the configuration bits revealed that 8.6% bits of the MicroBlaze core are sensitive, where 2.3% cause persistent errors. The average time duration to recover the processor in the enhanced lockstep is 23us, meanwhile in the basic lockstep is about 516us. In [9], authors propose lockstep architecture adopting a Virtex II-Pro target device which embeds two hard-core PowerPC processors. The reported results of faults injected in the processor's registers (user, special purpose, and control registers) show that the implemented approach was able to mitigate about 97% of the faults. Besides the showed DCLS solutions, there are some processors, like ARM Cortex-R5 processor [10], that already provides in its architecture a support to lockstep mode that could be configured to application reliability.

As one can see, DCLS can be implemented in soft-core or hard-core processors, although the majority of related works of DCLS in programmable devices uses soft-core processors. The main advantage of using soft-core processors is that these cores have open architecture, which the user can modify if needed. In the other hand, soft-core embedded in SRAM-based FPGAs are susceptible to persistent soft errors in the configuration bitstream, so periodically reconfiguration (scrubbing) must be performed to correct these persistent bit flips errors. Our proposed DCLS approach uses an hard-core processor embedded in APSoC that can take advantages of the programmable matrix, at the same time taking advantage of the high-performance hard-core processor. Thus, it is avoided persistent errors in the embedded processors caused by bit flips in the program-mable configurable blocks as occur with soft-core processors.

3   Proposed DCLS Technique in Zynq ARM-A9

The proposed DCLS architecture, showed in Fig. 1, is based on Zynq-7000 APSoC that provides on the PS a 32-bit 666 MHz dual-core ARM Cortex-A9 processor, which has two cache level (L1 and L2) embedded. In our approach, all processors' caches are disabled, since the sensitive area they introduce compro-mises the system reliability. According to [11], the addition of any cache memory affects the cross section of the ARM processor. In order to avoid single point of failures in the data memory and to minimize both ARM CPUs (CPU0 and CPU1) to contending to shared memory resources, each CPU is connected to its own private dual-port 64 KB BRAM memory, which stores the application data as well as the processor's context, that is only shared with the checker module IP. The BRAM's size strongly depends on the application and should be resized if needed. The two BRAM memories and the checker module are implemented in the PL part of Zynq, which runs at a frequency of 100MHz. Besides the BRAM memories, both CPUs are connected to an external shared DDR memory, which contains both CPUs' instruction memory and, in addition, can be used as an alternative safe memory to store the checkpoint of the system. In this paper, we explore two approaches of storing the checkpoint states, one storing only in BRAMs and other storing also a copy in the DDR. Although BRAM and DDR memories have EDAC capability, Multiple-Bit Upsets (MBUs) can occur and the reliability could be compromised. Thus, we consider alternative approaches to store the consistent states of the processors. By replicating the consistent state of the CPUs on the DDR memory, it is possible to increase the system relia-bility, once we can compare both stored values to detect errors. It is important to notice that the access time to the DDR memory is usually slower than the access to the BRAM memories, so the number of stores in the DDR should be analyzed to avoid compromising the system performance.

The DCLS functional flow is described in Fig. 2, where we can observe the application flow in each ARM CPU combined with the Checker module IP. The behavioral flow of the original program without lockstep is illustrated in Fig. 2(a). The Fig. 2(b) represents the application divided in code blocks, which is a section of code of the original program, besides the additional code necessary for lockstep implementation as the verification points, represented by the signatures status, and the checkpoint and the rollback routine. The number of code blocks that the original program is divided can be adjusted depending on the application requirements and it is directly connected with the number of verification points. When CPUs reach a verification point, the application execution is stalled, the cores are locked and the checker is activated to compare the results. If the outputs match, it is assumed that the processors do not have any errors, thus the current system state is consistent and can be saved for future reuse. This consists on a checkpoint operation that stores the processors' context, which includes all data

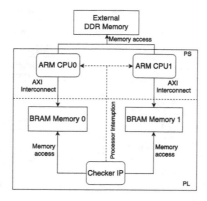

Fig. 1. Proposed lockstep architecture for dual-core ARM Cortex-A9.

resources used in the application execution (i.e. registers, main memory), on a memory considered safe and without errors. Then, the CPUs are unlocked and continue to run the application until they reach the next verification point. If the checker module IP detects any difference between the outputs, which implies in the occurrence of errors, a recovery method is applied and both processors roll back to a previous state. In the rollback operation, the CPUs' context are restored to a correct saved state. This means that the main memory and registers are replaced with the fault-free copy. Therefore, the entire system rolls back to a state without errors and restart the application execution from this point.

3.1 Checker Module

The checker module (Checker IP), which is a customized IP designed in HDL and implemented in the PL of the Zynq-7000 FPGA, snoops the operations performed by the two ARM CPUs by accessing both BRAM memories. Figure 2(c) presents an overview of the Checker behavior. The data verification is required when both CPUs reach to a verification point, which is indicated by writing a signature status (current processor's state) on the BRAM memory. To make sure that the CPUs are in a correct state, besides the outputs verification, the Checker compares the processors' registers. If there is any mismatch, an interruption is generated to both ARM CPUs indicating a rollback operation. Otherwise, it is launched an interruption to perform a checkpoint.

   Regarding the verification of the processors' registers, it is required to consider some characteristics. First, owing to the fact that after the reset the ARM registers are in undefined state, it is necessary to clean the general-purpose registers at the beginning of the program execution. Second, each CPU is connected to an independent BRAM memory implemented in the FPGA logic, which is mapped to different address. Third, both CPUs run the same application, however the program instructions of each one is stored in distinct addresses of the DDR memory. Fourth, it is defined in the architecture of the ARM processor [12] that general-purpose registers (R0 to R12) can be used by the software when the

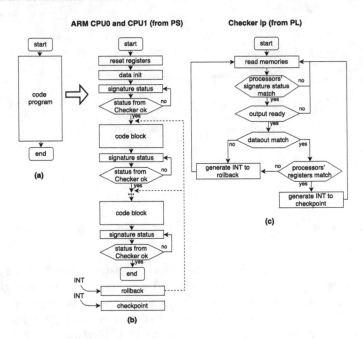

Fig. 2. Lockstep functional flow for ARM Cortex-A9 dual-core: (a) original code, (b) code with lockstep technique running in both CPUs and (c) the checker functionality.

CPU is in user mode, although there are systems modes that could access some of these registers to store instructions or system information. Finally, the ARM deprecates the use of the special registers - stack pointer (SP), link register (LR) and program counter (PC) registers - for any purpose other than as they are specified for; the incorrect handling of these registers could lead the system to an unpredictable behavior.

To guarantee that the application will not be locked on the code block execution due a fault in the system, it is configured a watchdog timer with twice the time required to run each code block. Therefore, if a CPU did not reach the verification point before the watchdog timer is over, it is considered a system inconsistency and the Checker operates the rollback mechanism.

3.2 Checkpoint Implementation

A checkpoint is performed to save a consistent state of the processors. When the Checker verifies that the system is error-free, it generates an interruption request to each CPU, which allows them access and save their context. For the sake of this paper, we assume as processor's context the following ARM CPU registers: general-purpose registers (R0 to R12); stack pointer (SP); link register (LR); and program counter (PC). The interruption mechanism provides a way to access the registers of the processor. When an interrupt is processed by a processor, the following actions are performed [13]:

1. The execution of the actual thread is stalled.
2. The registers of the processor are saved into the stack.
3. The interruption routine is executed.
4. The processor restores its context from the stack at the end of the interruption routine.
5. The processor continues the execution of previous thread.

Thus, when the *checkpoint interrupt routine* is executed, at point three, it accesses the processor's stack and makes a copy of the registers to the memory. Our approach considers two setups to save the processors' context. The *DCLS accessing BRAM memory only (DCLS_BR)* that uses the BRAM memories to store the processor's context. Therefore, the registers of CPU0 and CPU1 are stored in the BRAM0 and BRAM1, respectively. And the setup *DCLS accessing BRAM and DDR memories (DCLS_BR_DDR)* that saves the processor's context in both BRAM and external DDR memory. Besides, it is saved in the DDR all the data application stored in the BRAMs, as a way to improve the data reliability.

To deal with errors that could occur between the verification point and the context storage, we save the first checkpoint in two different memory address (just in *DCLS_BR* setup). In which the first is overwritten in every checkpoint and the other still unchanged. If it is necessary perform two consecutive rollbacks, without context storage between them, this indicates that the actual checkpoint has an error. Thus, the system is recovered to the first context saved, returning to the application begin. Although this approach has a performance penalty, it avoids a hang in the system caused by infinite rollback to a wrong context.

3.3   Rollback Implementation

A rollback consists in recovering the system to a safe state previously saved in the memory. This operation is performed when the Checker detects a mismatch in the CPU's data output at a verification point. In the application flow of the ARM CPU, after a code block execution, a signature with the processor's status is saved in the BRAM memory and the processor stays locked at the verification point. Meanwhile, the Checker verifies both CPUs. In case of any mismatch, the Checker generates an interruption request to each processor and the rollback operation is performed. As in the checkpoint, the interruption mechanism is used to access the processor's context. In the *rollback interrupt routine* the processor's stack is overwritten with the registers saved on the memory. When the processor restores the context from the stack, as presented at point four of the interruption request sequence, the system returns to a consistent state. In our approach, the execution program returns to the point just after the checkpoint and re-executes the code block, as expressed by the dotted line in the Fig. 2(b). Depending of the setup used to save the processor's context, the *rollback interrupt routine* has different behaviors. In the *DCLS_BR* the processor's stack is overwritten with the registers saved on the BRAM memory. And in the *DCLS_BR_DDR* the context is read from the DDR memory and in sequence the data on the BRAMs and the registers on the processor's stack are overwritten.

The critical aspect of this approach is to define the number of verification points and to identify all the required resources to save in the processors' context, saving only the information relevant to restore the processors' state in case of error recovery. The efficiency of the methods depends on these decisions. Although, frequently interrupting the processors affects directly the system's performance, it is necessary to perform the checkers as often as possible to minimize the fault latency [9]. Therefore, the system designer must find the tradeoff that minimizes the performances loses for the verification and for recover time.

4   Fault Injection Methodology

To validate the efficiency of the proposed lockstep approach, we implemented a fault injector method, which randomly injects bit flips at the registers of the dual-core ARM processor directly in the board by interruption. The ARM registers susceptible to upsets from the fault injector are: the general-purpose (R0 to R12) and the specifics SP (stack pointer), LR (link register) and PC (program counter) registers. The faulty injection strategy adopted aims to be less intrusive as possible by using interrupt mechanisms to inject faults in the processor registers [14–16]. The fault injection experiment setup used for gathering the results is presented in Fig. 3(a). The system is composed by the following modules: the *Power Control*, a electrical device responsible for power up the board; the *System Controller*, a software application located at a host computer that manages the Power Control and stores the fault injection logs receive by serial communication; and the *Injector Module*, a customized IP designed in HDL and implemented in the PL part of the Zynq-7000 that perform the fault injection procedure. Figure 3(b) shows the flow diagram of the fault injection procedure. In the first step, the Injector is configured with a random injection data, which contains the injection time and the fault target location (the ARM CPU and register in which the fault must be injected, besides the specific bit to be flipped). Due to the complexity of generating random numbers in FPGA logic, the injection configuration is rendered by the ARM CPU0 before it starts the application and then it is read by the Injector Module. It is important to note that the injection time is defined based on the execution time of the application, which means that a fault could be inserted at any moment during the application time as in real scenarios. Once the injector module has been configured, it starts to count clock cycles until it reaches the injection time. Then, the injector module launches an interruption to the specific CPU indicated by the configuration. In the *injection interrupt routine*, the target register is read, a XOR mask with the appropriated bit to flip is applied to its value and, then, the register is overwritten.

After the fault injection, the injector module starts a watchdog timer with twice the value of the application time and it remains waiting for the end of the application. If the application does not end before the watchdog timer is over, it is considered a occurrence of a *HANG*, which is defined as a crash in the system or an infinite loop in the application. In case of the application finished on time, the injector module compares the results generated by both CPUs with the gold

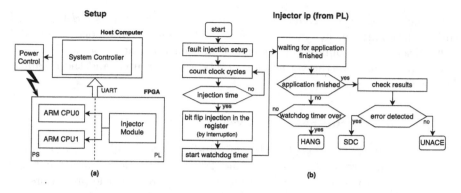

Fig. 3. Fault injection: (a) experiment setup and (b) procedure flow.

results. If there is any mismatch, it is indicated that a *SDC* occurred. Otherwise, it is indicated an *UNACE*, which represents that the bit flip was effectless or the fault was detected and corrected by the implemented lockstep.

5   Experimental Results

We selected applications based on a set of matrix multiplications operations as benchmark to evaluate the proposed DCLS in the ARM-A9. Both CPUs execute the bare-metal application in hand-shake. Each full matrix multiplication operation is considered one code block defined in Fig. 2(b). Each matrices operation multiplies different matrices inputs, which contains data of 32 bits, that are stored in BRAM memory. As the objective is investigating the effect of the code block size and the number of code blocks in the application in terms of performance and soft error correction, we consider applications with five matrix sizes $(3 \times 3, 10 \times 10, 20 \times 20, 30 \times 30$ and $40 \times 40)$ and composed of three (short application) or six (long application) code blocks. To validate the proposed DCLS, it was used the setups *DCLS_BR* and *DCLS_BR_DDR*, and the *UNHARDENED* version, which is not protected against soft errors and runs its applications only on CPU0. The CPU's L1 and L2 caches are disabled, and it is connected to a BRAM memory, which stores the application data, and to the external DDR memory, which stores the program instruction.

The versions of the application use the following ARM general-purpose registers: R0 to R5, R8, and R11; besides the specifics: SP, LR and PC. This represents the usage of 68% of the register file. Although all versions were compiled allocating the same registers, the exposure time and functionalities during the execution time are different, which affects the reliability as verified in the fault injection experiments. In all versions, *UNHARDENED* and DCLS setups, the R0 to R3 and R11 registers are used in the matrix multiplications operations and the R4 and R5 registers are used in the *printf* function to show the performance information. Furthermore, the R0 to R3 and R11 registers are also used to save and restore the context in the DCLS setups. To verify the flow execution consistency, we defined a counter stored on the R8 register. In *UNHARDENED* versions the counter is incremented after a matrix multiplication operation. And, in DCLS setups the counter is incremented in each verification point. Thus, it is possible to check if all the verification points were executed and the reliability of the rollback operation.

5.1 Area and Performance Analysis

The area resources in terms of LUTs and flip-flops are detailed in Table 1. One can observe the area overhead is around 280% for the logic implemented in the CLBs, which is consistent with related works [7,8]. For the processors and memories, the area overhead is 100%. Table 2 reports the results in terms of performance comparing the execution times of different matrix sizes, distinct setups and also for two application sizes. The execution time obtained depends on several factors as following: the time required to both CPUs execute the application in hand-shake; the application size; the number of checkpoints performed; the time needed to run the interrupt routine that implements the context saving, which is directly affected by the amount of data stored; and the execution time of the rollback operation (just in case of errors). As described in the Table 2, the performance overhead is significantly higher, around 425% to *DCLS_BR* and 625% to *DCLS_BR_DDR*, when the execution time of the application is much smaller compared to the time to perform the checkpoint and the rollback routines. For large applications, the time overhead of *DCLS_BR* is less than 25%, which can be an acceptable overhead in many applications that require high reliability and availability. When considering the setup *DCLS_BR_DDR* the time overhead in all versions is higher compared to *DCLS_BR*, as expected, due the time to access the DDR memory.

5.2 Fault Injection Analysis

In order to evaluate the impact of soft errors in a dual-core ARM processor and to validate the efficiency of the proposed DCLS approach, we run an extensive fault injection campaign in the Zedboard. We tested long and short applications performing 3×3, 10×10 and 20×20 matrix multiplications in *UNHARDENED*, *DCLS_BR* and *DCLS_BR_DDR* setups. Table 2 shows the fault injection results. For the *UNHARDENED* versions, up to 70% of the injected faults are UNACE. For the DCLS setups, one can observe that the DCLS approach is able to recover around 91% of the injected faults in the *DCLS_BR* and 90.5% in *DCLS_BR_DDR*

Table 1. Area overhead analysis

Setup	Area (LUTs/FFps)	# ARM CPUs	# BRAM
UNHARDENED	833/996	1	1
DCLS_BR	3,130/3,425 (275% / 243%)	2	2
DCLS_BR_DDR	3,130/3,425 (275% / 243%)	2	2

Table 2. Performance overheads and fault injection analysis for each setup running different matrix sizes

Setup			Performance info	Fault injection		
Version	App. size (# M × M)	Matrix sizes	# Clock cycles (% overhead)	UNACE [%]	SDC [%]	HANG [%]
UNHARDENED	Short (3)	3 × 3	98,280	69.6	12.0	18.4
		10 × 10	2,207,018	64.8	8.5	26.7
		20 × 20	15,763,012	67.0	13.2	19.8
		30 × 30	51,343,884	-	-	-
		40 × 40	119,758,930	-	-	-
	Long (6)	3 × 3	182,876	66.3	8.3	25.4
		10 × 10	4,291,642	63.6	7.3	29.1
		20 × 20	30,827,142	64.6	9.1	26.3
		30 × 30	99,950,676	-	-	-
		40 × 40	231,917,552	-	-	-
DCLS_BR	Short (3)	3 × 3	516,296 (425.3%)	90.9	1.3	7.8
		10 × 10	2,930,374 (32.8%)	88.3	0.0	11.7
		20 × 20	19,896,474 (26.2%)	88.3	0.0	11.7
		30 × 30	63,689,580 (24.0%)	-	-	-
		40 × 40	148,497,868 (23.6%)	-	-	-
	Long (6)	3 × 3	707,732 (287.0%)	90.8	0.2	9.0
		10 × 10	5,780,740(34.7%)	88.2	0.0	11.8
		20 × 20	38,618,858(25.3%)	89.4	0.0	10.6
		30 × 30	124,760,012(24.8%)	-	-	-
		40 × 40	287,243,296(23.9%)	-	-	-
DCLS_BR_DDR	Short (3)	3 × 3	712,544 (625.0%)	86.4	0.1	13.5
		10 × 10	4,088,692 (85.3%)	86.4	0.2	13.4
		20 × 20	23,319,986 (47.9%)	90.2	0.4	9.4
		30 × 30	71,256,642 (38.8%)	-	-	-
		40 × 40	161,541,952 (34.7%)	-	-	-
	Long (6)	3 × 3	1,009,842 (452.2%)	90.5	0.1	9.4
		10 × 10	7,336,424 (70.9%)	88.6	0.0	11.4
		20 × 20	44,173,342 (43.3%)	90.1	0.0	9.9
		30 × 30	137,032,766 (37.1%)	-	-	-
		40 × 40	311,447,120 (34.3%)	-	-	-

setup. Up from 8% of the bit flips that could not be recovered provoke hangs in the DCLS system. This result can be explained by two facts. First, there are some registers (R0, R1, R11 and R12) that could not be protected by our solution because these registers have distinct values in CPU0 and CPU1 during the normal program execution. Therefore, if a bit flip affect one of them during a code block execution and its effect is masked, witch consequently does not affect the outputs, the Checker will not detect the error in those registers. This will lead to store the actual context with the wrong values as a safe state. Thus, the fault can manifest itself at the next code block execution leading a rollback operation that will restore the wrong context causing, then, an infinite loop in system. The hang or timeout can be identified, but only can be recovered by reset. In addition, if a fault affect any of the special registers (SP, LR or PC), generating an illegal data or instruction value, the processor will be directed to a data or prefect abort leading to a system crash. Finally, the number of injected faults in our approach that produce SDCs (wrong outputs values) is negligible, even so they can be explained by bit flips in the LR or PC registers that can direct the program pointer to the end of the application. Thus, when the outputs results are compared with the gold ones they mismatch and a SDC is indicated.

6   Conclusion

This paper presents a lockstep approach to mitigate radiation-induced soft errors in embedded processors. The proposed DCLS was implemented on Zynq-7000 APSoC from Xilinx, to protect the embedded dual-core ARM Cortex-A9 processor. As results, we observed that for larges applications the use of the technique has an acceptable effect in the system's performance. By fault injection experiments we observed that the presented DCLS approach improved the reliability and dependability of the dual-core ARM processor. As future work, we will extend the technique to protect all of the processors' registers and to reset the application when a hang is detected. Besides, we will submit the system to real radiation experiments to compare the fault injection results and validate the approach in a harsh environment.

References

1. Siegle, F., et al.: Mitigation of radiation effects in sram-based fpgas for space applications. ACM Comput. Surv. **47**(2), 37:1–37:34 (2015)
2. Normand, E.: Correlation of inflight neutron dosimeter and seu measurements with atmospheric neutron model. IEEE Trans. Nucl. Sci. **48**(6), 1996–2003 (2001)
3. Azambuja, J., et al.: Hybrid Fault Tolerance Techniques to Detect Transient Faults in Embedded Processors. Springer International Publishing, Switzerland (2016)
4. Bowen, N.S., Pradham, D.K.: Processor- and memory-based checkpoint and roll-back recovery. Computer **26**(2), 22–31 (1993)
5. Reorda, M.S., et al.: A low-cost see mitigation solution for soft-processors embedded in systems on pogrammable chips. In: DATE, pp. 352–357, April 2009
6. Violante, M., et al.: A low-cost solution for deploying processor cores in harsh environments. IEEE Trans. Ind. Electron. **58**(7), 2617–2626 (2011)
7. Gomez-Cornejo, J., et al.: Fast context reloading lockstep approach for SEUs mitigation in a FPGA soft core processor. In: IECON, pp. 2261–2266, November 2013
8. Pham, H.M., et al.: Low-overhead fault-tolerance technique for a dynamically reconfigurable softcore processor. IEEE Trans. Comput. **62**(6), 1179–1192 (2013)
9. Abate, F., et al.: A new mitigation approach for soft errors in embedded processors. IEEE Trans. Nucl. Sci. **55**(4), 2063–2069 (2008)

10. Cortex-R5 and Cortex-R5F Technical Reference Manual. Rev: r1p1 (2010–2011)
11. Tambara, L.A., et al.: Analyzing the impact of radiation-induced failures in programmable SoCs. IEEE Trans. Nucl. Sci. **63**(4), 2217–2224 (2016)
12. ARM® Architecture Reference Manual. ARMv7-A and ARMv7-R edition (2012)
13. Taylor, A.: How to use interrupts on the Zynq SoC. Xcell J. **87**, 38–43 (2014)
14. Rezgui, S., et al.: Estimating error rates in processor-based architectures. IEEE Trans. Nucl. Sci. **48**(5), 1680–1687 (2001)
15. Velazco, R., et al.: Predicting error rate for microprocessor-based digital architectures through C.E.U. (code emulating upsets) injection. IEEE Trans. Nucl. Sci. **47**(6), 2405–2411 (2000)
16. Lins, F., et al.: Register file criticality on embedded microprocessor reliability. In: Proceedings RADECS (2016)

Applying TMR in Hardware Accelerators Generated by High-Level Synthesis Design Flow for Mitigating Multiple Bit Upsets in SRAM-Based FPGAs

André Flores dos Santos[✉], Lucas Antunes Tambara,
Fabio Benevenuti, Jorge Tonfat, and Fernanda Lima Kastensmidt

Instituto de Informática – PGMICRO,
Universidade Federal do Rio Grande do Sul (UFRGS), Porto Alegre, Brazil
{afdsantos, latambara, jltseclen, fglima}@inf.ufrgs.br,
fabio.benevenuti@ufrgs.br

Abstract. This paper investigates the use of Triple Modular Redundancy (TMR) in hardware accelerators designs described in C programming language and synthesized by High Level Synthesis (HLS). A setup composed of a soft-core processor and a matrix multiplication design protected by TMR and embedded into an SRAM-based FPGA was analyzed under accumulated bit-flips in its configuration memory bits. Different configurations using single and multiple input and output workload data streams were tested. Results show that by using a coarse grain TMR with triplicated inputs, voters, and outputs, it is possible to reach 95% of reliability by accumulating up to 61 bit-flips and 99% of reliability by accumulating up to 17 bit-flips in the configuration memory bits. These numbers imply in a Mean Time Between Failure (MTBF) of the coarse grain TMR at ground level from 50% to 70% higher than the MTBF of the unhardened version for the same reliability confidence.

Keywords: FPGA · Soft error · Fault injection · HLS

1 Introduction

SRAM-based FPGAs are susceptible to radiation-induced upsets, more specifically Single Event Upsets (SEUs) in their configuration memory bits and embedded memory cells. SEUs can also occur in the Flip-Flops (FFs) of the Configuration Logic Blocks (CLBs) used to implement the user's sequential logic. In this case, the bit-flip has a transient effect and the next load of the flip-flop can correct it. Multiple Bit Upsets (MBUs) can also occur in SRAM-based FPGAs due to charge sharing and accumulation of upsets. Thus, the majority of the errors observed in SRAM-based FPGAs used in harsh environments come from bit-flips (SEUs, MBUs) in the configuration memory bits and, therefore, Triple Modular Redundancy (TMR) with majority voters is commonly used to mask errors combined with reconfiguration [1]. Bit-flips in the bitstream are only corrected by partial or full reconfiguration. However, according to the reconfiguration rate, upsets can accumulate in the FPGA configuration memory of FPGAs.

© Springer International Publishing AG 2017
S. Wong et al. (Eds.): ARC 2017, LNCS 10216, pp. 202–213, 2017.
DOI: 10.1007/978-3-319-56258-2_18

TMR is usually applied at Register Transfer Level (RTL) or gate-level descriptions in the FPGA design flow. It can be implemented manually or automatically if appropriate tools are available. There are many challenges on applying TMR in a design that will be synthesized into an SRAM-based FPGA. The first one is to ensure that commercial synthesis tools will not remove any logic redundancy [2]. The second one is to explore the TMR implementation in a way that it can achieve high error coverage with an efficient area and performance overhead. Depending on the architecture of the design implemented into SRAM-based FPGAs, more or less configuration bits are used and more or less susceptible bits may be responsible for provoking an error in the design output. However, it is not only the number of used bits that determine the sensitivity of a design. The error masking effect of the application algorithm and the TMR implementation play an important role. Moreover, there are trade-offs in the architecture such as area, performance, execution time, and types of resources utilized that may direct contribute to SEU susceptibility analysis in FPGAs.

Hardware accelerators are built from SRAM-based FPGAs to improve the performance of applications running on embedded hard-core and soft-core processors. In this context, High-Level Synthesis (HLS) is widely used for reducing the development time and exploring efficiently the design space of algorithms with different architectures. HLS is an automated design process that starts interpreting an algorithm described in a high-level software programmable language (e.g. C, C++) to automatically produce an RTL hardware that performs the same function.

However, SRAM-based FPGAs and APSoCs are demanded in many high reliability applications such as satellites, autonomous vehicles, servers, and others. Therefore, the code executed in the processor and the hardware accelerator must be able to mitigate SEUs. With regard to HLS-based designs, applying TMR in the high-level algorithm so that the resulted RTL code is protected is challenging, because there are different ways to implement the TMR scheme and its voters, as well as the input and output interfaces of the design.

This work investigates the use of TMR in HLS-based designs for mitigating multiple bit upsets. TMR schemes are implemented directly in the algorithms described in C programming language to be synthesized in the Xilinx Vivado HLS [3] tool for use in Xilinx SRAM-based devices. Nevertheless, we believe the proposed approach and the achieved results are capable to be generic and extendable to other HLS tools. Our objective is to evaluate different TMR implementations at C-level under soft errors. Area resources, performance overheads, and error rate for multiple bit upsets are evaluated for different TMR approaches. TMR can mitigate SEUs but not necessarily MBUs. However, since the implemented voters mask signals bit by bit, many errors due to MBUs that do not affect the same bit are still capable of being masked. Previous works [4] have shown that the use of Diverse TMR (DTMR) may work properly under SEU accumulation in the configuration memory bits. In this work, we observe how TMR implemented at C-level is also able to mitigate accumulated upsets.

Some previous studies related to HLS have investigated the trade-offs among performance, area, and types of resources used [5–7]. Other studies have investigated the use of TMR in RTL designs generated by HLS for use in Application Specific Integrated Circuit (ASIC) devices [8]. However, from the best of our knowledge, there is no study that have investigated the use of TMR applied at C language level to be synthesized in HLS and evaluated in SRAM-based FPGAs for SEUs.

The case-studied FPGA is a 28-nm Artix-7 FPGA from Xilinx. Different TMR approaches were implemented in a matrix multiplication algorithm described in C language connected to a soft-core Microblaze responsible for sending and receiving the workload data stream. Bit-flips were injected into the FPGA bitstream by a fault injection framework developed in our research group [5]. Several fault injection campaigns were performed for all the designs in order to identify the error rate under accumulated bit-flips. Results show that the TMR can mask multiple errors as expected, but redundancy in the voters and in the interface is mandatory to increase reliability. Results show that by using a coarse grain TMR with triplicated inputs, voters, and outputs, it is possible to reach 95% of reliability by accumulating up to 61 bit-flips and 99% of reliability by accumulating up to 17 bit-flips in the configuration memory bits. These numbers imply in a Mean Time Between Failure (MTBF) of the coarse grain TMR at ground level from 50% to 70% higher than the MTBF of the unhardened version for the same reliability confidence.

2   TMR in Hardware Accelerators Generated by HLS

The concept of TMR is to have three identical copies processing data and a majority voter voting their outputs to mask errors in one of the copies. TMR can be implemented in hardware at gate level, for instance, where each module is triplicated and voters are added, but it can also be implemented in software, where part of the code is triplicated and its outputs are voted. According to the granularity of the TMR and the location of the majority voters, there is the coarse grain TMR (CGTMR), in which voters are placed only at the outputs of the design, and there is the fine grain TMR (FGTMR), in which voters are placed at the outputs of all or selected flip-flops and/or combinational logic, according to the design requirements. In this work, we are implementing TMR in a piece of high-level code to generate a hardware block through HLS. Thus, after synthesis, redundant hardware and majority voters are automatically generated. The input/output interfaces can be triplicated or not. However, if the interface is not triplicated, single point of failures can be observed in the TMR design.

When describing an algorithm to be synthesized by an HLS tool, one can consider that the algorithm source code is composed of operations, conditional statements, loops, and functions. Therefore, TMR must be implemented in these code structures. The question is how to triplicate all these structures to generate coarse or fine grain TMR in an efficient way, ensuring that the redundant logic will not be removed and, at the same time, being able to take advantage of some of the optimization strategies usually provided by HLS tools.

By default, an HLS tool translates each high-level function call in an RTL block. As consequence, if a function is called three times, three identical RTL blocks will be generated and the HLS tool will interpret that they can be executed in parallel if no data dependencies exist among them. Conversely, if we perform an operation three times in sequence inside a same function, the HLS tool will generate a serial hardware in which each operation will be executed sequentially, one at a time. With regards to the majority

voters, since they are always implemented as a function call, they are always synthesized as independent RTL blocks. These are the main principles in which our
investigation relies. Lastly, based on these approaches, one can observe that in a
modularized design (parallel), the majority voters are placed separately of the TMR
blocks, while in a non-modularized design (serial), the majority voters are placed
together with the TMR circuitry. In this work, we investigate coarse grain TMR
implemented in parallel, named CGPTMR.

For hardware accelerators, the interface to receive the workload data stream is very
important. In Xilinx devices, high-performance hardware accelerators are usually connected to soft- or hard-core processors through a Direct Memory Access (DMA) interface and Advanced eXtensible Interface Stream (AXI-S) ports. This interconnect
infrastructure provides a pipelined control that enables the software running on the
processor to queue multiple tasks requests, reducing its latency. According to [9], each
accelerator operates as an independent thread, synchronized in hardware at the transport
level by AXI-S handshaking, with the input arrival and accelerator hardware
"start/done" synchronization barriers realized by the Stream interface of the DMA.

The architecture of the proposed evaluation setup is composed of the design generated by the HLS (here referred as the Design Under Test - DUT), a Microblaze
soft-core processor, which is a 32-bit 5-state pipeline Reduced Instruction Set Computer (RISC) soft processor, Advanced eXtensible Interface (AXI) units, memories
(BRAM), Direct Memory Access (DMA) unit and the fault injector framework, as
described in Fig. 1. Note that in Fig. 1(a) there is only one interface for communication, while the setup in Fig. 1(b) the input and output interfaces are triplicated.

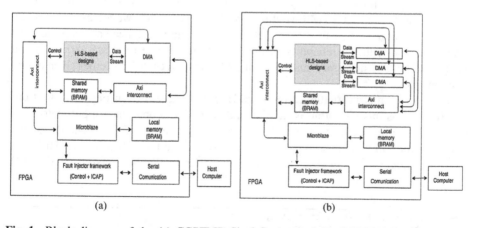

(a)   (b)

Fig. 1. Block diagram of the (a) CGPTMR SingleStream and (b) CGPTMR MultipleStream
case-study designs connected to the Microbaze soft-core processor and fault injection framework.

Figure 2 shows an execution time representation of a piece of code implemented in
an HLS tool in terms of the number of steps to perform input reads, execution, and
outputs writes. Each step can take several clock cycles. The algorithm execution
contains the read of inputs, the main execution code, and the write of outputs

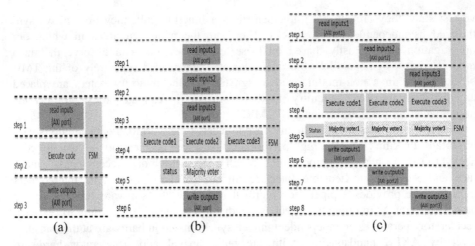

Fig. 2. The three versions of the M × M implementations: Unhardened with single stream(a), CGPTMR with single stream(b) and CGPTMR with multiple stream(c) represented in the number of steps to run the applications.

(Fig. 2(a)). In case of TMR, the redundancy can be implemented in parallel by triplicating the functions as represented in Fig. 2(b) and maintaining the single stream AXI port interface. In this case, each function is triplicated and a single voter is placed at the end of the code to vote out the data outputs. This scheme is named coarse grain parallel TMR with single stream (CGPTMR SingleStream). The voters and interfaces can also be triplicated, as shown in Fig. 2(c). This scheme is named coarse grain parallel TMR with multiple stream (CGPTMR MultipleStream). In this work, we are exploring these two implementations to analyze how area and performance overhead are impacted and comparing also with the reliability of the TMR scheme. The resource allocation and binding select the necessary and efficient RTL resources to implement behavioral functionalities.

We selected matrix multiplication (MxM) algorithm, shown in Fig. 3, to start our investigation, as this algorithm is rich in parallelism and loops. Each input matrix is a 6 × 6 8-bits array generating a 6 × 6 16-bits array output. Three versions of the M × M algorithm were implemented and generated using the Xilinx Vivado HLS tool from the C algorithm source code: TMR Coarse Grain Parallel version (CGPTMR)

```
read data from the input stream: a, b
void matrixmul(matrix a, matrix b, matrix res){
    for(i=0; i<MAT_DIM; i++){
        for(j=0; j<MAT_DIM; j++){
            res[i][j] = 0;
            for(k=0; k<MAT_DIM; k++){
                res[i][j] += a[i][k] * b[k][j];
}}}}
write data to the output stream: res
```

Fig. 3. Unhardened matrix multiplication algorithm without optimizations.

without optimization and single stream input, output data, TMR Coarse Grain Parallel version (CGPTMR) without optimization and multi stream input and output data, and the unhardened version without optimization single stream input, output data.

It is important to mention that for TMR implementations, it is not advised to use the Vivado HLS optimization option named *function inline*, which optimizes designs for area. Function inline removes the function hierarchy aiming to improve area by allowing the components within the function to be better shared or optimized with the logic in the calling function, which is something that is not recommended for redundant circuits.

The *CGPTMR version* code is represented in Fig. 4 with single stream and in Fig. 5 with multiple streams. Each function call is replicated. Optimizations performed in the

```
read the data from the stream: a0, b0, a1, b1, a2, b2
matrixmul(a0, b0, mat_res0);
matrixmul(a1, b1, mat_res1);
matrixmul(a2, b2, mat_res2);

// voter
for(i=0; i<MAT_DIM; i++){
    for(j=0; j<MAT_DIM; j++){
        voter_func(mat_res1[i][j],mat_res2[i][j],mat_res3[i][j],voterOutput);
        mVoter[i*MAT_DIM+j] = voterOutput.mVoter;
        status[i*MAT_DIM+j] = voterOutput.mStatus;
            }
        }
write the data to the stream: mVoter
write the data to the stream: mStatus
```

Fig. 4. Coarse Grain Parallel TMR (CGPTMR) with single stream.

```
read the data from input the stream0: a0, b0
read the data from input the stream1: a1, b1
read the data from input the stream2: a2, b2

matrixmul(a0, b0, res0);
matrixmul(a1, b1, res1);
matrixmul(a2, b2, res2);

// voter
for(i=0; i<MAT_DIM; i++){
    for(j=0; j<MAT_DIM; j++){
    voter_func(res1[i][j], res2[i][j], res3[i][j], mVoter1[i*MAT_DIM+j]);
    voter_func(res1[i][j], res2[i][j], res3[i][j], mVoter2[i*MAT_DIM+j]);
    voter_func(res1[i][j], res2[i][j], res3[i][j], mVoter3[i*MAT_DIM+j]);
    status_func(res1[i][j], res2[i][j], res3[i][j], mSstatus[i*MAT_DIM+j]);
}}
write data to the output stream0: mVoter1
write data to the output stream1: mVoter2
write data to the output stream2: mVoter3
write data to the output stream3: mStatus
```

Fig. 5. Coarse Grain Parallel TMR (CGPTMR) with multi stream.

function are extended to all the replicas. The majority voter votes the data output bit by bit after the call of the three redundant functions. The status is used to check bit by bit if there is any difference among the three modules. Status equal to zero means that all bits match, otherwise status is equal to one.

3 Fault Injection Method for Accumulated SEUs

Fault injection (FI) by emulation is a well-known method to analyze the reliability of a design implemented in an SRAM-based FPGA. The original bitstream configured into the FPGA can be modified by an embedded design or a computer program by flipping one of the bits of the bitstream, one at a time. This bit-flip emulates an SEU in the configuration memory.

The fault injector platform used in this work is based on the work presented in [5]. Our fault injection platform is composed of an ICAP controller circuit embedded in the FPGA and a script running on a monitor computer. The ICAP controller circuit controls the Internal Configuration Access Port (ICAP) and is connected to the script, which defines the injection area and type of fault injection (sequential or random) and controls the campaign. Faults are only injected in the area of the DUT and in their configuration bits related to CLBs (LUTs, user FFs, and interconnections), DSP resources (DSP48E), and clock distribution interconnections. Faults are not injected in BRAM configuration bits in order not to affect the inputs and outputs of the DUT. The flow and the design floorplanning are shown in Fig. 6.

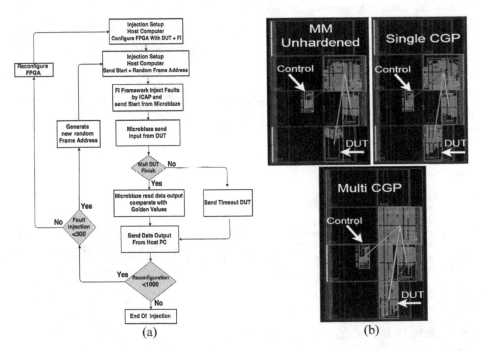

Fig. 6. The fault injection methodology in (a) and the FPGA floorplanning of designs in (b).

The Microblaze is responsible to send the input data as a data stream through AXI connections, receive the data output stream, and to compare the received values with the reference ones. The data is sent in 288 bits (6 × 6 8-bit matrix data) through the AXI interface. All the system runs at 100 MHz. The execution time of the Microblaze is around 175,727 clock cycles, which includes the time to send the control to the DUT, send the data inputs, wait for the DUT execution, read data outputs, compare the values, and wait for the fault injection framework next injection. For the DUT design, the execution time contains the number of clock cycles for reading the input data, execute the multiplication of matrix, voting, and writing data output. As an example, for the CGPTMR SingleStream, it is needed 216 clock cycles for reading the input data, 710 clock cycles to execute the HLS application, 156 clock cycles to execute the majority voter, 36 clock cycles to write the voter data, and 36 clock cycles to write the status data. The total time spent to perform all operations is 1,154 clock cycles.

4 Experimental Results

Table 1 presents the area resources and performance. The area can be evaluated by the number of LUTs, flip-flops, and DSP blocks. One can notice that the TMR designs present very similar areas. In this work, we mapped all the designs to the same target area of 388 frames. The area overhead of the TMR designs is three times or more, as expected. The maximum overhead is reached when the inputs and outputs AXI interfaces are triplicated. In terms of performance, each TMR design presents a very different execution time compared to the unhardened version. As explained, the execution time is calculated by the number of clock cycles needed to read the input matrices, execute, vote, and write the output matrices. The performance overhead of the TMR designs comes from the fact that the data input and data output is now triplicated in time as well, and the voting phase also takes several clock cycles of the total execution time, as shown in Fig. 2.

Accumulated SEUs where injected as described in Sect. 3. Although each design uses a different amount of resources as detailed in Table 1, the fault injection campaigns considered the same injection area for all designs. Thus, we stablish a condition similar to all designs, which emulates a same fluence of particles on its surface, for instance.

In this work, each DUT was implemented in a rectangular physical block of 388 configuration memory frames. Since a frame on Xilinx Artix-7 FPGA has 3,232 bits,

Table 1. Resource usage and performance results of each case-study design

Design version	Area resources			Performance
	# LUTs/FFs	# DSP48E	# essential bits	Exec. time (clock cycles)
CGPTMR SingleStream	1216/692	3	234,884	1,154
CGPTMR MultiStream	1791/1122	3	371,950	1,228
Unhardened	497/340	1	107,930	849

the total inject area comprises 1,254,016 bits. The value of essential bits is obtained from the Vivado Design Suite tool [3]. In this case, it is only considered the HLS accelerator design under fault injection. In the fault injection campaigns, the number of SEUs injected was limited up to 300 bits. Since the number of faults injected is small compared to the total number of configuration bits in the fault injection area, the likelihood of the same bit getting hit more then once is small allowing the error rate to be estimated as the average of errors over total injected faults. The average error rate for the different design, aside its upper and lower quartile, is presented in Fig. 7.

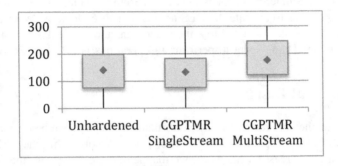

Fig. 7. Average number of bit flips required to provoke an error.

A more detailed comparison of the designs can be seen in Fig. 8, where reliability is presented as the complement of the cumulative failure distribution ($R(t) = 1-F(t)$). The failure rate $F(t)$ of the system is the probability of one or more modules have failed by time t. In our case, Fig. 8 represents the reliability in terms of the accumulated bit-flips.

The inferiority of the CGPTMR SingleStream design, even when compared to the unhardened design, can be related to the amount of data that is serialized through the stream, as can be seen in Fig. 2(b) CGPTMR Single Stream steps and the single point

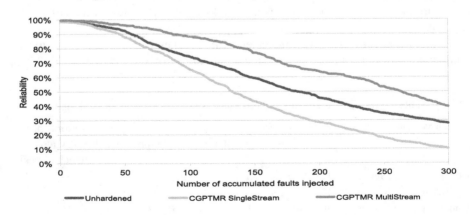

Fig. 8. Observed reliability on the different designs

of failures of the DMA interconnection. Being a single point of failure, not only a communication failure is more likely due to larger amount of data being serialized, but also it jeopardizes the efforts placed on the TMR implementation. On the other hand, the CGPTMR MultipleStream gives clearly a reliability improvement over the unhardened along the range of SEUs injected on this experiment. Notwithstanding, as with to any TMR implementation, that may be a crossing point ahead in the reliability curves where the unhardened performs better than the TMR implementation.

Even with these experiments limited to 300 SEUs injected, the expected exponential behavior of reliability curves and the relationship among the reliability of the design can be seen when we look at this same data in semi-log coordinate, as presented in Fig. 9. Two useful observations can be extracted from Fig. 9 contributing to further engineering decisions. First, if any recovery strategy, such as scrubbing or system reconfiguration by reset, is to be is activated before the expected time when up to approximately 10 SEUs are accumulated, then the power of TMR will not be exploited and no profit is given by its implementation on the system. Second, as we can see a trend that the crossing from better TMR performance to better unhardened performance occurs somewhere between 300 and 1,000 SEUs, that defines the upper bound limit of TMR performance.

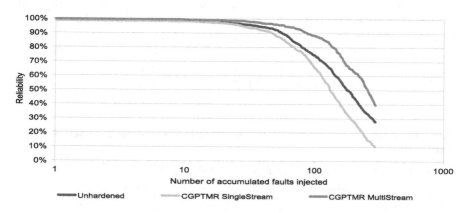

Fig. 9. Semi-log view of the observed reliability of the different designs.

Considering the neutron flux at New York as reference (13 n/cm^2.h) [10] and the static neutron cross-section of Artix-7 FPGAs (7 $\times$ 10^{-15} cm^2/bit) [11], we can estimate the static neutron cross-section of the target area (388 frames $\times$ 3232 bits = 1,254,016 bits), which is 8.78 $\times$ 10^{-9} cm^2. The expression to obtain static neutron cross-section of the target area is:

$$\sigma_{static,target\ area} = \sigma_{static,device} \times Bits_{target\ area}$$

Failure rate is the most common reliability metric. The failure rate itself is either time-dependent or time-independent [12]. The failure rate target area (1.14 $\times$ 10^{-7} h^{-1})

is calculated by multiplying the value of the static neutron cross-section by the neutron flux at New York, as follows:

$$Failure\ rate_{target\ area} = \sigma_{static,target\ area} \times Flux$$

Mean time between failure (MTBF) is defined as the average amount of time a device or product works before it fails. We calculate the MTBF of bit-flips (8.7×10^6 h) for the target area as follows:

$$MTBF_{target\ area} = \frac{1}{Failure\ rate_{target\ area}}$$

Then we can calculate the MTBF of the design as follows:

$$MTBF_{design} = MTBF_{target\ area} \times Accumulated\ bits$$

For instance, at a reliability of 99%, the unhardened version can accumulate in average up to 10 bit-flips, which implies in a MTBF of 8.7×10^7 h, while the CGPTMR MultiStream can accumulate in average up to 17 bit-flips in the configuration memory, which implies in a MTBF of 1.48×10^8 h, 70% higher. The improvement in MTBF reduces as the percentage of reliability reduces. For instance, at a reliability of 95%, the unhardened version can accumulate in average up to 41 bit-flips, which implies in a MTBF of 3.6×10^8 h, while the CGPTMR Multi-Stream can accumulate in average up to 61 bit-flips in the configuration memory, which implies in a MTBF of 5.4×10^8 h, 50% higher (Table 2).

Table 2. Reliability of accumulated bit-flips and MTBF for the unhardened version and the CGTMR multistream version

Reliability	Accumulated bit-flips		MTBF$_{design}$	
	Unhardened	CGPTMR	Unhardened	CGPTMR
99%	10	17	8.7×10^7	1.48×10^8 (+70%)
95%	41	61	3.6×10^8	5.4×10^8 (+50%)
90%	55	87	4.8×10^8	7.6×10^8 (+58%)

5 Conclusions

This work demonstrated the feasibility of generating hardware design or hardware accelerators intrinsically hardened based on the introduction of that hardening in a high level specification, in this case in the form of C/C++ language to be processed by high level synthesis. The methodology adopted of accumulated SEUs injection allowed the characterization and comparison of alternative design and evidenced design pitfalls, such as in the case of the CGPTMR SingleStream. This methodology also allows the proper calibration of recovery mechanisms and allowed further analysis on the voting mechanism operating point.

References

1. Carmichael, C.: Triple Module Redundancy Design Techniques for Virtex FPGAs. Xilinx, Application Note XAPP197, July 2006
2. Habinc, S.: Functional Triple Modular Redundancy (FTMR). Gaisler Research, Design and Assessment Report FPGA-003-01, December 2002
3. Xilinx: Vivado Design Suite - User Guide - High-Level Synthesis. UG902 (v2014.3), 1 October 2014
4. Tambara, L.A., Kastensmidt, F.L., Rech, P., Frost, C.: Decreasing FIT with diverse triple modular redundancy in SRAM-based FPGAs. In: Proceedings of IEEE International Symposium on Defect and Fault Tolerance in VLSI and Nanotechnology Systems, pp. 1–6, November 2014
5. Tonfat, J., Tambara, L., Santos, A., Kastensmidt, F.: Method to analyze the susceptibility of HLS designs in SRAM-based FPGAs under soft errors. In: Bonato, V., Bouganis, C., Gorgon, M. (eds.) ARC 2016. LNCS, vol. 9625, pp. 132–143. Springer, Heidelberg (2016). doi:10.1007/978-3-319-30481-6_11
6. Winterstein, F., Bayliss, S., Constantinides, G.A.: High-level synthesis of dynamic data structures: a case study using Vivado HLS. In: Proceedings of International Conference on Field-Programmable Technology, pp. 362–365, December 2013
7. Tambara, L.A., Tonfat, J., Santos, A., Lima Kastensmidt, F., Medina, N.H., Added, N., Aguiar, V.A.P., Aguirre, F., Silveira, M.A.G.: Analyzing reliability and performance trade-offs of HLS-based designs in SRAM-based FPGAs under soft errors. IEEE Trans. Nucl. Sci. **1**, 1–8 (2017). ISSN: 0018-9499
8. Chan, X., Yang, W., Zhao, M., Wang, J.: HLS-based sensitivity-induced soft error mitigation for satellite communication systems. In: 2016 IEEE 22nd International Symposium on On-Line Testing and Robust System Design (IOLTS), pp. 143–148 (2016). ISSN 1942-9401
9. Xilinx: AXI4-Stream Accelerator Adapter v2.1. PG081 18 November 2015
10. JEDEC: Measurement and Reporting of Alpha Particle and Terrestrial Cosmic Ray-Induced Soft Errors in Semiconductor Devices JEDEC Standard (2006). http://www.jedec.org/sites/default/files/docs/jesd89a.pdf
11. Xilinx Inc.: Device Reliability Report, UG116 (v9.4) (2015)
12. Crowe, D., Feinberg, A.: Design for Reliability (2001). ISBN 13:978-1-4200-4084-5. https://www.crcpress.com/

FPGA-Based Designs

FPGA Applications in Unmanned Aerial Vehicles - A Review

Mustapha Bouhali[1(✉)], Farid Shamani[2], Zine Elabadine Dahmane[3],
Abdelkader Belaidi[1], and Jari Nurmi[2]

[1] Ecole Nationale Polytechnique d'Oran, Es Senia, Algeria
{mustapha.bouhali,abdelkader.belaidi}@enp-oran.dz
[2] Tampere University of Technology, P.O.Box 553, FIN-33101 Tampere, Finland
{farid.shamani,jari.nurmi}@tut.fi
[3] Ecole Nationale Polytechnique d'Alger, El-harrach, Algeria
zine_elabadine.dahmane@g.enp.edu.dz

Abstract. Most of the existing Unmanned Aerial Vehicles (UAVs) in different scales, use microcontrollers as their processing engine. In this paper, we provide a wide study on how employing Field Programmable Gate Arrays (FPGAs) alters the development of such UAV systems. This work is organized based on the application's criticality. After surveying recent products, we reviewed significant researches concerning the use of FPGAs in high-level control techniques necessary for navigation such as path planning, Simultaneous Localization and Mapping (SLAM), stereo vision, as well as the safety-critical low-level tasks such as system stability, state estimation and interfacing with peripherals. In addition, we study the use of FPGAs in mission-critical tasks, including target tracking, communications, obstacle avoidance, etc. In this paper, we mainly review other research papers and compare them in different terms such as speed and energy consumption.

1 Introduction

Unmanned Aerial Vehicles (UAVs) gained a tremendous interest during last decade in both academic field and the industry. Their wide range of potential applications are growing day by day. UAVs are widely used in military, transportation, search and rescue operations, etc. With respect to the electronic system of the UAV, almost all existing platforms used in experiments are based on sequential approaches, deploying either microcontrollers or Digital Signal Processors (DSPs). For instance, most of commercially available autopilot devices have a microcontroller-based architecture. On the other hand, FPGAs are well-known for their processing speed and hardware flexibility. Moreover, FPGA's technology has advanced significantly in last years to offer more hardware features such as embedded processors, floating point calculation, Analog-Digital converters (ADC, DAC) and memory controllers [1]. In parallel, software resources have matured enough to reduce the design time and rise the level of abstraction (Intellectual Properties and design tools) [2]. During the last decade, several researches

© Springer International Publishing AG 2017
S. Wong et al. (Eds.): ARC 2017, LNCS 10216, pp. 217–228, 2017.
DOI: 10.1007/978-3-319-56258-2_19

have been carried out to verify the versatility of the FPGAs in each real-time part of an UAV system. As a result, some products have already appeared in the market. This led us to take a look back to explore the suitability of FPGAs in high-level control techniques (such stereo vision, Simultaneous Localization and Mapping (SLAM) and path planning), as well as the low-level critical tasks (such as stability, data acquisition and motor control). We also explore FPGA usage in mission critical tasks such as object recognition and tracking. This paper presents a wide study on FPGA applications in every task concerning on-board processing of UAVs. We aim to provide researchers and designers significant information which can help enhancing their design strategy. We structured this paper as follows. The commercial products are studied in Sect. 2. Section 3 deals with high-level control techniques leveraging FPGA's advantages. Then, in Sect. 4, we present recent studies in which FPGAs are used in low-level control. The use of FPGA in mission-critical tasks is presented in Sect. 5. Finally, we conclude our work in Sect. 6 with a summary and future challenges.

2   Hardware of UAV and Commercial Platforms

UAVs can be found in different mechanical structures, mainly divided into fixed-wing and rotary-wing UAVs. Multirotors are mostly used in the market due to their wide range of potential applications, as well as their flight flexibility such as vertical take-off and landing (VTOL) and the rotation around their 3 axes (roll, pitch, yaw). Figure 1 shows a general design of a Quadrotor with its rotational axes. Like many embedded systems, they are mainly constituted of sensors, actuators (motors) and a processing system. Technically, critical sensors of an UAV are known as accelerometers, gyroscopes and magnetometers (which are located in the Inertial measurement Unit (IMU)), and the ultrasound height and pressure sensors to calculate the altitude. Cameras (monocular, stereo and omni-directional) and laser scanners are the sensors that could highly expend the autonomy of the UAVs. A GPS receiver could also be employed for location-estimating applications such as *Fly Home* or *Land* where the drone takes emergency actions. The actuator side of an UAV is mainly composed of motors with their drivers and Electronic Speed controllers (ESCs). Since the main power source of an UAV is batteries, different Direct-Current motors can be used. In this category, the use of brushless DC motors is more efficient due to their high speed and low weight.   The processing system is responsible for acquiring data from sensors and maybe receiving control commands from a ground station via Radio-Control receiver. Thereafter, the processing system sends the calculated control data to the motor drivers. Most of the commercial platforms use two microcontrollers such as "MikroKopter" developed by the HiSystems GmbH [3]. The first microcontroller is configured in a baremetal mode for low-level control tasks such as stability & altitude control, sensor processing and motor control. The other one runs an operating system for high-level applications. Those include the navigation system's algorithms such as the *path planner* or *stereo vision*. It also executes mission-critical tasks such as *target tracking*. A general illustration

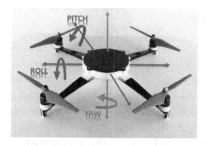

Fig. 1. Quadrotor and its rotational axes

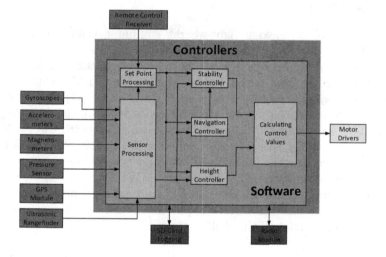

Fig. 2. Tasks, peripherals and data dependencies

of tasks and peripherals with data dependencies is presented in Fig. 2. During last years, Xilinx and Intel FPGA (Altera previously) launched their hybrid platforms, Zynq and Cyclone V, incorporating of an FPGA and an embedded processor on the same die. Konomura and Hori [4] developed "Phenox", the first Zynq-based quadrotor where the FPGA fabric was used for the on-board image and sound processing, generation of Pulse Width Modulation (PWM) signals used for motor control, as well as the interfacing with sensors. Currently, the quadrotor is available on demand costing 1,800 USD [5]. In the beginning of 2016, Aerotenna launched "Octagonal-Pilot-On-Chip" (OcPoC), a Flight Control System (FCS) based on a Zynq-7000 SoC board. The system is able to run Ardupilot software platform and is intended to overcome the limitation of the number of pins in standard processors. The high number of I/Os in FPGA served to add many video feeds (up to 8 video feeds) and the possibility to add more sensors [6]. Then, in August 2016, Aerontena unveiled OcPoC-Cyclone, an open source FCS based on Intel FPGA Cyclone V. The two products provide the opportunity for designers with expertise on Intel FPGA or Xilinx products [7].

3   High-Level Control

High-level control techniques refers to tasks that enable the autonomous navigation. Data dependencies in Fig. 2 show that the navigation system is the first decision maker in the hierarchy, hence we considered them as high-level control tasks. Deploying image processing and machine learning algorithms is common in such algorithms. Moreover, these tasks can take advantage of the parallelism in computation which makes FPGAs and Application-Specific-Integrated-Circuits (ASIC) suitable candidates for hardware implementations.

3.1   Stereo Vision

Honegger et.al [10] designed a light-weight computer vision platform based on an FPGA and a mobile CPU suitable for UAVs. A dense disparity map is created based on semi-global matching algorithm implemented on the FPGA fabric. It runs at 60 Frames Per Second (FPS) with 752×480 resolution. The system was used further in their work [11] to perform low latency obstacle avoidance system running on a Micro-Aerial Vehicle. Later on, the system was compared in performing stereo vision with the Pushbroom system (based on ARM processor, developed in MIT) [12]. The FPGA-based architecture outperforms the Pushbroom system in term of latency (2 ms against 16.6 ms) and power consumption (5 W against 20 W). Both systems have a high synchronization speed. While FPGA system is more flexible in the way that the stereo core can be replaced for other applications, the Pushbroom platform is easy to adapt commercial off-the-shelf parts.

3.2   SLAM

In [8], a Zynq-7000 is used for accurate real-time SLAM based on visual-inertial sensors. The FPGA fabric was used in the detection phase, where the implementation of corner detection algorithm in FPGA has shown a significant acceleration compared to the CPU-based algorithm. Features from Accelerated-Segment-Test (FAST) and Harris corner detection algorithms were implemented interchangeably. In addition, the fixed-pointed version of the algorithm was used. The drift accumulated in a 700 m distance is 5 m horizontally, and 1 m vertically. Potential improvement could be made using modern FPGAs incorporating hardware DSP Blocks for implementing floating point versions. Despite the traditional feature-based SLAM and visual odometry algorithms, the work in [9] presents potentially the first contributions into accelerating one of the state-of-the-art SLAM techniques, large-scale direct SLAM. Although the hardware implementation has shown 2× speed-up alongside a significant reduction in power, the frame rate is still at low level due to the existence of memory latencies.

3.3   Path Planning

In [13], the authors demonstrated that the genetic algorithms offer more accurate solution for path planning. Therefore, they proposed a hardware architecture-based both on the FPGA and a general purpose processor. In [14], Kok proposed an architecture for path planning based on evolutionary algorithm totally in hardware. It reached to 10 Hz update rate required by a typical autopilot. Furthermore, it is more resource efficient than its predecessors as it occupies only 32% of the logic slices available on a Xilinx Virtex-4 FPGA.

3.4   Ego-Motion Estimation

Ego-motion estimation deals with finding the camera pose in a 3D environment. In [16], the authors developed a vision-based ego-motion estimation using an FPGA device along with a low-power processor. Most of the algorithm was implemented in a Xilinx Virtex-II 6000, while other high-level control parts were implemented in the processor. It occupies 41% of the available logic resources and it achieves up to 200 fps with 320×240 resolution. Schmidt et al. employed an FPGA for designing a stereo vision system [15]. The system was used to perform ego-motion calculation at 15 Hz. However, the communication overhead between the processor and the FPGA (planar rectification and post processing in the processor, disparity calculation in the FPGA) led to a relatively high overall latency of 250 ms. The latency problem is the main reason why such systems are unusable for some applications which require low data latency (e.g. obstacle avoidance).

3.5   Feature Extractor and Matcher

Feature Extractor and Matcher (FEM) algorithms are computationally intensive, and could benefit highly from the hardware acceleration. In addition, FEMs are the most important algorithms for vision-based navigation systems such as ORB-SLAM. This subsection mainly concentrates on reviewing papers which focus only on these type of algorithms. A very recent FPGA implementation and cross-platforms comparison of feature detectors and descriptors algorithms is presented in [17]. They designed and optimized FAST detector with BRIEF and BRISK descriptors in the FPGA of a Zynq-7020, and compared it to software implementations in CPU and GPU. The advantages of FPGA were clear in terms of runtime and power consumption which makes it well suited for UAVs. One of the most advantageous feature of the modern FPGAs, compared to other platforms, is the capability of performing real time *dynamic reconfiguration*, either fully or partially [18]. A very good example of exploiting dynamic partial reconfiguration (DPR) feature can be found in [19]. In [20], the author leverages the advantages of DPR in the design of an adaptive FEM. The technique was used only in a part of the algorithm, namely the reconfigurable Gaussian filter to adapt the noise created by harsh dynamic environments in space. It achieves a throughput of 33 fps while occupying around 10% of logic and memory resources in a Xilinx Virtex 4-QV VLX200 FPGA showing significant improvement over an FEM developed in university of Dundee called "Feature-Extractor-Integrated-Circuit". In [21] van der Wal et al. designed a hardware add-on for drones where they implemented their FEM in the Programmable Logic (PL) part of a Zynq-7000 platform. The algorithms were chosen at the basis of rotation and scale invariance. The implementation can achieve 30 fps of 1080p resolution. Compared to a quad-core CPU, it achieves 5x of latency reduction. The whole infrastructure took more than 70% of a Zynq-7020 and less than 20% in a Zynq-7045 of logic and memory resources (flip-flops, lookup tables, DSP slices and RAM). Fowers et al. also proposed an FPGA implementation of an FEM named BAsis Sparse-coding Inspired Similarity (BASIS) [22]. Although, the proposed implementation is not rotation and scale invariant, the authors focus on providing reduced size descriptors based on sparse coding. BASIS outperforms Speeded Up Robust Features (SURF) FEM and "Scale-Invariant Feature Transform" (SIFT) FEM algorithms implemented in software in terms of power consumption and speed. It operates at 60 fps for 1000 features and it occupies 21% of the logic in a Xilinx Virtex 6 VLX761 FPGA platform.

4   Low-Level Control

Sensor processing, state estimation, stability and motor control are the most safety-critical tasks in UAVs as they are used in all existing platforms and perform the basic processing in UAVs. Their role is to send data and receive decisions from high-level control algorithms like the path planner, hence we regrouped them as low-level control tasks. In researches, the use of FPGA was also significant for these tasks.

4.1   Stability Control

The role of stability systems is to maintain a desired state of UAV via a number of controllers. Each controller is responsible of one of the angles (roll, pitch, yaw), angular velocities and the altitude. Although the use of FPGA-based controllers is widespread in industrial applications [23], only few researchers used FPGAs in this specific area. Custom hardware implementation in FPGA of a proportional integral controller for the rotation axes of a small-scale quadrotor is proposed in [24]. It outperforms the software approach using ARM7 microcontroller, achieving 4.3 MHz control loop rate compared to 0.71 MHz in software. The same group implemented proportional-integral-derivative controller in a Zynq FPGA controlling a micro-UAV, while using HW/SW approach for their motion planning algorithm [25]. In mixed criticality system, the need for a good hardware separation between critical and non-critical tasks is necessary. In [26] a Zynq-7000 was used as the hardware of a multi-rotor. Safety-critical tasks, including the stability system, were implemented in the PL using two Microblaze processors, while mission critical tasks were implemented in the Processing System (PS). For the good functioning of UAVs in unknown dynamic environments, the need of more accurate control algorithms is necessary. Many Non-linear Adaptive controllers have shown more accurate results. However, creating customized hardware for these algorithms is a cumbersome task, mainly because such algorithms have a sequential structure that is unsuitable for FPGAs. Furthermore, most of existing UAVs are based on microcontrollers which makes working on another architecture insignificant. In [27], Fowers claimed that imperfections in Inertial Measurement Units (IMUs) could be overcome by using a reduced vision system based on FPGA for drift control. He proposed an architecture where Harris corner detection is implemented in FPGA, and returns results to IMU and motor controllers for further regulation.

4.2 State Estimation

The use of state estimation is a very important task in UAV systems for which Kalman filters are the mostly used [28]. The literature provides several application-specific implementations of the Kalman filter in FPGAs. For more general purposes, Soh and Wu [29] proposed a HW/SW co-design of Unscented Kalman Filter. The algorithm was divided in a way that the hardware part is application-independent. The author stated the results of different scenarios according to the number of Processing Elements (PEs) (1,2,5 and 10). The algorithm was implemented in a Xilinx Zynq-7000 series XC7Z045 showing a speed improvement of over 2x compared to a software approach, while consuming less energy (131 mW using only a single PE, increasing PEs increases speed at the expense of energy consumption).

4.3 Interfacing with Sensors

FPGA provides a significant flexibility and a huge number of I/Os. Researchers exploited this feature to design flexible communication interfaces with sensors helpful for sensor fusion and easier system upgrade [4,26,30]. Other few researches look into replacing commercial off-the-shelf (COTS) IMUs. In [31], digital controllers for Micro-Electro-Mechanical Systems (MEMS) gyroscopes are implemented in an FPGA in order to compensate thermal effects for accuracy. The design could benefit from modern FPGAs with their internal DACs, ADCs and phase-locked loops. In [32], the author used FPGA to acquire data from Fiber Optical Gyro, synchronize it, and then output it over an RS-422 communication interface.

4.4 Motor Control

Small UAVs mostly use Brushless DC motors. FPGA was used in previous researches to control such motors in two ways: First, the FPGA board generates PWM signal to COTS Electronic Speed Controllers. The latter is composed of a microcontroller that runs specific control algorithms, and a power circuit. This technique was used in [4,26]. Second, the FPGA generated PWM signals and ran control algorithms, with the external power circuit [33]. Essentially, the algorithms require the speed and position of the rotor. Different techniques were used either with or without sensors [34,35]. Another interesting approach was proposed in [36]. The author deployed DPR to implement an adaptive controller that switches between multiple fly modes of an octocopter. Due to the fact that the UAV used can operate with 3, 4, 6 or 8 motors, they designed customized hardware for PWM generator modules of modes. Then, they used DPR to switch between modules. The whole stability system was implemented in a Zynq-7000 platform using the HW/SW co-design.

5   Mission-Critical Tasks

Other than essential algorithms for UAV's FCS, many works have been done for other mission-dependent processing. The use of FPGAs was significant in these research area, especially on obstacle avoidance, object recognition and communications.

5.1   Obstacle Avoidance

In [37], Gohl et al. proposed a perception system based on FPGA for micro aerial vehicle that is able to perform omnidirectional obstacle detection. The work is an extension of their previous work [8], reviewed in the third section. It is able to perform computation up to 80 fps with less power consumption than conventional techniques.

5.2   Object Recognition and Tracking

In [38], Real-time moving target detection is implemented using FPGA. The whole system was prototyped in a Terasic DE2 Board with an Altera Cyclone IV FPGA. Most of the computation was done in hardware, while a soft-core processor Nios II handles part of the ego-motion algorithm, Random Sample Consensus (RANSAC). The system achieves a rate of 30 fps with 640 × 480 pixels of resolution, and it occupies 13% of logic and memory. Biologically-inspired hardware with FPGA also was used for object tracking. SIFT algorithms for feature detection was implemented in [39] using a mixed analog/digital implementation, and an FPGA implementation of Retinal Ganglion Cell model was shown in [40]. Both works have shown significant improvement in terms of latency and power consumption. In [41] a vision system based on FPGA was proposed for a small UAV performing aerial manipulation. Its role is to align the UAV with bar-like object. FPGA was dedicated for image processing pipeline, and for generating PWM signal to control yaw. This could be applied for preserving energy by parking the drone in high altitude places. Giitsidis et al. [42] proved that FPGA is well suited for implementing Cellular Automaton algorithms. Then, the author describes their applications in human and fire detection from high altitude images taken by UAVs. In [43], the author proposed a hybrid architecture using FPGA and CPU to reduce computation latency in an UAV Synthetic Aperture Radar.

5.3 Communication System

Recently, the use of FPGA in Software Defined Radios (SDR) has gained a significant interest. In this subsection we reviewed researches focused on UAV communication system based on SDR concepts. In [44], an SDR based flight termination system (FTS) using FPGA is proposed. The design is supposed to overcome the use of bulky FTSs. Also, it enhances cost of upgrading through the flexibility of FPGAs. In this application, a Xilinx Virtex 5 FPGA was used to implement Digital Up Conversion and Digital Down Conversion for the transmitter and the receiver. The whole implementation took 86% of resources. It could be enhanced by using modern FPGAs like Xilinx Virtex 7 AMS with their analog resources (XADC block). Other researches proposed implementations of different communication protocols and scenarios. In [45], an UAV is used as a relay to create a unidirectional communication link between an unmanned ground vehicle and the ground control station using SDR Orthogonal Frequency-Division Multiplexing (OFDM). The hardware stack mounted on UAV is based on a hybrid platform of two FPGAs and an Intel Atom processor. In [46], the author claimed that Single-Carrier Frequency-Division-Multiplexing (SCFDM) modulation is suitable for UAV's communication system. Their hardware design is based on SDR concepts using an FPGA board.

6 Conclusion and Future Challenges

Like most of the embedded systems, Unmanned Aerial Vehicles (UAVs) require power efficiency, low latency and small weight. Therefore, the Field Programmable Gate Array (FPGA) has such characteristics to provide fine-grained parallelism. Some studies have proven that employing FPGAs as a processing engine of the UAVs has tremendously grown in the last years. The most important role of the FPGAs were the vision system based on the computer vision algorithms. Our work also showed that employing embedded processors in FPGA-SoC platforms has already been exploited for many functions. Furthermore, we have shown that many previous studies have the potential to be improved using modern FPGAs' features such as dynamic reconfiguration and hardwired DSP blocks. This paper also reviewed some studies leveraging the advantages of FPGA to provide flexible interfaces with peripheral devices. FPGA-SoC platforms seemed promising platforms for designing UAVs. However, scientists are still encountering challenges such as how to efficiently use the FPGA-SoC. The first challenge is how to schedule applications between their Processing System (PS) and Programming Logic (PL). In addition, more dynamic control of the PL is required. For example, in cases where time-multiplexed tasks are based on hardware resources in FPGAs, a reconfiguration manager is needed inherent with the Robotic Operating System. FPGA is used and well-suited for implementing Convolutional Neural Networks (CNNs) due to the parallel nature of the algorithms. However, there are still a lot of works to be done targeting UAV's vision system with FPGA-based CNNs for Visual Odometry, SLAM, target tracking, etc. Moreover, enhanced design tools which facilitate HW/SW co-design are highly required, as we saw that most of the computational algorithms are based on HW/SW co-design. Finally, this review has shown how FPGAs fulfill the requirements needed in designing UAVs and similar embedded systems.

References

1. Shamani, F., Sevom, V.F., Nurmi, J., Ahonen, T.: Design, implementation and analysis of a run-time configurable memory management unit on FPGA. In: Nordic Circuits and Systems Conference (NORCAS): NORCHIP & International Symposium on System-on-Chip (SoC), Oslo, pp. 1–8 (2015)
2. Rodriguez-Andina, J.J., Valdes-Pena, M.D., Moure, M.J.: Advanced features and industrial applications of FPGAs – a review. IEEE Trans. Ind. Inform. **11**(4), 853–864 (2015)
3. HiSystems GmbH: MikroKopter-Boards. http://wiki.mikrokopter.de/en/MK-Board
4. Konomura, R., Hori, K.: Phenox: Zynq 7000 based quadcopter robot. In: Inter Confererence on ReConFigurable Computing and FPGAs (ReConFig), pp. 1–6 (2014)
5. Phenox lab. http://phenoxlab.com/
6. Aerotenna. http://aerotenna.com/ocpoc/
7. Aerotenna User and Developer Hub. https://aerotenna.readme.io
8. Nikolic, J., Rehder, J., Burri, M., Gohl, P., Leutenegger, S., Furgale, P.T., Siegwart, R.: A synchronized visual-inertial sensor system with FPGA preprocessing for accurate real-time SLAM. In: IEEE International Conference on Robotics and Automation (ICRA), pp. 431–437 (2014)
9. Boikos, K., Bouganis, C.S.: Semi-dense SLAM on an FPGA SoC. In: 26th International Conference on Field Programmable Logic and Applications (FPL), pp. 1–4 (2016)
10. Honegger, D., Oleynikova, H., Pollefeys, M.: Real-time and low Latency embedded computer vision hardware based on a combination of FPGA and mobile CPU. In: IEEE/RSJ International Conference on Intelligent Robots and Systems, pp. 4930–4935 (2014)
11. Oleynikova, H., Honegger, D., Pollefeys, M.: Reactive avoidance using embedded stereo vision for MAV flight. In: IEEE International Conference on Robotics and Automation (ICRA), pp. 50–56 (2015)
12. Barry, A.J., Oleynikova, H., Honegger, D., Pollefeys, M., Tedrake, R.: FPGA vs. pushbroom stereo vision for MAVs. In: Vision-Based Control and Navigation of Small Lightweight UAVs, IROS Workshop (2015)
13. Allaire, F.C.J., Tarbouchi, M., Labonté, G., Fusina, G.: FPGA implementation of genetic algorithm for UAV real-time path planning. J. Intell. Robot. Syst. **54**(1–3), 495–510 (2008)
14. Kok, J., Gonzalez, L.F., Kelson, N.: FPGA implementation of an evolutionary algorithm for autonomous unmanned aerial vehicle on-board path planning. IEEE Trans. Evol. Comput. **17**(2), 272–281 (2013)
15. Schmid, K., Tomic, T., Ruess, F., Hirschmüller, H., Suppa, M.: Stereo vision based indoor/outdoor navigation for flying robots. In: IEEE/RSJ International Conference on Intelligent Robots and Systems, pp. 3955–3962 (2013)
16. Angelopoulou, M.E., Bouganis, C.S.: Vision-based ego-motion estimation on FPGA for unmanned aerial vehicle navigation. IEEE Trans. Circuits Syst. Video Technol. **24**(6), 1070–1083 (2014)

17. Ulusel, O., Picardo, C., Harris C.B., Reda, S., Bahar, R.I.: Hardware acceleration of feature detection and description algorithms on low-power embedded platforms. In: 26th International Conference on Field Programmable Logic and Applications (FPL), pp. 1–9 (2016)
18. Shamani, F., Airoldi, R., Ahonen, T., Nurmi, J.: FPGA implementation of a flexible synchronizer for cognitive radio applications. In: Conference on Design and Architectures for Signal and Image Processing (DASIP), Madrid, pp. 1–8 (2014)
19. Shamani, F., et al.: FPGA implementation issues of a flexible synchronizer suitable for NC-OFDM-based cognitive radios. J. Syst. Architect. (2016)
20. Carlo, S.D., Gambardella, G., Prinetto, P., Rolfo, D., Trotta, P.: SA-FEMIP: A self-adaptive features extractor and matcher IP-Core based on partially reconfigurable FPGAS for space application. IEEE Trans. Very Large Scale Integr. (VLSI) Syst. **23**(10), 2198–2208 (2015)
21. Van der Wal, G., Zhang, D., Kandaswamy, I., Marakowitz, J., Kaighn, K., Zhang, J., Chai, S.: FPGA acceleration for feature based processing applications. In: IEEE Conference on Computer Vision and Pattern Recognition Workshops (CVPRW), pp. 42–47 (2015)
22. Fowers, S.G., Lee, D.J., Ventura, D.A., Archibald, J.K.: The nature-inspired BASIS feature descriptor for UAV imagery and its hardware implementation. IEEE Trans. Circuits Syst. Video Technol. **23**(5), 756–768 (2013)
23. Monmasson, E., Idkhajine, L., Cirstea, M.N., Bahri, I., Tisan, A., Naouar, M.W.: FPGAs in industrial control applications. IEEE Trans. Ind. Inform. **7**(2), 224–243 (2011)
24. Eizad, B., Doshi, A., Postula, A.: FPGA based stability system for a small-scale quadrotor unmanned aerial vehicle. In: Proceedings of the 8th FPGA World Conference, NY, USA, pp. 3:1–3:6 (2011)
25. Doshi, A.A., Postula, A.J., Fletcher, A., Singh, S.P.N.: Development of micro-UAV with integrated motion planning for open-cut mining surveillance. Microprocess. Microsyst. **39**(8), 829–835 (2015)
26. Schlender, H., Schreiner, S., Metzdorf, M., Grüttner, K., Nebel, W.: Teaching mixed-criticality: multi-rotor flight control and payload processing on a single chip. In: Proceedings of the WESE: Workshop on Embedded and Cyber-Physical Systems Education, NY, USA, pp. 9:1–9:8 (2015)
27. Fowers, S.G., Lee, D.J., Tippetts, B.J., Lillywhite K.D., Dennis, A.W., Archibald, J.K.: Vision aided stabilization and the development of a quad-rotor micro UAV. In: International Symposium on Computational Intelligence in Robotics and Automation, pp. 143–148 (2007)
28. Chen, S.Y.: Kalman filter for robot vision: a survey. IEEE Trans. Ind. Electron. **59**(11), 4409–4420 (2012)
29. Soh, J., Wu, X.: A FPGA-based unscented Kalman filter for system-on-chip applications. IEEE Trans. Circuits Syst. II: Express Br. **PP**(99), 1 (2016)
30. Christopherson, H., Pickell, W., Koller, A., Kannan, S., Johnson, E.: Small adaptive flight control systems for UAVs using FPGA/DSP technology. In: Proceeding of AIAA "Unmanned Unlimited", Technical Conference, Workshop and Exhibit (2004)
31. Wang, X., Li, B., Yang, L., Huang, L., Wang, S.: A prototype of MEMS gyroscope based on digital control. In: International Conference on Automatic Control and Artificial Intelligence (ACAI), pp. 275–278 (2012)
32. Bai, C., Zhang, Z., Han, X.: A design and realization of FPGA-based IMU data acquisition system. In: International Conference of Electron Devices and Solid-State Circuits (EDSSC), pp. 1–2 (2011)

33. Tefay, B., Eizad, B., Crosthwaite, P., Singh, S., Postula, A.: Design of an integrated electronic speed controller for agile robotic vehicles. Presented at the Australasian Conference on Robotics and Automation (ACRA), pp. 1–8 (2011)
34. Sathyan, A., Milivojevic, N., Lee, Y.J., Krishnamurthy, M., Emadi, A.: An FPGA-based novel digital PWM control scheme for BLDC motor drives. IEEE Trans. Ind. Electron. **56**(8), 3040–3049 (2009)
35. Lin, C.T., Hung, C.W., Liu, C.W.: Position sensorless control for four-switch three-phase brushless DC motor drives. IEEE Trans. Power Electron. **23**(1), 438–444 (2008)
36. Thomas, N., Felder, A., Bobda, C.: Adaptive controller using runtime partial hardware reconfiguration for unmanned aerial vehicles (UAVs). In: International Conference on ReConFigurable Computing and FPGAs (ReConFig), pp. 1–7 (2015)
37. Gohl, P., Honegger, D., Omari, S., Achtelik, M., Pollefeys, M., Siegwart, R.: Omnidirectional visual obstacle detection using embedded FPGA. In: IEEE/RSJ Inter Conference on Intelligent Robots and Systems (IROS), pp. 3938–3943 (2015)
38. Tang, J.W., Shaikh-Husin, N., Sheikh, U.U., Marsono, M.N.: FPGA-based real-time moving target detection system for unmanned aerial vehicle application. Int. J. Reconfig. Comput. (2016)
39. Yasukawa, S., Okuno, H., Ishii, K., Yagi, T.: Real-time object tracking based on scale-invariant features employing bio-inspired hardware. Neural Netw. **81**, 29–38 (2016)
40. Moeys, D.P., Delbrück, T., Rios-Navarro, A., Linares-Barranco, A.: Retinal Ganglion Cell Software and FPGA Model Implementation for Object Detection and Tracking. In: IEEE International Symposium Circuits and Systems (ISCAS), pp. 1434–1437 (2016)
41. Shimahara, S., Ladig, R., Suphachart, L., Hirai, S., Shimonomura, K.: Aerial manipulation for the workspace above the airframe. In: IEEE/RSJ International Conference on Intelligent Robots and Systems (IROS), pp. 1453–1458 (2015)
42. Giitsidis, T., Karakasis, E.G., Gasteratos, A., Sirakoulis, G.C.: Human and fire detection from high altitude UAV images. In: 23rd Euromicro International Conference on Parallel, Distributed, and Network-Based Processing, pp. 309–315 (2015)
43. Lou, Y., Clark, D., Marks, P., Muellerschoen, R.J., Wang, C.C.: Onboard radar processor development for rapid response to natural hazards. J. Sel. Top. Appl. Earth Obs. Remote Sens. **9**, 2770–2776 (2016)
44. Panda, A.R., Mishra, D., Ratha, H.K.: FPGA implementation of software defined radio-based flight termination system. IEEE Trans. Ind. Inform. **11**, 74–82 (2015)
45. Blümm, C., Heller, C., Weigel, R.: SDR OFDM waveform design for a UGV/UAV communication scenario. J. Signal Process. Syst. **69**, 11–21 (2012)
46. Mikó, G., Németh, A.: SCFDM based communication system for UAV applications. In: 25th International Conference on Radioelektronika, pp. 222–224 (2015)

Genomic Data Clustering on FPGAs for Compression

Enrico Petraglio[1](✉), Rick Wertenbroek[1], Flavio Capitao[1], Nicolas Guex[2], Christian Iseli[2], and Yann Thoma[1]

[1] REDS Institute, HEIG-VD School of Business and Engineering Vaud, HES-SO
University of Applied Sciences Western Switzerland,
1400 Yverdon-les-Bains, Switzerland
{enrico.petraglio,rick.wertenbroek,flavio.capitaocantante,
yann.thoma}@heig-vd.ch
[2] Vital-IT, SIB Swiss Institute of Bioinformatics, 1015 Lausanne, Switzerland
{nicolas.guex,christian.iseli}@sib.swiss

Abstract. Current sequencing machine technology generates very large and redundant volumes of genomic data for each biological sample. Today data and associated metadata are formatted in very large text file assemblies called FASTQ carrying the information of billions of genome fragments referred to as "reads" and composed of strings of nucleotide bases with lengths in the range of a few tenths to a few hundreds bases. Compressing such data is definitely required in order to manage the sheer amount of data soon to be generated. Doing so implies finding redundant information in the raw sequences. While most of it can be mapped onto the human reference genome and fits well for compression, about 10% of it usually does not map to any reference [1]. For these orphan sequences, finding redundancy will help compression. Doing so requires clustering these reads, a very time consuming process. Within this context this paper presents a FPGA implementation of a clustering algorithm for genomic reads, implemented on Pico Computing EX-700 AC-510 hardware, offering more than a 1000× speed up over a CPU implementation while reducing power consumption by a 700 factor.

1 Introduction

With the advent of high throughput sequencing, genomics has entered a new era where massive amounts of data are produced (∼2–40 ExaBytes/year are to be expected in 2025 [9]). The sequencing of one human genome generates in the order of 300 GB of raw data. This data is composed of small sequences randomly located in the genome, with high redundancy (typically 30–50×). Processing data in a timely fashion is imminently important for the future of genomics. Another issue is the storage space required. Currently, many different data formats are used and most of them are far from optimal (cf. [2,4,7]). Each format has different characteristics, and so a universal standard is required to facilitate the development of algorithms. This would for instance allow sharing the same input/output logic. The authors are currently working on such a new format,

© Springer International Publishing AG 2017
S. Wong et al. (Eds.): ARC 2017, LNCS 10216, pp. 229–240, 2017.
DOI: 10.1007/978-3-319-56258-2_20

and to that end, clustering, as it will be presented in this paper, can improve and speed up genomic data compression. Especially for the compression of sequences that do not share similarities with the reference human genome.

To better understand the context of genomic algorithms, and particularly the compression of such data, the next subsection describes the data specificities.

1.1   Genomic Data

Currently, sequencing machines (for instance from Illumina[1]) apply the following process: (1) The DNA is cut into small sequences. (2) If needed they are amplified by PCR (Polymerase Chain Reaction) to create redundancy. (3) Finally sequences are read from both ends and two outputs are generated: A file containing the DNA read from the first end of the sequence, and another one from the other end (Fig. 1 illustrates the sequence structure).

The reads are typically quite small (from 50 up to 200 base pairs) and the size of the unread part of the sequence is typically in the range of 100–300 base pairs. At the end of the process every read is written into a text based file in FASTQ format. Each read is composed of an ID line, a line composed of the sequence bases, an optional redundancy line and a line with the quality values for the second line. Sequencing of a whole genome with $\sim 40\times$ coverage typically generates two text files of roughly 150 GB each (uncompressed).

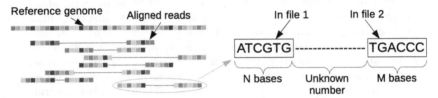

Fig. 1. Paired reads mapped onto the reference genome

Efficient compression algorithms obviously exploit data redundancy. The first step is to identify known sequences and to map them onto the reference genome (this artificial human genome was built as an average of multiple human genomes). The result of this process, shown in Fig. 1, allows to easily compress these mapped sequences, using their relative location to the reference. Current compression algorithms already take advantage of this. However, not all the reads can be correctly aligned onto the reference genome, and typically $\sim 10\%$ of the sequences remain unaligned. This can be caused by the fact that the individual genome differs from the reference, by errors in the sequencing or because reads are part of various other entities found in the body, such as bacteria, viruses, fungus, archea, etc. Nevertheless these sequences remain important, they could be sign of a specific genetic disease or mutation, thus be interesting for analysis and should not be discarded. One way to compress this data is to group similar reads together and only encode their differences. In order to group these sequences a clustering algorithm is needed.

---

[1] http://www.illumina.com.

The work presented in this paper aims at reducing the processing time of clustering, since software solutions suffer from the algorithms high complexity, $O(n^2)$, and the data set gigantic size. Our approach exploiting FPGAs dramatically reduces up the processing time needed.

The rest of this paper is organized as follows: The next section introduces the concept of clustering applied to genomic data. Section 3 presents the current implementation focusing on hardware. Then Sect. 4 shows results. Finally Sect. 5 lists conclusions and introduces future work.

2   Clustering

Clustering data is a well known field of research, usually designing algorithms with the goal of finding a number k of clusters grouping data with respect to a neighbourhood function [3,6]. Clustering algorithms have been designed and tailored for different domains including genomics [8], nevertheless no specific clustering algorithm has been proven to be particularly useful for compression of genomic data. Compression will benefit more from algorithms that define clusters with highly correlated data, rather than having an exact number k of clusters. Therefore, instead of doing k-clustering, such as k-means, k-medians or k-medoids algorithms, it would be better to seek clusters, regardless of the total number of clusters, using a small threshold neighbourhood function. The following *match* function is used and shows how cluster membership is defined. *match* returns *true* if both sequences should be in the same cluster and *false* otherwise.

$$match(s1, s2, N) \Leftrightarrow \exists d \in [-N, N]:$$
$$s1(max(0, -d)..min(le-1, le-1-d)) = s2(max(0, d)..min(le-1, le-1+d))$$

Where le is the size of the sequences to be compared, d the distance between them and N is the distance threshold. Figure 2 illustrates the results of the *match* function for three sequences of $le = 8$ and threshold $N = 2$.

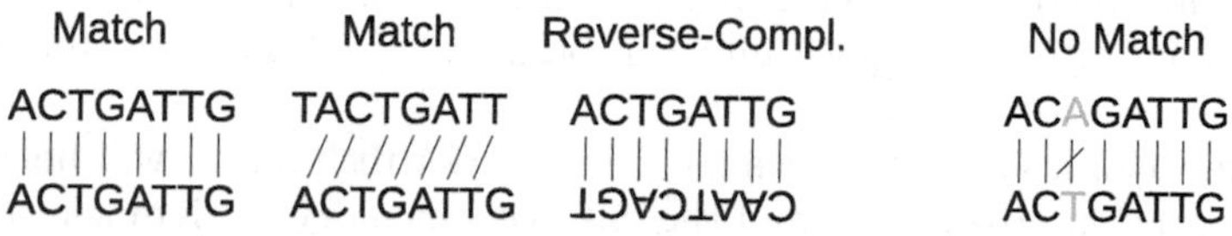

Fig. 2. Examples of matches and mismatches

If $N = 0$ *match* becomes the $=$ operator and will only return *true* if two sequences are the same. With $N > 0$ two sequences can match with a distance up to N, represented by a shift between them[2]. Since DNA consists of a complementary double helix, matching sequences with a reverse complement makes

---

[2] Ignoring the non-overlapping ends of length d.

sense. Allowing reverse complement matching would lead to more populated clusters and requires very few ressources to encode.

Having this *match* function, a first approach can be described as follows: Algorithm 1: Every sequence is tested for membership using the function *isInCluster(seq, cluster)* against all current clusters. If a sequence does not match any existing cluster a new one is created taking the sequence as its reference. This is repeated until there are no more sequences to process. Algorithm 1 has a complexity $O(n^2)$, where n is the number of sequences.

Algorithm 1. Clustering algorithm

1: **function** CLUSTERING(*seqs*)
2:      *clusters* ← ∅
3:      **while** *seqs* ≠ ∅ **do**
4:          *calcClusters* ← NC *seqs*; Remove these sequences from *seqs*
5:          **for all** *seq* ∈ *seqs* **do**
6:              **for all** *cluster* ∈ *calcClusters* **do**
7:                  **if** *isInCluster(seq, cluster)* **then**
8:                      *cluster* ← {*cluster, seq*}; Remove *seq* from *seqs*
9:          *clusters* ← {*clusters, calcClusters*}
10:      **return** *clusters*

Considering that current sequencing outputs contain more than a billion sequences, even 10% of it still accounts for 100 million sequences, and clustering even only this 10% would require more than 2 years on a Intel core i7 4790. This estimation is based on real measurements of an optimized clustering software developed during this project (See Sect. 3.1).

2.1   Parallel Clustering

Running a clustering algorithm in a purely sequential manner is extremely time consuming. Exploiting parallelism is one way to speed up processing. One sequence can be compared with multiple cluster references at the same time. Therefore lines 6 to 8 of Algorithm 1 can be parallelized onto multiple computing cores.

An implementation of Algorithm 1 using FPGA technology will benefit from the parallelization possibilities and the on-board memory to significantly reduce processing time.

The *match* function, when comparing two sequences, has to check every single base to decide if they match or not, or at least until a difference is found. DNA sequences are composed of four bases, however the sequencing machines sometimes provide a fifth value, N, as unknown[3]. Since the base is unknown, we use it as a wildcard and therefore N matches all four other bases. A very interesting result for FPGA implementation with this kind of data is that the

---

[3] This usually means the sequencing machine could not determine the exact nucleotide.

5 values can be stored using 3 bits, and so the base-to-base matching function can be done using a single 6-bit input look up table (LUT). This renders the hardware implementation extremely efficient, as Altera and Xilinx FPGAs offer such 6-bit input LUTs as basic hardware building blocks.

To the best of our knowledge, FPGA implementations of K-clustering such as [5,10] have been published, but nothing compared to the proposed solution.

3   Design Implementation

This section will start with the software framework and its modular architecture. Then the FPGA architecture implementing the clustering algorithm is detailed.

3.1   Software Setup

A C++11 software has been designed as an interface to perform clustering with FPGA accelerators as well as a reference benchmark. A modular architecture allows to use the same software with or without an FPGA subsystem. The software takes care of the general data flow. It has three main stages, namely a reading stage a processing stage and a writing stage, as shown in Fig. 3.

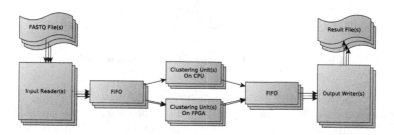

Fig. 3. Software with modular architecture.

The reading stage gathers sequences from a FASTQ file. The processing stage does the clustering of the sequences and the writing stage collects the results in an output file. Each stage is realized by one or more threads and the communication between the stages is done with one or more FIFO buffers (blocking queues). This allows for a highly modular and performance oriented setup.

A version of the clustering unit has been implemented in software. It is optimized using Intel's AVX2 256-bit SIMD instructions. The software architecture allows for easy deployment of multiple threads implementing this unit. Therefore it can take full advantage of multi-core CPUs. The CPU and FPGA clustering units are interchangeable allowing performance and result comparisons.

The typical setup for our FPGA board has six reader threads reading from different portions of a FASTQ file feeding six clustering units each one on a separate FPGA and threads collecting the results as they come in.

The FPGA board is connected using a `PCIe x16` slot on an Intel Haswell core i7 based PC running GNU/Linux. The communication between the software and the FPGAs is done using the `PCIe` bus. The drivers and API are provided by Micron Pico Computing (the target platform being an EX-700 backplane with AC-510 modules) but the software can easily be adapted for other hardware.

3.2 FPGA Architecture

This section details the hardware architecture, and specifically the internal data flow. Moving data is critical because of the tremendous amount of sequences to be processed. Figure 4 shows the top hierarchy of our implementation.

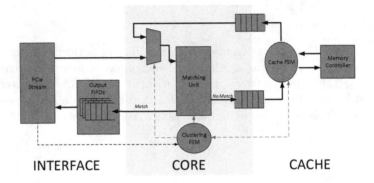

Fig. 4. Top hierarchy of the FPGA implementation.

In order to analyze the data stream flowing through the design, the latter was cut off in three different parts: the interface, the core and the cache. The first part implements the communication with the outside world, in which the `PCIe` interface receives the reads coming from the CPU and sends them to the clustering unit. This part of the design is also in charge of storing the clustering results and sending them back to the CPU. The central block contains the clustering algorithm itself. It decides if the current sequence belongs to the present clusters or not. In case of a positive match the ID and the score (alignment information) of the sequence are sent back to the output FIFOs, otherwise the sequence is forwarded to the FPGA cache. The latter is mainly composed of the memory controller, which will store all the unmatched sequences from the clustering unit into the external memory. During a run, data flows through two different paths and the algorithm can be separated into two different phases.

Phase One. At the very beginning, the system receives sequences from the `PCIe` interface. The latter directly forwards this information to the core block. The clustering unit then starts. It flags the first non-matching sequences as references and then compares the following sequences to these references. When a sequence matches with a reference, the result is sent to the output FIFOs, and if it does

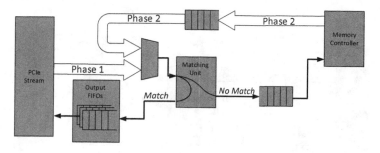

Fig. 5. In 1st phase the data is coming from the outside while in 2nd phase it is coming from the cache.

not match any cluster the sequence is stored in the cache memory (Fig. 5). It has to be noted that the size of the memory used to store the unmatched sequences will directly limit the maximum number of sequences that a single FPGA can handle. In the worst case, which is, none of the sequences match the references of the current clusters, the FPGA has to be able to store all the sequences into its cache. This issue can be resolved by adding more external memory to the FPGA subsystem or by cutting the FASTQ file into smaller pieces whose sequences can fit into the cache memory. This can be done sequentially with a single FPGA or in parallel with a group of FPGAs. It is noteworthy to add that this process could lead to a sub-optimal clustering result but would allow handling files of any size even on hardware settings with limited memory capacity.

Phase Two. When all the sequences in the FASTQ file have been sent to the FPGA and were tested against all current clusters, the FPGA starts to work on the sequences stored in the cache. These sequences are sent to the core module once again. The latter will use the first non-matching sequences as new references for the clusters and restart the clustering process. Again, if a sequence matches a reference, its ID and score are sent to the output FIFOs, otherwise the sequence will return to the cache in order to be processed during the next run of phase two (Fig. 5). Phase two is repeated until all the sequences have been placed into a cluster, leaving the cache empty.

Although phase one is executed only once, phase two is repeated a certain number of times. This high number of executions combined with the memory latency will slow down the clustering process. Two stratagems have been used to minimize the slowdown. Firstly, using the fastest memory elements on the market (i.e. HMC modules[4]) helps to decrease the store/load time of each sequence[5]. Secondly, using the maximum number of parallel clustering units as possible decreases the number of executions of phase two since there will be less sequences for each run of phase two.

---

[4] http://hybridmemorycube.org/files/SiteDownloads/HMC_Specification_1_0.pdf.

[5] The memory is used as a circular buffer and only written to or read from in bursts to maximize the read/write speeds.

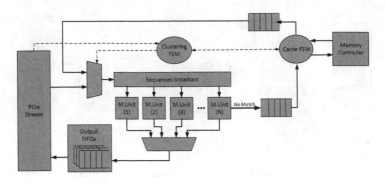

Fig. 6. Multi cluster implementation.

3.3 Parallel Clustering

Implementing the clustering units, who decide whether a sequence is part of a given cluster or not, in parallel, as is shown in Fig. 6, helps reducing processing time tremendously. However doing so has a few drawbacks. First, arbitration is needed. When a sequence matches the references of multiple clusters it should be decided of which single cluster the sequence will be a member. This is easily solved with priority based on the smallest matching distance. If multiple sequences match with the same priority we simply take the first one. A possible improvement on this would be to use the cluster size as a second order priority. Second the number of clustering units is limited by the FPGA size and by the latency of the sequence distribution over the FPGA surface. These drawbacks are however greatly restrained through clever hardware design.

3.4 Hardware Setup

The integration was done on a Micron Pico Computing hardware setting composed of an EX-700[6] backplane with AC-510[7] modules. The EX-700 can accomodate up to six modules and is composed of a x16 `PCIe` GEN 3 switch and a Spartan 6 FPGA. The latter is in charge of programming and configuring the FPGA modules. The AC-510 modules are the computational cores of the system. Each one consists of a Kintex Ultrascale 060 FPGA[8] directly connected to a 4GB HMC.

The most complex design implemented into a single AC-510 module so far is a design counting 70 clustering units with a matching function that is able to match reads with a position shift up to ±16 nucleotides and includes reverse complement matching. The matching of reads is fully parallelized with respect to the number of shifts and reverse complement using 21 nucleotide wide comparators. Therefore checking two 126 nucleotide reads for matches on all the possibilities takes 6 clock cycles. Everything is running at 125 MHz and the resource utilization is summarized in Table 1.

---

[6] http://picocomputing.com/products/backplanes/ex-700/.

[7] http://picocomputing.com/ac-510-superprocessor-module/.

[8] https://www.xilinx.com/products/silicon-devices/fpga/kintex-ultrascale.html.

Table 1. Resource usage for a design counting 70 matching units with ±16 shifts and reverse complement matching capability @ 125 MHz on a Kintex Ultrascale 060

Logic utilization	Used	Avail.	Usage
Number of slice registers	178'141	663'360	26.85%
Number of slice LUTs	227'394	331'680	68.56%
Number of occupied slices	40'714	41'460	98.20%
Number of BlockRAM/FIFO	221.5	1'080	20.51%

4   Tests and Results

This section summarizes the performance results and shows the speed gain achieved thanks to hardware acceleration on FPGA. Three hardware designs and three software versions were used. Each FPGA based version runs at 125 MHz, The software version runs on an Intel core i7-4790 Haswell 4-core hyper-threaded processor running at 4 GHz. All versions have reverse complement matching. The versions differ on the maximum number of shifts tolerated for the *match* function. This maximum number has a direct impact on the clustering units complexity, the lower the maximum number of shifts the smaller the hardware unit and the faster the software *match* function running time. This allows for hardware implementations with more clustering units in the same FPGA. It is also to be noted that by reducing this number a given sequence is less likely to be a member of an existing cluster. This will lower the average size of the final clusters and make the algorithm go through more passes of phase two. However as can be seen on Fig. 7 having more clustering units outweights the fact that the sequences are less likely to fit a cluster. This gives us a choice between bigger sized final clusters and faster processing. Figure 8 shows the number of clusters relative to their size (number of sequences in the cluster).

The sequences used during the experiments are unmapped paired sequences of 126 bases. They were generated using an Illumina sequencer on a real human sample.

The timing measurements shown in Fig. 7 were done using a single FPGA module and multi-threaded software using a single thread for the clustering algorithm. Both versions can benefit from more parallelism, having the hardware run on six modules and using more threads for the CPU version. Running the algorithm with six modules allowed us to process six times more data with the same timing results. This was possible because there is no dependency and no I/O bottleneck since the unmatched sequences reside in the HMC local to the modules. Having six threads for the clustering units on our 4-core CPU (8 logical cores thanks to hyper-threading) processed six times more sequences but also ran slower due to resource sharing (memory) resulting in a speedup of only 3.53 compared to the speedup of 6 on the multi FPGA version.

In order to do clustering on a real case, around 100 million sequences would have to be processed (~24GB FASTQ file). To do this the file would be split between six FPGA modules or 6 CPU cores limiting the amount of time needed

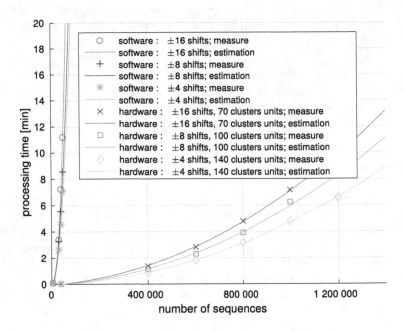

Fig. 7. System running time depending on input file size.

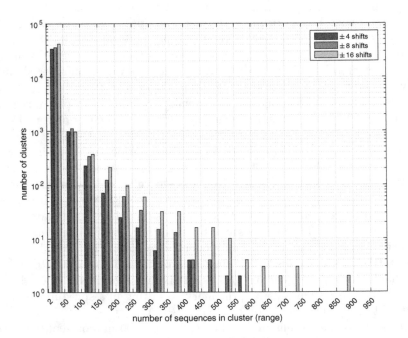

Fig. 8. Number of clusters depending on the number of matched sequences.

to process it. Table 2 shows the time needed to achieve this. The values were measured or extrapolated[9] from real timing measurements using a FASTQ file of unaligned sequences (with respect to the reference genome).

All in all, the software versions take so much time they rapidly become unusable. However the results using FPGA acceleration seem reasonable.

Table 2. Proc. time needed to cluster a real case file of $\sim 100 \times 10^6$ unaligned sequences

	24GB FASTQ	6×4GB FASTQ
Software config.	1 core	6 cores
±16 shifts	≈ 95 years	≈ 2.6 years
Hardware config.	1 AC-510	6 AC-510
±16 shifts, 70 clusters units	≈ 37 days	14.8 hours
±8 shifts, 100 clusters units	≈ 31 days	14.0 hours
±4 shifts, 140 clusters units	≈ 26 days	12.6 hours

The effective speed gain between using software running on CPU and using FPGA based accelerators is colossal. It takes more than a 1000 times longer in software, leading to an impressive 2.6 years of CPU processing, to cluster unaligned sequences of a single person's genome. This becomes much more acceptable using FPGA based acceleration and now requires only around half a day of processing time. It is to be noted that while the FPGAs are processing the sequences the CPU is almost at idle, where its only task is to collect results and to write them to a file. The CPU potential processing power could be used, e.g., joining cluster results from different FPGAs.

In terms of power consumption, running the software on the same PC draws around 100 W of power (without FPGA card installed). Running the software with FPGA accelerators, the PC draws around 220 W of power. In terms of energy needed for the task the CPU version needs 100 W for 2.6 years and the FPGA based version 220 W for under a day. This is almost 700 times less energy.

5   Conclusions and Future Works

The goal of this paper was to introduce a clustering framework based on FPGA acceleration, with the idea of providing clusters of sequences to ease genomic data compression. A solution for clustering unaligned genomic sequences has been found and verified. This solution already offers a massive speed gain against processor based implementations (×1000) as well a significant energy savings (×700). The framework is modular enough to be easily modified and further developped. This allows to explore new (compression) algorithms using clustering as well as to research new algorithms for general genomic data processing.

---

[9] The values following the $\approx$ sign in Table 2 are extrapolated.

To improve on and go further with this work several paths could be taken. Having a `PCIe` switch on the FPGA board makes it possible for the modules to communicate using `PCIe x8` links without interfering with the PC. Communication between units could allow for better clustering results. Using heterogenous accelerators in this setup would grant even more possibilities. Future work should also include quantifying compression rates relative to the clustering algorithm in order to determine the best implementation (in number of shifts and clusters).

This work provides a solid basis to further expand research in the field of genomic data processing and proved possible to run algorithms of high complexity, such as $O(n^2)$, on big datasets in reasonable time.

Acknowledgments. The reasearch presented in this paper was funded by the Swiss PASC initiative in the framework of the PoSeNoGap (Portable Scalable Concurrency for Genomic Data Processing) project. The authors would like to thank all the participants for the fruitful discussions, namely Ioannis Xenarios, Thierry Schüpbach and Daniel Zerzion from SIB, Marco Mattavelli and Claudio Alberti from EPFL.

References

1. Cox, A.J., Bauer, M.J., Jakobi, T., Rosone, G.: Large-scale compression of genomic sequence databases with the burrows-wheeler transform. Bioinformatics **28**(11), 1415–1419 (2012)
2. Deorowicz, S., Grabowski, S.: Compression of DNA sequence reads in FASTQ format. Bioinformatics **27**(6), 860–862 (2011)
3. Du, K.L.: Clustering: a neural network approach. Neural Netw. **23**(1), 89–107 (2010)
4. Fritz, M.H.Y., Leinonen, R., Cochrane, G., Birney, E.: Efficient storage of high throughput DNA sequencing data using reference-based compression. Genome Res. **21**(5), 734–740 (2011)
5. Hussain, H.M., Benkrid, K., Seker, H., Erdogan, A.T.: FPGA implementation of k-means algorithm for bioinformatics application: an accelerated approach to clustering microarray data. In: 2011 NASA/ESA Conference on Adaptive Hardware and Systems (AHS), pp. 248–255, June 2011
6. Jain, A.K.: Data clustering: 50 years beyond k-means. Pattern Recogn. Lett. **31**(8), 651–666 (2010). Award Winning Papers from the 19th International Conference on Pattern Recognition (ICPR) 19th International Conference in Pattern Recognition (ICPR)
7. Pinho, A.J., Pratas, D., Garcia, S.P.: Green: a tool for efficient compression of genome resequencing data. Nucleic Acids Res. **40**(4), e27 (2011)
8. Pollard, K.S., van der Laan, M.J.: Bioinformatics and computational biology solutions using R and bioconductor. In: Gentleman, R., Carey, V.J., Huber, W., Irizarry, R.A., Dudoit, S. (eds.) Cluster Analysis of Genomic Data, pp. 209–228. Springer, New York (2005)
9. Stephens, Z.D., Lee, S.Y., Faghri, F., Campbell, R.H., Zhai, C., Efron, M.J., Iyer, R., Schatz, M.C., Sinha, S., Robinson, G.E.: Big data: astronomical or genomical? Plos Biol. **13**(7), e1002195 (2015)
10. Winterstein, F., Bayliss, S., Constantinides, G.A.: FPGA-based k-means clustering using tree-based data structures. In: 23rd International Conference on Field programmable Logic and Applications. pp. 1–6, September 2013

A Quantitative Analysis of the Memory Architecture of FPGA-SoCs

Matthias Göbel[1]([✉]), Ahmed Elhossini[1], Chi Ching Chi[2],
Mauricio Alvarez-Mesa[2], and Ben Juurlink[1]

[1] Embedded Systems Architecture, Technische Universität Berlin, Berlin, Germany
{m.goebel,ahmed.elhossini,b.juurlink}@tu-berlin.de
[2] Spin Digital Video Technologies GmbH, Berlin, Germany
{chi,mauricio}@spin-digital.com

Abstract. In recent years, so called *FPGA-SoCs* have been introduced by Intel (formerly Altera) and Xilinx. These devices combine multi-core processors with programmable logic. This paper analyzes the various memory and communication interconnects found in actual devices, particularly the Zynq-7020 and Zynq-7045 from Xilinx and the Cyclone V SE SoC from Intel. Issues such as different access patterns, cache coherence and full-duplex communication are analyzed, for both generic accesses as well as for a real workload from the field of video coding. Furthermore, the paper shows that by carefully choosing the memory interconnect networks as well as the software interface, high-speed memory access can be achieved for various scenarios.

1 Introduction

HW/SW-codesign is a common approach applied in domains where neither pure hardware nor pure software implementations offer a satisfying solution. It combines the advantages of both hardware and software and therefore delivers an elaborated solution to a given problem. FPGA manufacturers such as Xilinx and Intel are offering devices, often called *FPGA-SoCs*, that combine an FPGA logic fabric and a dedicated processor, which in the end allows for a significant performance gain when using HW/SW-codesign compared to pure software solutions.

In order to achieve high speedup, it is clearly important to achieve high performance of both the hardware and the software. However, without having sufficient memory bandwidth it is not possible to unleash the full potential of such a solution. In fact, the memory bandwidth often poses the bottleneck in HW/SW-codesigns and therefore limits the overall performance: While it is possible to achieve a very high throughput in an FPGA, the memory interface is in many cases not able to provide input and store output data fast enough [1,2]. Therefore, many research papers are only presenting the throughput inside the FPGA while disregarding the memory bandwidth [3,4]. For this reason, this work presents an analysis of the memory architecture of FPGA-SoCs.

Two representative low-cost FPGA-SoCs have been chosen for the analysis, particularly the *Zynq-7020* from Xilinx and the *Cyclone V SE* SoC from Intel.

© Springer International Publishing AG 2017
S. Wong et al. (Eds.): ARC 2017, LNCS 10216, pp. 241–252, 2017.
DOI: 10.1007/978-3-319-56258-2_21

Furthermore, the same benchmarks have been performed on the *Zynq-7045* from Xilinx to show the memory bandwidth of a high-performance FPGA-SoC. These results have also been compared to a system using a configurable soft-core memory controller from Xilinx. This allows for a comparison of the memory bandwidth of FPGA-SoCs with soft-core SoCs using Xilinx's *Microblaze* or Intel's *Nios II*. The best configurations for all these devices are discussed and their respective strengths are highlighted.

The main contribution of this paper is the evaluation of the memory subsystems of the Zynq-7000 SoC from Xilinx and the Cyclone V SoC from Intel, taking into account all of the following:

1. Memory access from software as well as from hardware
2. Coherent as well as non-coherent access
3. Independent read and write transactions
4. Coupling of multiple memory ports
5. Fine-grained, two-dimensional transactions that are often found in video coding and image processing kernels
6. Evaluation of the available memory bandwidth for H.265/HEVC motion compensation as a representative for such video coding kernels

The paper is structured as follows: First, some related work is presented in Sect. 2 to give an overview of the current state-of-the-art. Then, in Sect. 3, a short introduction to the FPGA-SoCs from Intel and Xilinx is given with a focus on their memory interface. This is followed in Sect. 4 by a description of the implemented memory engines that are used to measure the bandwidth under various circumstances. In Sect. 5, the Zynq-7020 and the Cyclone V SE SoC are evaluated and compared, followed by an analysis of the Zynq-7045 and Xilinx's soft-core memory controller. Finally, the paper is concluded in Sect. 6.

2   Related Work

Some other work already evaluated the memory bandwidth of FPGA-SoCs. First results are given by Sadri et al. [5]. They analyzed the memory interfaces of the Zynq-7020 with a focus on the *Accelerator Coherency Port* (ACP), which allows coherent access from IP cores implemented in logic to main memory. The results show that it is possible to achieve a full-duplex throughput of up to 1.7 GB/s when using a single port between memory and programmable logic, with the IP core running at a fixed frequency of 125 MHz.

Sklyarov et al. [6] also evaluated the Zynq-7020. Although the maximum bandwidth at the chosen frequency of 100 MHz is not given explicitly, it can be derived from the results that the achieved maximum bandwidth is significantly lower than the theoretical maximum (e.g. 284 MB/s for a 64-bit port when reading and writing 32 KB instead of the theoretically possible 800 MB/s).

Furthermore, Tahghighi et al. [7] present a mathematical model that allows to estimate the latency of a memory access from the programmable logic. While the model covers several parameters, it is currently limited to the Zynq-7000. It also does not give an overview of the available memory bandwidth for different access patterns. Similar to [5], it does not cover the combination of multiple ports to increase the overall memory bandwidth.

Although these papers provide valuable information, several of our questions remain unanswered. For instance, the combination of multiple ports yields a significant increase in bandwidth thus expanding the field of applications suitable for FPGA-SoCs to a broader range. While this is analyzed in [6], their results are surprisingly low. In comparison, our results show a significantly higher bandwidth when combining multiple ports. Furthermore, to the best of our knowledge, our work is the first to include multiple devices that cover a large part of the market (Xilinx's Zynq-7020 and Zynq-7045 + Intel's Cyclone V SE SoC + Xilinx's Microblaze) while all the related papers only use the Zynq-7020 for their evaluations thus limiting their impact.

3   FPGA-SoCs

FPGA-SoCs are devices that contain a dedicated hard-core processor with various peripherals and programmable logic. Both components are located on the same chip, which allows them to be tightly coupled. Such devices are offered by Xilinx [8] and Intel [9]. Both combine a 32-bit dual-core ARM Cortex-A9 based CPU with programmable logic. This CPU uses the ARMv7-A architecture and support NEON SIMD instructions. A two-level cache hierarchy is available that provides 32 KB of L1 per core and a shared 512 KB L2 cache.

Xilinx offers the Zynq-7000 family of so-called *All-programmable SoCs* while Intel offers SoCs as part of their Cyclone, Stratix and Arria product lines to cover the whole market. Both vendors have already announced successors to their current FPGA-SoCs, featuring a 64-bit quad-core ARM Cortex-A53 CPU and more logic resources. However, as they were not publicly available at the time of this work, they could not be included.

While Xilinx devices use only support the ARM AXI standard, Intel supports AXI as well as their own Avalon standard. For the sake of comparison, only the AXI mode of Intel's devices was taken into account. Both vendors offer a variety of master and slave ports suitable for different applications. As the master ports (i.e. the CPU is the master) cannot be used directly to access the DDR memory from the programmable logic, these ports will not be discussed in this work.

Xilinx's Zynq-7000 devices offer the following ports for the programmable logic to access memory:

1. **General-purpose** (GP) ports
   These two ports have a fixed width of 32 bits and no internal buffers, making them a good choice for low-throughput applications.
2. **High-performance** (HP) ports
   Four slave ports with widths of either 32 or 64 bits with built-in FIFOs are available for high-throughput applications.
3. **Accelerator Coherency Port** (ACP)
   This additional 64-bit port resembles the HP ports. However, the ACP allows cache-coherent access to the memory.

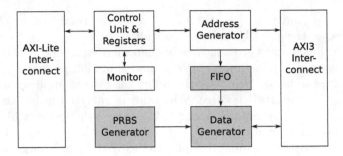

Fig. 1. The engines that are used to perform one- or two-dimensional accesses to main memory. A register-based AXI-Lite interface for control tasks and a full-scaled AXI master interface for data transfer connect the engine to the CPU and the main memory. Note that the gray blocks are only required for the write engine.

For Intel's SoCs, the layout of the ports for accessing memory is as follows:

1. **FPGA-to-HPS** (F2H) port
   This port has a configurable width of 32, 64 or 128 bits.
2. **FPGA-to-SDRAM** (F2S) port
   Instead of offering four ports like the Zynq's HP ports, the Intel SoCs have one port which is directly connected to the memory controller. This port, however, can be split into up to three independent AXI ports with a combined port width of up to 256 bits (e.g. 1×256-bit or 1×128-bit + 2×64-bit).
3. **Accelerator Coherency Port** (ACP)
   This port matches the ACP of the Zynq regarding DDR memory access.

4   Architecture of Memory Engines

In this section, the designs and implementations of the so-called *memory engines* are presented briefly. These engines allow to gain the required insights into the potential bandwidth of the different ports. They are designed to support one- and two-dimensional access to memory with a fixed stride, as well as trace-based inputs, i.e. a list of specific memory transactions. As this work focuses on high-throughput applications, the GP ports of the Zynq-7000 and the F2H port of Intel's SoC are not evaluated.

Figure 1 shows the general structure of the *Write Engine* that is used to determine the achievable write bandwidth for different scenarios. It has two different AXI interfaces: a full-scale AXI master interface for the actual memory access connected to one of the ports mentioned in Sect. 3 and a register-based AXI-Lite interface for control and configuration purposes. The latter is connected to the CPU using dedicated AXI ports that are not suitable for memory access. While Xilinx and Intel offer IP cores supporting AXI4, their FPGA-SoCs only support AXI3 for memory access. Therefore, the maximum number of bursts in one request is 16. By using the control interface, the specific scenario in terms of height and width of the access as well as the stride for two-dimensional access, i.e. the offset between two bytes in the same column, can be controlled.

The parameters stored in these registers are used by a *Control Unit*, which splits the two-dimensional block into one-dimensional transactions if necessary. These requests are afterwards converted into AXI transactions by an *Address Generator*. This unit is connected to the address lines of the AXI interface and drives the required signals. In addition, it deals with alignment issues. The requests are buffered in a FIFO from which they are read by a *Data Generator*. It writes the requested amount of data from a *Pseudo-Random Binary Sequence* (PRBS) generator to main memory.

To accurately measure the throughput of each operation, a *Monitor* has been added that measures the number of cycles the operation takes. It communicates with the CPU by using the register interface.

The implemented *Read Engine* for reading data from main memory has a very similar structure. However, as no data has to be generated and written for reading data, the corresponding generator and the FIFO are not required in this case.

5   Experimental Design and Performance Analysis

The implemented read and write engines have been used to evaluate the bandwidth of the interconnect ports and the memory system of the chosen FPGA-SoCs. In particular, two different benchmarks have been designed for this purpose:

1. A synthetic benchmark for one- or two-dimensional transactions. Performing a two-dimensional transaction can be understood as reading or writing a block of data (e.g. a part of an image) from/to memory with each row of the block consisting of one or multiple one-dimensional transactions.
2. A trace-based benchmark that simulates the memory transactions that are performed during H.265/HEVC motion compensation.

While the first benchmark gives an overview of the bandwidth that can be expected for a given width and height, the latter allows to measure the bandwidth for a real-world scenario with a mix of different block sizes. In this section, a comparison of the Zynq-7020 and the Cyclone V SoC will be discussed, as these are two chips in the same price segment. Later, the same benchmarks will be used to evaluate a high-performance FPGA-SoC, the Zynq-7045, in order to show the difference between low-cost FPGA-SoCs and high-performance FPGA-SoCs. Finally, a comparison to a system which uses Xilinx's soft-core memory controller instead of the hard-core memory controller of an FPGA-SoC will be presented. This allows comparing the bandwidth of the memory controller of an FPGA-SoC with that of a soft-core SoC such as Xilinx's Microblaze or Intel's Nios-II running on an FPGA.

All the benchmarks used in this work are optimized for high bandwidth. As a result, the highest possible number of data beats per burst is used.

5.1 Synthetic Benchmark

Cyclone V SoC and Zynq-7020. The experiments in this part have been performed using the *DE1-SoC Board* from Terasic that features Intel's Cyclone V SoC and the *Zedboard* from Digilent with Xilinx's Zynq-7020. The bandwidth is given in MiB/s, i.e. 2^{20} *bytes/s*, and not in 10^6 *bytes/s*.

In order to get an overview of the achievable throughput for accessing different patterns in main memory, a synthetic benchmark has been used. It takes the width and height of the block being processed as well as the stride as parameters. The analyzed configurations include cached and non-cached software implementations as well as hardware implementations with different number of HP ports (Xilinx) or different widths of the F2S port (Intel) and with the ACP.

To have a reasonable baseline, the software implementations are NEON-accelerated, i.e. they use SIMD memory instructions to maximize the throughput. The non-ACP hardware implementations have been performed using a fixed frequency of 110 MHz for both the memory engine and the AXI bus, while the ACP implementation uses a frequency of 100 MHz. These are the maximum frequencies, i.e. the highest frequencies for which the memory engines could be placed and routed on all devices. The CPU on the Intel device is running at 800 MHz and also uses 800 MT/s for the memory controller. Xilinx uses a CPU with a frequency of 666 MHz, but 1066 MT/s to access the DDR memory. Due to the different memory data rates, the theoretical maximum bandwidth for DDR memory access is higher for the Zynq-7020 (4066 MiB/s) than for the Cyclone V SoC (3052 MiB/s). For all hardware experiments, the memory controller has been configured to prioritize the programmable logic memory ports and therefore minimize the impact of parallel memory accesses from software.

Figure 2(a)-(f) shows the results for the software and the non-ACP hardware scenarios. In this figure, a fixed stride of 1 MiB and a fixed height of 50 rows have been used while the width in bytes is the variable parameter with a range from 1 byte to 1 MiB. The choice of a height of 50 rows has been made as heights in this range are found quite often in video coding applications, an important domain when analyzing two-dimensional memory accesses. An example is the block structure of HEVC/H.265 [10]. A fixed stride of 1 MiB has been used as the stride must be larger or equal to the width. Thus, this choice allows for evaluating different memory accesses with a width of up to 1 MiB while using the same stride. Due to the choices of height and stride, this can either be interpreted as a single two-dimensional access with a height of 50 and a stride of 1 MiB or as 50 one-dimensional accesses with a fixed distance of 1 MiB between them. Therefore, it provides information for one- as well as two-dimensional access.

For reading, the non-cached SW baseline has the lowest throughput for both devices with a maximum bandwidth of 256 MiB/s on the Zynq-7020 and 150 MiB/s on the Cyclone V SoC. On the other hand, for the cached SW baseline, the Intel device has a significantly higher bandwidth of up to 996 MiB/s compared to a maximum of 751 MiB/s for its Xilinx counterpart. These differences are probably caused by the lower frequency of the Xilinx CPU and therefore of the caches. However, starting at around 16 KiB, i.e. the width where the 512 KiB L2

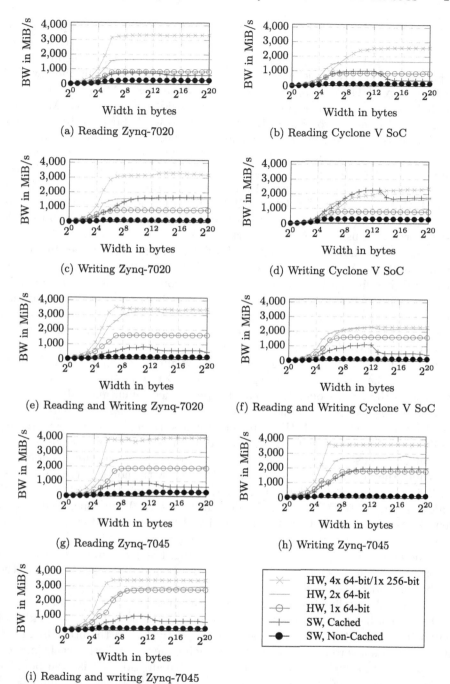

(a) Reading Zynq-7020

(b) Reading Cyclone V SoC

(c) Writing Zynq-7020

(d) Writing Cyclone V SoC

(e) Reading and Writing Zynq-7020

(f) Reading and Writing Cyclone V SoC

(g) Reading Zynq-7045

(h) Writing Zynq-7045

(i) Reading and writing Zynq-7045

Fig. 2. The bandwidth (BW) for a fixed stride of 1 MiB and a height of 50 rows. The HW implementations are running at 110 MHz (Zynq-7020 and Cyclone V SoC) and 214 MHz (Zynq-7045 4x/2x) or 250 MHz (Zynq-7045 1x). The CPUs are running at 666 MHz (Zynq-7020) or 800 MHz (Zynq-7045 and Cyclone V SoC). Note that for the combined read and write transactions the added bandwidth for reading and writing is given.

Cache can no longer hold the entire 50 rows, the Zynq-7020 again outperforms it counterpart. The stride of 1 MiB induces several cache misses in this case, which allows for comparing it to the other non-cached accesses in this benchmark.

For the 64-bit HW implementation, both devices are limited by the low AXI bus frequency of 110 MHz resulting in a bandwidth of 839 MiB/s. By using all four HP ports or a 256-bit F2S port, higher bandwidths of up to 3337 MiB/s for the Zynq-7020 and up to 2590 MiB/s for the Cyclone V SoC can be achieved. The difference is caused by the higher memory data rate for the Zynq-7020 of 1066 MT/s. It can also be seen that the 256-bit F2S port of the Cyclone V SoC requires a higher block width to reach its maximum bandwidth. Both devices behave similarly when using two 64-bit ports in parallel, reaching a maximum of 1644 MiB/s (Cyclone V SoC) and 1689 MiB/s (Zynq-7020), respectively. In particular, for small block widths it turns out to be more reasonable to use two 64-bit ports than using one 256-bit port.

Figure 2 also shows the writing results for the same settings, again for the software and non-ACP hardware scenarios. The main difference is the improved cached SW baseline for both devices. For the Cyclone V SoC it is even comparable to the 256-bit HW implementation. In general, for the HW implementations, the same behavior as for reading can be seen: The 64-bit implementation is limited by the AXI interconnect frequency, while the 256-bit solution of Xilinx outperforms the Intel one.

The plots (e) and (f) in Fig. 2 show the result of reading and writing in parallel. As the read and write signals of an AXI interface are independent from each other, both operations can be performed simultaneously. This has been accomplished by instantiating a read and a write engine in parallel. For the 64-bit and the 2 × 64-bit HW implementations, the bandwidth has increased significantly. This is caused by the increase of the bus width: As two independent data busses are used for reading and writing, the effective bus width is doubled.

While the former experiments deal mostly with non-coherent accesses, Fig. 3(a)-(d) compares reading from main memory using the ACP in coherent mode running at 100 MHz to the NEON-accelerated SW baseline. The chosen scenario uses a stride of 1 MiB and a height of 5, 10, 20 or 100 rows. The different heights are required to analyze the impact of the cache architecture on the bandwidth. To see the full impact of caching, the same operation has been performed 100 times before starting the actual measurements as this reduces the number of cold cache misses.

For the SW baseline it can be seen that caching is especially useful for small heights. For a height of 5 rows and a fixed width of 4096 bytes a bandwidth of 3839 MiB/s and 5441 MiB/s can be seen, respectively. On the other hand, for larger heights some rows are removed from cache due to conflicting cache misses, which results in a higher miss rate. In fact, for small widths it is even possible on the Cyclone V SoC to achieve bandwidths higher than the maximum DDR bandwidth of 3052 MiB/s.

For the ACP, the bandwidth is significantly lower compared to the SW baseline. The data bus width of 8 bytes and the employed frequency of 100 MHz

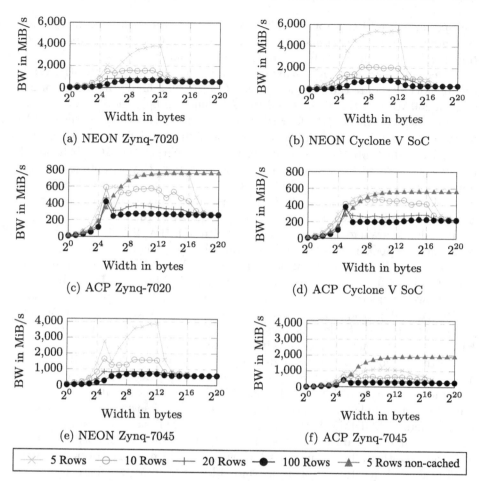

Fig. 3. The cached read bandwidth (BW) for a fixed stride of 1 MiB. Note the different scale for the Zynq-7045. For all scenarios, the same transactions have been performed 100 times before starting the measurement in order to fill the caches and therefore maximize the throughput.

limit the bandwidth to 763 MiB/s. In fact, for widths smaller than 256 bytes, a higher bandwidth can simply be reached by performing non-coherent accesses on the ACP. Anomalously high is the ACP bandwidth for a width of 32 bytes. As this behavior occurs on both devices, it indicates a general limitation of the ACP port.

Zynq-7045 and Soft-Core Memory Controller. The previous part of the evaluation deals with two low-cost FPGA-SoCs. More powerful FPGA-SoCs are also available, however. Furthermore, HW/SW-codesign can also be realized by using soft-core SoCs. In this part, the *Zynq-7045* as an example of a high-performance FPGA-SoC as well as Xilinx's soft-core memory controller are evaluated. The same benchmarks as before have been used. The *ZC706 Evaluation Board* from Xilinx has been employed for evaluation.

The results for the Zynq-7045 are depicted in Figs. 2(g)-(i) and 3(e)-(f). While the memory ports are the same as for the Zynq-7020, a higher frequency of 214 or even 250 MHz for the engines and the AXI bus can be achieved. As a result, the bottleneck when using the four HP ports in parallel is not located in the AXI interconnect as before, but caused by the maximum bandwidth of the memory controller of 4066 MiB/s. Furthermore, when comparing the ACP benchmark results for all three FPGA-SoCs, it can be seen that the advantage of using non-coherent accesses for larger blocks compared to coherent accesses is even more significant for the Zynq-7045. Besides these aspects, the results for the Zynq-7045 qualitatively match the results for the Zynq-7020.

In order to evaluate the memory bandwidth of a HW/SW-codesign running on a soft-core SoC, a soft-core memory controller [11] has been evaluated. This memory controller can be instantiated in various Xilinx FPGAs which are connected to DDR memory. In this case, the same ZC706 board as before has been used. However, instead of using the memory connected to the hard-core memory controller of the Zynq, an external 1 GB DDR3 SODIMM is connected to the soft-core memory controller. As a result, the Zynq-7045 behaves like an ordinary FPGA in this evaluation, i.e. one without a hard-core CPU.

As the memory controller is highly configurable, it can use an AXI bus with a data width of up to 512 bits. The design could be placed and routed with a maximum frequency of 166 MHz for the AXI interconnect, resulting in a maximum read or write bandwidth of 10132 MiB/s. In fact, as the ZC706 Evaluation Board offers an SODIMM with a data rate of 1600 MT/s and a bus width of 64 bits, a maximum bandwidth of even 12207 MiB/s could be obtained in theory. The same synthetic benchmarks as for the hard-core memory controllers have been evaluated, resulting in a peak bandwidth of 9230 MiB/s for reading and 8754 MiB/s for writing. This is significantly higher than the maximum memory bandwidth for any of the current FPGA-SoCs.

5.2   H.265/HEVC Trace-Based Benchmark

HEVC motion compensation has been evaluated as a representative real benchmark. It processes blocks (i.e. parts of video frames) of size between 4×2 and 128×64 bytes. As it also requires a different number of neighboring pixels of these blocks, it actually has to read blocks of size between 7×5 and 142×71 bytes. Furthermore, it has to write blocks between 32×32 and 128×64 bytes.

A trace of the application's memory transactions has been generated. Afterwards, these memory accesses have been performed on different FPGA-SoCs. The results are depicted in Fig. 4. On the two Zynq systems, two or four HP ports have been used to process different parts of the same frame in parallel. Otherwise, each frame has been processed sequentially. For benchmarking the Zynq-7045, a frequency of 214 MHz has been employed, with a frequency of

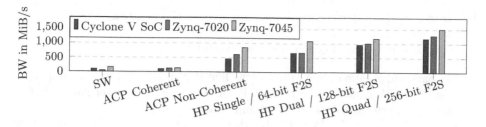

Fig. 4. The achievable read bandwidth (BW) for a trace-based simulation of the memory accesses of the motion mompensation stage of an H.265/HEVC decoder. A Full HD video stream with a medium bitrate has been used.

100 MHz for the other two SoCs. Again, these frequencies pose the maximum on each device for this implementation.

It can be seen that both the SW baseline and the coherent ACP implementation offer a very low bandwidth of less than 200 MiB/s. In comparison, non-coherent HW solutions offer a significantly higher throughput. While the bandwidth does not scale perfectly with the number of ports (Zynq) or the port width (Cyclone V), it allows to increase the bandwidth significantly this way. As the difference for 256-bits between the 100 MHz solution on the low-cost FPGA SoCs and the 214 MHz solution on the Zynq-7045 is rather small, the bottleneck is apparently not located in the AXI bus, but instead in the memory controller itself. For the HP Quad solution on the Zynq-7045, a bandwidth of 1515 MiB/s can be reached, which is sufficient for real-time Full HD decoding [12].

The theoretical maximum of 4066 MiB/s on the Zynq cannot be reached, however. This can be explained with the different block sizes: As can be seen in Fig. 2(g), the expected bandwidth when using four HP ports is below 1000 MiB/s for those blocks with the smallest width (5 bytes) in this workload. On the other hand, a bandwidth of almost 4000 MiB/s can be reached for those blocks with the largest width (142 bytes). As a result, the actual bandwidth is in between these two extremes. An analysis of the block sizes for the workload shows that almost 50% of the blocks have a width smaller than 16 bytes and more than 80% of the blocks have a width smaller than 32 bytes. Therefore, the small memory accesses dominate which results in a relatively low bandwidth.

6   Conclusions

In this paper, three different FPGA-SoCs from Xilinx and Intel have been evaluated regarding their memory bandwidth. In particular, two low-cost devices, the *Zynq-7020* from Xilinx and the *Cyclone V SoC* from Intel, have been compared. The *Zynq-7045* from Xilinx has been evaluated as an example for a high-performance FPGA-SoC. By using several synthetic benchmarks, it has been possible to determine the memory bandwidth for various scenarios. A real workload from the field of video coding has been applied as well. Finally, the bandwidth of these devices has been compared to the bandwidth of a soft-core memory controller.

The following general conclusions can be drawn:

- For bandwidth-demanding applications like H.265/HEVC motion compensation, HW/SW-codesigns on recent FPGA-SoCs have the potential to significantly outperform SW solutions running on the same CPU.
- High-performance FPGA-SoCs like the *Zynq-7045* offer significantly higher bandwidth than low-cost devices. However, the maximum bandwidth of the memory controller of 4066 MiB/s can pose a bottleneck in this case.
- For applications with demanding memory bandwidth requirements and moderate CPU performance requirements, a soft-core SoC system might be a reasonable choice as it offers up to 9230 MiB/s.

References

1. Fu, H., Clapp, R.: Eliminating the memory bottleneck: an FPGA-based solution for 3D reverse time migration. In: 19th ACM/SIGDA International Symposium on Field Programmable Gate Arrays (FPGA), Monterey, USA (2011)
2. Naylor, M., Fox, P., Markettos, A., Moore, S.: Managing the FPGA memory wall: custom computing or vector processing? In: 23rd International Conference on Field Programmable Logic and Applications (FPL), Porto, Portugal (2013)
3. Dobai, R., Sekanina, L.: Image filter evolution on the Xilinx Zynq platform. In: NASA/ESA Conference on Adaptive Hardware and Systems (AHS), Turin, Italy (2013)
4. Ishikawa, S., Tanaka, A., Miyazaki, T.: Hardware accelerator for BLAST. In: 6th IEEE International Symposium on Embedded Multicore SoCs (MCSoC), Aizu-Wakamatsu, Japan (2012)
5. Sadri, M., Weis, C., Wehn, N., Benini, L.: Energy and performance exploration of accelerator coherency port Using Xilinx Zynq. In: ACM 10th FPGAWorld Conference, Copenhagen, Denmark, Stockholm, Sweden (2013)
6. Sklyarov, V., Skliarova, I., Silva, J., Sudnitson, A.: Analysis and comparison of attainable hardware acceleration in all programmable systems-on-chip. In: 2015 Euromicro Conference on Digital System Design (DSD), Funchal, Portugal (2015)
7. Tahghighi, M., Sinha, S., Zhang, W.: Analytical delay model for CPU-FPGA data paths in programmable system-on-chip FPGA. In: 12th International Symposium on Applied Reconfigurable Computing (ARC), Mangaratiba, Brazil (2016)
8. Zynq-7000 All Programmable SoC Technical Reference Manual by Xilinx. http://www.xilinx.com/support/documentation/user_guides/ug585-Zynq-7000-TRM.pdf
9. Altera's User-Customizable ARM-based SoCs by Altera. http://www.altera.com/literature/br/br-soc-fpga.pdf
10. Sullivan, G., Ohm, J.-R., Han, W.-J., Wiegand, T.: Overview of the High Efficiency Video Coding (HEVC) standard. IEEE Trans. Circuits Syst. Video Technol. **22**(12), 1649–1668 (2012)
11. 7 Series FPGAs Memory Interface Solutions User Guide by Xilinx
12. Chi, C.C., Alvarez-Mesa, M., Bross, B., Juurlink, B., Schierl, T.: SIMD acceleration for HEVC decoding. IEEE Trans. Circuits Syst. Video Technol. **25**, 841–855 (2014)

Neural Networks

Optimizing CNN-Based Object Detection Algorithms on Embedded FPGA Platforms

Ruizhe Zhao[1]([✉]), Xinyu Niu[1], Yajie Wu[2], Wayne Luk[1], and Qiang Liu[3]

[1] Imperial College London, London, UK
{ruizhe.zhao15,niu.xinyu10,w.luk}@imperial.ac.uk
[2] Corerain Technology, Shanghai, China
james.wu@corerain.com
[3] Tianjin University, Tianjin, China
qiangliu@tju.edu.cn

Abstract. Algorithms based on Convolutional Neural Network (CNN) have recently been applied to object detection applications, greatly improving their performance. However, many devices intended for these algorithms have limited computation resources and strict power consumption constraints, and are not suitable for algorithms designed for GPU workstations. This paper presents a novel method to optimise CNN-based object detection algorithms targeting embedded FPGA platforms. Given parameterised CNN hardware modules, an optimisation flow takes network architectures and resource constraints as input, and tunes hardware parameters with algorithm-specific information to explore the design space and achieve high performance. The evaluation shows that our design model accuracy is above 85% and, with optimised configuration, our design can achieve 49.6 times speed-up compared with software implementation.

1 Introduction

Object detection is a fundamental and difficult computer vision problem that requires the solution not only to tell what the image is about, but also to recognise the objects inside the image. A typical object detection algorithm consists of two major steps: bounding boxes regression and inner object classification. Traditional approaches like sliding window and region-based algorithms suffer from low accuracy and long execution time. Recently, several new CNN-based algorithms, which inherit successful image classification CNN architectures (e.g. VGGNet, GoogLeNet, etc.) and integrate them into object detection problem, beat old ones in accuracy (best mean average precision 83.6% on PASCAL VOC 2007 from R-FCN [3]) and in execution time (155 frames per second for Fast YOLO [9]).

While these state-of-the-art CNN-based object detection algorithms look promising, they may not be suitable to be deployed on embedded systems without modification. There are three main challenges: (1) Most of the CNN architectures for object detection algorithms do not have identical layer parameters

© Springer International Publishing AG 2017
S. Wong et al. (Eds.): ARC 2017, LNCS 10216, pp. 255–267, 2017.
DOI: 10.1007/978-3-319-56258-2_22

(e.g. different convolution layers can have different kernel sizes, such as 3 × 3, 7 × 7 and 11 × 11), which increases the difficulty of designing generic hardware modules that can be adapted to varying parameters. (2) Object detection algorithms use deep and complex CNN architectures, which makes it hard to fit the network into an FPGA and to decide the optimal parameters of hardware modules. (3) Multiple **backbone** CNN architectures are available to an object detection algorithm, and the more accurate an architecture can achieve, the more hardware resources it will require.

Our main contribution in this paper is a CNN accelerator design customised for object detection algorithms on an embedded FPGA platform. This design can tackle those three aforementioned challenges: (1) This design is built upon parameterised hardware modules that can be configured for different layer parameters. (2) We develop design models for estimating resource usage of deep CNN architectures. (3) We present an optimisation flow that treats two CNN-based object detection algorithms (YOLO and Faster RCNN) and their backbone CNN architectures as candidates, in order to find the optimal hardware design under different optimisation targets (e.g. speed or accuracy). At the end of this paper, we provide evaluation results for both the design model accuracy and the performance of the optimal hardware design. To the best of our knowledge, this is the first work to support end-to-end development of CNN-based object detection applications with FPGA accelerators.

2   Background and Related Work

Background. A typical CNN contains multiple computation layers which are concatenated together. There are 3 different kinds of layers that are frequently found in CNN architectures: Convolution layer (conv layer), fully-connected layer (fc layer), and max pooling layer (pooling layer). Details of these three layers are as follows.

1. **Convolution layer** mainly performs convolution operation between the input matrix - a representation for the input image or a feature map (will be discussed later), and the convolution kernel - a tiny coefficient matrix.

   Given f is the filter index, c is the channel index and C is the total number of channels, then the convolution layer can be described as follows:

$$O_f = \sum_{c=1}^{C} \text{conv}(I_c, K_{f,c}) + b_f \tag{1}$$

   This equation means that each output filter will sum up all convolution results between each channel of the input feature map (I_c) and the kernel ($K_{f,c}$). In many architectures, an activation function can be applied to the result elements, like Rectified Linear Unit (ReLU).

2. **Fully-Connected layer** is an affine transformation of the input feature vector. Fully-connected layer contains a single matrix-vector multiplication followed by a bias offset.

3. **Max-Pooling layer** performs a sub-sampling method that takes only the maximum value of each small region in the input matrix. These regions can be constructed by performing sliding window operations on the input matrix.

4. **Feature map** is the core idea to understand how CNN works. Every input and output matrix inside the CNN can be viewed as a feature map, which contains extracted features for the given image. Image classification aims at transforming the whole feature map into object classification scores by using fully-connected layers, and object detection aims at exploring region information.

Popular CNN Architectures. There are many CNN architectures, but only a few of them have been validated on well-known datasets, and they are viewed as state-of-the-art CNN architectures. The following are some CNN architectures used in object detection algorithms. (1) **VGG16** [11] is one of the VGGNet versions with 16 convolution layers and 2 pooling layers. An appealing feature of VGGNet is that it has homogeneous kernel size (3×3) for all convolution layers, and is easy to implement on hardware accelerators. (2) **Zeiler-and-Fergus (ZFNet)** [15] is the winner of Image-Net Large-Scale Vision Recognition Challenge (ILSVRC) 2013. It is shallower than the VGGNet, and has different kernel size for different convolution layers. (3) **GoogLeNet** [14] is the winner of ILSVRC 2014. It discovers strategies to reduce the number of parameters in convolution layers, and replaces the fully-connected layers with the Average Pooling layer.

CNN-Based Object Detection Algorithms. There are two CNN-based object detection algorithms discussed in this paper. One is YOLO [9], which is designed for real-time object detection; the other one is Faster RCNN [10], which extends Fast RCNN [5] with Region Proposal Network (RPN).

Both algorithms have two major components in their network architectures. The first one is the **backbone** CNN network, which is extracted from a typical CNN architecture; the second consists of extra layers that process the backbone CNN's output feature map. YOLO can choose to use GoogLeNet or a trimmed version, Faster RCNN can choose VGG16 or ZFNet as the backbone network.

Faster RCNN introduces extra layers like RoI pooling and RPN. It has been discovered that Faster RCNN is more accurate than YOLO but about 20 times slower. Deciding which algorithm to use will be introduced in the Sect. 5.

Related Work. There is much work related to CNN accelerator design on FPGA. Zhang et al. [16] use the roofline model and data dependencies analysis to optimise a convolution-only CNN architecture. Qiu et al. [7] successfully deploy VGGNet on an embedded FPGA platform, with several optimisation techniques like data quantisation and coefficient matrix decomposition. Chakradhar et al. present their dynamic configurable architecture among different CNN layers [2]. They also devise a compiler to work with their architecture. Farabet et al. [4] introduce NeuFlow, which is a runtime reconfigurable dataflow processor, and a compiler LuaFlow to compile high level dataflow representation to machine code. Similarly, Suda et al. [12] present a method to compile CNN configuration files into RTL code. They also introduce a systematic throughput optimisation methodology for OpenCL-based FPGA CNN accelerators [13]. In this work, we target object detection applications based on CNN algorithms, and explore the optimisation flow for various CNN backbone architectures and algorithms.

3   Architecture

This section presents the basic architecture of our hardware design, which consists of two kernels: conv kernel and fc kernel (Fig. 1). Each kernel contains an input buffer to cache data for further re-use, a computation kernel to perform convolution (conv) or matrix vector multiplication (fc), and an output buffer to store partial result before the final result is ready. Here we introduce these three components for each kernel in detail.

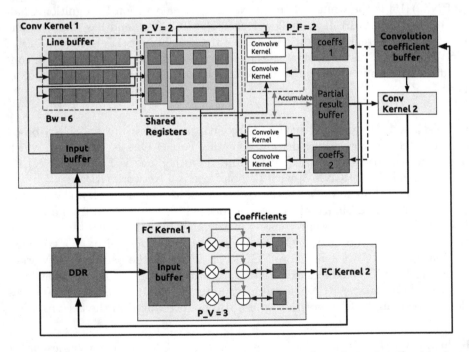

Fig. 1. A general architecture for the convolution layer (kernel size 3×3) with three different level of parallelism (P_P, P_V, and P_F). The top-left part is the line buffer.

The computation kernel inside `conv` contains several convolution kernels running in parallel, which consists of multiple multipliers followed by an adder tree. Suppose the width of a coefficient kernel is k, then the number of multipliers is k^2, and the depth of the adder tree is $\log(k)$. Multipliers take input from a customised input buffer called **line buffer** [1], which enables k data read in one clock cycle from the input feature map. The other side of the line buffer connects to a larger input buffer that partly or fully contains the input feature map. Multipliers also connect to another input buffer that caches coefficients. The output buffer in the `conv` kernel stores the partial convolution result. In each cycle the result from the adder tree will be used to update the partial result. Data type in the `conv` kernel is single-precision floating-point.

The major functionality of the `fc` kernel is to perform dot product between the reshaped input feature vector and the coefficient matrix. The computation kernel contains several multipliers in parallel to calculate the dot product between each row of the coefficient matrix and the feature vector. There are two ways to organise buffers: to cache the whole feature vector and store no partial output, or to store the partial result and no input buffer. These two methods are related to the computation sequence we choose for the `fc` (row major or column major), which will be discussed in Sect. 4. Because there is a feedback loop within the dot product, we use fixed-point data type to enhance performance. The bit width of the fixed-point data type used is 32, which contains 23 fraction bits and 8 integer bits.

4   Design Model Analysis

This section introduces the design model of `conv` and `fc`, which can predict the resource usage from given CNN architecture parameters. This design model provides an important insight into how different strategies and hardware parameters affect the usage of hardware resources, and how we could optimise performance with these model parameters. Table 1 summarises the parameters used in this paper.

The convolution layer design model takes 3 aspects into consideration. The first is **blocking**, which divides the input feature map into several parts to reduce buffer usage; the second is **data access pattern**, which is related to the exchangeable nested loops in the convolution layer. The third is computation **kernel design re-use**. Since our hardware needs to support some irregular CNN architectures with different kernel size in each layer, it is effective to re-use the same design.

Blocking Strategy. Blocking is essential when implementing `conv` kernel on FPGA. Since convolution layer's parameters are usually large in real life CNN architectures, data access patterns often cannot fit their buffer usage into the BRAM resource constraints on board. We introduce two parameters B_H and B_W to indicate the shape of the blocked input feature map. The following discussions will assume $B_H \times B_W$ blocking is applied, i.e. we will use B_H and B_W rather than H and W to indicate the input feature map's shape.

Table 1. A summary of the parameters in the design model analysis

Parameter	Kernel	Description
H	conv	Height of the input feature map
W		Width of the input feature map
N_C		Number of channels in the input feature map
N_F		Number of filters in the output feature map
k		Height and width of the kernel
s		Stride of the convolution layer
B_H		Height of the blocked feature map
B_W		Width of the blocked feature map
M	fc	Length of the output feature vector
N		Length of the reshaped feature vector

Data Access Pattern. Data access pattern is critical to conv kernel implementation, because we could choose to compute the convolution either by **channels** in the feature map, or by **filters** in the output. Each of these patterns has a trade-off between the input and output buffer size.

Algorithm 1: Convolution layer computation with two nested loops.

> **input** : A feature map I of shape $N_C \times B_H \times B_W$
> **input** : A coefficient matrix K of shape $N_F \times N_C \times B_H \times B_W$
> **output**: A feature map O of shape $N_F \times B_H \times B_W/s^2$

> **for** $f \leftarrow 0$ **to** N_F **do**
>   **for** $c \leftarrow 0$ **to** N_C **do**
> $O[f] \leftarrow O[f] + \text{conv}(I[c], K[f, c])$

Consider two nested loops in Eq. 1, one iterates the channel and the other iterates the filter (Algorithm 1). Thus we have two access patterns: **filter major** and **channel major**. The main difference between these two patterns lies in memory usage. The following will calculate the input and output buffer size. (1) **Filter major**: Algorithm 1 presents the filter major pattern. Once we complete the inner reduce add loop of channels for each output filter f in the filter major pattern, the final result for this filter will be ready. Thus, we only need to store $B_H B_W/s^2$, which is the shape of one output filter, in the output buffer. However, it needs to iterate through all the channels of the input feature map and the associated coefficient kernel, so the input buffer size of the filter major pattern is $(B_H B_W + k^2)N_C + kB_W$, where kB_W is the **line buffer** size. (2) **Channel major**: In this case, the channel iteration is the outer loop. After each iteration in the outer loop, only partial results for **all** N_F filters are available and they will be updated in the following iterations. Thus the output buffer is required to have size $N_F \times B_H B_W / s^2$. For the input buffer, only one channel of the input feature map needs to be cached, but all the coefficients for this channel should also be stored in the input buffer. Hence the input buffer size is $B_H B_W + k^2 N_F + k B_W$. The line buffer is also required for this case.

Table 2 summarises the buffer usage for these two data access patterns. With these parameterised analyses, it is convenient to decide which data access pattern should be used based on the parameter values. In general, although these two patterns have similar buffer usage, it is better to choose channel major as it has simpler control logic.

Table 2. Summary of two data access patterns

Access pattern	Output buffer size	Input buffer size
Filter major	$B_H B_W / s^2$	$(B_H B_W + k^2) N_C + k B_W$
Channel major	$B_H B_W / s^2 \times N_F$	$B_H B_W + k^2 N_F + k B_W$

Kernel Design Reuse. According to state-of-the-art CNN-based object detection algorithms, our CNN architectures should not be restricted to VGG16, other networks like ZFNet and GoogLeNet which contain convolution layers of different kernel shapes should also be supported in our hardware design. In order to efficiently adapt to different kernel size without re-synthesis of the design, we configure the `conv` kernel with the largest kernel size at first, and fully reuse it by adding control logic to enable computation with multiple smaller kernels. Figure 2 illustrates how this adaptive technique works.

A Fully-Connected layer is implemented as the `fc` kernel. As mentioned in Sect. 3, `fc` kernel buffer usage is mainly decided by the computation sequence, which is either **row major** or **column major**: (1) **Column major** means that we multiply all the elements in the column of the coefficient matrix to the same input value, and update the partial output with size M. (2) **Row major** requires the input vector with length N to be buffered on-chip, and reuses it to perform dot product with all the rows in the matrix. According to the discussion above, it is obvious that the computation strategy is determined by M and N: if $M \geq N$, we will use row major; and use column major when $M < N$.

5   Optimisation Flow

This section presents our optimisation flow for CNN-based object detection algorithms. The optimisation flow has three major steps: strategy selection, parameter tuning, and algorithm-specific optimisation.

Strategy Selection. Once we have the CNN network architecture configuration, we are able to select which strategy to use for each layer. There are two aforementioned strategies, one is the data access pattern for the `conv` kernel, and the other one is the computation sequence for the `fc` kernel. The selection will be based on this algorithm: For each layer i,

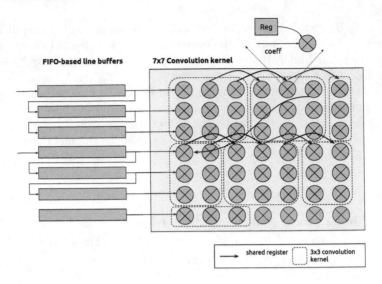

Fig. 2. Reusing 7×7 configuration for 3×3 kernel size computation. There are 49 multipliers on board, and they connect directly to the FIFO line buffer and the coefficient input port. The 7 FIFOs are split into two groups, each containing 3 FIFOs. At most, we could compute 5 3×3 kernels in parallel without reconfiguring the 7×7 kernel design. Curved arrows in the figure illustrate how the register sharing works.

1. If layer i is a `conv` layer, then compare the buffer usage of all data access patterns and find the one uses minimal buffer in total.
2. If layer i is a `fc` layer, then compare M_i and N_i to decide whether to use the row major or the column major strategy.

After selecting strategies for each layer, we can derive exact expressions of the maximum BRAM usage and the maximum level of parallelisation, which are decided by both Table 2 and `fc`'s M_i and N_i.

Parameter Tuning. Suppose we are using the channel major data access pattern and row major strategy, which are suitable for most cases, we need to further tune several parameters to optimise the amount of parallelism.

1. **Pipeline depth** (P_P): For `conv` or `fc`, P_P represents the number of **kernels** to support in hardware. The supported layers can be connected as a pipeline, with the output of a layer to be the input for the next layer.
2. **Filter width** (P_F): For `conv` only, P_F represents the number of **filters** processed in parallel, which has an upper bound N_F.
3. **Vector width** (P_V): For `conv` or `fc`, P_V represents the amount of **input data** processed in parallel. While computing convolution between one kernel and one channel's feature map, it is possible to compute multiple kernels in parallel. This level of parallelisation can be measured by the width of input vector in each cycle.

Convolution Layer. Based on the above parallelism parameters, we need to modify the line buffer size, which should be $P_V B_W$ to support P_V read operations in parallel. Besides, we derive the expression for the on-chip (BW_i^{conv}) and DDR ($\overline{BW}_i^{conv}$) **bandwidth**, estimated to be:

$$BW_i^{conv} = BW_i^{out} + BW_i^{in} = P_V \times P_F + P_F \tag{2}$$

$$\overline{BW}_i^{conv} = \overline{BW}_i^{out} + \overline{BW}_i^{in} = \frac{P_V \times P_F}{F_i} + \frac{P_V \times P_F}{C_i} \tag{3}$$

It is a constrained optimisation problem to find the best P, P_F, and P_V for a given FPGA. We model resource usage of our design in two parts:

1. **Logic resources.** It covers the usage of LUT, FF, and DSP, which will linearly increase with respect to $P_P \times P_F \times P_V$ by a constant factor (L^c) decided by the layer configuration and the strategy we choose to use.

$$L^{conv} = L^c(P_P \times P_F \times P_V) \tag{4}$$

2. **Memory.** Memory usage is decided by two terms, one is buffer size (BS^{conv}), which can be calculated as follows:

$$BS_i^{conv} = (\underbrace{B_H B_W/s^2 \times N_F}_{output\ buffer} + \underbrace{B_H B_W + k^2 N_F}_{input\ buffer} + \underbrace{P_V B_W}_{line\ buffer}) \times P_P \tag{5}$$

The other is **on-chip bandwidth** (BW_i^{conv}). Buffer size decides the minimum number of BRAMs to store the data, and on-chip bandwidth decides the required number of ports as each BRAM has a limited number of ports to read and write. Thus, the memory usage for the convolution layer is:

$$M^{conv} = \max(\frac{BS_i^{conv} \times DW}{\text{BRAM}_{size}}, \frac{BW_i^{conv} \times DW}{\text{BRAM}_{bandwidth}}) \tag{6}$$

Fully-Connected Layer. The `fc` kernel can be analysed in a way similar to the `conv` kernel. As the `fc` kernel does not contain filter-wise parallelisation, there are only two parameters P_P and P_V to be decided. The **logic usage** will also linearly increase with respect to $P_P \times P_V$, and **memory size** is decided by N_i as we choose to use row major strategy. In our design, **on-chip bandwidth** for `fc` is simply $2P_V$. The **DDR bandwidth** requirement is to load coefficient data from DDR, and the input and output read and write at each cycle. Results are shown in Table 3.

Algorithm-Specific Optimisation. Algorithm-specific information in this context covers two algorithms: YOLO and Faster RCNN, and backbone CNN architecture candidates include VGG16, ZFNet, and GoogLeNet. At this level of optimisation, the whole application's constraints such as system capacity and real-time requirement will be taken into consideration.

Our approach is to provide two strategies: **speed priority** and **accuracy priority** for optimisation. For any object detection application, speed priority means that real-time response is important, while accuracy priority means that the estimated detection accuracy is beyond 70%. According to [9], the YOLO algorithm is suitable for speed priority, and Faster RCNN is for accuracy priority.

Table 3. Summary of resource usage for `conv` and `fc` kernels

	conv	fc
Logic	$L^c(P_P \times P_F \times P_V)$	$L^f(P_P \times P_V)$
Memory	$\max\left(\dfrac{BS_i^{conv} \times DW}{\text{BRAM}_{size}}, \dfrac{BW_i^{conv} \times DW}{\text{BRAM}_{bw}}\right)$	$\max\left(\dfrac{N_i \times DW}{\text{BRAM}_{size}}, \dfrac{2P_V \times DW}{\text{BRAM}_{bw}}\right)$
DDR	$P_V P_F \left(\dfrac{1}{F_i} + \dfrac{1}{C_i}\right)$	$P_V \left(\dfrac{1}{M_i} + \dfrac{1}{N_i} + 1\right)$

When we select the algorithm-specific optimisation strategy and which algorithm to use, the optimisation flow will iterate all the possible backbone CNN architectures for each algorithm, and will try to use these configurations to get the optimal result and will then compare them in order to select the best CNN architecture.

6   Evaluation

This section describes our evaluation and performance analysis of the hardware design with specific resource constraints and network architecture. We choose to measure the performance for the YOLO algorithm with the GoogLeNet backbone.

Implementation Details. We briefly introduce the implementation detail of our hardware design. We present the overall architecture in Sect. 3. The proposed architecture and optimisation flow can target various FPGA platforms. To illustrate our approach, our hardware design is built for the Xilinx Zynq platform (zc706), which contains two main components: PS and PL. PS is the processing system with an ARM CPU and a DDR memory, while PL refers to the FPGA, which contains logic resources, on-chip memory, and DMA support. In our case, CNN hardware design targets the PL part, with some complex software algorithms running on the PS part. We use the AXI to connect between PS and PL.

The CNN hardware design can be split into `conv` kernel and `fc` kernel. They are parameterised and are connected to each other through FIFO. They use our streaming protocol to control and schedule tasks. Coefficients and other external data will be loaded through DDR from the external memory.

Design Model Accuracy. We estimate the design model accuracy from the synthesis report and the estimated resource usage on 3 different cases: $P_V = 1, 4, 8$ (Fig. 3). Here the kernel size of the `conv` module is 7×7, and the column number of the `fc` module is 4096. The estimation is based on equations in Table 3. The design model accuracy is beyond 85%, and therefore it can support our optimisation flow. The dotted line stands for available resources in our target chip. Thus, we select $P_V = 4$ in this design.

Algorithm Evaluation. Based on the optimisation model, we derive the optimal design parameters for both YOLO (GoogLeNet) and Faster RCNN

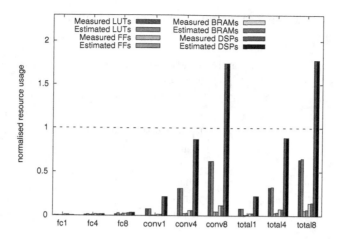

Fig. 3. Design model accuracy measured with the synthesis report and the model estimation results. Resource usage is normalised against available resources in the target chip. The last digit of each label is the P_V value.

(VGG16), and predict the best performance for these two algorithms. In addition, we also evaluate the software performance on x86 CPU and ARM CPU. We use Darknet [8] and Caffe [6] as the software reference for YOLO and Faster RCNN evaluation. Results are listed in Table 4.

Based on the optimization model, we make a few decisions. (1) Input and output buffers are necessary so that the design has the appropriate bandwidth. (2) For the 1×1 kernel, the 25 BRAM requirement is not the major limitation in resource usage. (3) At current precision, the DSPs are the limiting resources for `conv` kernels. We can set $P_V = 4$ and $P_P = P_F = 1$ in this case. (4) `fc` kernel also uses $P_V = 4$ to coordinate with the `conv` kernel's output.

We estimate that the overall execution time for YOLO (GoogLeNet) is **0.744** s, and for Faster RCNN (VGG16) is **0.875** s. Compared with the best software performance on ARM (**36.92** s), the speed-up is **49.6** times. Even compared with the x86 CPU there is a 1.5 times speed-up. Although the GPU version is much faster than our implementation, the GPU (Titan X) is not suitable for embedded systems. Also the total energy cost of the FPGA version (0.868J) is much smaller than the GPU version (23J).

7   Summary

This paper presents our novel approach to optimise CNN-based object detection algorithms on embedded FPGA platforms, which consists of a design model for the basic CNN hardware architecture, and an optimisation flow which takes into account both FPGA optimisation strategies and algorithm-specific optimisation strategies. Our evaluation shows that an optimised hardware design for the YOLO algorithm with GoogLeNet backbone can reach 49.6 times speed-up

Table 4. Algorithm evaluation on 4 platforms

	x86 CPU	ARM CPU	FPGA	GPU
Platform	Intel Core i7	ARMv7-A	Zynq (zc706)	GeForce Titan X
Num. of Cores	8 (4 used)	2 (2 used)	-	-
Compiler	GNU GCC	GNU GCC	Vivado (2016.2)	CUDA (v7.5)
Compile Flags	-Ofast	-Ofast	-	-Ofast
Clock	3.07 GHz	Up to 1 GHz	200 MHz	1531 MHz
Technology	45 nm	28 nm	24 nm	16 nm
YOLO (Tiny)	**1.12 s**	**36.92 s**	-	0.0037 s (178 W)
YOLO (GoogLeNet)	13.54 s	430.6 s	**0.744 s (1.167 W)**	0.010 s (230 W)
Faster RCNN (ZF)	2.547 s	71.53 s	-	0.043 s (69 W)
Faster RCNN (VGG16)	6.224 s	Failed	0.875 s (1.167 W)	0.062 s (81 W)

compared with software on ARM. Also our design model accuracy is above 85%. Future work includes evaluating the object detection application with multiple real world datasets, introducing automatic data quantisation, and enhancing the optimisation flow to support CNN training.

Acknowledgement. The support of the European Union Horizon 2020 Research and Innovation Programme under grant agreement number 671653, UK EPSRC (EP/I012036/1, EP/L00058X/1, EP/L016796/1 and EP/N031768/1), Corerain Technologies, the State Key Laboratory of Space-Ground Integrated Information Technology, and Xilinx, Inc. is gratefully acknowledged.

References

1. Bosi, B., et al.: Reconfigurable pipelined 2-D convolvers for fast digital signal processing. IEEE Trans. VLSI Syst. **7**(3), 299–308 (1999)
2. Chakradhar, S., et al.: A dynamically configurable coprocessor for convolutional neural networks. In: ISCA (2010)
3. Dai, J., et al.: R-FCN: object detection via region-based fully convolutional networks. arXiv preprint (2016). arXiv:1605.06409
4. Farabet, C., et al.: NeuFlow: a runtime-reconfigurable dataflow processor for vision. In: ECVW (2011)
5. Girshick, R.: Fast R-CNN. In: ICCV (2015)
6. Jia, Y., et al.: Caffe: convolutional architecture for fast feature embedding. arXiv preprint (2014). arXiv:1408.5093
7. Qiu, J., et al.: Going deeper with embedded FPGA platform for convolutional neural network. In: FPGA (2016)
8. Redmon, J.: Darknet: open source neural networks in C (2013–2016). http://pjreddie.com/darknet/
9. Redmon, J., et al.: You only look once: unified, real-time object detection (2015). https://arxiv.org/abs/1506.02640
10. Ren, S., et al.: Faster R-CNN: towards real-time object detection with region proposal networks. In: NIPS (2015)

11. Simonyan, K., Zisserman, A.: Very deep convolutional networks for large-scale image recognition. ImageNet Challenge (2014)
12. Suda, N., et al.: Scalable and modularized RTL compilation of convolutional neural networks onto FPGA. In: FPL (2016)
13. Suda, N., et al.: Throughput-optimized OpenCL-based FPGA accelerator for large-scale convolutional neural networks. In: FPGA (2016)
14. Szegedy, C., et al.: Going deeper with convolutions. In: CVPR (2015)
15. Zeiler, M.D., Fergus, R.: Visualizing and understanding convolutional networks. In: Fleet, D., Pajdla, T., Schiele, B., Tuytelaars, T. (eds.) ECCV 2014. LNCS, vol. 8689, pp. 818–833. Springer, Cham (2014). doi:10.1007/978-3-319-10590-1_53
16. Zhang, C., et al.: Optimizing FPGA-based accelerator design for deep convolutional neural networks. In: FPGA (2015)

An FPGA Realization of a Deep Convolutional Neural Network Using a Threshold Neuron Pruning

Tomoya Fujii[1], Simpei Sato[1], Hiroki Nakahara[1(✉)], and Masato Motomura[2]

[1] Tokyo Institute of Technology, Meguro, Japan
nakahara.h.ad@m.titech.ac.jp
[2] Hokkaido University, Sapporo, Japan

Abstract. For a pre-trained deep convolutional neural network (CNN) for an embedded system, a high-speed and a low power consumption are required. In the former of the CNN, it consists of convolutional layers, while in the latter, it consists of fully connection layers. In the convolutional layer, the multiply accumulation operation is a bottleneck, while the fully connection layer, the memory access is a bottleneck. In this paper, we propose a neuron pruning technique which eliminates almost part of the weight memory. In that case, the weight memory is realized by an on-chip memory on the FPGA. Thus, it achieves a high speed memory access. In this paper, we propose a sequential-input parallel-output fully connection layer circuit. The experimental results showed that, by the neuron pruning, as for the fully connected layer on the VGG-11 CNN, the number of neurons was reduced by 89.3% with keeping the 99% accuracy. We implemented the fully connected layers on the Digilent Inc. NetFPGA-1G-CML board. Comparison with the CPU (ARM Cortex A15 processor) and the GPU (Jetson TK1 Kepler), as for a delay time, the FPGA was 219.0 times faster than the CPU and 12.5 times faster than the GPU. Also, a performance per power efficiency was 125.28 times better than CPU and 17.88 times better than GPU.

1 Introduction

1.1 Convolutional Deep Neural Network (CNN)

Recently, for embedded computer systems, a convolutional deep neural network (CNN), which consists of the 2D convolutional layers and the fully connected neural network, is widely used. Since the CNN emulates the human vision, it has a high accuracy for an image recognition. For example, a human face recognition [22], a human and object detection [12], a human pose estimation [25], a string recognition in a scene [13], a road traffic sign recognition [6], a sport scene recognition [16], a human action recognitions [8,15], are reported. These researches showed that the CNN outperforms conventional techniques.

With the increase of the number of layers, the CNN can increase classification accuracy. Thus, a large-scale CNN is desired. To keep up with the real-time

S. Wong et al. (Eds.): ARC 2017, LNCS 10216, pp. 268–280, 2017.
DOI: 10.1007/978-3-319-56258-2_23

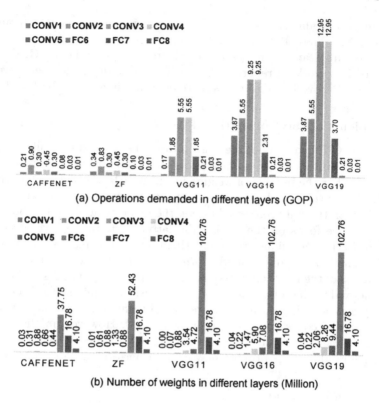

(a) Operations demanded in different layers (GOP)

(b) Number of weights in different layers (Million)

Fig. 1. The complexity distribution of state-of-the-art CNN models: (a) distribution of operations by theoretical estimation; (b) distribution of weight number [26].

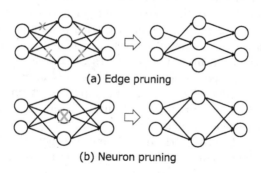

(a) Edge pruning

(b) Neuron pruning

Fig. 2. Comparison of pruning techniques.

requirement of the embedded vision system, since the existing system using a CPU is too slow, the acceleration of the CNN is necessary [17]. Most software-based CNNs use the GPUs [2,3,7,23,24]. Unfortunately, since the GPU consumes much power, they are unsuitable for the embedded system [9]. Thus, FPGA-based CNNs are required for a low-power and a real-time embedded vision system. As for the classification accuracy, the CNN using a fixed-point representation has almost the same accuracy as one using a floating-point representation [11]. The FPGA can use a minimum precision which reduces the hardware resources and increases the clock frequency, while the GPU cannot do it. A previous work [9] reported that, as for the performance per power, the FPGA-based CNN is about 10 times more efficient than the GPU-based one.

1.2   Problems of the Conventional CNNs

Typically, the CNN consists of the convolutional layers and the fully connected layers. Figure 1(a) shows that operations demanded in different layers, while that for (b) shows that the number of weights in different layers [26]. As shown these figures, in the convolutional layers, the multiply accumulation operation is a bottleneck, while in the fully connected layers, the memory accesses is a bottleneck. In the paper, we focus on the solving the latter part, that is, we propose the memory reduction techniques to realize them on-chip memories on the FPGA. Figure 2(a) shows an example of edge pruning of the fully connected layer. The memory access of the fully connected layer is a sequentially reading of the weights that are indexed to the corresponding edges. Thus, by pruning edges, the amount of memory can be reduced. In the conventional techniques, the randomly pruning techniques of edges have been proposed [1,14]. However, in the hardware realization point of view, since the memory access of the sequential address is suitable, the random edge pruning may cause a performance degradation.

1.3   Proposed Method

In the paper, we propose a neuron pruning instead of the edge pruning. Figure 2(b) shows an example of neuron pruning of the fully connected layer. Since by pruning all the incoming and the outgoing edges of a neuron is equivalent to the neuron pruning, in general, the edge pruning can eliminate more edges than neuron pruning. However, even if the neuron pruning is applied, since it maintains the sequential memory access, it is suitable for the hardware realization. Since the proposed neuron pruning can eliminate almost edges, we can store all the remainder edges into the on-chip memory on the FPGA. In the paper, we propose the serial-input parallel-output circuit for the fully connected layer. To realized a high-performance circuit, it efficiently uses on-chip memories and DSP slices on the FPGA. In the experiment, we show that the FPGA based realization outperforms than the CPU and the GPU realizations.

1.4   Contributions of the Paper

Contributions of the paper are as follows:

1. We proposed the threshold based neuron pruning techniques for the FPGA realization of the fully connected layer on the deep neural network. The proposed one is suitable to the on-chip realization of the FPGA. The experimental result showed that as for the 99% accuracy, it eliminated the number of neurons by 89.3% for the VGG-11 CNN.

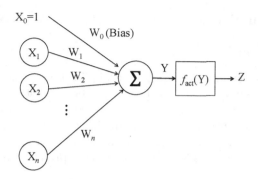

Fig. 3. Artificial neuron.

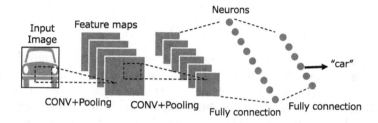

Fig. 4. Example of the convolutional neural network (CNN).

2. We proposed the sequential-input parallel-output circuit for the fully connected layer. It efficiently uses on-chip memories and DSP slices on the FPGA. Since the proposed circuit can store all the weights of the fully connected layer, it can realized a wide band of the memory access. Our technique is a complementary to the conventional techniques that accelerates the convolutional layers for the FPGA. We expanded the applicability of the CNN using the FPGA.
3. We applied the neuron pruning for the fully connected layers on the VGG-11 CNN, then implemented them on the Digilent Inc. NetFPGA-1G-CML board. Comparison with the CPU (ARM Cortex A15 processor) and the GPU (Jetson TK1 Kepler), as for a delay time, the FPGA was 219.0 times faster than the CPU and 12.5 times faster than the GPU. Also, a performance per power efficiency was 125.28 times better than CPU and 17.88 times better than GPU.

1.5   Organization of the Paper

The rest of the paper is organized as follows: Sect. 2 introduces the convolutional deep neural network (CNN); Sect. 3 introduces the neuron pruning in the fully connected (FC) layer on the CNN; Sect. 4 shows the serial-input parallel-output FC circuit; Sect. 5 shows the experimental results; and Sect. 6 concludes the paper.

2   Convolutional Deep Neural Network (CNN)

2.1   Artificial Neural Network

Let n be a bit precision, $x_i, y_i, w_i, z_i \in \{0,1\}$ be binary variables, $X = (x_0, x_1, \ldots, x_n)$ be the input, $Y = (y_0, y_1, \ldots, y_n)$ be the internal variable, $W = (w_0, w_1, \ldots, w_n)$ be the weight, f_{act} be the activation function, and $Z = (z_0, z_1, \ldots, z_n)$ be the output. Note that, in this paper, a capital letter denotes an integer, while a small letter denotes a binary value. Figure 3 shows a circuit for **an artificial neuron (AN)**. The following expression shows an operation for the AN:

$$Y = \sum_{i=0}^{n} W_i X_i,$$
$$Z = f_{act}(Y),$$

where X_0 is a constant one and W_0 denotes **a bias** which corrects the deviation of the given data. Typically, the activation function is realized by a sigmoid, a tanh, a ReLU [18], and so on. In the paper, we use the ReLU function which is suitable to a hardware realization. **A convolutional deep neural network (CNN)** has multiple **layers**. Figure 4 shows an example of the CNN. The typical layer consists of **a 2D convolutional layer**, **a pooling layer**, and **a classification layer**. Each layer consists of multiple **feature maps**. To recognize the input image, first, the feature map reacts corresponding subdivided training data by 2D convolutional layers with pooling layers. Then, the classifier selects the appropriate reactions from feature maps. Usually, the classifier is realized by the fully connected neural network. In this paper, for layer i, K_i denotes the kernel size, N_i denotes the number of feature maps, and L_i denotes the feature map size. Figure 5 shows the 2D convolution operation. It computes the output by shifting

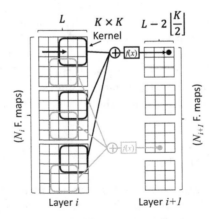

Fig. 5. Convolutional operation.

Table 1. Specifications for the VGG-11 [21].

Layer #	Type	Kernel size	# Feat. maps
1	Conv + maxpool	3	64
2	Conv + maxpool	3	128
3	Conv	3	256
4	Conv + maxpool	3	256
5	Conv	3	512
6	Conv + maxpool	3	512
7	Conv	3	512
8	Conv + maxpool	3	512
9	FC	1	4096
10	FC	1	4096
11	FC	1	1000

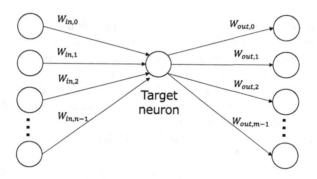

Fig. 6. Model of a neuron pruning.

a $K \times K$ size **kernel**. For (x, y) at the output feature map value $i + 1$, the following MAC (multiply-accumulation) operation is performed:

$$Y_{i+1,x,y} = \sum_{k=0}^{N_i-1} \left(\sum_{m=0}^{K-1} \sum_{n=0}^{K-1} X_{k,x+m,y+n} W_{k,m,n} \right) \quad (1)$$

$$Z_{i+1,x,y} = f_{act}(Y_{i+1,x,y}).$$

In the 2D convolutional operation, Z is mapped to (x, y) at the output feature map $i + 1$. In the fully connected layer, $L_i = 1$ and $K_i = 1$. By inserting the non-linear and low-imaging operations into the convolution layers, we can reduce the number of computations in the convolution layers, while we can obtain the movement invariance. We call this **a pooling operation**, which can be realized by a simple circuit. In this paper, we implement the max-pooling operation. Its operation can be realized by a comparator for selecting the maximum value in the kernel. It is much smaller than the 2D convolution operation circuit.

2.2   VGG-11 CNN

Table 1 shows specifications for the VGG-11 benchmark CNN [21], which is widely used in the computer vision system. The VGG-11 consists of 11 layers. The basic layers consist of multiple 2D convolution (Conv) layers with $K = 3$ and max-pooling (maxpool) layers, while the rear layers consist of fully connected (FC) layers. First, it receives a normalized 32×32 image, which consists of 8-bit RGB color data.

Almost CNN researches have been proposed to improve the performance, power consumption for the convolutional layer only on the CNN [4,20,27]. Only a few work [26] tried to improve both the convolutional layer and the fully connected layer. In this paper, we consider a high-speed and a low-power circuit for the fully connected layer with a neuron pruning technique. Our technique can be applied to the previous work.

3   Threshold Neuron Pruning

In the paper, we propose the threshold neuron pruning instead of the edge pruning. Figure 6 shows that a model for the neuron pruning. Suppose that a target neuron is connected to n incoming edges with weight $W_{in,k}$ and m outgoing edges with weight $W_{out,k}$, where k denotes the index variable. If all the incoming edges and the outgoing ones of a neuron are eliminated, it means the neuron pruning itself. Therefore, generally, the edge pruning eliminates more edges than the neuron pruning. However, since the edge pruning randomly eliminates edges, it is not suitable for the hardware realization, which requires sequentially memory

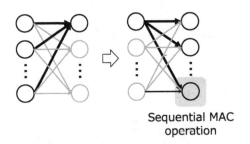

Fig. 7. Serial-input parallel-output (SIPO) fully connected layer [10].

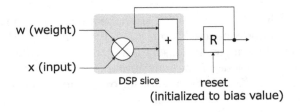

Fig. 8. Sequential multiply accumulation (MAC) circuit.

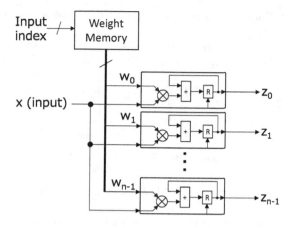

Fig. 9. Circuit for a SIPO fully connected layer.

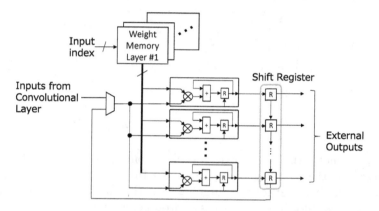

Fig. 10. Circuit for SIPO fully connected layers with the threshold neuron pruning.

access. On the other hand, since the neuron pruning eliminates all the incoming and outgoing edges, it maintains the sequentially memory access of weights. Thus, it is suitable for the hardware realization.

First, we define the neuron pruning.

Definition 3.1. A neuron pruning *eliminates all the incoming and outgoing edges for a neuron.*

In the paper, we propose a threshold neuron pruning.

Definition 3.2. A threshold neuron pruning *performs the neuron pruning when the sum of the input weights or that of outputs is lower than the threshold.*

There are various decisions of thresholds for the neuron pruning. In the paper, the threshold neuron pruning is performed, when one of the following conditions is satisfied:

Table 2. Number of neurons corresponding to the accuracy (%).

Layer #	Original	99% accuracy	95% accuracy
1	4096	941	891
2	4096	354	74
3	4096	31	31
4	10	10	10
Total	12298	1336	1006
Ratio	1.000	0.107	0.082

Table 3. Number of 18 KB BRAMs corresponding to the accuracy (%).

Layer #	Original	99% accuracy	95% accuracy
1–2	7280	145	29
2–3	7280	5	1
3–4	18	1	1
Total	14578	151	31
Ratio	1.000	0.010	0.002

1. $\sum_{k=1}^{n} |w_{in,k}| < \mu_i \times n$
2. $\sum_{k=1}^{m} |w_{out,k}| < \mu_o \times m$,

where $w_{in,k}$ denotes the k-th weight for the incoming edge, $w_{out,k}$ denotes the k-th weight for the outgoing one, μ_i denotes the threshold for the incoming edge, and μ_o denotes that for the outgoing edge (Fig. 6). In this paper, different thresholds are used for incoming edges and outgoing ones.

4   Circuit for the Fully Connected Layers After Threshold Neuron Pruning

Figure 7 shows the serial-input parallel-output (SIPO) fully connected layer [10]. As shown in Fig. 7, it can reduces the memory bandwidth for the primary input. To realize the SIPO fully connected layer, it requires the sequentially multiply accumulation (MAC) circuit to emulates the artificial neuron shown in Fig. 3 sequentially. Figure 8 shows a sequential MAC circuit, which consists of the MAC unit and the register. Initially, it reset the value for the register to the bias value. Then, it updates the value for the neuron with performing the MAC operation sequentially. Finally, it sends the value to the external output. The MAC operation is realized by the DSP slice on the FPGA. Figure 9 shows the circuit for the SIPO fully connected layer. In the circuit, **the weight memory** stores the weight value, and it is read for corresponding input x_i. The sequential MAC circuit updates the value for neurons sequentially. Figure 10 shows the circuit for SIPO fully connected layers with the threshold neuron pruning. The most of weights is eliminated by the neuron pruning, and only a few part of weights is packed in the weight memories. Since the FPGA can realize the appropriate size of the memory with the block RAMs (BRAM) and the distributed memories, it is suitable to realize the neuron pruning. All the weights for each layer are read, and the output neurons are updated at a time. After all the inputs are evaluated, it transfer the values for the output neurons to the shift register. Then, the next layer is evaluated by shifting the value for the shift register. When all the layers are evaluated, the values for the output neurons are send to the external output.

5 Experimental Results

5.1 Threshold Neuron Pruning

We designed the CNN using a Chainer which is a deep neural network framework [3], and the target task is the CIFAR-10 [5] which is an image recognition task. In the experiment, we set an appropriate threshold μ by manually, and applied the threshold neuron pruning for each fully connected layer.

Table 2 compared the number of neurons for each fully connected layer. Note that, generally, when the number of neurons decreases, then recognition accuracy also decreases. In the comparison, we measured the number of neurons for the original CNN, the 99% accuracy, and the 95% accuracy compared with the accuracy for the original one. From Table 2, as for the 99% accuracy, the number of neurons decreased by 89.3%, while as for the 95% accuracy, it decreased by 91.8%. Table 3 compared the number of 18 Kb BRAMs for each fully connected layer. From Table 3, as for the 99% accuracy, the number of BRAMs decreased by 99.0%, while as for the 95% accuracy, it decreased by 99.8%. Let n_i be the number of incoming edges for each layer, n_o be that of outgoing edges, and w be the bit precision (in the experiment, we used 8-bit). Since the amount of weight memory for each layer is $n_i n_o w \simeq O(n^2)$, the neuron pruning exponentially reduces the amount of memory. In our experiment, for the VGG-11 CNN, we can realized the weight memory for the fully connected layer by the on-chip memory on the FPGA. In that case, since it reads weights with a width band-width memory access, it can operate the fully connected layer with a high-speed. Also, since it requires no extra off-chip memory, it reduces the power consumption and costs.

5.2 FPGA Implementation

We applied the threshold neuron pruning with the 99% accuracy. Then, we implemented the fully connected layers on the Digilent Inc. NetFPGA-1G-CML evaluation board (It has a Xilinx Inc. Kintex 7 XC7K325T FPGA: 50,950 slices, 890 18 Kb BRAMs, and 840 DSP slices). We used the Xilinx Inc. Vivado 2016.2 with timing constrain 100 MHz. Our implementation used 4,241 Slices, 151 18 Kb BRAMs, and 145 DSP slices. Also, it satisfied the timing constraint for real-time applications. The delay time for the fully connected layer was 29.0 usec.

We measured the power consumption without that for the power sources on the board: It was 7 W. Since the implemented fully connected layer operated with 29.0 usec delay time, its performance was 34482.7 (images/usec). Thus, the performance per power efficiency is 4926.10.

Table 4. Comparison with the CPU and the GPU.

Device	CPU	GPU	FPGA
Platform	Jetson TK1		NetFPGA 1G-CML
Device	Cortex A15@2.5 GHz	Kepler@950 MHz	Kintex 7@100 MHz
Delay time [usec]	6354	363	29
Performance [images/usec]	157.3	2754.8	34482.7
Power [W]	4	10	7
Performance/power	39.32	275.48	4926.10

5.3   Comparison with the CPU and the GPU

We applied the threshold neuron pruning fully connected layer, we compared with the CPU and the GPU. As for the CPU, we used the ARM Corp. Cortex A15 running at 2.5 GHz on the nVidia Corp. Jetson TK1 evaluation board, while that for the GPU, we used the nVidia Corp. Kepler running at 950 MHz, which has 192 CUDA cores on the same board. As for software based one, we used Ubuntu 14.04 LTS as an operating system, and used framework was the Chainer. Table 4 compared the FPGA realization with the CPU and the GPU ones. From Table 4, the delay time for the CPU was 6,354 usec, and its power consumption was 4 W, while the delay time for the GPU was 363 usec, and its power consumption was 10 W. Note that, we measured the power consumption excepting for the standby power consumption. The experimental results showed that as for the delay time, the FPGA realization was 291.0 times faster than the CPU one, and it was 12.5 times faster than the GPU one. As for the performance per power efficiency, the FPGA realization was 125.28 times better than the CPU, and it was 17.88 times better than the GPU one.

6   Conclusion

In the paper, we proposed the threshold neuron pruning which eliminates almost part of the weight memory, which was a bottleneck of the conventional realization. By applying the threshold neuron pruning, we could realize the weight memory by on-chip memory on the FPGA. Thus, it operated with a high-speed memory access. In the paper, we showed the SIPO fully connected layer circuit, which is efficiently access to on-chip memories on the FPGA. In the comparison, we measured the number of neurons for the original CNN, as for the

99% accuracy, the number of neurons decreased by 76.4%, while as for the 95% accuracy, it decreased by 91.7%. That is, as for the 95% accuracy, the number of BRAMs decreased by 96.2%, while as for the 95% accuracy, it decreased by 99.7%. We implemented the neuron pruning fully connected layer on the Digilent Inc. NetFPGA-1G-CML FPGA board, and compared with the ARM Cortex A15 processor and the Kepler GPU. As for a delay time, the FPGA was 219.0 times faster than the CPU and 12.5 times faster than the GPU. Also, a performance per power efficiency was 125.28 times better than CPU and 17.88 times better than GPU.

The future project is to apply the pruning technique to the binarized CNN [19].

Acknowledgments. This research is supported in part by the Grants in Aid for Scientistic Research of JSPS, and an Accelerated Innovation Research Initiative Turning Top Science and Ideas into High-Impact Values program (ACCEL) of JST.

References

1. Anwar, S., Hwang, K., Sung, W.: Structured pruning of deep convolutional neural networks. Computer Research Repository (CoRR), December 2015. https://arxiv.org/ftp/arxiv/papers/1512/1512.08571.pdf
2. Caffe: Deep learning framework. http://caffe.berkeleyvision.org/
3. Chainer: a powerful, flexible, and intuitive framework of neural networks. http://chainer.org/
4. Chakradhar, S., Sankaradas, M., Jakkula, V., Cadambi, S.: A dynamically configurable coprocessor for convolutional neural networks. In: Annual International Symposium on Computer Architecture (ISCA), pp. 247–257 (2010)
5. The CIFAR-10 data set. http://www.cs.toronto.edu/kriz/cifar.html
6. Ciresan, D.C., Meier, U., Schmidhuber, J.: Multi-column deep neural networks for image classification. In: Proceedings of CVPR (2012)
7. CUDA-Convent2: Fast convolutional neural network in C++/CUDA. https://code.google.com/p/cuda-convnet2/
8. Donahue, J., Hendricks, L.A., Guadarrama, S., Rohrbach, M., Venugopalan, S., Saenko, K., Darrell, T.: Long-term recurrent convolutional networks for visual recognition and description. In: Proceedings of CVPR (2015)
9. Dundar, A., Jin, J., Gokhale, V., Martini, B., Culurciello, E.: Memory access optimized routing scheme for deep networks on a mobile coprocessor. In: HPEC 2014, pp. 1–6 (2014)
10. Farabet, C., Poulet, C., Han, J.Y., LeCun, Y.: CNP: an FPGA-based processor for convolutional networks. In: FPL 2009, pp. 32–37 (2009)
11. Farabet, C., Martini, B., Akselrod, P., Talay, S., LeCun, Y., Culurciello, E.: Hardware accelerated convolutional neural networks for synthetic vision systems. In: ISCAS 2010, pp. 257–260 (2010)
12. Girshick, R., Donahue, J., Darrell, T., Malik, J.: Rich feature hierarchies for accurate object detection and semantic segmentation. In: Proceedings of CVPR (2014)
13. Goodfellow, I.J., Bulatov, Y., Ibarz, J., Arnoud, S., Shet, V.: Multi-digit number recognition from street view imagery using deep convolutional neural networks (2013). arXiv preprint: arXiv:1312.6082

14. Han, S., Mao, H., Dally, W.J.: Deep compression: compressing deep neural networks with pruning, trained quantization and Huffman coding. In: ICLR 2016 (2016)
15. Ji, S., Xu, W., Yang, M., Yu, K.: 3D convolutional neural networks for human action recognition. IEEE Trans. Pattern Anal. Mach. Intell. **35**(1), 221–231 (2013)
16. Karpathy, A., Toderici, G., Shetty, S., Leung, T., Sukthankar, R., Li, F.: Large-scale video classification with convolutional neural networks. In: Proceedings of CVPR, pp. 1725–1732 (2014)
17. Lecun, Y., Bottou, L., Bengio, Y., Haffner, P.: Gradient-based learning applied to document recognition. Proc. IEEE **86**(11), 2278–2324 (1998)
18. Nair, V., Hinton, G.E.: Rectified linear units improve restricted Boltzmann machines. In: ICML, pp. 807–814 (2010)
19. Nakahara, H., Yonekawa, H., Sasao, T., Iwamoto, H., Motomura, M.: A memory-based realization of a binarized deep convolutional neural network. In: The International Conference on Field-Programmable Technology (FPT 2016), pp. 273–276 (2016)
20. Peemen, M., Setio, A.A.A., Mesman, B., Corporaal, H.: Memory-centric accelerator design for convolutional neural networks. In: ICCD 2013, pp. 13–19 (2013)
21. Simonyan, K., Zisserman, A.: Very deep convolutional networks for large-scale image recognition. In: ICLR 2015 (2015)
22. Taigman, Y., Yang, M., Ranzato, M., Wolf, L.: DeepFace: closing the gap to human-level performance in face verification. In: Proceedings of CVPR, pp. 1701–1708 (2014)
23. Theano. http://deeplearning.net/software/theano/
24. Torch: A scientific computing framework for LUTJIT. http://torch.ch/
25. Toshev, A., Szegedy, C.: DeepPose: human pose estimatiion via deep neural networks. In: Proceedings of CVPR (2014)
26. Qiu, J., Wang, J., Yao, S., Guo, K., Li, B., Zhou, E., Yu, J., Tang, T., Xu, N., Song, S., Wang, Y., Yang, H.: Going deeper with embedded FPGA platform for convolutional neural network. In: FPGA 2016, pp. 26–35 (2016)
27. Zhang, C., Li, P., Sun, G., Guan, Y., Xiao, B., Cong, J.: Optimizing FPGA-based accelerator design for deep convolutional neural networks. In: FPGA 2015, pp. 161–170 (2015)

Accuracy Evaluation of Long Short Term Memory Network Based Language Model with Fixed-Point Arithmetic

Ruochun Jin[✉], Jingfei Jiang[✉], and Yong Dou[✉]

National Laboratory for Parallel and Distributed Processing,
National University of Defense Technology, Changsha 410073, Hunan, China
{jinruochun,jingfeijiang,yongdou}@nudt.edu.cn

Abstract. Long Short Term Memory network based language models are state-of-art techniques in the field of natural language processing. Training LSTM networks is computationally intensive, which naturally results in investigating FPGA acceleration where fixed-point arithmetic is employed. However, previous studies have focused only on accelerators using some fixed bit-widths without thorough accuracy evaluation. The main contribution of this paper is to demonstrate the bit-width effect on the LSTM based language model and the tanh function approximation in a comprehensive way by experimental evaluation. Theoretically, the 12-bit number with 6-bit fractional part is the best choice balancing the accuracy and the storage saving. Gaining similar performance to the software implementation and fitting the bit-widths of FPGA primitives, we further propose a mixed bit-widths solution combing 8-bit numbers and 16-bit numbers. With clear trade-off in accuracy, our results provide a guide to inform the design choices on bit-widths when implementing LSTMs in FPGAs. Additionally, based on our experiments, it is amazing that the scale of the LSTM network is irrelevant to the optimum fixed-point configuration, which indicates that our results are applicable to larger models as well.

Keywords: LSTM network · Fixed-point arithmetic · Bit-width · FPGA

1 Introduction

Language models, capturing the likelihood of words and phrases in text, are widely used in natural language processing. It has been shown by prior research that neural network based language models (NNLMs) [3,8] tend to outperform many other advanced techniques because neural networks, such as Long Short Term Memory (LSTM) Network [5], have the expressive ability to "remember" the sequential information and patterns of sentences. However, the training and prediction procedures require significantly more storage and computation cost, which has limited the proliferation of their applications, especially in the field of embedded systems [9].

© Springer International Publishing AG 2017
S. Wong et al. (Eds.): ARC 2017, LNCS 10216, pp. 281–288, 2017.
DOI: 10.1007/978-3-319-56258-2_24

Thus, in order to satisfy the real-time demands of language model users, hardware acceleration has been introduced and a variety of solutions based on different platforms, such as ASICs, GPUs and FPGAs [7,9], have been explored. Among them, FPGA based acceleration is more promising because of its high design flexibility and low energy cost. However, it is too resource-consuming to support a large number of floating-point units on chip and store values using the standard floating-point representation in on-chip RAMs. As a result, most previous designs implemented fixed bit-widths of 8 bits, 16 bits or 32 bits. However, all reported LSTM hardware designs on FPGA simply selected fixed-point arithmetic with a certain bit-width without deeply analyzing the impact of this choice on computational accuracy [4]. So it remains unclear that whether the selected fixed bit-width is the most suitable and area efficient for LSTMs. Similarly, as it is expensive to implement exponential functions and division operations directly on FPGA, it is important to thoroughly understand and evaluate the approximation of the required tanh function in LSTMs.

There are three main contributions in this paper as follows.

- We have proposed a mixed bit-width fixed-point solution for LSTM hardware implementation through extensive experiments and analysis.
- The effect of the linear approximation of tanh function has been explored through experiments, which guides the hardware design.
- We have discovered that the fixed-point configuration is insensitive to the scale of the LSTM based language model, which indicates that our results are applicable to larger scale models.

2   LSTM in a Nutshell

The core idea of vanilla LSTM [5] can be expressed by the equations as follows:

$$i_t = \sigma(W_{xi}x_t + W_{hi}h_{t-1} + b_i) \tag{1}$$

$$f_t = \sigma(W_{xf}x_t + W_{hf}h_{t-1} + b_f) \tag{2}$$

$$o_t = \sigma(W_{xo}x_t + W_{ho}h_{t-1} + b_o) \tag{3}$$

$$\tilde{c}_t = tanh(W_{xc}x_t + W_{hc}h_{t-1} + b_c) \tag{4}$$

$$c_t = f_t \odot c_{t-1} + i_t \odot \tilde{c}_t \tag{5}$$

$$h_t = o_t \odot tanh(c_t) \tag{6}$$

where σ is the logistic sigmoid function, $\odot$ is element wise multiplication, x is the input vector, W is the model parameter, c is the memory cell activation, $\tilde{c}$ is the candidate memory cell gate, h is the output vector. The subscript $t-1$ indicates the output from the previous time step and i, f and o denote the input gate, the forget gate and the output gate respectively. The knowledge learnt from the historical sequence are embedded in the parameter matrixes or vectors on the right hand of the equations. In this model, each module has four gates with element-wise operations and non-linear activation functions, which will dramatically increase the computation time and the complexity of the model if more layers are cascaded or more modules are expanded in each layer.

3 Experimental Methodology

In our experiments, we modified the floating-point versions of the vanilla LSTM network into fixed-point versions to explore the effect of this modification and the most suitable fixed-point solution for LSTMs. The fixed-point version took bit-widths as parameters, including bit-widths of neural units, weights, activation functions, so it could run in any bit-width configuration. Only testing was translated into a fixed-point version while training and verification were still computed with the standard floating-point arithmetic. All fixed-point experiments were conducted in Matlab2016a with Fixed-Point Designer toolbox. The software version of the vanilla LSTM based language model and the corresponding data set in our experiment were borrowed from Zaremba et al.'s work [10]. As the fixed-point simulation in Matlab was approximate 30 times slower than floating-point computation, we chose the small scale and medium scale model in [10] for illustration purpose. The floating-point training process was completed by python under the Tensorflow framework [1].

The modification of the testing process consisted three main steps. Firstly, the pre-trained weight and parameters of the model were converted to fixed-point numbers. Secondly, when a word was fed to the model, all arithmetic operations such as matrix multiplication and element-wise operation were modified to operate on fixed-point numbers. Thirdly, for hardware implementation, special approximation should be applied to non-linear activations functions, which will be thoroughly discussed in Sect. 5. During testing, we used perplexity (PPL), which is a common metric for language prediction accuracy, to capture the quality of a sentence or a paragraph and the lower the PPL value is, the better the language model is. The absolute error of our fixed-point modification was quantified by the absolute value of the difference between the PPL output from the original floating-point version and that from the fixed-point version. The error rate was further calculated by dividing the absolute error by the PPL output from the corresponding floating-point version.

All experiments were completed on a PC equipped with a 3.2 GHz AMD CPU and 8 GB memory. The first 1000 words of the original testing set were selected as the testing sample and fed into the model in sequence. Based on the PPL errors generated under different fixed-point configurations, we explored bit-width configurations from 8 bits to 32 bits in detail and found noticeable turning points.

4 Influence of Shortened Bit-Width

Overflow of the integer part will significantly affect the language model's performance because the integer part primarily determines the representation scope. Thus, we need firstly figure out the most suitable integer length before investigating the error of precision resulted from the shrinkage of the fractional part.

Before the modification, we firstly tested the floating-point model on the selected testing sample and the PPL values were approximate 111.4334 for the small model and 79.5194 for the medium model. Then for all values in the model, fixing the length of the fractional part as 16 bits and shortening the integer part from 16 bits to 4 bits, we ran the fixed-point model on the same 1000 testing words in sequence and compared the PPL output with the baseline PPL derived from the floating-point version. The linear approximation of non-linear activation functions has not been implemented in this section so far.

As is shown in Fig. 1, it is noticeable that the 4-bit integer was not wide enough for both the small model and the medium model in terms of scope representation. So the errors were extremely large and unstable. When the integer width increased one or two bits, the representation scope was mostly satisfied. Thus, the length of fixed-point numbers' integer part in both models should never be less than 5 bits. Otherwise, the limit of scope representation would lead to disastrously huge error.

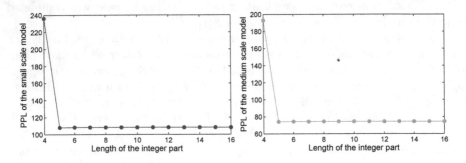

Fig. 1. The PPL of both models under different fixed-point configurations where the length of the fractional part is fixed as 16 bits and the length of the integer part is shortened from 16 bits to 4 bits.

Then, with similar method, we fixed the integer length at 6 bits and shortened the fractional part from 16 bits to 4 bits. Though the 5-bit long integer part was wide enough for scope representation according to previous experiments, we still decided to use 6-bit long integers to cover larger scope because there might exist unexpected outliers. As is shown in Fig. 2, in order to guarantee the precision during calculation, the length of the fractional part should be no less than 6 bits and the corresponding error rate was approximate 1.95% for the small scale model and 6.43% for the medium scale model.

In order to maintain the precision of the network and save the storage space at the same time, based on our experiments, we believed that the 12-bit long number with 6-bit fractional part was theoretically the best trade-off for both models. In addition, both of the models showed similar trends and had exact the same turning point when shortening the fixed-point numbers. This indicates that the scale of the LSTM network had little influence on the choice of fixed-point configuration. Thus, it can be inferred that our methodology and experimental results are compatible with large scale models as well.

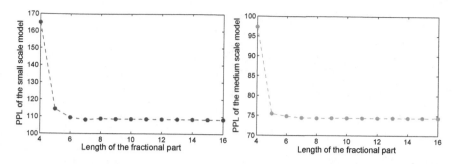

Fig. 2. The PPL of both models under different fixed-point configurations where the length of the integer part is fixed as 6 bits and the length of the fractional part is shortened from 16 bits to 4 bits.

5 Effect of Tanh Function Approximation

As it is very expensive to implement exponential functions directly on FPGAs, the approximation of the tanh function should be considered. However, there has been few thorough analysis of the tanh function's implementation on FPGAs. Contrarily, the sigmoid function, which is similar to the tanh function in terms of using exponential functions, has been analyzed and implemented on various hardwares [6]. Thus, inspired by the prior work on sigmoid functions, we can borrow the ideas and methods to accomplish our own analysis on tanh function.

The FPGA implementation of LSTM networks requires thousands of exponential function units to execute in parallel. Thus, Piecewise Linear Approximation (PLA) of nonlinearity algorithms [2] is preferred in this situation because this method consumes much less hardware resource, which is suitable for implementing vastly replicated units. In order to study how the precision of PLAs would harm the language model's performance, we used two PLA algorithms with different number of line segments, which are shown in Table 1, in our experiment.

Table 1. Two Piecewise Linear Approximation algorithms of tanh function.

PLA1		PLA2	
x	y	x	y
$0 \leqslant |x| < 11/16$	$y = |x|$	$0 \leqslant |x| < 1/2$	$y = |x|$
$11/16 \leqslant |x| < 57/32$	$y = (16|x|+33)/64$	$1/2 \leqslant |x| < 5/4$	$y = (2|x|+1)/4$
$57/32 \leqslant |x| < 97/32$	$y = (32|x|+927)/1024$	$5/4 \leqslant |x| < 8/4$	$y = (8|x|+46)/64$
$97/32 \leqslant |x|$	$y = 1$	$8/4 \leqslant |x| < 195/64$	$y = (2|x|+58)/64$
		$195/64 \leqslant |x|$	$y = 1$
$x < 0$	$y = -y$	$x < 0$	$y = -y$

Based on Table 1, with the configuration of 6-bit integer and different lengths of fractional parts, we built a fixed-point version of both PLAs and Fig. 3 shows the maximum and mean absolute value of errors of both PLAs. It turned out that, for both PLAs, the errors were stable when the fractional part was longer than 9 bits.

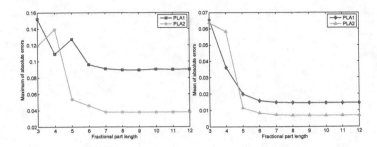

Fig. 3. Maximum (left) and mean (right) absolute errors of PLA1 and PLA2, configured with 6 bits integer and varying lengths of the fractional part.

We also compared the performance between PLA1 and PLA2 when they were applied to the language model. As is shown in Fig. 4, the length of the integer part was fixed at 6 bits and the fractional part varied from 9 bits to 11 bits. The absolute error of the PPL value was used to evaluate the performance of each solution. The rest of the numbers, such as neuron values and connection matrix, in the model were operated with 22-bit (6-bit integer part and 16-bit fractional part) fixed-point numbers. Though the difference was minor, it was obvious that PLA2 outperformed PLA1 at every fixed-point configuration. However, If the hardware resource is limited, PLA1 is recommended as it consumes less.

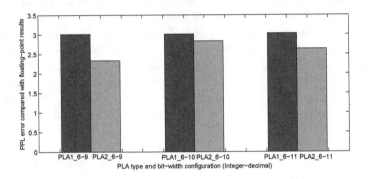

Fig. 4. Performance of the LSTM language model with different fixed-point configurations using PLA1 (blue) and PLA2 (red). (Color figure online)

6   Mixed Bit-Widths

Modern FPGAs supply built-in primitives to support basic operations, such as accumulation and multiplication, which are widely used in the LSTM network. Moreover, these primitives have their own favorite bit-width that benefits the hardware implementation. One DSP48E slice, for instance, contains one 25×18 two's complement multiplier, an adder, and an accumulator. Although different devices have their own favourite bit-width, 8-bit numbers or 16-bit numbers are more suitable for the whole system due to two main reasons. Firstly, the length that is integer multiples of the machine word-length usually leads to efficient memory management and communication. Secondly, most ASICs employ machine word-length numbers. With 8-bit or 16-bit numbers, it will be easier for the FPGA-based system to cooperate with other ASIC-based systems. Eventually, we decided to use 8-bit fixed-point numbers to represent all parameter matrixes of the model and 16-bit numbers for the rest.

With similar methods introduced in Sect. 4, we have also conducted a variety of experiments to search for the best bit-width choice. The only difference was that we used linear approximation of both the sigmoid function and the tanh function in this section. The PPL error rate was used to quantify the performance of the model and the results of the experiments are illustrated in Fig. 5.

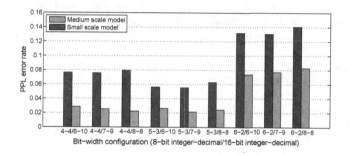

Fig. 5. The PPL error rate of the model under different mixed bit-width configurations.

Based on these experiments, the 8-bit number with 3-bit fractional part along with the 16-bit number with 9-bit fractional part was the best configuration for both models and the corresponding PPL error rates for the small scale model and the medium scale model were around 5.54% and 2.14% respectively. This result proves again that the fixed-point configuration is insensitive to the scale of the models.

7   Conclusion

Our work gives a comprehensive evaluation for implementing a LSTM network based language model on FPGAs by studying a wide range of bit-width, achieving best performance and area efficiency. Theoretically, for both the small scale model and the medium scale model, the 12-bit fixed-point configuration is the best choice balancing the accuracy and storage saving, which indicates that the scale of the model has little influence on the choice of fixed-point configurations. Both PLAs of the tanh function are acceptable for the model and PLA1 is more suitable if the hardware resource is limited while PLA2 is better if the model needs to be more precise. Eventually, based on these results, in order to obtain efficient memory management and communication, a mixed bit-widths solution combing 8-bit numbers and 16-bit numbers is proposed and evaluated.

Acknowledgement. This work was supported by the Natural Science Foundation of China under the grant No. 61303070.

References

1. Abadi, M., Agarwal, A., Barham, P., Brevdo, E., Chen, Z., Citro, C., Corrado, G.S., Davis, A., Dean, J., Devin, M., et al.: Tensorflow: large-scale machine learning on heterogeneous distributed systems (2016). arXiv preprint arXiv:1603.04467
2. Hesham Amin, K., Curtis, M., Hayes-Gill, B.R.: Piecewise linear approximation applied to nonlinear function of a neural network. IEE Proc.-Circuits, Devices Syst. **144**(6), 313–317 (1997)
3. Bengio, Y., Ducharme, R., Vincent, P., Jauvin, C.: A neural probabilistic language model. J. Mach. Learn. Res. **3**(Feb), 1137–1155 (2003)
4. Chang, A.X.M., Martini, B., Culurciello, E.: Recurrent neural networks hardware implementation on FPGA (2015). arXiv preprint arXiv:1511.05552
5. Hochreiter, S., Schmidhuber, J.: Long short-term memory. Neural Comput. **9**(8), 1735–1780 (1997)
6. Jiang, J., Rongdong, H., Mikel, L., Dou, Y.: Accuracy evaluation of deep belief networks with fixed-point arithmetic. Comput. Model. New Technol. **18**(6), 7–14 (2014)
7. Li, S., Chunpeng, W., Li, H., Boxun Li, Y., Wang, Q.Q.: FPGA acceleration of recurrent neural network based language model. In: 2015 IEEE 23rd Annual International Symposium on Field-Programmable Custom Computing Machines (FCCM), pp. 111–118. IEEE (2015)
8. Mikolov, T., Karafiát, M., Burget, L., Cernockỳ, J., Khudanpur, S.: Recurrent neural network based language model. In: Interspeech, vol. 2, p. 3 (2010)
9. Nurvitadhi, E., Sim, J., Sheffield, D., Mishra, A., Krishnan, S., Marr, D.: Accelerating recurrent neural networks in analytics servers: comparison of FPGA, CPU, GPU, and ASIC. In: 2016 26th International Conference on Field Programmable Logic and Applications (FPL), pp. 1–4. EPFL (2016)
10. Zaremba, W., Sutskever, I., Vinyals, O.: Recurrent neural network regularization (2014). arXiv preprint arXiv:1409.2329

FPGA Implementation of a Short Read Mapping Accelerator

Mostafa Morshedi and Hamid Noori[✉]

Faculty of Engineering, Electrical Engineering Department,
Ferdowsi University of Mashhad, Mashhad, Iran
morstafa@yahoo.com, hnoori@um.ac.ir

Abstract. Recently, due to drastically reducing costs of sequencing a human DNA molecule, the demands for next generation DNA sequencing (NGS) has increased significantly. DNA sequencers deliver millions of small fragments (short reads) from random positions of a very large DNA stream. To align these short-reads such that the original DNA sequence is determined, various software tools called short read mappers, such as Burrows BWA, are available. Analyzing the massive quantities of sequenced data produced using these software tools, requires a very long run-time on general-purpose computing systems due to a great computational power it needs. This work proposes some methods to accelerate short read alignment being prototyped on an FPGA. We use a seed and compare architecture based on FM-index method. Also pre-calculated data are used for more performance improvement. A multi-core accelerator based on the proposed methods is implemented on a Xilinx Virtex-6. Our design performs alignment of short reads with length of 75 and up to two mismatches. The proposed parallel architecture performs the short-read mapping up to 41 and 19 times faster than parallel programmed BWA run on eight-core AMD FX9590 and 6-cores Intel Extreme Core i7-5820 k CPUs using 8 and 12 threads.

1 Introduction

Recently, processing massive data generated by NGS (Next Generation Sequencing) methods [1] has become the main bottleneck in genetic researches. Based on the moore's law [2] the available data that needs to be processed in genetic researches, massively exceeds the computational power of the modern processors.

Using the NGS methods, millions of small DNA fragments of length 20 to 100 base pairs (bp) named *short read*, are generated in each run. In short read mapping, short reads have to be aligned according to a larger DNA stream, named *reference genome*. Older alignment approaches such as Smith-Waterman (SW) [3] and BLAST [4] are not suitable for short read mapping due to searching the whole reference for each short read. Recent methods like BWT [5] and soap3 [6], make short read mapping a lot more faster compared to the previous approaches, by generating an index from the reference genome before alignment. These approaches mainly use two major methods including FM-index [7] and Hash-table [8]. Between these two methods, FM-index is more popular due to lower memory footprint and being independent of the length of reference genome during the search operation.

© Springer International Publishing AG 2017
S. Wong et al. (Eds.): ARC 2017, LNCS 10216, pp. 289–296, 2017.
DOI: 10.1007/978-3-319-56258-2_25

Despite all the progress and improvements, due to massive amount of data that need to be processed, still short read mapping is a time consuming process on modern computers. To solve this problem many recent works try to accelerate short read mapping on other platforms like FPGAs due to the high parallelism and customization they provide. Researches such as [8–13] accelerate short read mapping using FPGAs. In this work an FPGA-based fully pipelined accelerator for short read mapping is proposed. The proposed hardware supports up to two mismatches in short read with 75 base-pairs (up to 100 bp). Our design uses the FM-index and the seed and compare methods. The main concepts of our design are:

- Pre-calculated data along using one memory controller for top and bot pointers.
- Extracting three identical and non overlapping seeds from each short read in the inexact match unit and comparing them with the reference.
- Through smart implementation, searching one of the three extracted seeds from each short read is done in the exact match unit.
- A multi-core system is presented to maximize the efficiency of the design.

2 Related Works

In the following subsection we briefly discuss the FM-index approach and after that review some recent short read mapping accelerators.

2.1 FM-index

To use FM-index method, the borrows-wheeler transform (BWT) [14] has to be generated from the reference genome (Fig. 1a). The suffix array (SA) values show the position of each suffix in the original reference stream (Fig. 1b). Using BWT stream, the occurrence array $O(x,i)$ and the characters count $C(x)$ are generated from the BWT (Fig. 1c). Then, searching any short read in the reference genome is done using Eqs. 1 and 2 with n steps, where n is the length of the short read.

The search operation uses two pointers named top and bot (bottom). These pointers needs to be updated n times. To find the location of a short read in the reference genome, top pointer is used as the address to read the SA values (Fig. 1d is an example of searching GA in ACTGA). This is very important to note that finding SA values using the top and bot values is not done in the FPGA accelerators and it is assumed that this step is done in software. Also to reduce the memory size required to store the $O(x, i)$, the rows of $O(x,i)$ are sampled with a factor of (d) and the rest of values $(d-1$ values) are calculated online using the sampled values and the BWT.

$$top_{new} = O(x, top_{old}) + C(x) \tag{1}$$

$$bot_{new} = O(x, bot_{old}) + C(x) \tag{2}$$

	(a)			(b)			(c)			

Reference Genome: ACTGA	
Rotations:	Sorted Rotations:
ACTGA$	$ACTG**A**
CTGA$A	A$ACT**G**
TGA$AC	ACTGA**$**
GA$ACT	CTGA$**A**
A$ACTG	GA$AC**T**
$ACTGA	TGA$A**C**
Borrows Wheeler transform: AG$ATC	

Reference Genome: ACTGA		
i	Suffixes:	SA
0	$	5
1	A$	4
2	ACTGA$	0
3	CTGA$	1
4	GA$	3
5	TGA$	2

Occurrence Array: O(x,i)					
i	BWT	A	C	G	T
0	A	0	0	0	0
1	G	1	0	0	0
2	$	1	0	1	0
3	A	1	0	1	0
4	T	2	0	1	0
5	C	2	0	1	1
6	total	2	1	1	1

Character Count: C(x)			
A	C	G	T
1	3	4	5

(d)	Short Read = GA Initial values: top = 0, Bot = 6	
1st step (A)	2nd step (G)	Result
Top = 0 + 1 = 1	Top = 0 + 4 = 4	i = 4
Bot = 2 + 1 = 3	Bot = 1 + 4 = 5	SA = 3

Fig. 1. An example of generating the BWT, SA values, O(x,i) and C(x) from a reference genome and finding GA in the reference.

2.2   Recent FPGA Accelerators

While searching a short read in the reference genome (A = 00, C = 01, G = 10, T = 00) two cases can happen including: (1) exact match and (2) inexact match. Also it is known that more than 70% of the short reads can be exactly matched to the reference genome [12]. Among the FPGA implementations using FM-index, [9] is the first implementation which only supports exact matching. Actually, the FM-index method can only support exact matching which is the drawback of this method.

To support inexact matching with FM-index, software tools such as BWA [5] and FPGA implementations such as [11–13] mainly use the backtrack version of FM-index to support mismatches. Another method to support mismatches is the seed and extend method. The original seed and extend method was presented by [4] and its combination with FM-index was implemented on FPGA by [10]. Also, there is another version of BWA [5] which uses this method. In [10] smaller streams named seeds are extracted from each short read. These seeds are searched in the reference genome using FM-index and the SA values extracted from the seeds present the candidate locations. In the final step the short read is compared to the reference genome (in the candidate location) using SW algorithm and the results are streamed to output. In [12] a seed and compare module is used which directly compares some short reads to the reference genome.

3   Proposed Architecture

In this section the proposed architecture to implement short read mapping on FPGA is discussed in details. The fully pipelined design consists of two main modules: the exact match unit and the inexact match unit. Short reads enter the exact match unit and the short reads that cannot be aligned in the exact match unit, are transferred to the inexact match unit. The proposed inexact match unit does not use backtrack version of FM-index. Instead, it extracts seeds from each short read and searches them in the reference genome using simple FM-index. This section consists of four major sub-sections: (1) Exact match unit architecture. (2) Pre-calculated values. (3) Inexact match unit architecture. (4) Multi-core implementation of the design.

3.1 Exact Match Unit

To begin short read mapping operation, short reads are streamed to the exact match unit and searched in the reference genome using FM-index (Fig. 2a). The current top and bot for a short read are used as addresses to read O(x,i) values. The sampled O(x,i) is stored in BRAMs with d = 64 and C(x) values are stored in FPGA registers.

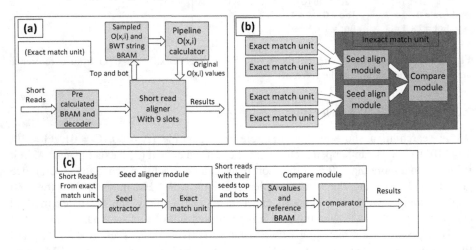

Fig. 2. Top view of exact match unit, inexact match unit and the quad-core design

Our design needs nine clock cycles to update a single top and bot (due to memory latency, generating O(x,i) values and adding O(x,i) to C(x)). To hide the nine clock cycles latency [10], we search nine short reads concurrently in the exact match unit. While other short reads are waiting for new data (top_{new} & bot_{new}), new short reads generate and send their requests for their corresponding tops and bots. As a result, searching any short read with the length of n can be done in n clock cycles in average.

Another important consideration is the memory interface. Basically, to implement Eqs. 1 and 2, two connections to two separate memories are needed, one for top (Eq. 1) and one for bot (Eq. 2), respectively. If only one memory is used for both top and bot, two memory accesses are needed to read $O(x, top_{old})$ (Eq. 1) and $O(x, bot_{old})$ (Eq. 2) values (and their BWTs). Therefore, the required memory size is decreased to the half but the delay for reading O(x,i) becomes doubled and the speedup decreases by half. In FM-index, top and bot have the maximum distance at the beginning. The distance decreases in each search step. Hence, in many cases the top and bot will hit at the same sampled $O(x,i)$ and the original $O(x,i)$ can be calculated for both top and bot, in one clock cycle by reading one memory address.

Our design uses one memory for both top and bot instead of two to reduce the number of memory interfaces. Through doing experiments for 10 K short reads we learn that after first seven steps (in average) the top and bot can be calculated using the same sampled $O(x,i)$ which requires one memory access (around 13 steps when the reference is the whole human genome [12]). With this method (using one memory for top and bot instead of two), the number of memory controllers is reduced to one for each exact match unit. However, the speedup for each exact match unit with one memory controller decreases at most by 0.15x for short reads with the length of 75 compared to the exact match unit with two memory controllers.

3.2   Pre-calculated Data

Every DNA string, similar to short reads of length n, has 4^n different combinations. Therefore, if the top and bot for all combinations of length m (where $m < n$) are pre-calculated before the short read mapping operation, the m initial search steps can be skipped for all of the short reads by replacing this data with the initial values for top and bot. Also, when only one memory connection is used for both top and bot, the initial steps need two memory accesses to read $O(x, top_{old})$ (Eq. 1) and $O(x, bot_{old})$ (Eq. 2), because their distance is more than $d = 64$. Therefore, the speedup obtained by using pre-calculated data would be more, when one memory connection is used.

Pre-calculated values are stored in FPGA embedded RAMs (BRAMs). Obviously, there is a limitation for available BRAM memories in any FPGA. According to the limitation of BRAM modules in Virtex 6 LX240T FPGA, we assume $m = 9$ for our design. Pre-calculated data are compressed more than 5 times in our design. As a result pre-calculated data with $m = 9$ can are used in our FPGA but another pipeline stage is needed to obtain the original pre-calculated data from compressed data. The speedup for searching short reads with 75 base pairs using pre-calculated data for $m = 9$ is 1.28x.

3.3   Inexact Match Unit

The proposed inexact match unit (Fig. 2c) is fed by the exact match unit. In this unit three identical seeds (25 bp each) are extracted from each short read and they are searched in the reference genome by an exact match unit. If a seed successfully aligns to the reference genome, the SA values are obtained which specify the locations where the seed exactly matches to the reference genome. These locations are called candidate locations. After reading the candidate locations from the reference genome these locations are compared to the short read which the corresponding seed was extracted from. This comparison is performed using a pipelined comparator and the outputs are the number and the locations of mismatches between the short read and the candidate location.

The pre-calculated data is also used in this module. Because of the smaller length of seeds (25) comparing to the short reads (75) the effect of using pre-calculated data is much more than its effect in the exact match unit in terms of speedup. For the seeds with 25 base pairs, the speed-up while using pre-calculated data is 2x (m = 9).

Another enhancement used in our design, is that the seed aligner needs to search only two seeds instead of three seeds. In our design, additional counters and registers are added to the exact match unit so that when the search steps reach to the one third of the short read, the related top and bot are stored in a register. These data is sent to the inexact match unit. The seed aligner in inexact match unit reuses these data and therefore, does not need to search one of the seeds again. Using this technique and pre-calculated data, searching the seeds in the seed aligner module becomes 3x faster, which is always the slowest module in the inexact match unit pipeline stages.

3.4   Multi-core Version

In order to achieve higher performance, a multi-core accelerator is designed and implemented on the FPGA (Fig. 2b). By considering two changes and applying them to the design we could fit a quad-core design on the target FPGA. (1) Due to lower percentage of short reads with mismatch, two exact match units are connected to a single seed aligner. (2) The seed aligner is the slowest part in our design therefore two seed aligners are connected to a single compare module in the inexact match unit and design works exactly like two separated simple inexact match units. As a result the final design works exactly like four separated simple cores.

4   Implementation and Experimental Results

4.1   Experimental Setup

The aim of this section is to evaluate the proposed methods discussed in Sect. 3. A reference genome with the length of 128 k base pairs is used as the reference genome which is extracted from chromosome 22 (available in [15]). Our design is implemented on the ML605 development board including a Xilinx Virtex-6 LX240T FPGA. Each module is modeled and developed in VHDL language in ISE design suite. The BWT, SA values, O(x,i) and pre-calculated data are generated offline from the reference genome. In our experiment, 10 K short reads with 75 base pairs are extracted directly from the reference genome and 1–3 mismatches are injected randomly into 30% of short reads. Our experiments are done for one million short reads by saving these 10 K short reads in the BRAMs and processing them 100 times.

4.2   Evaluating the Performance

Our design speed is limited to the exact match units. The information about area, number of BRAMs and the run time for processing one million short reads is reported in Table 1. The quality of alignment in FPGA is exactly similar to software and both versions of BWA are tested and the faster result is chosen to be compared with FPGA results.

Table 1. Area and BRAM usage and the run time for searching one million short reads.

	LUT	Register	32 Kb BRAM	Run time (sec)
Quad core design	29554 (19%)	31091 (10%)	361 (87%)	0.095

According to the recent works discussed in Sect. 2, searching the smaller percentage of the short reads which contains mismatches is the most time consuming part in short read mapping. Using the optimization techniques proposed in our design, searching the short reads with mismatches has become much faster than searching the short reads in the exact match unit.

4.3   Comparing the Results with Software

To compare the results with software implementation, short reads are searched in the reference genome by the BWA tool on the following two platforms: (1) AMD FX9590 (an eight cores processor) and (2) Intel Extreme Core i7-5820 k (a six cores processor that can handle 12 threads). In this experiment, 100 K short reads are processed by both software and FPGA (using the same reference). The results are compared to the parallel programmed version of the software that supports 8 and 12 threads against the four cores design on the FPGA. The results are shown in Table 2. For a fair comparison the run time for the BWA software is measured only for the align step which only calculates the top and bot values and the number of mismatches.

Table 2. Comparing software and FPGA run time for searching 100 thousand short reads.

	Number of threads	Clock freq. (MHZ)	Run time (sec)	Speed up
AMD FX9590	8	4600	0.39	41
Intel core-i7 5820 k	12	3300	0.18	19

4.4   Comparing with Other Designs

Our design is compared with [14] which also use a small reference genome. Similar to this paper, [14] uses FPGA memory to store values such as O(x,i), but it uses the backtrack version of FM-index. In [14] one million short reads with 72 bp are searched in the reference with one million base pair and our quad core design is 126 times faster than the six core design in [14] ([14] supports one open gap).

5   Conclusion

In this paper an FPGA implementation of an accelerator with parallel architecture is proposed to solve the long run-time of short read mapping algorithm. The accelerator has been designed based on FM-index algorithm and considers multiple optimizations to enhance the short read alignment speedup such as multi-core structure, multithreading, pipelining and using pre-calculated data. Our paper uses a modified seed and compare version of FM-index to align short reads with 75 bp (up to two mismatches) which does not use the backtrack version of FM-index which is more complex.

References

1. Mardis, E.R.: The impact of next-generation sequencing technology on genetics. Trends Genet. **24**(3), 133–141 (2008)
2. Wetterstrand, K.: DNA sequencing costs, data from the NHGRI Genome Sequencing Program (GSP) (2014). http://www.genome.gov/sequencingcosts
3. Smith, T.F., Waterman, M.S.: Identification of common molecular subsequences. J. Mol. Biol. **147**(1), 195–197 (1970)
4. Altschul, S.F., et al.: Basic local alignment search tool. J. Mol. Biol. **215**(3), 403–410 (1990)
5. Li, H., Durbin, R.: Fast and accurate short read alignment with Burrows-Wheeler transform. Bioinformatics **25**(14), 1754–1760 (2009)
6. Liu, C., et al.: SOAP3: ultra-fast GPU-based parallel alignment tool for short reads. Bioinformatics **28**(6), 878–879 (2012)
7. Ferrragina, P., Manzini, G.: An experimental study of an opportunistic index. In: Proceeding of 12th ACM-SIAM Symposium on Discrete Algorithms, pp. 269–278 (2001)
8. Olson, C.B., et al.: Hardware acceleration of short read mapping. In: 2012 IEEE 20th Annual International Symposium on Field-Programmable Custom Computing Machines (FCCM), pp. 161–168. IEEE (2012)
9. Fernandez, E., Najjar, W., Lonardi, S.: String matching in hardware using FM-index. In: 2011 IEEE 19th Annual International Symposium on Field-Programmable Custom Computing Machines (FCCM), pp. 218–225. IEEE (2011)
10. Arram, J., Tsoi, K.H., Luk, W., Jiang, P.: Reconfigurable acceleration of short read mapping. In: 2013 IEEE 21st Annual International Symposium on Field-Programmable Custom Computing Machines (FCCM), pp. 210–217. IEEE (2013)
11. Arram, J., Luk, W., Jiang, P.: Ramethy: reconfigurable acceleration of bisulfite sequence alignment. In: Proceedings of the 2015 ACM/SIGDA International Symposium on Field-Programmable Gate Arrays, pp. 250–259. ACM (2015)
12. Arram, J., et al.: Leveraging FPGAs for accelerating short read alignment. IEEE/ACM Trans. Comput. Biol. Bioinform. (2016). http://ieeexplore.ieee.org/document/7422003/
13. Xin, Y., et al.: Parallel architecture for DNA sequence inexact matching with Burrows-Wheeler Transform. Microelectron. J. **44**(8), 670–682 (2013)
14. Burrows, M., Wheeler, D.: A block-sorting lossless data compression algorithm. Digital Equipment Corporation. Technical report (1994)
15. UCSC Genome Bioinformatics. http://hgdownload.cse.ucsc.edu

Languages and Estimation Techniques

dfesnippets: An Open-Source Library for Dataflow Acceleration on FPGAs

Paul Grigoras$^{(\boxtimes)}$, Pavel Burovskiy, James Arram, Xinyu Niu, Kit Cheung, Junyi Xie, and Wayne Luk

Department of Computing, Imperial College London, London, UK
{paul.grigoras09,w.luk}@imperial.ac.uk

Abstract. Highly-tuned FPGA implementations can achieve significant performance and power efficiency gains over general purpose hardware. However the limited development productivity has prevented mainstream adoption of FPGAs in many areas such as High Performance Computing. High level standard development libraries are increasingly adopted in improving productivity. We propose an approach for performance critical applications including standard library modules, benchmarking facilities and application benchmarks to support a variety of use-cases. We implement the proposed approach as an open-source library for a commercially available FPGA system and highlight applications and productivity gains.

1 Introduction

Highly tuned FPGA implementations can achieve performance and power efficiency gains for many problems [1]. However, development productivity is limited compared to other acceleration alternatives such as GPUs or Xeon Phi processors [2].

Recently, higher-level programming facilities based on High Level Synthesis [3,4] or domain specific languages [5–7] have improved productivity of FPGA development significantly. High-quality standard development libraries are becoming essential to improve productivity further. However, FPGA development environments may not provide standard development libraries. Fundamental operations such as floating point reductions may not be supported, and depending on the available resources and desired performance are nontrivial to implement, as we show in Sect. 2.

It is therefore necessary to provide well-designed component libraries to facilitate the development of applications and tools. However, in addition to these facilities, and as a point of departure from conventional approaches, given the performance-critical nature of the FPGA environment, component and application benchmarks should also be part of the library to facilitate the development of high-performance designs. To increase developer productivity for FPGA accelerators at all levels, libraries might provide: *(1)* library components which serve as the building blocks for developing real-world applications. These library components should be efficient in terms of latency, throughput and resource usage,

S. Wong et al. (Eds.): ARC 2017, LNCS 10216, pp. 299–310, 2017.
DOI: 10.1007/978-3-319-56258-2_26

and provide a useful and customisable interface; *(2)* benchmarking utilities which aid in tasks such as determining system performance and resource utilisation. These utilities are essential for rapid prototyping, and assessing the scalability and feasibility of FPGA designs; *(3)* applications which can be used as benchmarks, or case studies for framework and tool development. These applications can also be adapted to accelerate closely related problems, considerably reducing development time.

In this work we present `dfesnippets`,[1] the first community driven open-source library for Maxeler DataFlow Engines (DFEs). The library is available under the MIT License. Table 1 provides an overview of the components:

1. A library component which contains useful reusable cores such as reduction, sorting and I/O circuits; these cores are tested and optimised, and have been used in several published designs [8–11].
2. A benchmarking component which facilitates quantitative evaluation and simplifies the process of modelling and estimating resource and performance properties, speeding up the design process.
3. An application component which provides a collection of full applications to be used as case-studies for the development of frameworks and tools for FPGA based programming. These applications have been used in several research projects and publications [12–16].

Table 1. Overview of components in `dfesnippets`

Component	Block	Refs
Library	Input/output – ALBP, Inter-FPGA	[8]
	Linear algebra – SpMV, power iteration	[17,18]
	Reductions – tree, PCBT, LogAdder	[9]
	Sorting – bitonic sorter	[13]
Benchmarks	Infiniband/PCIe throughput	–
	Custom memory controller throughput	–
	Default memory controller throughput	–
	Component resource utilisation	–
Applications	Quantitative phase imaging	[19]
	Genetic sequence alignment	[16,20]
	Monte carlo finite difference option pricing	[13]
Software utilities	Build tool (python)	–
	Project template tool (python)	–
	Results extraction (python)	–
	Sparse matrix utilities (C++)	–
	Scheduling utilities (C++)	–

[1] https://github.com/custom-computing-ic/dfe-snippets.

Although we will not cover this in greater detail due to lack of space, the library also contains: *(1)* header only C++ libraries implementing useful functionality for managing and benchmarking DFE projects ranging from timing utilities to APIs for reordering sparse matrix data in preparation for FPGA execution; *(2)* tools for creating and managing projects such as to compile, generate and manage multiprocess and multi-node hardware compilation, and automatically extract and tabulate resource usage and generate reports; *(3)* comprehensive, automated test suite, testing each design to ensure it is functionally correct and it meets timing and resource usage constraints.

A community driven library of open-source implementations, component and application benchmarks can increase the productivity of researchers and professional programmers. It can also improve the quality of results, and pave the way for broader FPGA adoption in areas where productivity has been a key limiting factor, such as High Performance Computing.

2   Library Components

Library components are the building blocks for developing more complex real world applications. **dfesnippets** includes a range of components such as generic reduction, I/O blocks, linear algebra blocks (sparse product, matrix vector and matrix-matrix-multiply, power iteration kernels, sparse matrix vector multiplication for banded matrices), and generic configuration and connectivity utilities such as inter-FPGA communication blocks. Despite being fundamental components, they are challenging to implement on FPGAs due to the resource constrained nature and high emphasis on performance and resource efficiency.

To be used effectively in large scale designs, library components must be parametric, provide a useful interface, and be efficient in terms of latency, throughput, and resource utilisation. Pure encapsulation, in software terminology, is difficult to achieve, therefore the internals of many cores may have to be customised in order to fit into the resource and performance constraints of a particular application. This makes source code availability important for component reuse.

We implement **dfesnippets** for the Maxeler FPGA platform [21]. The platform constitutes of a hardware implementation, a compiler from a high-level dataflow language, MaxJ, to FPGA bitstream, and a runtime environment. MaxJ [22] provides explicit control of the design of the hardware architecture itself, which is critical in delivering good performance and effectively exploiting customisation opportunities available for FPGA designers. It is conceptually close to Verilog, but with increased productivity due to the abstraction of low-level vendor IPs; MaxJ provides good support for software-only simulation and interfacing with many available programming languages. These features make MaxJ a good choice for implementing an open-source library: it provides a high level of control and flexibility without being verbose while the similarity to other hardware description languages simplifies porting components to other languages. In the rest of this Section we provide a more in-depth look at certain components of **dfesnippets**. For a full list please see the project page[2].

---

[2] https://github.com/custom-computing-ic/dfe-snippets.

2.1 Reductions

A *reduction* is the application of an associative binary operator to an initial value and a list of values in order to collapse the list to a single value. The deeply pipelined nature of the arithmetic units on FPGAs, such as those for floating point, make reduction operators non-trivial to implement, and much research has gone into efficient reduction circuits [23–25].

Reduction implementations must balance throughput, resource usage and latency. From this perspective, we can define at least three types of reduction circuits. First, a fully parallel *reduction tree* which can reduce k values per clock cycle, assuming fully pipelined operators. Trees have the highest throughput, but also the largest resource usage of $O(k)$. To reduce large data streams of size n, reduction trees of size n are required. This is fast but not practical from a resource utilisation standpoint. Second, a *C-slowed accumulator* may reduce one value per clock cycle, with a latency depending on the latency L of the reduction operator. This is a resource efficient approach requiring a single reduction operator, but the throughput is limited: one value per clock cycle may make the reduction circuit a performance bottleneck of the entire design. For example a modern FPGA architecture may read 48 double precision values from DRAM per clock cycle. Also, the C-slowed accumulator does not fully compute the reduction, as L partial sums are left to be reduced in the pipeline. Third, more complex reduction circuits have been proposed such as the *partially compacted binary reduction tree*, PCBT [26]. These blocks are more complex to implement but can achieve good resource efficiency when high throughput is not a concern. Circuits such as the PCBT solve the issue of only partially reducing the data set, and they typically require more resources than a C-slowed implementation but fewer resources than a tree.

Many designs, such as implementations of sparse matrix vector circuits [8], iterative solvers [10] and power iteration kernels [17] may require a combination of all three circuits to achieve maximum performance: *(1)* a full tree performs the initial reduction at high throughput reducing k values per cycle, *(2)* each output of the reduction tree is fed and accumulated in a C-slowed accumulator and finally *(3)* each output of the C-slowed accumulator may be reduced using a PCBT.

Our implementation of the PCBT is shown in Fig. 1. It consists of a chain of blocks, each implementing its own level of a binary reduction tree using a state machine, a buffer and an adder. The state machine has two states: *no arguments* and *one argument*. When one argument is present in the buffer and the second argument is an enabled input, the adder produces their sum as the output signal with the valid signal high, then flushes the internal state to *no arguments*. At the transition to the *one argument* state the output valid is low, whilst the output is a sum of a stored argument with zero. The valid signal of a block is connected to the enable signal of the next block so that each level of the PCBT is waiting for the complete accumulation at the previous level. It also enables the PCBT to stall but preserve its internal state if necessary (when enable is low). The external reset signal forces all state machines to produce the valid signal high regardless of their internal state, thus finalising the reduction with whatever number of inputs are internally present in our PCBT circuit. This enables accumulating an arbitrary number of terms in a reduction set.

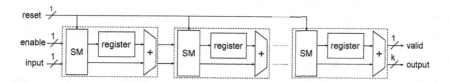

Fig. 1. PCBT based on state machines

To conclude the reduction case study, we note that, in principle, the reduction operation is probably one of the most fundamental building blocks required for implementing more complex applications. However, due to the broad range of design choices with varying throughput, resource utilisation and functionality, this operation is not trivial to implement. Having easy access to multiple variants of reduction circuit, as provided by dfesnippets, can therefore improve productivity.

2.2 Input and Output Blocks

I/O blocks are commonly used to manage the connection between the computational kernel implemented on the FPGA accelerator and off-chip components such as DRAM, the host CPU (PCIe, Infiniband), or other FPGA devices.

In the case of DRAM and CPU communication, the I/O blocks may be required to convert the fixed width output interface of the communication channel to a different input width of the computational kernel. This is a common requirement, particularly for applications which process an irregular, runtime dependent input size at each cycle such as a sparse matrix vector multiplication kernel [8]. The I/O blocks are required to be efficient from a resource utilisation perspective but the logic they implement is often complex and the control heavy nature does not map well to dataflow style accelerators and languages. If unoptimised, these blocks can use substantial on-chip resources, particularly memory resources such as BRAMs.

Blocks such as the Arbitrary Length Burst Proxy (ALBP) included in dfesnippets and used in previous work [8] can help address these issues. The ALBP architecture contains k FIFOs to store bursts retrieved from off-chip memory. Once a burst is retrieved, data are pushed in the FIFOs such that the i-th element of a burst is assigned to FIFO $o+i$ mod k. o is the position after processing the previous burst. $m_t < k$ data items may be simultaneously requested from the ALBP by the compute kernel, where m_t is runtime-determined. If fewer than k items are requested, the output is zero-padded to the fixed width k to match with the fixed, regular k width of the compute kernel's input interface.

Other I/O blocks may be required for inter-device communication. In computing clusters with multiple FPGAs, light-weight and easy-to-use communication modules for inter-FPGA data transfer help to reduce the latency and overhead of the whole system. In a number of HPC systems, such as the Maxeler system used in this work, direct built-in inter-FPGA links are used for transferring large amounts of data with low latency. dfesnippets builds on top of these inter-FPGA links to implement an interchangeable communication kernel which creates a one-dimensional systolic array, unrolled across multiple FPGAs. The kernel uses counters to keep track of the amount of data sent and received, which are used to control input and output switches, allowing data to be rapidly transferred among the FPGAs. dfesnippets implements an all-to-all broadcasting protocol using this systolic array by alternating the direction of the data transfer in successive turns. Interchangeable inter-FPGA communication modules provide greater flexibility in distributing workload among the accelerators, hence such a library of modules is extremely useful for applications requiring large-scale multi-FPGA systems.

2.3 Other Blocks

In addition to the components presented in this section, dfesnippets includes a range of components such as sorting and linear algebra blocks, more generic configuration and connectivity utilities and a substantial number of CPU based functionalities, to handle pre-processing and integration of the accelerator designs within larger application frameworks. Leveraging these blocks, there are many possibilities for developing, optimising and including more library components within the proposed approach, which will further increase the productivity and applicability.

3 Benchmarking

Benchmarking utilities are especially helpful for the research community. They help establish a baseline for the system performance or resource efficiency, facilitate quick estimation and prototyping (for example to assess the scalability of various designs with respect to memory bandwidth, resources etc.), provide sanity checks and highlight empirically the impact of some optimisations which may not be entirely transparent to the end user. Two types of benchmarks are particularly important for FPGA development: (1) performance benchmarks which can be used to measure the throughput and latency of FPGA designs and memory and interconnect subsystems (2) resource utilisation benchmarks which demonstrate the resource efficiency of particular cores and are essential for assessing the scalability and feasibility of FPGA designs.

Performance. dfesnippets provides three system level performance benchmarks which can be used to measure the achievable throughput of various links. The *Default DRAM Benchmark* instantiates a default memory controller, with customisable clock frequency which reads and writes data in a linear access fashion. This can be used to determine the peak memory bandwidth performance of a given device, which can serve as a baseline for measuring the achieved performance of user applications. The *Custom DRAM Benchmark* instantiates a more complex design with a custom memory command generator and associated host code to drive the benchmarking. This can be used for evaluating the memory access speed using custom memory commands and linear access patterns. It fetches parallel data streams from DRAM and then routes them to DRAM and/or host, behaviour which is configurable by the user. The major configuration options are parameterised so users can change the number of bursts per command, size of memory to access, width of memory interface and number of parallel DRAM streams to match existing properties in their own designs. This enables rapid experimentation with application specific data placement and access scheduling techniques to improve DRAM performance. The *Infiniband/PCIe DRAM Benchmark* instantiates a simple pass through design which matches the PCIe input width (128 bits). Together with the associated software to run on the CPU, the design can be used to measure throughput over the CPU to FPGA interconnect.

The library allows users to easily adjust the number of measurements, data size, memory controller frequency, on-chip frequency, and architecture for each benchmark. This reduces the possibility for error and promotes good practices.

Resource Utilisation. dfesnippets includes a synthetic resource utilisation benchmark to measure the resource usage of various blocks using the MaxCompiler builtin resource usage annotations. These reports are openly available as part of the library and can provide the basis for rapid resource usage estimation models without the need to sit through long compilation times. This can greatly reduce the time to prototype designs. The benchmarks are provided for both the Xilinx Virtex 6 based Vectis boards and the Stratix V Maia boards. This provides a quick method to highlight differences between the two (such as different resource usage profile of DSPs) or provide insight into hidden properties, which can probably only be discovered by significant empirical exploration, such as the considerable resource savings achieved by reducing pipelining factors on the Stratix V Maia boards.

4 Applications

dfesnippets also includes a set of full applications which can be used as reusable components in other applications or as benchmarks and case studies for framework and tool development. The broader availability of such applications can help researchers and developers focus more on their area of expertise and avoid typical pitfalls stemming from the complexity of designing FPGA based applications. These applications themselves contain reusable blocks which can be adapted in other designs, or can be reused directly in other applications, perhaps as one stage of a complex pipeline or multi FPGA design. Overall, the availability of these larger designs can increase the productivity of researchers and tool developers.

Genomic Data Analysis. dfesnippets includes an FM-index [27] design which can be used to accelerate a variety of genomic data analysis applications such as sequence alignment [28], sequence assembly [29], and reference-based compression [30]. Several works which make use of the FM-index design have been published [15,16]. The FM-index is a full-text compressed index which supports substring searching in time proportional to the search string length. The FM-index is built upon the Burrows-Wheeler transform [31], a permutation of a text generated from its Suffix Array [32].

A single FPGA outperforms the fully-optimised software version running on dual Intel Xeon CPUs with 16 threads. The largest performance improvement is for the hg38 data set where the FPGA is *3.7 times faster* than the software version. With the performance gains presented, the FM-index design has great potential for integration into many genomic data analysis applications or to be used as a reference benchmark application for tool development.

Monte Carlo Finite Difference Option Pricing. dfesnippets includes a multi-FPGA dynamic Monte Carlo design for bond options pricing. This design is particularly useful as a case study for resource management frameworks or environments for FPGAs [13,14] as it demonstrates good scalability and performance. To accelerate the payoff evaluation for the bond option, the Monte Carlo paths and the payoff evaluation functions are implemented on the FPGA accelerator. The finite difference method [33] is applied to solve the resulting equations and estimate the payoff of the bond at some time in the future.

The design operates in a map-reduce fashion, using OpenMP to parallelise the calls to the Maxeler API which load and execute the Monte Carlo evaluation over a configurable number of FPGAs. A final reduction step is implemented on the CPU to aggregate the results of the computation corresponding to different Monte Carlo paths. On the FPGA accelerator, an optimised random number generator [34] is used to generate the random numbers required for the Monte Carlo computation. A baseline design with 4 parallel processing elements, uses less than 20% of the resources on the Virtex 6 chip of the Maxeler Vectis DFE. This makes the design easy to place and route, and therefore ideal for experimental workloads where a short iteration time is essential, for example when developing tests and benchmarks for more complex tools. The design achieves linear scalability [13] and can therefore be used to benchmark load distribution tools, scheduling strategies and cloud-like environments for heterogeneous systems, such as FPGAs.

Quantitative Phase Imaging (QPI) on FPGAs. dfesnippets also includes a block for image processing based on the newly developed quantitative asymmetric-detection time-stretch optical microscopy (Q-ATOM) which offers ultrafast and high-sensitivity quantitative phase cellular imaging. Retrieved phase images provide essential information of cells and potentially benefits medical diagnostics. However, performing backend phase retrieval and cell image classification is extremely computationally intensive. With the aid of FPGAs researchers can push QPI phase retrieval and cell image classification to near real-time speed [19].

The QPI phase retrieval and cell image classification design is composed of a spatial domain module, a frequency domain module and a linear SVM classifier. The spatial domain module performs background subtraction, intensity normalization and complex phase shift extraction. The frequency domain module performs low-pass filtering to reduce noises and retrieves final phase images. The Winograd 16-point algorithm is used in the frequency domain module to perform forward and inverse 2D fast Fourier transform (FFT). The sequential Winograd algorithm has low resource consumption and is suitable for a wide range of applications involving frequency spectrum analysis.

The QPI application has *a throughput of 32.08 GOPS* when running on a single Altera Stratix V GS 5SGSD8 FPGA [19], which is equivalent to retrieving and classifying around 2497 phase images of 256×256 size. Classification accuracy of unstained and live human chondrocytes (OAC), human osteoblasts (OST) and mouse fibroblasts (3T3) increases when using retrieved phase images.

5   Evaluation

dfesnippets totals approximately 6000 lines of CPU utilities and tests and 7000 lines of MaxJ in the library and benchmarking components and 4000 lines of CPU and MaxJ code in the applications components. We estimate the development time of each library component to be of the order of one to two weeks while the development effort for applications is on the order of 1–2 months. Both library and application development usually involve two developers, of which one is typically experienced (more than two years) in the MaxJ programming language.

Even in a relatively high level language such as MaxJ, approximately 600 lines of library code including comments are required to implement the three alternative reduction strategies described in Sect. 2.1 plus an additional 700 lines for setting up the CPU test bench that is vital to verify the correctness of these implementations, particularly for the more complex designs. By using dfesnippets almost 1300 lines of code can be replaced by several lines to instantiate the required reduction circuits directly in the user design. Therefore the productivity gains resulting from the proposed library component of our approach are substantial, particularly since reduction circuits are generic blocks, commonly used in many applications. Table 2 shows several applications where we have used dfesnippets and observed a substantial reduction in source lines of code (SLOC) for the hardware design.

To illustrate the productivity gains achievable by the applications components we note that recent software frameworks such as experimental compilers [12] and resource management frameworks [13] for FPGA based systems can utilise these applications directly as benchmarks. Prototypes for these projects require 4123 and 3880 lines of code respectively, while the benchmarks require 2050 and 2924 lines of code respectively. Therefore a substantial productivity gain comes from the ability to directly reuse these benchmarks and avoid spending substantial time on redeveloping complex designs. We estimate the development time of application components in dfesnippets to be between 1–2 months

Table 2. Examples of projects using `dfesnippets` and estimated productivity improvement measured in a reduction in source lines of code (SLOC), including only the hardware components and thus excluding comments, test code, CPU interfaces etc.

Application	Components used	SLOC reduction
SpMV tuning framework [8]	Reductions, I/O, configuration	710
Biomedical acceleration [15]	Bitwise operation, FM index	361
FEM accelerator [11]	Reductions, I/O	490
Elastic cloud framework [13]	Option pricing app benchmark	590
Linear solver [10]	Benes network, reductions	250
SpMV accelerator [18]	Reductions, I/O	490

each for an experienced MaxJ developer. These applications often require complex, specialised and state of the art blocks such as high throughput random number generators, Fast-Fourier Transforms, and custom memory controllers. Such blocks are not only complex and non-trivial to optimise for FPGA implementation, they are also difficult to develop and debug. It is clear that from a tool developer perspective, it is not productive to spend as much time developing the benchmark as developing the tool itself.

Not only is the development time reduced substantially by avoiding the need to redevelop benchmarks, but the parametric design supports customisation effectively, leading to additional productivity gains. All applications can be built with minimal configurations to verify correctness or with full replication and optimisations to verify performance and energy efficiency. This approach simplifies debugging and testing in the early stages of project development by reducing the compilation time.

6   Conclusion

We present `dfesnippets`, an open source library of reusable components: cores, benchmarks, applications and tools. It improves the productivity of FPGA development by providing fundamental blocks for any real world application as well as system, component and application benchmarks. By providing `dfesnippets` directly as open source software to the research community, we hope that a substantial improvement in productivity can be achieved. This may pave the way for supporting exciting and sophisticated research and applications, while enhancing the adoption of FPGAs in High Performance Computing, embedded systems and other domains.

Acknowledgement. The support of UK EPSRC (EP/I012036/1, EP/L00058X/1, EP/L016796/1 and EP/N031768/1), the European Union Horizon 2020 Research and Innovation Programme under grant agreement number 671653, the Maxeler University Programme, Altera, Intel and Xilinx is gratefully acknowledged.

References

1. Todman, T.J., Constantinides, G.A., Wilton, S.J., Mencer, O., Luk, W., Cheung, P.Y.: Reconfigurable computing: architectures and design methods. IEE Proc.-Comput. Digit. Tech. **152**(2), 193–207 (2005)
2. Jones, D.H., Powell, A., Bouganis, C., Cheung, P.Y.: GPU versus FPGA for high productivity computing. In: Proceedings of the FPL, pp. 119–124 (2010)
3. Zhang, Z., Fan, Y., Jiang, W., Han, G., Yang, C., Cong, J.: AutoPilot: a platform-based ESL synthesis system. In: Coussy, P., Morawiec, A. (eds.) High-Level Synthesis, pp. 99–112. Springer, Heidelberg (2008)
4. Canis, A., Choi, J., Aldham, M., Zhang, V., Kammoona, A., Anderson, J.H., Brown, S., Czajkowski, T.: LegUp: high-level synthesis for FPGA-based processor/accelerator systems. In: Proceedings of the FPGA, pp. 33–36. ACM (2011)
5. Kulkarni, C., Brebner, G., Schelle, G.: Mapping a domain specific language to a platform FPGA. In: Proceedings DAC, pp. 924–927. ACM (2004)
6. George, N., Lee, H., Novo, D., Rompf, T., Brown, K.J., Sujeeth, A.K., Odersky, M., Olukotun, K., Ienne, P.: Hardware system synthesis from domain-specific languages. In: Proceedings of the FPL, pp. 1–8. IEEE (2014)
7. Cong, J., Sarkar, V., Reinman, G., Bui, A.: Customizable domain-specific computing. IEEE Des. Test Comput. **28**(2), 6–15 (2011)
8. Grigoras, P., Burovskiy, P., Luk, W.: CASK: open-source custom architectures for sparse kernels. In: Proceedings of the FPGA, pp. 179–184 (2016)
9. Grigoras, P., Burovskiy, P., Hung, E., Luk, W.: Accelerating SpMV on FPGAs by compressing nonzero values. In: Proceedings of the FCCM (2015)
10. Chow, G., Grigoras, P., Burovskiy, P., Luk, W.: An efficient sparse conjugate gradient solver using a benes permutation network. In: Proceedings of the FPL (2014)
11. Burovskiy, P., Grigoras, P., Sherwin, S.J., Luk, W.: Efficient assembly for high order unstructured FEM meshes. In: Proceedings of the FPL (2015)
12. Grigoras, P., Niu, X., Coutinho, J., Luk, W., Bower, J., Pell, O.: Aspect driven compilation for dataflow designs. In: Proceedings of the ASAP (2013)
13. Grigoras, P., Tottenham, M., Niu, X., Coutinho, J.G.F., Luk, W.: Elastic management of reconfigurable accelerators. In: Proceedings of the ISPA, pp. 174–181. IEEE (2014)
14. Coutinho, J.G.F., Pell, O., O'Neill, E., Sanders, P., McGlone, J., Grigoras, P., Luk, W., Ragusa, C.: HARNESS project: managing heterogeneous computing resources for a cloud platform. In: Goehringer, D., Santambrogio, M.D., Cardoso, J.M.P., Bertels, K. (eds.) ARC 2014. LNCS, vol. 8405, pp. 324–329. Springer, Heidelberg (2014). doi:10.1007/978-3-319-05960-0_36
15. Arram, J., Pflanzer, M., Kaplan, T., Luk, W.: FPGA acceleration of reference-based compression for genomic data. In: Proceedings of the ICFPT, pp. 9–16. IEEE (2015)
16. Arram, J., Luk, W., Jiang, P.: Ramethy: reconfigurable acceleration of bisulfite sequence alignment. In: Proceedings of the FPGA, pp. 250–259. ACM (2015)
17. Burovskiy, P., Girdlestone, S., Davies, C., Sherwin, S., Luk, W.: Dataflow acceleration of Krylov subspace sparse banded problems. In: Proceedings of the FPL, pp. 1–6. IEEE (2014)
18. Grigoras, P., Burovskiy, P., Luk, W., Sherwin, S.: Optimising sparse matrix vector multiplication for large scale FEM problems on FPGA. In: Proceedings of the FPL, pp. 1–9. EPFL (2016)

19. Xie, J., Niu, X., Lau, A.K., Tsia, K.K., So, H.K.: Accelerated cell imaging and classification on FPGAS for quantitative-phase asymmetric-detection time-stretch optical microscopy. In: Proceedings of the ICFPT, pp. 1–8. IEEE (2015)

20. Arram, J., Tsoi, K.H., Luk, W., Jiang, P.: Hardware acceleration of genetic sequence alignment. In: Brisk, P., Figueiredo Coutinho, J.G., Diniz, P.C. (eds.) ARC 2013. LNCS, vol. 7806, pp. 13–24. Springer, Heidelberg (2013). doi:10.1007/978-3-642-36812-7_2

21. Lindtjrn, O., Clapp, R.G., Pell, O., Mencer, O., Flynn, M.J.: Surviving the end of scaling of traditional micro processors in HPC. In: IEEE HOT CHIPS 22 (2010)

22. Pell, O., Mencer, O.: Surviving the end of frequency scaling with reconfigurable dataflow computing. SIGARCH Comput. Archit. News 39(4), 60–65 (2011)

23. Morris, G.R., Zhuo, L., Prasanna, V.K.: High-performance FPGA-based general reduction methods. In: Proceedings of the FCCM, pp. 323–324 (2005)

24. Zhuo, L., Morris, G.R., Prasanna, V.K.: Designing scalable FPGA-based reduction circuits using pipelined floating-point cores. In: Proceedings of the ISPDP (2005)

25. Wilson, D., Stitt, G.: The unified accumulator architecture: a configurable, portable, and extensible floating-point accumulator. Trans. Reconfigurable Technol. Syst. (TRETS) 9(3), 21 (2016)

26. Zhuo, L., Morris, G.R., Prasanna, V.K.: High-performance reduction circuits using deeply pipelined operators on FPGAs. IEEE Trans. PDS 18(10), 1377–1392 (2007)

27. Ferragina, P., Manzini, G.: An experimental study of an opportunistic index. In: Proceedings of the Twelfth Annual ACM-SIAM Symposium on Discrete Algorithms, pp. 269–278. Society for Industrial and Applied Mathematics (2001)

28. Langmead, B., Salzberg, S.L.: Fast gapped-read alignment with Bowtie 2. Nat. Methods 9(4), 357–359 (2012)

29. Simpson, J.T., Durbin, R.: Efficient de novo assembly of large genomes using compressed data structures. Genome Res. 22(3), 549–556 (2012)

30. Zhang, Y., Li, L., Yang, Y., Yang, X., He, S., Zhu, Z.: Light-weight reference-based compression of FASTQ data. BMC Bioinform. 16(1), 1 (2015)

31. Burrows, M., Wheeler, D.J.: A Block-sorting Lossless Data Compression Algorithm (1994)

32. Manber, U., Myers, G.: Suffix arrays: a new method for on-line string searches. SIAM J. Comput. 22(5), 935–948 (1993)

33. Mitchell, A.R., Griffiths, D.F.: The Finite Difference Method in Partial Differential Equations. Wiley, Hoboken (1980)

34. Thomas, D.B., Luk, W.: High quality uniform random number generation using LUT optimised state-transition matrices. Vlsi Sig. Process. 47(1), 77–92 (2007)

A Machine Learning Methodology for Cache Recommendation

Osvaldo Navarro, Jones Mori$^{(\boxtimes)}$, Javier Hoffmann, Fabian Stuckmann,
and Michael Hübner

Ruhr-University Bochum, Universitästr. 150, 44801 Bochum, Germany
{Osvaldo.Navarro,Jones.MoriAlvesDaSilva,Javier.Hoffmann,fabian.Stuckmann,
Michael.Huebner}@rub.de
http://www.ruhr-uni-bochum.de

Abstract. Cache memories are an important component of modern processors and consume a large percentage of the processor's power consumption. The quality of service of this cache memories relies heavily on the memory demands of the software, what means that a certain program might benefit more from a certain cache configuration which is highly inefficient for another program. Moreover, finding the optimal cache configuration for a certain program is not a trivial task and usually, involves exhaustive simulation. In this paper, we propose a machine learning-based methodology that, given an unknown application as input, it outputs a prediction of the optimal cache reconfiguration for that application, regarding energy consumption and performance. We evaluated our methodology using a large benchmark suite, and our results show a 99.8% precision at predicting the optimal cache configuration for a program. Furthermore, further analysis of the results indicates that 85% of the mispredictions produce only up to a 10% increase in energy consumption in comparison to the optimal energy consumption.

Keywords: Cache design · Machine learning cache · Cache tuning ·
Cache prediction · Cache recommendation

1 Introduction

The cache memory is a critical component of modern processors because it avoids the latency generated by accessing the main memory. The quality of service of this element changes with the memory demands of the software running on the system. An application might benefit more from a cache configuration which is highly inefficient for another application. Moreover, this component can consume a significant percentage of the system's power consumption [13]. Therefore, choosing the right cache system that fulfills the application's memory requirements with the minimum resources would not only improve performance, but it would also provide energy savings. This is particularly important in the case of embedded systems, which usually have high area and energy constraints while also demanding high performance.

© Springer International Publishing AG 2017
S. Wong et al. (Eds.): ARC 2017, LNCS 10216, pp. 311–322, 2017.
DOI: 10.1007/978-3-319-56258-2_27

Furthermore, it is not a trivial task to choose the optimal cache for a system. Normally, the architecture designer would choose a cache configuration such that it yields an average performance and energy consumption for a series of programs, which leads to non-optimal cache performance for a specific application. Usually, configuring a cache parameter involves a tradeoff between performance, cost and energy consumption. For example, on the one hand, having a small block size enables a faster data transfer from the main memory to the cache than a larger block size. On the contrary, having a large block size favors the spatial locality of the data, as data with consecutive addresses are usually accessed sequentially, therefore requiring fewer data transfers. However, if the block size is too large, unnecessary data will be transferred, which may also decrease the performance.

Furthermore, the design space exploration involves evaluating the effect that the different cache parameters (e.g. cache size, associativity, line size, replacement policy, among others) have on the performance. This is usually done using simulators such as Gem5 [3], Simplescalar [4], SMPCache [16], Dinero IV [5], etc., and even data mining techniques [11].

Statistical classification is a Machine Learning technique which, given a set of observations, it aims to identify to which of a set of predefined categories or classes each of these observations belong. Examples of the applications of this technique are: classifying emails into *Spam* or *No Spam* classes, classifying texts into different literary genres, classifying symptoms of medical patients into possible diseases, and so on. Furthermore, one can define the problem of cache design into a statistical classification problem. On cache design, one wants to determine which cache configuration (or cache class) is optimal for every application (or observation). Thus, using statistical classification techniques can be an effective solution to narrow down the design space for cache design.

In this paper, we propose a methodology for predicting the optimal cache configuration for a program given as input. The methodology uses classification, a supervised machine learning technique. Our methodology starts by obtaining the execution trace of the input program, then generating a feature vector which contains the information regarding the frequency of a subset of the dynamic instructions and then feeding this vector to a series of previously trained classification models. The models take the feature vector as input and output a cache configuration predicted to be optimal for this program, concerning energy consumption and performance.

We evaluated our methodology with 488 applications using different input data. Our results show that our methodology reaches approximately a 99.8% precision rate. Furthermore, a deeper analysis of our results indicates that the misclassified programs were in 75% of the cases still assigned a suboptimal cache configuration that increased the energy consumption up to only 10% in comparison with the optimal cache configuration. These results suggest that our methodology is a promising technique to narrow the design space exploration when choosing the right cache memory for a set of applications.

This paper has the following contributions:

- A novel methodology for cache recommendation based on supervised learning.
- A classification model for cache recommendation based on the relative frequencies of the applications' dynamic instructions.
- An analysis of the misclassified instances which shows the increase in energy consumption of the chosen suboptimal cache configurations in comparison with the optimal ones.

The rest of this paper is organized as follows. We summarize the related work in Sect. 2. In Sect. 3 we described our proposed approach. We describe the experimental setup used for our evaluation on Sect. 4. Furthermore, our results and their analysis are outlined in Sect. 5. Finally, our concluding remarks appear in Sect. 6.

2   Related Work

There have been several approaches that use data mining techniques for computer architecture design. For example, there are approaches which focus on improving branch prediction [10,18] or dynamic resource allocation [7].

Regarding cache memories, there have been very few data mining approaches to recommend parameters of the cache system. CHIDDAM [6] is a methodology based on a decision tree combined with a greedy algorithm to determine the best cache hierarchy, i.e. number of cache levels, and the size of each cache level. This methodology simulates a number of applications, then, an algorithm scans the simulation data iteratively and determines the best number of cache levels, based on the performance of the system. Moreover, a decision tree is built from the simulation data, which determines the contribution of each cache level to the overall performance. Finally, a greedy algorithm is used to find the best cache size of each level. Unfortunately, this approach was evaluated with only two applications, so it remains uncertain if the methodology works for other applications. [11] proposed a methodology to predict the block size of a cache for data mining applications. The methodology uses the tool *Pin* [12] to obtain memory traces of the applications. These memory traces were divided into blocks of 10 million traces each and then fed to SMPCache [16], a cache simulator. The miss rates of each block were obtained and used to measure the performance of the chosen cache configuration. Then a feature dataset was created using the frequencies of co-occurrences of memory traces as well as the frequencies of the traces with contiguous memory addresses. The feature dataset was then used to train a neural network. This methodology was also evaluated with very few applications, in this case three; therefore it is not clear how effective it would be for any other data mining application. In this paper, we focused on the first cache level of an embedded processor, and considered 3 parameters in our methodology: cache size, line size and associativity. Instead of focusing only on cache misses to measure the quality of our methodology, we use a model that considers a Pareto optimal point between energy consumption and cache hits. Furthermore, to provide a good evaluation, we used a much larger dataset, consisting of 488 applications.

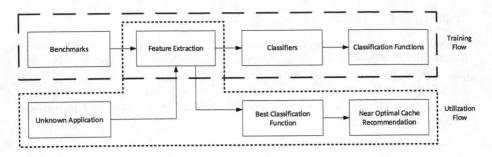

Fig. 1. The proposed methodology for automatic cache structure recommendation.

3   Proposed Methodology

In this work, we present a methodology based on machine learning to determine the near-optimal cache configuration for a given application, without the need to profile its execution on actual hardware. Figure 1 shows an overview of the proposed methodology, in three stages: (a) Database generation; (b) Classifier's training; (c) Test and refinement; each one explained as follows.

The methodology starts with the profiling of several benchmarks over a standard processing architecture, to generate the *Profiling Database*. The profile goals were: (a) Hits and Miss rates, (b) Application's Energy Consumption, (c) Total execution time. Each benchmark's application was run with different cache configurations to determine how sensitive the profiling goals are to each configured parameter and to determine the optimal cache configuration. For this paper, we focused on the level 1 data cache, and considered the following parameters: cache size, line size and associativity. Table 1 shows the parameter values considered.

Table 1. Classifiers used in the evaluation.

Cache size (bytes)	512, 1024, ..., 131072
Line size (bytes)	16, 32, 64
Associativity	1, 2, 4, 8

To find the optimal cache configuration for each program, we implemented an energy model commonly utilized by cache reconfiguration approaches [14,17,19]. This energy model considers the number of hits and misses and the energy consumed by the cache, to find the best tradeoff between small caches that consume less energy but have a higher miss rate and a large cache that has a better miss rate but consumes more energy. The energy model is represented by Eq. 1, which considers the dynamic energy consumption, or E_d, which refers to the energy consumed by logic switching and also static energy consumption, or E_s, which refers to the energy consumed by the current leakage. E_s is calculated as the static energy consumed by the cache per cycle times the number of elapsed cycles, as shown in Eq. 2. E_d is calculated as the energy consumed by the cache on a hit times the number of hits, plus the energy consumed by the cache on a miss times the number of misses, as shown in Eq. 3.

$$E_{Cache} = E_s + E_d \tag{1}$$

$$E_s = cycles * E_{StatPerCycle} \tag{2}$$

$$E_d = E_{hit} * cacheHits + E_{miss} * cacheMisses \tag{3}$$

Next, in the feature extraction phase, as shown in Fig. 2, a representation of the applications is chosen, with which will be used as input for the classifiers. For this, we used assembly instruction's sequences with variable lengths (*n-grams*) as features. The generated *Profiling Database* is then composed by the data sets shown in Table 2. Each *N-gram* appears with different frequencies in each application (the frequency can be zero if the *N-gram* is not present in the application).

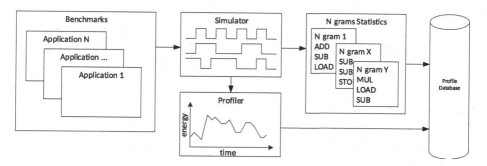

Fig. 2. Profile database generated from the N-gram statistics and energy profiles.

The features generated (the *N-gram*) are used to determine a correlation among their frequencies and the profiling results (Cache Hit and Miss rates, Energy Consumption and Execution Time), Fig. 3. The correlations extracted can then be used to select a Cache Configuration for a new given application. Several different classifiers were used for this process, each one generating a different correlation among the *N-grams* and the profiling results. The results of training part are functions in the format shown in Eq. 4.

$$f_{classifierK} \begin{pmatrix} freq_{ngram1} \\ freq_{ngram2} \\ ... \\ freq_{ngramZ} \end{pmatrix} = \begin{cases} Level\,1\,Instruction\,Cache = X\,KBytes \\ Level\,1\,DataCache = Y\,KBytes \end{cases} \tag{4}$$

Each classifier is a function of the *N-gram*'s frequencies and gives as output the cache configuration which generate the near-optimal solution, based on the design constraints (application's execution time and energy consumption).

Table 2. Profiling database structure

Application	Hits	Misses	Energy (nJ)	Exec. time (s)	*N-gram*	Frequency
App_1	4387	1244	352	34		
					Ng_1	132
					Ng_2	75
					...	...
					Ng_n	21
...	...	...	...	...	...	...
App_z	1063	957	43	210		
					Ng_1	7
					...	...
					Ng_m	379

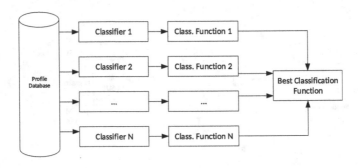

Fig. 3. Selecting the best classification function generated by the learned classifiers.

After the end of the training, the execution tests are used to determine the quality of the prediction functions created by the classifiers. For a new given application, we extract the *N-gram*'s frequencies and check whether each classifier generates or not the desired near-optimal solution, Fig. 4.

4   Experimental Setup

We used Gem5 [3] to obtain the dynamic instructions used to generate the features to train our model and also to get the optimal cache configurations. Gem5 is a platform for architecture research, which enables cycle accurate processor simulation using several different cache parameters. Table 3 shows the configuration used for Gem5.

We used CACTI 4.1 [15] to obtain several values employed by the energy model to calculate the power consumption of a cache. CACTI is a cache model which provides estimations regarding access time, cycle time, area, etc. We use the API from Weka 3.8 [9] to train and evaluate our model. Weka is a data

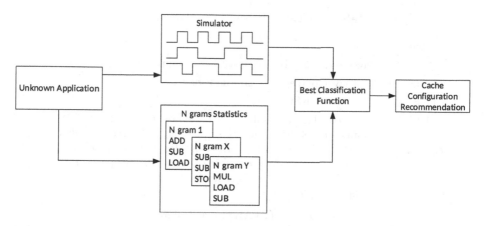

Fig. 4. Using the best classification function to recommend a cache configuration for a given unknown application.

Table 3. Gem5 configuration.

Parameter	Value
System clock	1 GHz
Memory	Mode: timing accesses, address range: 4096 MB
Cache memory bus	Coherent XBar
System memory bus	Coherent XBar
Interrupt controller	Directly connected to the bus and not cached
DDR3 memory controller	DDR_1600_x64

mining tool set developed in Java that includes several machine learning algorithms, filters, and evaluation tools. Table 4 shows the classifiers used to evaluate our approach. Each experiment was run with all the classifiers. The execution time of the classifiers, including training and evaluation phases, was of 6 min in average. To evaluate the classifiers, we used the measures *precision, recall* and *F-measure*, which are commonly used in statistical classification. These measures are calculated as shown in Eqs. 5, 6 and 7, where tp represents the number of true positives, fp refers to the number of false positives and fn represents the number of false negatives.

$$Precision = \frac{tp}{tp + fp} \tag{5}$$

$$Recall = \frac{tp}{tp + fn} \tag{6}$$

$$F_{measure} = 2 * \frac{Precision * Recall}{Precision + Recall} \tag{7}$$

Table 4. Classifiers used in the evaluation.

Type	Classifier
Bayes	BayesNet, naive bayes, naive bayes multinomial
Functions	Multilayer perceptron, simple logistic, SMO
Lazy	LBK, LWL, KStar
Meta	AdaBoostM1, attribute selected classifier, bagging, CV parameter selection, filtered classifier, iterative classifier optimizer, LogitBoost, multiclass classifier, multischeme, multischeme, random committee, random subspace, randomizable filtered classifier, stacking, vote
Misc	Input mapped classifier
Rules	Decision table, JRip, PART, OneR, ZeroR
Trees	Decision stump, hoeffding tree, J48, LMT, random forest, random tree, REPTree

Regarding the applications used to train and evaluate our model, we built a data set of 488 programs from the miBench [8] benchmark suite and from a group of C programs provided in the Florida State University's Website [1]. The applications' domains range from arithmetic programs, route planning, image processing, etc. We built a script to automatically compile and simulate each program with Gem5 using each cache configuration from Table 1.

5   Results and Discussion

We carried out a series of experiments to evaluate our methodology. Figure 5 shows a histogram with the number of applications ordered according to their optimal cache configuration. As the figure shows, there are many configurations which got only one application assigned to them. Considering these configurations in our model would not bring any improvements, since one instance brings not enough information to train our model on that particular cache configuration. Thus, we chose a threshold of 5 instances, so that only those cache configurations which have 5 or more programs assigned to them are used to train our model, remaining a data set of 488 applications and 6 cache settings. In this histogram the format *cacheSize_lineSize_associativity* is used to indicate each cache configuration. It is worth mentioning that all the remaining configurations have an associativity of 1. This does not mean that this parameter is not relevant. It rather depends on the characteristics of the applications of the dataset we used for our evaluation. As Fig. 5 shows, there are 6 applications which optimal cache configurations have an associativity other than 1. Furthermore, we used Weka to perform classification using this data set and the list of classifiers shown in Table 4. The 10 Fold Cross-validation method provided by Weka was used to produce statistically reliable results. Table 5 displays the results of the best performing classifiers for this data set. The best classifier was *RandomSubSpace* which obtained an F-Measure of 0.683 (an F-Measure closer to 1 is better).

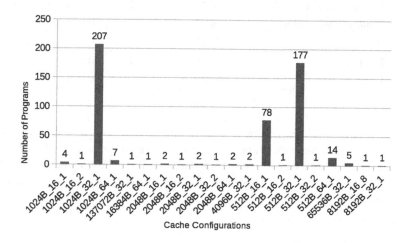

Fig. 5. Histogram of applications per class (cache configuration).

Table 5. Classifiers used in the evaluation.

Classifier	Precision %	Recall %	F-measure
RandomSubSpace	68.6	69.5	0.683
LMT	68.0	68.9	0.682
Simple logistic	68.0	68.9	0.682
SMO	67.5	69.1	0.681
Multilayer perceptron	66.3	67.6	0.669

Next, we carried out another experiment where we applied the Resample [2] filter provided by Weka to the data set, to have a more balanced data set. The results of this experiment are shown in Table 6. Here we see an overall improvement in our results. In this experiment, the best performing classifier was *RandomizableFilterClassifier*, with a precision value of 99.52%, a recall value of 79.74 and an F-measure of 0.866. The rest of the classifiers show a very high precision and F-measure values as well. These results are very promising since even with an unbalanced data set our model can generate very accurate results.

Furthermore, we analyzed the misclassified programs to find out how far from the optimal configurations did our model perform in these cases. To observe this, we calculated the increase in energy consumption that would be generated when choosing the suboptimal classes predicted by our model in the previous experiment. The results are shown in Fig. 6. As the figure shows, 85% of the misclassified applications would have an increase in energy consumption up to

Table 6. Classification's results from data set with resample filter

Classifier	Precision %	Recall %	F-measure
RandomizableFilterClassifier	99.52	79.74	0.866
RandomCommittee	99.47	79.94	0.864
IBK	99.67	78.51	0.858
LMT	98.46	78.10	0.848
RandomForest	99.80	77.68	0.843

10% in comparison with the optimal cache configuration. 12% of the misclassified applications would generate an increase in energy consumption from 11% to 25%, what suggests that even though the model misclassified these instances, it chose cache configurations which are close in energy efficiency to the optimal cache configurations.

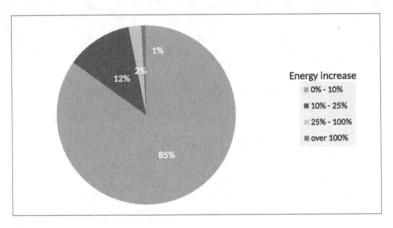

Fig. 6. Increase of energy consumption of misclassified instances in comparison with the optimal cache configurations.

6   Concluding Remarks and Future Work

In this paper, we propose a methodology based on statistical classification to predict the optimal cache configuration for an application. Our methodology uses simulation to obtain the optimal cache configuration for each application's execution trace. Then the relative frequency of the dynamic instructions of each application is calculated and used as features, and the optimal cache configuration is the class, which then are used to train a group of classifiers. We used 488 applications to evaluate our model. Our results show that our methodology has a precision of approximately 99.8% to predict the optimal cache configuration for an application. Furthermore, an analysis of the misclassified instances revealed that on 85% of the misclassified programs the energy consumption of the misclassified applications increased only up to 10% in comparison with the optimal cache configuration and on 12% of the misclassified programs this growth was from 11% to 25%. These results are promising and open several paths of research to improve the precision of our methodology and further narrow down the design space for cache memories.

As future work, we will carry out a deep analysis of the code of the misclassified instances to obtain specific information about the reasons for the misclassification and generate new features from this information to include into our model. We will also add more applications from different domains to our data set to train a more robust model and have a more accurate evaluation.

Acknowledgements. The authors of this paper would like to thank CONACyT (grant number 359472) and CAPES Foundation for their support.

References

1. C source codes benchmark. http://people.sc.fsu.edu/~jburkardt/c_src/c_src.html
2. Weka's resample filter. http://weka.sourceforge.net/doc.dev/weka/filters/super vised/instance/Resample.html
3. Binkert, N., Beckmann, B., Black, G., Reinhardt, S.K., Saidi, A., Basu, A., Hestness, J., Hower, D.R., Krishna, T., Sardashti, S., et al.: The gem5 simulator. ACM SIGARCH Comput. Archit. News **39**(2), 1–7 (2011)
4. Burger, D., Austin, T.M.: The simplescalar tool set, version 2.0. ACM SIGARCH Comput. Archit. News **25**(3), 13–25 (1997)
5. Dinero IV, T.D.U.C.: Simulator (2012). http://www.cs.wisc.edu/markhill/DineroIV
6. Elakkumanan, P., Liu, L., Vankadara, V.K., Sridhar, R.: CHIDDAM: a data mining based technique for cache hierarchy determination in commercial applications. In: 48th Midwest Symposium on Circuits and Systems, pp. 1888–1891. IEEE (2005)
7. Gomez, F.J., Burger, D., Miikkulainen, R.: A neuro-evolution method for dynamic resource allocation on a chip multiprocessor. In: Proceedings of the International Joint Conference on Neural Networks, IJCNN 2001, vol. 4, pp. 2355–2360. IEEE (2001)
8. Guthaus, M., Ringenberg, J., Ernst, D., Austin, T., Mudge, T., Brown, R.: MiBench: a free, commercially representative embedded benchmark suite. In: Proceedings of the Fourth Annual IEEE International Workshop on Workload Characterization, pp. 3–14. WWC-4 (Cat. No. 01EX538) (2001)
9. Hall, M., Frank, E., Holmes, G., Pfahringer, B., Reutemann, P., Witten, I.H.: The weka data mining software: an update. ACM SIGKDD Explor. Newsl. **11**(1), 10–18 (2009)
10. Jiménez, D.A., Lin, C.: Neural methods for dynamic branch prediction. ACM Trans. Comput. Syst. (TOCS) **20**(4), 369–397 (2002)
11. Khakhaeng, S., Chantrapornchai, C.: On the finding proper cache prediction model using neural network. In: 2016 8th International Conference on Knowledge and Smart Technology (KST), pp. 146–151. IEEE (2016)

12. Luk, C.K., Cohn, R., Muth, R., Patil, H., Klauser, A., Lowney, G., Wallace, S., Reddi, V.J., Hazelwood, K.: Pin: building customized program analysis tools with dynamic instrumentation. In: ACM Sigplan Notices, vol. 40, pp. 190–200. ACM (2005)
13. Mittal, S.: A survey of architectural techniques for improving cache power efficiency. Sustain. Comput.: Inform. Syst. 4(1), 33–43 (2014)
14. Navarro, O., Leiding, T., Hübner, M.: Configurable cache tuning with a victim cache. In: 2015 10th International Symposium on Reconfigurable Communication-centric Systems-on-Chip (ReCoSoC), pp. 1–6. IEEE (2015)
15. Tarjan, D., Thoziyoor, S., Jouppi, N.P.: Cacti 4.0. Technical report, Technical report HPL-2006-86, HP Laboratories Palo Alto (2006)
16. Vega, M.A., Martín, R., Zarallo, F.A., Sánchez, J.M., Gómez, J.A.: Smpcache: simulador de sistemas de memoria cache en multiprocesadores simétricos. Granada, XI Jornadas de Paralelismo (2000)
17. Wang, W., Mishra, P., Gordon-Ross, A.: Dynamic cache reconfiguration for soft real-time systems. ACM Trans. Embed. Comput. Syst. (1) (2012). http://dl.acm.org/citation.cfm?id=2220340
18. Wang, Y., Chen, L.: Dynamic Branch Prediction Using Machine Learning. ECS-201A, Fall (2015)
19. Zhang, C., Vahid, F., Najjar, W.: A highly configurable cache architecture for embedded systems. In: 2003 Proceedings of the 30th Annual International Symposium on Computer Architecture, pp. 136–146. IEEE (2003)

ArPALib: A Big Number Arithmetic Library for Hardware and Software Implementations. A Case Study for the Miller-Rabin Primality Test

Jan Macheta, Agnieszka Dąbrowska-Boruch, Paweł Russek[✉],
and Kazimierz Wiatr

AGH University of Science and Technology, Mickiewicza Av. 30,
30-059 Krakow, Poland
{macheta,adabrow,russek,wiatr}@agh.edu.pl

Abstract. In this paper, we present the Arbitrary Precision Arithmetic Library - ArPALib, suitable for algorithms that require integer data representation with an arbitrary bit-width (up to 4096-bit in this study). The unique feature of the library is suitability to be synthesized by HLS (High Level Synthesis) tools, while maintaining full compatibility with C99 standard. To validate the applicability of ArPALib for the FPGA-enhanced SoCs, the Miller-Rabin primality test algorithm is considered as a case study. Also, we provide the performance analysis of our library in the software and hardware applications. The presented results show the speedup of 1.5 of the hardware co-processor over its software counterpart when ApPALib is used.

Keywords: Big numbers · Primality tests · High-Level Synthesis · FPGA

1 Motivation

The big numbers - the integer numbers in computer data representation that comprise of hundreds of bits, are a foundation for security solutions of today's computer systems. Although, some of the modern programming languages allow programmers to choose an arbitrary variable size, the majority of modern C language compilers, supports the maximum integer size of 64-bits only. Therefore, it is necessary to define the custom big data types and create functions for arithmetic operations from scratch. Alternatively, a developer can benefit from one of the ready-to-use big number libraries that are offered either commercially or as open sources [1, 2].

The FPGAs have been used for security enhancement algorithms before [3–6]. Meanwhile, the role of the Programmable SoC (PSoC) solutions, that incorporate a CPU subsystem and an FPGA structure in a single chip, is rapidly growing. Soon, such CPU-FPGA hybrid solutions will become ubiquitous, not

© Springer International Publishing AG 2017
S. Wong et al. (Eds.): ARC 2017, LNCS 10216, pp. 323–330, 2017.
DOI: 10.1007/978-3-319-56258-2_28

only for embedded systems but in server solutions as well. The major obstacle in deploying such systems is a cost of hardware development. Designing of hardware is time-consuming, cost-intensive, and requires extra developer skills. However, a shift towards high-level programming can be noticed in design tools today. Thanks to the High-Level Synthesis, C and C++ codes of the algorithms can be translated to their Register Transfer Level (RTL) representations and the process can be controlled by means of inserting pragmas into the source files. The HLS tools significantly speed up the FPGA system development and lead the way to CPU-FPGA systems spreading. Unfortunately, some of the software techniques (*i.e.* dynamic allocation or recursion) are prohibited by HLS. Thus, preparing the hardware synthesizable C code still requires some effort and care.

The main goal of this paper is to introduce the Arbitrary Precision Arithmetic Library (ArPALib) that was developed by the authors. Its main advantage over other available arithmetic libraries is that it can be implemented both in software and HLS synthesized hardware, allowing the developer to swiftly create CPU-FPGA based solutions. It is worth highlighting that the source code of ArPALib is available online in the repository provided by the authors [7].

2   The Big Number Libraries

For a proper background we will first overview the three big number libraries that are available for C programmers. We will refer to the GMP [1] and BigDigits [2] libraries, *ap_cint.h* - built-in library from Xilinx's Vivado HLS.

GMP library is considered to be one of the fastest big number library available today. It covers an arbitrary bit-width for signed and unsigned integers and fixed-point numbers. Its extraordinary performance comes from a variety of implemented algorithms that are selected according to the actual size of the used numbers. Additionally, the GMP's algorithms exploit aggressive optimizations for selected processor architectures (*e.g.* AMD K5/K10, Intel Sandy Bridge, ARM family).

The individual number is represented by the mpz_t structure that comprises the memory pointer to a dynamically-allocated array that stores the value of the number, and its current size. That kind of representation reduces the memory read/write operations, and induces basic pointer arithmetic to perform calculations. Unfortunately, the mentioned coding techniques exclude using GMP from a HLS design flow.

BigDigits library is an open source arithmetic library that conforms to ANSI C standard. The authors of BigDigit implemented mainly paper-and-pencil methods arithmetic algorithms, where arguments must be the same lengths. If the allocated space is bigger than the actual number length, zero-padding operation is performed to ensure the result correctness. BigDigits simplicity made this library a good candidate for HLS, however, some of its algorithms use a recursion, which is not supported by HLS tools.

In our experiments we used Xilinx's Vivado HLS environment, that provides built-in arbitrary precision integer library, included in *ap_cint.h* header.

It defines the [u]int *<precision>* type exclusively recognized by the Vivado's C compiler and HLS tool, that makes bit-accurate simulations possible.

The [u]int *<precision>* is implemented in hardware as a bit vector, which means that the width of hardware registers and functional elements fit the width of the number. That provides a one clock cycle for a single operation, but also leads to a limited clock frequency and the fast exhaustion of FPGA resources for large bit-widths (even a single multiplication of two 4096-bit numbers exceeds the capacity of Xilinx Artix-7 family of FPGAs). Therefore, the maximum precision of [u]int is restricted (by default) to 1024. Unfortunately, the Vivado HLS does not provide sequential processing of big numbers and the trade-off between performance and resources cannot be controlled.

3   ArPALib Introduction

To overcome problems mentioned in Sect. 2, we created ArPALib, which is fully synthesizable (by Vivado HLS 2015.4) and C99 compatible library for software and hardware implementations. Our goal was to propose a solution that enables sequential processing of big numbers in blocks of bits of a selected width to reduce. The code of ArPALib is publicly available under the GNU GPLv3 license [7].

The library can be parametrized to redefine the base integer type (named uint_t), which is used as an elementary computational block of the big number, and processed in sequential algorithm steps. The base type allows programmers to force such a bit-width of the co-processor architecture that fits the size of the selected FPGA device. Furthermore, it can be defined as [u]int for the Vivado HLS compiler, thus enabling optimization for speed or resources footprint.

A type for the unsigned integer big number is called uintBig_t in ArPALib. It contains an array of uint_t elements, and the length of the array is defined at compile time. Optionally, the uintBig_t can hold a variable that keeps the current size of the stored big number. Thanks to that, the number of read/write operations is reduced by excluding not used segments from computations, instead of zero padding operation. For example, the number of memory accesses is limited to the size of the smaller argument in the add operation. The bigger the difference of the arguments' length is, the more significant is the speed-up. Our approach requires tracking the arguments' size, so it introduces some extra operations. However, even if the arguments are of similar size, the overhead that ArPALib produces is small (*e.g.* only one comparison operation more for the addition than the algorithm without modification). The library supports dynamic data allocation for software implementations to prevent stack overflow problems.

Algorithms implemented in ArPALib are summarized in Table 1. The library implements all elementary binary operations, comparison and assignment operations. It also provides input/output tools that include conversion of binary strings of different formats to big number values and vice versa in the software version. Unfortunately, all the performed operations are integer-based only, therefore, the Schoenhage-Strassen algorithm or Barett reduction are not available. On the other hand, hardware implementations are modest thanks to that.

Table 1. Algorithms implemented in ArPALib

Addition	• Schoolbook addition with carry algorithm
Subtraction	• Schoolbook subtraction with borrow algorithm
Multiplication	• Karatsuba alg. (for the uint_t type)
	• Schoolbook long multiplication algorithm
Division	• Knuth's D algorithm ref
Exponentiation	• Exponentiation by squaring algorithm
Exponentiation modulo	• Right-to-left binary shift algorithm

4   Tests of ArPALib as Software

We compared the software efficiency of ArPALib (using uint32_t as a base type) to the GMP(v.6.1.1) and BigDigits(v.2.6) for numbers up to 4096-bit long. Tests were conducted on the AMD FX-6100@4 GHz, 32GB RAM DDR3-2400 machine (and compiled by MinGWv5.0RC2 with $-O2$ flag). To cope with a very short single computation time, and to mitigate the influence of the OS, the measurements were performed in 100,000 repeats. The average processing time for a single addition is given in Fig. 1. The multiplication and division are given in Figs. 2 and 3 respectively.

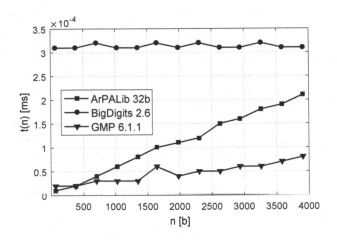

Fig. 1. A comparison of $n \times n$ unsigned integers addition/subtraction

5   A Case Study of ArPALib as Hardware

To present synthesizability and efficiency of ArPALib for FPGA hardware implementation, we will provide metrics of a custom co-processor for the Miller-Rabin

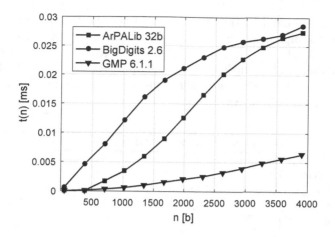

Fig. 2. A comparison of $n \times n$ unsigned integers multiplication

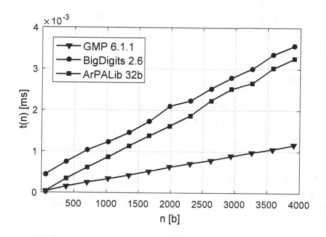

Fig. 3. A comparison of $n \times n$ unsigned integers division

algorithm that was created in the experiment, which is a well-known and widely-used number primality test that is used in security applications.

The implementation and experiments were performed on Xilinx's PSoC of Zynq-7000 family XC7Z020. The chip was a part of the Zedboard platform. Zynq combines the Cortex-A8 CPU of the ARM family and the small programmable logic of the Xilinx's 7 series FPGA. The HLS synthesis and design flow from Vivado 2015.4 development tool were used. In HLS, the architecture of the co-processor is formed according to the algorithm coded in the C programming language that is accompanied by special directives to steer the hardware synthesis (*e.g.* control parallelism or select IO interfaces). The coprocessor communication interface was built around the AXI4-Lite bus. The throughput of AXI-Lite is very modest, but it does not influence the performance of the system for the computational intensiveness of the Rabin-Miller algorithm. The goal was to implement the Rabin-Miller algorithm for the set of ten bases $a \in \{2, 3, 5, 7, 11, 13, 17, 19, 23, 29\}$, which guarantees the deterministic approach for the numbers up to 2^{63}, and the probabilistic test with less uncertainty than $4^{-10} \approx 9.5 \cdot 10^{-7}$ for larger numbers. The code for the implemented coprocessor is presented in Algorithm 1.

Algorithm 1. The algorithm implemented in the Miller-Rabin co-processor

---

Input: $n \in \mathbb{N}/\{1\}$ is the tested number
  procedure PROCPRIMALITYTEST(n)
      $K \leftarrow \{2, 3, 5, 7, 11, 13, 17, 19, 23, 29\}$ ▷ The constant set of primality witnesses
      if $d \mid 2$ **then**   ▷ Check if n is odd
         return *COMPOSITE*
      end if
      $s \leftarrow 0$
      $d \leftarrow$ BINARYSHIFTRIGHT(n)   ▷ n is odd, so $d = (n-1)/2$
      while LSB(d)=0 **do**   ▷ LSB() gets the least significant bit
         $s \leftarrow s + 1$
         $d \leftarrow d/2$
      end while
      for $i \leftarrow 1, 10$ **do**
         $a \leftarrow K(i)$ ▷ Get next element of K
         $result \leftarrow IsStrongPseudoprime(a, n, s, d)$
         if $result = COMPOSITE$ **then**
            return *COMPOSITE*
         end if
      end for
      return *PROBABLY_PRIME*
  end procedure

We created three versions of the 4096-bit coprocessor, differing in the bitwidth of the ArPALib base type uint_t (8, 16 and 32 bits). Figure 4 shows the corresponding resource usage of tested versions after FPGA implementation. Expectedly, as the uint_t size doubles, the resources requirement doubles as well. Unfortunately, any attempts to synthesize the coprocessor for the wider uint_t failed due to the FPGA resource shortage.

We also performed speed tests of co-processors. For the set of prime numbers in the range 2^{25} to 2^{4096}, the execution time of the Miller-Rabin coprocessor was measured against ARM Cortex-A9 running the software algorithm for the matching size of uint_t. Results are given in Fig. 5. The 32-bit version of hardware coprocessor runs 50% faster than its software counterpart. The speedup was even higher for the 8 and 16-bit versions, but results cannot be demonstrative as the CPU did not use its native data representation in those cases. It should be mentioned, that when the uint_t size doubles, the speed doubles as well. This scaling comes with the sequential behavior of the implemented big number operators.

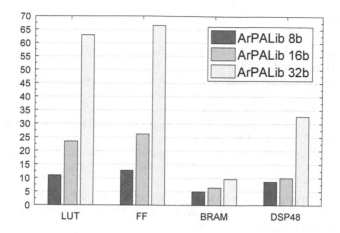

Fig. 4. Utilization of FPGA resources for Miller-Rabin co-processors in Zynq XC7Z020 FPGA. The size of the base type uint_t defined as 8, 16, and 32 bits

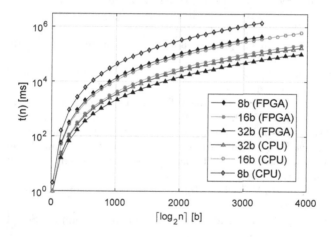

Fig. 5. ArPALib performance of the Miller-Rabin test in the hardware and software for n-bit numbers. The 8, 16, and 32-bits base type was tested and ARM Cortex-A8 (667 MHz) was used for the software version

6   Conclusions

The presented experiment proved that the hardware-software design symmetry come true thanks to HLS tools available today. At present, software routines can be positioned more easily in hardware to gain better performance. Although it requires the cautious coding style of the program, that drawback can be mitigated by the use of hardware and software compatible libraries like ArPALib.

Acknowledgements. This work was performed thanks to the funds for AGH statutory activity 11.11.230.017.

References

1. Granlund, T.: GNU MP 6.0 Multiple Precision Arithmetic Library. Samurai Media Limited, Hong Kong (2015)
2. Ireland, D.: BigDigits multiple-precision arithmetic source code. http://www.di-mgt.com.au/bigdigits.html. Accessed 29 Sept 2016
3. Gielata, A., Russek, P., Wiatr, K.: AES hardware implementation in FPGA for algorithm acceleration purpose. In: International Conference on Signals and Electronic Systems, pp. 137–140 (2008)
4. Kryjak, T., Gorgon, M.: Pipeline implementation of the 128-bit block cipher CLEFIA in FPGA. In: International Conference on Field Programmable Logic and Applications, FPL 2009, pp. 373–378 (2009)
5. Dąbrowska-Boruch, A., Gancarczyk, G., Wiatr, K.: Implementation of a RANLUX based pseudo-random number generator in FPGA using VHDL and impulse C. Comput. Inf. **32**(6), 1272–1292 (2014)
6. Jamro, E., Russek, P., Dąbrowska-Boruch, A., Wielgosz, M., Wiatr, K.: The implementation of the customized, parallel architecture for a fast word-match program. Int. J. Comput. Syst. Sci. Eng. **26**(4), 285–292 (2011)
7. Macheta, J., et al.: ARPALib repository. https://git.plgrid.pl/projects/ARPALIB/repos/arpalib. Accessed 29 Sept 2016
8. Miller, G.L.: Riemann's hypothesis and tests for primality. J. Comput. Syst. Sci. **13**(3), 300–317 (1976)
9. Pommerening, K.: Cryptology. Part III. Primality Tests: RSA and Pseudoprimes 28 May 2000. Accessed 21 Feb 2016
10. Pomerance, C., Selfridge, J.L., Wagstaff, S.S.: The pseudoprimes to $25 \cdot 10^9$. Math. Comput. **35**(151), 1003–1026 (1980)
11. Walter, C.D.: Right-to-left or left-to-right exponentiation? International Workshop on Constructive Side-Channel Analysis and Secure Design, pp. 40–46 (2010)
12. Conrad, K.: FERMAT'S TEST. http://www.math.uconn.edu/kconrad/blurbs/ugradnumthy/fermattest.pdf
13. Solovay, R., Strassen, V.: A fast Monte-Carlo test for primality. SIAM J. Comput. **6**(1), 84–85 (1977)
14. Bach, E.: Number-theoretic algorithms. Annu. Rev. Comput. Sci. **4**(1), 119–172 (1990)

Author Index

Al-Ars, Zaid   36
Albuquerque, Glauberto   16
Ali, Karim M.A.   168
Ali, Muhammad   129
Alvarez-Mesa, Mauricio   241
Alves, Marco A.Z.   28
Arram, James   299
Avelino, Álvaro   16

Becker, Jürgen   141
Becker, Tobias   60
Belaidi, Abdelkader   217
Ben Atitallah, Rabie   168
Benevenuti, Fabio   202
Bobda, Christophe   47
Bollengier, Théotime   93
Börcsök, Josef   118
Bouhali, Mustapha   217
Brandon, Anthony   3
Burovskiy, Pavel   299

Capitao, Flavio   229
Carro, Luigi   28
Cheung, Kit   299
Chi, Chi Ching   241

Dąbrowska-Boruch, Agnieszka   323
Dahmane, Zine Elabadine   217
de Oliveira, Ádria Barros   189
Dekeyser, Jean-Luc   168
Ding, Weiqiao   141
dos Santos, André Flores   202
Dou, Yong   281
Dumitriu, Victor   177

Elhossini, Ahmed   241

Fakhfakh, Nizar   168
Farooq, Umer   129
Fiessler, Andreas   72
Figuli, Peter   141
Figuli, Shalina   141
Fujii, Tomoya   268
Funie, Andreea-Ingrid   154

Gaydadjiev, Georgi   60
Göbel, Matthias   241
Göhringer, Diana   106
Grigoras, Paul   299
Guex, Nicolas   229
Guilloux, Pierre   93
Guo, Liucheng   154
Guo, Qi   3

Hager, Sven   72
Harb, Naim   16
Hayek, Ali   118
Heij, Rolf   36
Hoffmann, Javier   311
Hoozemans, Joost   36
Hu, Sensen   3
Hübner, Michael   311

Iseli, Christian   229

Jiang, Jingfei   281
Jin, Ruochun   281
Juurlink, Ben   241

Kamhoua, Charles   47
Kastensmidt, Fernanda Lima   189, 202
Khan, Habib Ul Hasan   106
Khan, Sheraz Ali   81
Khatri, Abdul Rafay   118
Kim, Cheol-Hong   81
Kim, Jong-Myon   81
Kirischian, Lev   177
Kwiat, Kevin   47

Lagadec, Loïc   93
Le Lann, Jean-Christophe   93
Liu, Qiang   255
Loebenberger, Daniel   72
Luk, Wayne   154, 255, 299

Macheta, Jan   323
Mead, Joshua   47
Mencer, Oskar   60
Mori, Jones   311

Morshedi, Mostafa   289
Motomura, Masato   268

Najem, Mohamad   93
Nakahara, Hiroki   268
Navarro, Osvaldo   311
Nguyen, Ngoc-Hung   81
Niu, Xinyu   154, 255, 299
Noori, Hamid   289
Nurmi, Jari   217

Obac, Valentin   16
Oliveira, Geraldo F.   28

Pasha, Muhammad Adeel   129
Petraglio, Enrico   229
Possa, Paulo   16

Russek, Paweł   323

Salmon, Mark   154
Santos, Paulo C.   28
Sato, Simpei   268
Scheuermann, Björn   72

Shamani, Farid   217
Sharma, Dimple   177
Siddiqui, Bilal   129
Siozios, Kostas   141
Soudris, Dimitrios   141
Stuckmann, Fabian   311

Tambara, Lucas Antunes   189, 202
Thoma, Yann   229
Tonfat, Jorge   202

Valderrama, Carlos   16
van Straten, Jeroen   36
Voss, Nils   60

Wang, Yizhuo   3
Wertenbroek, Rick   229
Whitaker, Taylor J.L.   47
Wiatr, Kazimierz   323
Wu, Yajie   255

Xie, Junyi   299

Zhao, Ruizhe   255

Printed in the United States
By Bookmasters